Animal Welfare in China

ANIMAL PUBLICS

Melissa Boyde, Fiona Probyn-Rapsey & Yvette Watt, Series Editors

The Animal Publics series publishes new interdisciplinary research in animal studies. Taking inspiration from the varied and changing ways that humans and non-human animals interact, it investigates how animal life becomes public: attended to, listened to, made visible, included, and transformed.

Animal Death, ed. Jay Johnston and Fiona Probyn-Rapsey

Animal Welfare in Australia: Politics and Policy by Peter Chen

Animal Welfare in China: Culture, Politics and Crisis by Peter J. Li

Animals in the Anthropocene: Critical Perspectives on Non-human Futures, ed. The Human Animal Research Network Editorial Collective

Cane Toads: A Tale of Sugar, Politics and Flawed Science by Nigel Turvey

Dingo Bold: The Life and Death of K'gari Dingoes by Rowena Lennox

Engaging with Animals: Interpretations of a Shared Existence, ed. Georgette Leah Burns and Mandy Patersonn

Enter the Animal: Cross-species perspectives on grief and spirituality by Teya Brooks Pribac

Fighting Nature: Travelling Menageries, Animal Acts and War Shows by Peta Tait

The Flight of Birds: A Novel in Twelve Stories by Joshua Lobb

A Life for Animals by Christine Townend

Meatsplaining: The Animal Agriculture Industry and the Rhetoric of Denial, ed. Jason Hannan

Obaysch: A Hippopotamus in Victorian London by John Simons

Animal Welfare in China

Culture, Politics and Crisis

By Peter J Li

SYDNEY UNIVERSITY PRESS

First published by Sydney University Press
© Peter J. Li 2021
© Sydney University Press 2021

Reproduction and communication for other purposes

Except as permitted under the Act, no part of this edition may be reproduced, stored in a retrieval system, or communicated in any form or by any means without prior written permission. All requests for reproduction or communication should be made to Sydney University Press at the address below:

Sydney University Press
Fisher Library F03
University of Sydney NSW 2006
Australia
sup.info@sydney.edu.au
sydneyuniversitypress.com.au

A catalogue record for this book is available from the National Library of Australia.

ISBN 9781743324707 paperback
ISBN 9781743324714 epub
ISBN 9781743324721 mobi
ISBN 9781743327449 pdf

Cover image: Asiatic black bear, iStock.com/anankkml
Cover design by Agata Mrva-Montoya

Contents

Introduction: animals in contemporary China		1
1	Animal cruelty in contemporary China: is culture to blame?	31
2	Human–animal relations in Chinese history	63
3	China's "civil war" over dogs	109
4	Wildlife as a resource: the controversy of bear farming	149
5	Animal agriculture	179
6	Protection or utilisation: revising the wildlife protection law	217
7	China's animal protection NGOs	267
Conclusion		311
Acknowledgements		319
Appendix 1: offences and penalties in the revised Wildlife Protection Law		321
References		325
Index		365

Introduction: animals in contemporary China

In 1988, I was a graduate student from China studying international relations in the United States. In that year's hot summer, I visited the National Zoo in Washington D.C. What impressed me most were the letters to the pandas written by young American children. Perhaps no Chinese celebrity in the world, be it Jackie Chan or Yao Ming, is more famous than the giant panda, the unofficial national emblem of China. This adorable bear subspecies is the sweetheart of children around the world. It would be unforgivably negligent to allow this magnificent animal to go extinct. Since 1961, the World Wildlife Fund (WWF) has used the image of the panda in its logo, as it calls for global attention to the crisis confronting wildlife species around the world.

Coincidentally, in the same year, Chinese authorities were alerted to a runaway assault on the giant panda and other wildlife, triggered by a nationwide famine (1959–62) that had been caused by a misguided economic policy. To survive humanity's worst manmade famine, hungry people, including government officials, army officers and soldiers, took to the mountains looking for edible plants and animals (Huang Zheng 2006, 208; Geng Biao 1998, 163–67).[1] To stop this

---

1   The great famine of 1959–62 caused by Mao Zedong's ill-conceived Great Leap Forward campaign sent hundreds of thousands of Chinese people to the mountains to hunt wildlife. Memoirs of senior Chinese officials published in

indiscriminate hunting, the State Council (comparable to China's cabinet) placed the giant panda and other endangered species under state protection (State Council 1962).

The giant panda has since enjoyed celebrity status in China's zoos and other captive wildlife institutions. In the suburbs of Chengdu, the capital city of Sichuan Province, the Chengdu Research Centre of Giant Panda Breeding (CRCGPB) was home to 152 pandas, all of them bred in captivity, at the end of 2015. This 100-hectare institution is covered with thick vegetation. It draws three million domestic and international visitors every year.[2] The centre showcases not only the breathtakingly cute panda cubs, but also the unparalleled care and attention they receive from staff. Workers at the centre are the gentlest of animal-care providers; their attention to the smallest details of the pandas' needs is impeccable. The indoor enclosures are air-conditioned in summer, are clean, and provide climbing structures, scratching poles, and destructible objects. Stone structures mimic caves and water pools. The outdoor enclosures are designed with pandas' natural habitats in mind. Despite the controversial photo-ops and artificial breeding program, pandas at the centre receive the best care possible. The institution has invested handsomely to make the living quarters of their "privileged residents" as comfortable as possible.

The treatment of giant pandas is in stark contrast to that of all other animals. China's captive wildlife institutions, such as zoos, safari parks, and aquariums, have long been criticised for a host of practices that ignore the welfare of captive animals (Watts and Han 2010). At a north China zoo, tigers are caged individually in small, barren, concrete indoor dens in a big house designed by Soviet experts in the early 1950s. In most Chinese zoos, bears are displayed in pit enclosures, a design relic of the past. Pit enclosures with barren concrete floors allow

---

recent years have disclosed the scale of the assault on various species. The interview by Huang Zheng (2006) with the widow of Liu Shaoqi, President of the People's Republic of China and the memoir of Geng Biao, former Defence Minister of the PRC mentioned government involvement in the assault on the wildlife animals to get animal protein for government officials during that special period of time.

2   See the centre's official website at http://www.panda.org.cn/china/about/2013-01-10/54.html.

Introduction: animals in contemporary China

and even encourage visitors to look down upon the bears, who are often showered with snacks, soft-drink bottles, trash and even harmful substances such as concentrated acid in one incident at the Beijing Zoo in 2002. Discrimination even exists inside the CRCGPB, where 68 red pandas (*Ailurus fulgens*) were kept as of 2011. One expert observer called the centre's treatment of the red pandas "barbaric and unforgiveable." "Giant pandas in China are given everything and the rest of the animal kingdom seems to be regarded as unfeeling, no-class citizens of Earth," the observer added.[3]

The privileged status of the giant panda is even more pronounced when compared to farm animals. Farm animals, particularly farmed wildlife animals, are raised in conditions beyond the wildest imagination of the uninformed public. China's bear farming, in the eyes of animal protectionists around the world, is the most ethically questionable of all commercial wildlife farming operations.[4] Jill Robinson, founder of the Hong Kong-based Animals Asia Foundation and the first animal protectionist to expose China's bear farms to the world, called the practice "absolutely shocking." Standing inside a bear farm in 1993 in Guangdong province, Ms Robinson felt like she had been thrown into "a horror film" (Browne 2009). Across the country, 10,000 or more Asiatic black bears are farmed for the sole purpose of extracting bile from an open wound in their stomach. These bears, called farm bears or bile bears, are incarcerated individually in iron cages. In addition to being deprived of space and socialisation, they are purposely denied adequate and proper food.[5] In a crude surgery, a catheter is inserted into their bodies that links the open wound (or bile exit site) with the gallbladder. Catheter use is no longer legal. A

---

3 Electronic interview with an expert observer who visited the Chengdu Research Centre of Giant Panda Breeding, 11 November 2011.
4 Bear farming was first exposed in 1993 to the shocked international community. Since then, thousands of reports and stories by Chinese and foreign writers, journalists and veterinarians have been published that question the ethical and medicinal grounds of the commercial operation. For a recent foreign report, see Harrison, David. (2011). "Chinese doctors call for 'cruel' bear farms to be closed", *Telegraph*, 28 August, http://bit.ly/3bLIXOO.
5 My interview with two bear farm owners in Chengdu, Sichuan, China in January 2004.

so-called new technology, the creation of an artificial fistula, often in an uncontrolled environment, still causes health issues to the bears. Besides the painful daily bile extraction, they suffer from traumas caused by de-toothing, de-clawing, and the wearing of metal corsets, among other practices. The open wound is forever irritated and inflamed. Years of confinement, physical pain, and mental agony take a heavy toll, and self-mutilation is common. A high percentage of farm bears die of liver cancers, cholecystitis, cholelithiasis, polyp formations and other illnesses caused by years of bile extraction (Cochrane 2003).

Many who adore giant pandas would not imagine that black bears in China suffer in this way. "Every rescued farm bear at Chengdu Asiatic Black Bear Rescue Centre, not too far from the CRCGPB, is a testimony to the unequal treatment the black bears have received in comparison with their celebrity cousin, the giant panda," says Toby Zhang, general secretary of Beijing's Ta Foundation, a non-profit organisation created to raise awareness of animal protection. China's bear farming, although a massive business operation, is only the tip of the iceberg. China's breathtaking economic growth has been accompanied by an increasingly formidable animal welfare crisis.

An escalating crisis

The words "welfare" and "wellbeing," according to one interpretation, mean "(net) happiness, or total enjoyment minus total suffering" (Ng 1995, 255). Animal welfare generally refers to the basic conditions necessary for the maintenance of the physical and psychological wellbeing of animals, particularly those in captive institutions. One established standard for judging animal welfare is the "five freedoms." The idea of the "five freedoms" originated in the 1965 Brambell Report on intensive livestock practices in the United Kingdom and was formalised in a 1979 press statement by the British Farm Animal Welfare Council (Farm Animal Welfare Council 1979). The five conditions identified as essential for a farm animal's physical and psychological wellbeing were: freedom from hunger and thirst; freedom from discomfort; freedom from pain, injury or disease; freedom to express normal animal behaviour; and freedom from fear or distress. These standards have since been used by welfare groups and animal protection activists to judge not only farm animal welfare, but the conditions of other captive animals. More in-depth and specialised studies have brought attention to the welfare of animals held in other types of captivity and have argued for a higher benchmark of animal welfare. In their article on "Animal welfare perspectives on pain and distress management in research and testing," for example, Andrew N. Rowan et al. forcefully called not only for a reduction in suffering, but for other measures to enrich animals' welfare (Rowan et al. 2009).

The term "animal welfare" is not native to the Chinese language. However, the meaning embodied in the "five freedoms" was not new to Chinese people. In the early 1930s, when the Chinese government launched a nationwide social transformation campaign called the "New Life Movement," the educated elite called for measures against animal abuse. The movement aimed to create a modern Chinese culture that could converge with the progress of civilisation around the world. Care for animals and provision of basic conditions for farm and working animals were two of the objectives of the social transformation effort. Under the Republic of China (ROC) government, the movement led to encouraging developments. In 1934 the municipal government of Nanjing, the capital of the ROC, promulgated *Implementation Measures for Banning Cruelty to Animals* as a local policy. In the same year, an association for the prevention of cruelty to animals was established (Chang and Michaels 2010, 251–56). When the Chinese Communist Party (CCP) took power in 1949, Chinese history took a drastic turn. The phrases "animal protection" and "anti-cruelty" disappeared completely from any Chinese publications on the mainland in the 30 years following the creation of the People's Republic of China (PRC). During this era of totalitarian politics, the authorities struggled to satisfy, with limited success, the basic needs of the Chinese people. Widespread and prolonged human suffering overshadowed the plight of nonhuman animals. Animal cruelty never attracted public attention or appeared on the radar of policymakers. Admittedly, the kind of animal cruelty that is associated with Chinese farming and industry today did not exist in the pre-reform era. For example, cruelty to dogs in the course of long-distance transport did not exist in the pre-reform era because the large-scale transportation of dogs to supply massive dog-meat markets did not exist. It was not until the early 1980s, when China was opened to the outside world, that the term "animal welfare" and ideas for protecting animals started to appear again in translated foreign publications.[6]

Two milestone events signified the start of public awareness in China of the escalating animal welfare problems on the mainland. In 1992, the China Small Animal Protection Association (CSAPA), the first officially registered animal advocacy group in China, came to the public's attention as a voice against animal cruelty. Led by Lu Di, a veteran of the Korean War and retired university professor, CSAPA and its supporters throughout the country represented a force never before seen in the People's Republic. With the establishment of CSAPA, Chinese society was no longer a passive bystander to the many questionable and ethically problematic practices impacting nonhuman animals.

A second milestone was the exposure of bear farming in 1993. Bear farming had been enthusiastically endorsed by local and national authorities as a "get rich" shortcut and a panacea for fighting poverty. Jill Robinson, then China Director of the International Fund for Animal Welfare, was the first foreign animal protectionist to go inside a bear farm and reveal what she found to the startled international community. Ever since, perceived cruelty to animals in China has attracted the attention of animal lovers and the public at large. Domestic and international attention has, in the last two decades, produced a plethora of reports on the welfare crisis affecting nonhuman animals on the Chinese mainland. The magnitude of the challenges is such that even scholars and officials who might not otherwise have paid attention to the issue have been dragged into public discussions, because of its connection to other topics.[7]

---

[6] For example, Beijing's Science Publishing House published in 1984 *Progress on Studies of Livestock Behaviors*; K.A. Houpt and T.R. Wolski's *Domestic Animal Behavior for Veterinarians and Animal Scientists* (Ames: Iowa State University Press, 1982) was translated into Chinese and published in 1987; and A.F. Fraser's *Farm Animal Behaviour* (London: Bailliere Tindall, 1980) was also translated into Chinese and published in 1985.

[7] For example, Professor Zhao Nanyuan, a specialist in automation at Beijing's Tsinghua University, joined the public discussion of the ethics of raising

Introduction: animals in contemporary China

In the following pages, I shall briefly address the background of the crisis and how the crisis has affected different groups of animals. Let's take a look at companion animals first. Public debates and media reports have mostly focused on this group.

Companion animals

There is no official definition of companion animals in China. In fact, for decades following the founding of the People's Republic of China, pet-keeping was discouraged by the authorities. A sea change in attitude happened in April 2020 when a national government spokesman publicly referred to dogs as companion animals (Thomson 2020). This was a commended step forward from the designation of dogs and cats as "pets" in March by the city government of Shenzhen, Guangdong in its effort to outlaw the local dog and cat meat trade (The Paper 2020b). As in the rest of the world, people in China keep a range of animals as pets, including turtles, fish, birds, snakes, lizards, monkeys and non-native species from Africa and Latin America. Practices such as bird-caging, fishing, and the more shocking and recent act of sealing small live animals in key rings, criticised in media reports, are popular among some of the old and young pet "lovers" (CNN 2011).

In this book, when I discuss companion animals or pets I am referring specifically to dogs and cats. In China, there are no authoritative statistics about the total number of pets. Based on incomplete dog registration data for urban areas, China's 2016 State Statistical Bureau reported 27.4 million pet dogs in urban households (Central News of Korea 2017). According to one other estimate, China had in 2017 a total of 168 million dogs in both urban and rural

---

St Bernards, a Swiss dog breed, for meat when he opposed foreign criticism of China's dog-eating. For details on the exchange between Professor Zhao and his opponents, a search on google.com or baidu.com using key words of "Zhao Nanyuan", "dog eating", and " St Bernards" will produce some 290 entries. See, for example, Zheng Yi's article on Professor Zhao's views and his arguments with other scholars at https://bit.ly/2YgqFNK.

households. This number was believed to be a 900% increase since 2003 (China Industrial Information Network 2018).

Cruelty to dogs and cats has received significant public attention in China. Dog abandonment is widespread. Neglect is common (Song Yunxiao 2018). Dogs and cats are often victimised out of sheer malice. A college student microwaved a live puppy following an argument with his girlfriend (Zhang 2002). A man in Weihai, Shandong drove for miles dragging his dog behind his car to its brutal death (Li 2016). An 8000-man "kill dog" squadron was formed via social media.[8] These are believed to be die-hard dog haters who vow to kill dogs by poisoning, trapping and other brutal methods. Companion animals, particularly dogs and cats, are also subject to cruelty by businesses and government. Owned dogs and cats are stolen and shipped over great distances to the country's major dog meat markets. Shenyang's Xita Street of dog-meat restaurants is a bloody scene of public dog slaughter.[9] Massive and indiscriminate dog culls orchestrated by local authorities following occasional and sporadic dog-bite incidents have appalled animal lovers.

The case of a Changsha policeman who beat a golden retriever to death in broad daylight on the last day of 2017 revealed the general lack of competence among Chinese law enforcement in handling issues caused by human–animal conflicts. The incompetence has a lot to do with the authorities' failure to attach importance to training of officers in the best and modern practices of urban animal management. The Changsha case also revealed a source of conflict between the government and a society that is increasingly sensitive to how the government deals with animals and other issues that matter to average people (Lo 2019). China is experiencing a "civil war" between animal activists and those who defend or participate in acts of cruelty to dogs. Animal lovers have responded to incidents of cruelty to dogs. For example, outraged animal lovers confronted and beat up the Weihai man who towed his dog to death on a busy highway. They stormed dog slaughterhouses and staged protests in front of dog meat restaurants. They called on the authorities and the entire society to shut down

---

8 Interview with DD, an activist with Beijing Mothers Against Animal Cruelty, 19 September 2018.
9 Interview with Ms Liu, a Tianjin activist, 2 October 2018.

online youth chatrooms where videos of dog torture and live skinning of kittens were circulated. They campaigned against the " Yulin Dog Meat Festival" in southwest China's Guangxi Zhuang Autonomous Region. And they confronted dog-meat traders and took part in highway interceptions of trucks shipping live dogs and cats to the country's major dog and cat meat markets. Animal protection groups have actively sought to change the government's policy regarding dogs. The month of March every year is the occasion when Chinese animal protection NGOs lobby legislators of the National People's Congress and delegates to the Chinese People's Political Consultative Conference to outlaw the dog-meat trade.

How dogs should be treated divides the mainland Chinese society into two opposing camps. While no one openly defends dog abusers or animal abusers in general, hardcore supporters of dog meat consumption and the dog meat industry are largely in a defensive posture in contrast to the more vocal and active animal activists. The heated arguments between representatives of the two groups on live TV talk shows have revealed the vast divide in mainland China over dogs. Confrontation and physical conflicts between activists and dog-meat traders have caught much media and social media attention in the last decade. With the rise of the younger generation born in the 1990s and 2000s in China's animal protection movement, this "civil war" over the treatment of dogs will continue.

Farm animals

China is the world's biggest livestock producer. Industrialised animal farming has long been criticised for animal welfare problems, and China now has the world's biggest concentrated animal feeding operations (CAFOs).[10] Chinese public was first drawn to farm animal welfare by concerns over meat safety. In the late 1990s, reports of the

---

10   China in 2012 produced 79.4 million metric tonnes of meat, accounting for 26.2% of the world's total meat output (302 million tonnes). For primary livestock production data, see the UN FAOSTAT database at http://faostat.fao.org.

forced watering of pigs by long-distance livestock transporters alerted Chinese consumers to the related problems of contaminated animal products and animal suffering.[11]

In the reform era (1978 to the present), however, farming methods are out of sight of most consumers, particularly urban consumers with greater purchasing power. Industrialised animal production pushed farming operations to inland provinces, far from the major consumption centres in the coastal regions such as the Nanjing-Shanghai and Guangzhou-Hong Kong regions. Long-distance transport moves live farm animals from locations of production to these distant urban centres of consumption (Appleby et al. 2008, 288–323). A truckload of pigs travelling from Henan in Central China to Guangzhou 1400 kilometres away in the south-east, for example, can spend 48 hours or more on the road. Pigs who are denied water, food and rest in the course of transport can lose up to 10% of their body weight by the time they arrive at the slaughterhouse. To make up for the lost weight, truck drivers have been known to pump large quantities of water into the pigs' stomachs. The forced-watering process is unquestionably brutal. The pigs fight hard, often receiving injuries, to get away from the water hose. Pigs whose stomachs are filled with water, or whatever liquids the truck drivers can access, die slowly and painfully before slaughter. Recent news reports about the pumping of a large quantity of water over the course of twelve hours into the stomachs of cattle at a slaughterhouse in Anhui aroused worldwide condemnation. Consumers expressed outrage that the potentially contaminated meat was sold on the market. (Chen, Laurie 2018).

Forced watering of livestock for weight gain is not a new invention; it was practised in the past. As the practice deceives consumers and brutalises farm animals, it was outlawed in China's Qing dynasty (1644–1911). The revival in the contemporary era of this "barbaric practice," as a Chinese activist called it, is thought-provoking. "While China's economy has been modernising at an astounding rate, our lack of compassion for farm animals is equally shocking," commented Mme Qin Xiaona, founder of Beijing's Capital Animal Welfare Association.[12]

---

11 See for example the 2004 *Epoch Times* report "Chinese market produces a new profession of 'live pig watering workers,'" http://bit.ly/2M3DzvX.

Yet for the self-employed long-distance transporters, staying in business and maximising profit are overriding objectives. They conduct forced watering not for the fun of brutalising pigs, but to increase their profit margins. Although the practice does not violate any anti-cruelty laws, as there are none on the Chinese mainland, transporters who engage in it may be legally liable under food safety regulations and government policies against forced watering.[13] Forced watering is not the only weight-increasing practice. Injection of gelatin-like substance into beef is also used by some traders to increase the weight of frozen beef (Wu Hong 2015). If gelatin-infected beef is a violation of the state's food safety laws, shouldn't forced watering of pigs and cows, a practice that produces contaminated meat, be penalised?

When China adopted factory farming, it also embraced many associated practices that are challenged by animal protectionists. Growth-promoting additives are commonly used in industrialised animal farming. In China, the use of banned substances such as Ractopamine and Clenbuterol to induce faster weight gain and leaner meat has received much media attention. The earliest reported human case of Clenbuterol poisoning happened in Guangdong Province in 1996. Since then, residents in Hong Kong, Shanghai, Beijing, Chongqing, Guangzhou, Zhejiang and other provinces have also reported symptoms including abnormal heart rates, nausea and vomiting, believed to be associated with consuming meat contaminated with Clenbuterol. At least five Chinese athletes were banned from sports competitions due to testing positive for prohibited substances after consuming contaminated meat (Lotrade.com 2011). In November 2002, 480 people in a Guangdong city came down with Clenbuterol poisoning (Chen Fang et al. 2011). In the first half of 2003, 3,643 people suffered from illnesses caused by Clenbuterol-contaminated pork (Zhu Shu 2003).

---

12 Interview with Mme Qin Xiaona, 18 September 2009, Beijing.
13 See the 2007 six-ministry joint "Emergency notice on further strengthening the management of pork sales on the market" (guanyu jinyibu jiaqiang zhurou shichang guanli de jinji tongzhi) issued by the State Development and Reform Commission, Ministry of Public Security, Ministry of Agriculture, Ministry of Commerce, Ministry of Public Health and General Administration of Food and Drugs at https://bit.ly/2VUhv8n.

Media coverage and government crackdowns on Clenbuterol have led to heightened public awareness of the health hazards of contaminated meat products. The "five freedoms" may be foreign standards that China is not bound to abide by, but the Chinese government's ban on the use of Clenbuterol as a feed additive is unambiguous. Some may wonder why the Chinese government, arguably one of the most powerful regimes in the world, is incapable of enforcing its ban on Clenbuterol and other substances. However, pork in China is no ordinary commodity. It is a product of strategic importance. Fluctuation in pork supply has been known to create strong public reactions. Like petroleum in the West, pork is so important that Chinese authorities have established a national "meat reserve" system, an emergency response mechanism to deal with fluctuations in pork production and market supply (Ding Qi 2007; Ministry of Commerce 2007).

Food security has been the top priority of China's reformist state. Meat and dairy production is part of the state's food security strategy. Deng Xiaoping said in 1978 that food security was a matter of great importance to the legitimacy of the ruling Communist Party (Chinese Communist Party Central Document Research Institute 2004, 450–51). The fear that strict enforcement of quality control could slow down food production explains the frequency of food safety incidents and regulatory failures. The 2011 discovery that China's biggest meat processing plant, Shuanghui, had produced contaminated meat products was one indicator of the failure of the government's regulatory power (Dongfang Morning News 2011). In December 2011, the Shuanghui incident, together with other widespread violations, forced authorities to issue a six-ministry joint order reaffirming a national ban on the production and sale of Clenbuterol (Ma, Anyue 2011). The following year, reports that the suppliers of Kentucky Fried Chicken (KFC) in China had used illegal drugs in their chicken feed to promote faster weight gain suggested that producers were still not paying adequate attention to food safety and animal welfare (Yan, Alice 2012).

Forced watering and the use of banned additives are two of the most publicised problems for farm animal welfare. Most other factory farming practices that compromise animal welfare are not known to the public. Crowded housing, gestation crates, battery cages, tail docking,

Introduction: animals in contemporary China

beak trimming, ear tagging, early weaning, and forced feeding are all standard factory farming practices that run counter to the "five freedoms." In the mid-1980s, Chinese researchers and scholars started to translate Western publications on factory farms.[14] Peter Singer's *Animal Liberation* was translated into Chinese in Taiwan and introduced to the mainland. Singer's biting 1975 critique of the industrialised farming system introduced Chinese readers to the latest Western ethical challenge to modern food production. Professor Zu Shuxian, translator of the mainland Chinese version of Peter Singer's ground-breaking book, has observed that by the time *Animal Liberation* was introduced to mainland China, people had come to think that it was acceptable to use any means necessary to produce food.[15]

The true cost of industrialised animal farming is yet to attract the attention of Chinese policy makers. Market demand for animal products has grown exponentially in the last 40 years, and further expansion is likely to continue in the foreseeable future. Chinese officials have long believed that there is room to increase per capita meat consumption (Jia Youlin 2001, 6–9). The per capita meat (not including fish) consumption in China in 2010 was 60 kilograms less than that of the European Union member states and most other industrialised nations such as the United States, Canada, Australia and New Zealand (FAOSTAT 2011). In China, the income gap between urban and rural residents remains wide and there is consequently a difference in meat consumption. Demand for meat in rural areas is a major driving force behind livestock production. People who are

---

14 For example, in 1984 Beijing's Science Publishing House published *Progress on Studies of Livestock Behaviors*; K.A. Houpt and T.R. Wolski's *Domestic Animal Behavior for Veterinarians and Animal Scientists* (Iowa State University Press, 1982) was translated into Chinese and published in 1987; and A.F. Fraser's *Farm Animal Behaviour* (Bailliere Tindall, 1980) was also translated into Chinese and published in 1985. More recently, in 2011 Jinshun Zhan, Bing Zhang and Zhirui Wang published their scholarly article on factory farming in China, "The animal welfare problems in China's livestock production" (woguo xumu yangzhiye zhong cunzai de dongwu fuli wenti), *Hunan Journal of Animal Feed* (*hunan shiliao*), No. 4, pp. 35–37.
15 Conversation with Professor Zu Shuxian, 18 September 2009, Beijing.

familiar with China's contemporary history understand the prevailing consumption ethos in the country, particularly among certain age groups. Chinese media identified compensatory meat consumption to explain the increasing popularity of animal food in people's diet and the rising chronic health issues (Shan 2014). This compensatory consumption behaviour is more common among those who were born in the 1950s and 1960s. These are the people who were exposed to the Chinese famine and who lived through the Maoist era of extreme food deprivation. Medical researchers in various countries have found that early exposure to poverty or famine can cause metabolic and structural changes that impact insulin resistance, leading to common diseases such as type 2 diabetes in adulthood. Food availability and lifestyle of those who suffered hunger in their early life can also be a major contributing factor that should have been included in these studies.[16] To Chinese seniors, food security takes precedence over food safety or how animal food is produced. In contrast, a 2016 consumer survey found that respondents aged between 22 and 36 years old were most supportive of paying a higher price (a 5% to 10% increase) for pork from farms that provided better welfare conditions for the pigs (World Animal Protection Association, China Veterinary Medical Association, and Xinhua News 2016).

Wildlife farming and trade

China has a long history of wildlife use. But the large-scale trade of wildlife animals and the massive farming of wildlife species for commercial purposes are new developments. While investigators had already noticed wildlife trade and farming operations across the country, it was not until 2002, when Severe Acute Respiratory

---

16 For studies on early life exposure to famine and development of type 2 diabetes in adulthood, see Li et al. (2010), Exposure to the Chinese famine in early life and the risk of hyperglycemia and type 2 diabetes in adulthood, *Diabetes* 59(10): 2400–6; see also Thurner et al. (2013). Quantification of excess risk for diabetes for those born in times of hunger, in an entire population of a nation, across a century, in *Proceedings of the National Academy of Sciences of the United States of America* (PNAS) 110(12): 4703–7.

Syndrome (SARS) broke out in Guangdong Province, that the Chinese public and the international community were alerted to the existence of a massive and unregulated wildlife catering industry in China. Following the devastation of the SARS epidemic, journalists and investigators found that wildlife animals, either caught in the wild or bred in captivity, were being shipped to Guangdong from all over the country by various transportation means. In addition to the adverse impact on global wildlife conservation, Guangdong's wildlife markets have been criticised for animal welfare problems. Wild-caught animals, often with open wounds caused by debilitating traps, suffer for days before being sold to restaurants. A 2003 report described cages crammed with different species of wild or farmed animals and rusting with animal waste, blood, pus and other bodily liquids. Most of the wildlife animals on the market had spent days on the road without access to food or water (Chakraborty 2003).

China has also been the main destination of global wildlife trafficking and other controversial wildlife imports. In October 2019, despite international criticism and the outrage of Chinese animal protection groups, China imported 30 baby elephants from Zimbabwe (Chen, Quin and Liu, Juliana 2019). The shipment was strongly criticised as it was hastened to beat the date of 26 November when a new rule of the Convention on International Trade in Endangered Species of Wild Fauna and Flora (CITES) was to take effect against elephant export (Humane Society International 2019). China had already imported 118 African elephants between 2010 and 2017.[17]

China has seen the rise of a massive wildlife farming industry in the reform era. By the end of the 1990s, it had reportedly succeeded in domesticating 54 wildlife species (State Forestry Bureau 2003, 51–2). Yet success in captive breeding is yet to result in enhanced awareness of wildlife conservation or improved welfare for captive wildlife animals. As the world's conservationists have pointed out, there has been little evidence that China's huge success in captive panda breeding has done anything for the bottom line, i.e., boosting panda populations in the wild (Dell'Amore 2013). Bear farming is another huge success in terms

---

17 The data on wildlife trade can be retrieved from the CITES trade database at trade.cites.org.

of the revenue it generates and the number of bears farmed in captivity. However, it is the most problematic and criticised of all farming operations. Unknown to most in China and abroad, Chinese tiger farms and other captive institutions such as zoos, safari parks and circus owners have phenomenal reproduction figures. In 2017, it was estimated by a government newspaper that there were between 5,000 and 6,000 tigers of different subspecies in these facilities (People's Political Consultative News 2017). In 2005, a firearm producer in Northeast China began a rhinoceros farming operation with the aim of shaving their horns for use in traditional Chinese medicine.[18] Across the country, farms raising civet cats, turtles, ostriches, bamboo rats, deer, musket deer, and Chinese alligators also report impressive breeding figures. These farms have continued to grow despite SARS. In 2017, reporters uncovered a tiger-breeding village where 300 tigers were bred to be used for travelling circuses, a source of income for the village of 1,600 (Metropolitan Express 2017).

Fur-animal farming is undoubtedly China's biggest farming operation besides livestock production. Of the $15 billion worldwide sales of fur products in 2010–11, China reportedly accounted for one quarter. Some analysts predicted that China would emerge as the world's biggest market for fur products in 2015 (Song Xueliang 2014). However, after processing 87 million pelts in 2014, China's fur industry has been declining in pelt production. In 2019, it processed 39.71 million pelts, a drop by 54% in comparison with the pelt output of 2014 (Zhang Xiaohong 2020). The revenue of pelt sales reached 95.7 billion yuan in 2016 only to be followed by a consecutive three-year decline. In 2018, the sales revenue dropped to 77 billion yuan (Qian Zhan Industry Research Institute 2019). Conditions on the fur farms have long been criticised by Chinese activists. The slaughter of fur animals was a shocking practice. Live skinning of raccoon dogs in China's fur-farming regions, documented in a video by the Swiss Animal Protection group in 2004–5, horrified Chinese and international audiences (Hsieh-Yi et al. 2005). The video shocked

---

18 A rhino farming and horn shaving development plan was attributed to Longhui, a firearms producer in northeast China's Qiqihar of Heilongjiang province. The project plan is accessible at https://bit.ly/2LY85HI.

members of the European Parliament when it was screened there in the spring of 2006.[19] In response to the global condemnation following the Hsieh-Yi et al. report, the Chinese fur industry started to centralise slaughter in designated facilities where electric stunning was performed. However, fur-farm owners have continued to skin the animals soon after smashing their heads on the ground. Some foxes and raccoon dogs regain consciousness when skinning takes place. Besides animal welfare issues, the risk of disease outbreaks on Chinese fur farms has also been raised as a concern in the context of the COVID-19 pandemic (Huang Pien 2020).

Wildlife in the entertainment industry

In 2018, there were 185 large animal display institutions (136 urban zoos and 49 safari parks) displaying wildlife of various kinds (China Baogao 2019). Most of these zoological gardens are members of the China Association of Zoological Gardens, a government-affiliated professional organisation under the Ministry of Housing and Urban–Rural Development. There are also a large number of small, rural and roadside zoos across the country. The determination to build more animal display facilities shows no signs of diminishing. New facilities were completed and more were planned (Tordesillas 2015). China's enthusiasm for aquariums seems to be unaffected by SeaWorld's decision to shut down its orca shows and breeding program. On 16 November 2018, a Shanghai ocean park premiered the first killer whale show in China (Li Xiaoming 2018). While the general public may know very little about the welfare problems of industrialised animal farming, the Chinese and international media have reported some of the pronounced welfare problems in Chinese zoos. In 2010, the death of 11 Siberian tigers due to starvation at a private wildlife park in northeast China's Liaoning Province sent shock waves through the international community (qq.com 2011).

---

19 I was present as an invited speaker at the screening of the footage at the European Parliament in Strasburg, France in March 2006.

Neglect, lack of expertise, outdated veterinary techniques, poorly designed enclosures, lack of motivation to adopt new management methods, harassment and assault of animals by visitors, and the drive to maximise profits may explain the welfare problems in most Chinese zoos, particularly privately owned safari parks and ocean parks built since the mid-1990s. In a zoo in northern China, I saw two Tibetan yaks used to cooler weather tethered to a pole under the blazing hot summer sun without any shade. This could be a result of the zoo management's lack of knowledge of the animals and of their natural habitat. Or, it could be a result of sheer negligence.[20] Older veterinarians, graduates of agricultural colleges and now in management positions at Chinese zoos, are often resistant to the adoption of new veterinary techniques recommended by junior vets.[21] Compromised welfare conditions in Chinese zoos have attracted much domestic and international attention. Management problems and outdated enclosure designs encourage visitors to act disrespectfully to zoo animals. In December 2012, visitors hitting two lions with snowballs at a zoo in Hangzhou elicited a strong reaction from Chinese and international audiences.[22] Beijing's Badaling Wildlife Park, a safari park, is perhaps China's most dangerous captive institution. Visitor and staff deaths and injuries caused by tigers, elephants, bears and camels have hit headlines, and the park has been criticised for the poor conditions in which it keeps its animals (BBC 2016; BBC 2017; Wang Tianqi 2018). This is also the place where live feeding was conducted.

Performances featuring zoo animals have caused huge controversy in contemporary China. While zoo managers defended animal

---

20 Observation made on 18 June 2010 by the author during a field investigation of zoos in northern China.
21 Personal interview with an expatriate worker at a wildlife breeding institution in Sichuan, 12 December 2011.
22 Some recent incidents involving visitors included the death of a kangaroo at a zoo in Fuzhou of Fujian Province and the plucking of peacock feathers in another zoo in Jiangsu. See Keegan Elmer, "Chinese tourists pluck out live peacocks' tail feathers at zoo," *South China Morning Post*, 30 April 2018 at http://bit.ly/2K6sI0o, and Chris Buckley, "Kangaroo pelted with rocks dies in Chinese zoo, and fury flies," *New York Times*, 20 April 2018, https://nyti.ms/2LVHc5h.

performance as harmless and a way to attract visitors, activists and experts called on the public to boycott zoos that were staging the performance. In a 2005 report on China's safari parks, the activist group China Zoo Watch documented the various ways animals were forced to perform for long hours and under stressful conditions, especially during China's national holidays (China Zoo Watch 2005). Chinese activists have criticised photo-ops with lion cubs and tigers, who are often tethered, drugged, de-toothed and de-clawed. Despite the national government's policy against animal performance, zoos with performance programs have largely resisted the new policy. In April 2013, the Asia for Animals Coalition, composed of major animal protection groups such as the Humane Society International, the Royal Society for the Prevention of Cruelty to Animals, the International Fund for Animal Welfare, the Animals Asia Foundation, and others identified 84 Chinese zoos and aquariums that had animal performances. The coalition appealed to Chinese authorities to shut such programs down. These 84 zoos were in clear violation of the Chinese government policy against animal performance, a policy adopted in 2010 both by the State Forestry Bureau and the Ministry of Housing and Urban–Rural Development (Huanqiu 2010; Beijing Evening News 2010).

Animal welfare problems in zoos are partly a result of the growth in the number of wildlife display institutions since the early 1990s. While private owners see profits in zoo operations, most of them do not have the professional expertise needed to manage and maintain captive wildlife institutions. A zoo built in 2011 in China's Inner Mongolia was a major project, with a 2 billion yuan (about US$312 million) investment. The ambitious management team reportedly vowed to bring animals from across the world to an area with a long and brutal winter.[23] In south-eastern China, a city zoo built in the 1950s was relocated in 2011 to a new site at a cost of 1 billion yuan. To the disappointment of animal welfare experts, much of this money went into beautifying the environment for visitors while considerably less

---

23 Information about the new zoo was obtained from the author's conversation with two managers of the newly built zoo, and with government officials in charge of the nation's zoological gardens, Beijing, 9 June 2011.

was spent on enclosures for the animals. The new zoo is admittedly an architectural marvel. The thick vegetation, man-made lakes, bridges and facilities for visitors are all beautifully designed and constructed. However, the facilities for housing animals have much room for improvement from a welfare point of view. A US specialist in zoo enclosure design commented that "At least half of the investment should have been spent improving the holding and display conditions of the animals who will live the rest of their lives in the zoo."[24] A focus on the experience of human visitors rather than animal welfare was also evident in the renovation of a northern Chinese zoo. In this enormous zoological garden in a city close to Beijing, bridges, beautiful pavilions and huge statues of dinosaurs graced the wide-open space. Yet the animal enclosures were rudimentary and shockingly inadequate in size, comfort and other basic respects.[25]

Animals in research and product safety tests

Animals used in scientific research, medical experiments, and product safety evaluation used to be the least known to the public. The shocking conditions of dogs used in medical experiments have been exposed by researchers, students, and members of the public (Cheng, Frances 2016). China has been working to produce national welfare standards for lab animals in an attempt to promote best practices and to eradicate unprofessional, unethical and cruel procedures that are still common in labs and medical schools. In 2017, a total of 1,870 licences for lab animal production and use were held by 1,382 Chinese businesses and organisations. Of the licence holders, 84% reported having access to a lab animal ethics review committee. Businesses represented 53% of the licence holders while non-business and other agencies represented 47%; 60% of the licence holders were public health and pharmaceutical

---

24 Author's electronic communication with the expert, a captive wildlife enclosure design specialist and senior director of the Humane Society of the United States, 15 July 2011.

25 Observation by the author during investigative trips to the zoo in August 2004 and June 2010.

Introduction: animals in contemporary China

organisations. Research and educational institutes accounted for 14% and 11% of the licence holders respectively. Across the country, more than 44,700 people were employed in the breeding and production of animals for lab use and experimentation. Less than half of them (41.21%) held certificates of technical training required for working in lab-animal related jobs (Wang Xile et al. 2017a, 66–70).

China has been using an increasing number of lab animals. In 2013, 2014 and 2015, China used 8.88 million, 9.87 million and 12 million lab animals, from 22 animal species. In the same period, the number of dogs used as lab animals increased from 19,100 in 2013 to 24,700 in 2015. Of the 24,700 dogs used in 2015, 80% were Beagles (Wang Xile et al. 2017c, 42–54). To supply the country's rapidly expanding lab research work, 422 lab animal producers produced in 2013 a total of 22 million animals. In 2015, the number went up to 26 million. A considerable number of these animals were bred for export. In 2015, 14 provinces bred 94,300 primates (Wang Xile et al. 2017b, 63–70.). A majority of the primates and a great number of other lab animals were exported (China Lab Animal Information Network 2018).

China's *Regulation on the Management of Lab Animals* was adopted in 1988. This national government policy reflected the national drive for economic modernisation, in that the quality of animal experimentation and laboratory work were the main concerns. Animal welfare as a concept was not addressed in the regulation, although harassment and mistreatment of animals are prohibited. In the last 30 years, lab animal welfare has slowly received more attention as a result of pressure from animal protectionists. The "three Rs" principle for tackling animal cruelty in lab experimentation – "replacement," "reduction" and "refinement" – is no longer strange to the Chinese scientific community. Chinese lab researchers have also participated in international conferences on alternatives to animal experimentation, with the first Chinese academic work on non-animal alternatives published in 2003. In 2006, the State Scientific Development Bureau released *A Directive on Humane Treatment of Lab Animals* (He Zhengming et al. 2018).

For animal activists, the welfare of laboratory animals is a gigantic challenge. But they have had some success. In the summer of 2013, the Be Cruelty Free campaign, a global effort, was launched in China by a coalition of Chinese groups. The purpose of the campaign was to promote humane innovation and encourage the Chinese authorities to start phasing out redundant and unnecessary animal tests in cosmetic production. In November 2013, China's Food and Drug Administration announced plans to modernise its cosmetics regulatory framework, including phasing out mandatory animal testing for new, domestically manufactured ordinary cosmetic products (Humane Society International 2014a). Scandals involving the head of the country's drug approval authorities in 2007 and the pervasiveness of food safety problems have so far prevented the Chinese authorities from removing animal test requirements for most domestic and imported cosmetic products (Associated Press 2007). In June 2014, however, China's State Food and Drug Administration waived mandatory animal testing for non-specialist, domestically produced cosmetics. This suggested for the first time that Chinese cosmetics companies may choose to replace animal testing with advanced, internationally approved alternatives such as in vitro testing (Humane Society International 2014b). In July 2020, the Humane Society International reported that "China appears on track to end animal testing for imported 'ordinary' cosmetics." In a State Council decision, the Chinese government took a major step to modernise cosmetic safety assessment and lay critical groundwork for removing the longstanding requirement to animal test all imported ordinary cosmetics. The requirement was responsible for the suffering of up to 120,000 rabbits used each year to ensure the safety of imported products. The new policy will take effect on 1 January 2021 (Humane Society International 2020a).

In February 2018, China announced the adoption of the Laboratory Animal Guidelines for Ethical Review of Animal Welfare, a national standard (China General Bureau of Quality Inspection and National Standard Commission 2018). This was the result of 10 years of efforts by a team of Chinese scientists under Professor Sun Deming, chief of the Welfare and Ethic Committee of the Chinese Association of Lab Animal Science. Starting in 2014, the drafting of the guidelines went through eight major revisions and an opportunity for public comment. Importantly, the adoption of the guidelines also benefitted from exchanges with international experts such as the Sino-British

Introduction: animals in contemporary China

International Forums on Lab Animal Welfare and Ethics. The guidelines cover animal welfare and ethics requirements for every aspect of the breeding, transportation and use of animals for scientific research (Welfare and Ethic Committee of the Chinese Association of Lab Animal Science 2013).

Animal welfare and the developmental state

A main theme linking all the animal welfare issues discussed is that China's economic modernisation program has justified the emergence of a pro-business and pro-growth politics. Ideas, groups and activities perceived to obstruct or derail growth are to be neutralised or prevented. In contrast, individual behaviours or corporate actions conducive to short-term gains and fast growth, even if they have an adverse long-term impact on the environment, public health, social morality or sustainable growth, are tolerated or embraced, particularly by the authorities most pressured to produce growth. What underlies the state's pro-growth and pro-business policies is its obsession with catch-up and modernisation at the national level. While economic growth has been used by other states to counter external threats (in the case of Taiwan and South Korea) and to rebuild national pride (Japan), it has been pursued relentlessly by the PRC to defuse internal discontent caused by Mao's mismanagement of the national economy, and to rebuild the legitimacy of the CCP. The regime's stability is seen to depend on the success of its economic modernisation policy. This has translated into an expectation that local leaders will deliver growth: their career progression depends on it, and they race one another to achieve the highest local growth rates. "It does not matter, be it a white cat or black cat, it is a good cat as long as it catches mice," as Deng Xiaoping was famously quoted. Economic growth has been pursued relentlessly, with little or no regard for the many side effects the single-minded growth-oriented development has produced. The following chapters (except chapter two) develop this theme.

Chapter 1, "Animal cruelty in contemporary China: is culture to blame?", is a response to the perception that China has a culture of cruelty; that it has a legacy of nature exploitation; and that the Chinese are culturally programmed to animal cruelty. This chapter also serves to support the book's claim that Chinese culture is relevant to an understanding of the animal welfare crisis; that Chinese culture is complex and includes core values that reject extravagance, insensitivity, cruelty and unbridled exploitation of natural resources; and that China's animal welfare crisis can only be understood by looking at contemporary politics, rather than fixating on China's past.

Animal cruelty did exist in China in the past and was sometimes sanctioned by traditional beliefs, as in all other cultures. Yet ancient Chinese culture also valued compassion and kindness to all life forms. Going back to the earliest days of documented Chinese civilisation, Chapter 2 introduces readers to the forgotten, neglected or slighted parts of Chinese culture, the parts that call for respect for nature and compassion for nonhuman living creatures. By focusing its attention on Daoism, Buddhism and Confucianism, the three ancient thought systems that have shaped the Chinese national character for more than 2,000 years, Chapter 2 sheds light on both the richness of the Chinese legacy of compassion and the pull of pragmatism that characterises all other anthropocentric cultures. In doing so I hope to bring attention to the fact that, while Chinese culture may be silent on a host of practices that were cruel to animals, as in most other cultures, this silence should not be construed as an endorsement of cruelty to nonhuman animals. Importantly, progressive concepts of animal welfare similar to those of the contemporary era were expressed more than 2,000 years ago in China. Taoism, the indigenous religious and philosophical tradition of China was in fact one of the first thought systems in the world to challenge anthropocentrism.

Chapter 3 examines the Chinese "civil war" over dogs and the country's dog-meat industry. Dogs and the dog-meat trade in China have attracted much international attention. In 2010, a highly controversial event, the Yulin Dog Meat Festival, was launched in Yulin, Guangxi. This "festival" was promoted by the local authorities as a local culinary tradition. It has been condemned by animal lovers, who have in turn been criticised for holding China's food culture in contempt. Is dog meat part of mainstream food culture in China? China is after all the world's biggest dog eating nation.[26] Its dog-meat industry involves a production chain of dog dealers, transporters, slaughterhouse operators, meat processors, and restaurant owners. How has this production chain evolved, and how can we explain the controversy around dog eating? How has the industry managed to defy growing domestic and international criticism, and why has the government remained passive in response to the various charges against the industry? Has the cultural tradition of dog meat consumption, claimed by the dog-meat traders, allowed the controversial industry to persist, or is it the naked profit drive that has fuelled market demand for dog meat? In Chapter 3 I look at the sources of the "meat" dogs, at those who are engaged in the industry, and at the main markets for dog meat, particularly the economic development level of these regions, to find an explanation for the persistence of the dog-meat trade. The chapter revolves around the question of whether the dog-meat industry is connected with or serves the country's economic development purposes.

Chapter 4 addresses the challenge of wildlife protection in China at a time when the country is determined to achieve economic modernisation. Wildlife was officially pronounced a resource to be used for economic development in 1988 (National People's Congress of the PRC 1988). This position has remained unchanged despite the most recent changes in 2017 to the country's Wildlife Protection Law. With the adoption of the Wildlife Protection Law in 1989, China has seen an exponential expansion of its wildlife industry. The growth of the industry has continued despite the outbreak in 2002–2003 of SARS, a pandemic that was linked to the country's wildlife markets and wildlife consumption. In 2016, the total sales value of China's terrestrial wildlife industry reached 55 billion yuan (China Statistical Bureau 2018). A 2017 study by a group of Chinese wildlife scholars and wildlife industry representatives revealed that the country's wildlife industry generated a total revenue of 521 billion yuan ($77 billion) (Ma Jiangzhang et al. 2017, 103). Bear farming is arguably the most successful and the most controversial of these operations. It has since 1993 been discredited in the court of public opinion thanks to the campaign efforts of Animals Asia Foundation and its founder Jill Robinson. While most bear

---

26 There is no authoritative data on the total number of dogs killed for food in the world, but China is believed to be the country with the biggest dog meat market, consuming some 10 million dogs a year.

farmers have learned to keep a low profile and avoid publicity, Guizhentang, the biggest bear farm in south-east China's Fujian Province, took the audacious step of going public in the country's burgeoning stock market. As soon as Guizhentang's initial public offering was announced, the company drew worldwide criticism. China's bear farming industry and the country's wildlife policies were once again scrutinised by the public.

Chapter 4 considers how this controversy highlighted the tenacity of both the wildlife industry and its opponents in their struggle to out-manoeuvre each other and to win the ears of the Chinese government. The controversy also revealed the awkward position of the State Forestry Bureau, China's national wildlife management agency. Entrusted with responsibility for both wildlife conservation and wildlife business management, the State Forestry Bureau has been pulled in opposite directions. Staffed by graduates of the country's forestry universities, which are bastions of the utilitarian belief that wildlife exists for human use, the Bureau and the Chinese state as a whole have so far sided with the wildlife farming industry. This official position has emboldened Guizhentang and the industry more widely.

Chapter 5 looks at China's food security strategy and its impact on the country's livestock industry. As part of agricultural production, livestock farming received much policy support in the initial stages of the government's modernisation program, because of the urgency of ending the food security crisis. In 1978, the greatest threat to national security in China was not tensions between Beijing and Moscow, but hunger, caused by three decades of economic mismanagement. To the post-Mao reformist leadership, improving food supply in the shortest possible time was urgent to stop mass exodus and to quiet discontent. In a major policy change, the reforming state allowed peasant households to move into farming activities beyond food-grain production. The stabilisation of grain production in 1984 allowed livestock producers to expand production by adopting Western farming models and technologies, leading to greater productivity and efficiency. Western farming models and practices have served China's political objectives as a developmental state, but they have also introduced new challenges that did not exist on China's formerly traditional farms. In chapter 5, I review the state's concerns about political stability, its

Introduction: animals in contemporary China

food security strategy, policy incentives designed to promote livestock production and industry modernisation, the impact of these incentives on productivity and efficiency, and the resulting animal welfare, food safety, environmental and public health issues. The key question is: how has the state's rural growth strategy led to the expansion of modern concentrated animal feeding operations on the Chinese mainland?

Chapter 6 evaluates the Wildlife Protection Law (WPL). The WPL is China's first national legislation ostensibly for protecting terrestrial species in the wild. Adopted in 1989, the WPL was revised several times. The biggest revision took place in 2013–16, in response to pressure from a coalition of critics including legislators, NGOs, wildlife experts, animal activists, and representatives of the wildlife-use industry. To both the critics and defenders of the wildlife-use industry, the 1989 WPL was a disappointment. In the eyes of its critics, the 1989 WPL failed to stop the runaway assault on wildlife, a situation that had become increasingly serious by the time the law was enacted. Contrary to the stated objective of wildlife protection, the WPL has since 1989 seen a worsening of the wildlife crisis in China. An increasing number of Chinese nationals have been implicated in transnational wildlife-related crimes. The WPL, rather than protecting wildlife, became a wildlife business management law that officially endorsed wildlife use. However, to the wildlife businesses, the 1989 WPL had failed to protect or promote their business interests. Chapter 6 takes a close look at the 2013–16 WPL revision efforts and the end product.

Chapter 7 explores China's animal protection movement and its evolution. As a post-socialist developmental state, China in the reform era (1978 – the present) allows the emergence of social forces in the form of associations, societies and professional organisations outside the state to participate in public affairs. In 1992, mainland China's first animal protection group, the China Small Animal Protection Association (CSAPA), was established in Beijing. Since then, rescue operations, volunteer groups and animal-care teams have multiplied across the country. With the expansion of the Chinese economy and accelerated urbanisation, animal protection groups have increased in number, an unintended result of reform politics. Not only are these groups involved in animal rescue; they have also campaigned for changes to legislation and regulations.

***

This book is exploratory in nature. I hope to direct attention to the impact of China's economic reform program on nonhuman animals and on human–animal relations in contemporary China. I also hope to spark more academic interest in subjects related to nonhuman animals in China in particular. In the reform era, the economic goals of growth and prosperity have been used to justify the introduction of the productive but ethically questionable Western factory farming model. In the reform era, China displays tremendous faith in the power of science, technology and Western production methods in its efforts to modernise its economy and to catch up with the most advanced countries. Social injustices, environmental devastation and animal abuse are considered "necessary evils," to be addressed after the economy improves. The current Chinese government sees economic growth as its most important objective. Without rapid growth, authorities fear that social and political stability cannot be sustained.

Since 1998, when I first delved into the subject of the animal welfare crisis in China, I have made conscious efforts to collect information from different sources on human–animal relations. Included in my collection are journal articles, news stories, tourist eye-witness accounts, special reports by international organisations, government reports, official press releases, policy announcements, and statistics from the Chinese government and inter-governmental groups such as the United Nations Food and Agriculture Organization, the World Animal Health Organization, and the World Bank. With the expansion of online search engines and academic databases, I have been able to add to my collection an increasing volume of data, much of it used in this book.

Importantly, I have managed to collect data from a diverse range of sources. For example, I have tried to rely more heavily on sources containing Chinese critiques of Chinese culture and contemporary Chinese politics. In this way, this book avoids parroting Western views.

This is a study of China's animal welfare crisis from a political scientist's perspective. Studying Chinese politics from afar has advantages as well as disadvantages. Working in an environment of academic freedom, observers in the West have access to diverse sources of information that may be denied to mainland Chinese scholars. Yet we have difficulty accessing some of the key sources of information in China. Over the years, I have forged and maintained professional ties with Chinese scholars, activists and officials strategically positioned in research and law enforcement. They have generously but legally shared data and provided frequent updates about new developments. My field trips to China, formal and informal meetings, hundreds of hours of telephone interviews, thousands of emails, and countless social media conversations have also enriched my data collection. Importantly, I have made and led study trips to farms, captive wildlife institutions, markets, slaughterhouses, research labs, and other animal holding institutions in the Greater China region to get primary data. These field studies include six field studies of China's bear farming industry (2004, 2006, 2008, 2011 and 2013); field trips in 2005–06 and 2014 to study China's livestock industry and animal welfare on factory farms; a field study of zoos and other wildlife-holding institutions in 2008, 2010, 2011, 2012, 2014 and 2018; five other field trips to zoos, aquariums and other wildlife events in 2010, 2011 and 2013; fourteen visits to Chinese police units in charge of urban animal management (2009, 2010, 2011, 2012, 2013, 2014, 2015, 2016, 2017 and 2018); field investigations in Yulin, Guangxi (2014, 2015, 2016, 2018); and visits to dog-meat markets and slaughterhouses in Yanji, Jilin and Changchun, Jilin (2015, 2017 and 2019).

In the course of this research, I have also drawn on literature on human–animal relations in ancient China, scholarly work on environmental mismanagement in reform-era China, and other work on social and demographic changes that have transformed China during the reform era. The animal welfare crisis is a largely neglected topic in China studies. Although there have been many journalistic investigations and NGO reports on animal welfare problems in China, there have been few focused attempts to identify the underlying political, institutional, and commercial forces that are responsible for animal welfare conditions in the country. I have therefore looked to scholarly works on other social and environmental problems in the reform era for their insights on the connection between the country's post-socialist developmental state and animal welfare problems. These works helped to pinpoint the direction of my research and to identify the importance of China's post-socialist developmental state in explaining its animal welfare crisis.

This book asks: in what way has China's modernisation program affected the fate of nonhuman animals? Is the animal welfare crisis on the Chinese mainland linked to the country's development strategy? The situation cannot be understood without considering the role of the contemporary Chinese state and its development policies. Culture may also be relevant, but culture alone cannot explain the welfare challenges currently affecting the world's largest population of nonhuman animals.

1
Animal cruelty in contemporary China: is culture to blame?

Animal abuse happens everywhere. But media reports of animal cruelty in China have raised public awareness of the problem, both domestically and internationally. They have also provided ammunition for sweeping generalisations about China, Chinese people and Chinese culture. In the last two decades, since I began researching animal welfare issues as a college teacher, I have on many occasions been asked if Chinese culture is responsible for animal cruelty in China.

Online, reader reactions to reported animal cruelty cases frequently condemn the Chinese as "despicable," "cruel," and even "mentally disturbed." When a foreign reader asks, "Why are they so cruel to animals?" it is less a question than an accusation, expressing perhaps the reader's contempt for the Chinese nation as a whole. Commenting on a description of live feeding at a wildlife park close to the Great Wall in Beijing, where keepers threw young goats purchased by visitors to a pack of hungry lions, readers worldwide expressed shock, disbelief and anger. "This is absolutely barbaric! What type of human being or people in a culture gets their kicks off seeing such a brutality on INNOCENT animals? Obviously, the answer is the people of China," an American reader wrote.[1] "The Chinese have always been very cruel to animals they should be ashamed" was a typical comment on a similar story.[2] Other commenters described the Chinese as "heartless" and "uncivilised." A Danish reader of the UK's *Daily Mail* saw animal cruelty as a sign that China had failed to progress with the rest of the world. Commenting on the alleged 500-year-old practice of horse fighting in China's southwest Guizhou Province, she wrote:

> Truly disgusting. The phrase "but we've done it for 500 years" just makes it worse. Wow, you were equally cruel, barbaric and horrible 500 years ago? Culture is about developing, moving on and becoming more civilized. Congratulations, you failed.[3]

Criticism of incidents of animal cruelty in China is often extended to Chinese culture and tradition. "I have a huge problem with their culture," declared a *Houston Chronicle* reader after learning about the illegal trafficking of Texas freshwater turtles to Guangdong to be made into turtle soup.[4] "Cruelty against animals is tragic, but China was a brutally sadistic society long before it was open to the outside world," wrote one reader in response to a 2008 story about dog eating.[5] At a 2009 social sciences conference in New York, a scholar in the audience of an animal-related panel argued that research efforts should focus on Chinese culture and what she called the Chinese propensity for animal cruelty because of their cultural tradition.

---

1   See reader comments on the story written by Danny Penman, "Animals torn to pieces by lions in front of baying crowds: the spectator sport China DOESN'T want you to see," 5 January 2008, http://dailym.ai/3lYRhfp.
2   See reader comments on the story written by Nick McDermott, "Live animals thrown to the tigers – for the amusement of the crowd," *Daily Mail*, 2 October 2006, http://dailym.ai/3n3eVZM.
3   See readers' comments on the story written by Bill Mouland, "China not ready to give up 'barbaric' horse fighting," *Daily Mail*, 11 July 2006, http://dailym.ai/3mUx77E.
4   In a *Houston Chronicle* article on the declining numbers of freshwater turtles in Texas, half of the 22 people interviewed questioned Chinese culture. See Shannon Tompkins, "Where have all the turtles gone", *Houston Chronicle*, 2 February 2007, https://bit.ly/3lYk9EA.
5   For readers' comments on China's dog eating culinary subculture, see Ted Kerasote "An Olympic disgrace: the current spotlight on China's human rights record fails to illuminate its cruel and inhumane treatment of dogs and cats", 24 March 2008, https://bit.ly/36YRBa0.

1 Animal cruelty in contemporary China: is culture to blame?

This tendency to use culture as an explanation seems to have been reinforced by two developments. First, as a result of China's increasing integration into the global economy and its becoming Asia's biggest centre of global media presence, international readers have read more stories about animal cruelty cases and practices in China. A Google search on animal cruelty in China is likely to generate more results than a similar search for most other countries. The outbreak of SARS and its connection to the wildlife trade may have helped to perpetuate the perception that China is culturally more tolerant of social injustice, political repression and cruelty to nonhuman animals. Second, with the disintegration of the Soviet Union and the end of the Cold War, academic efforts to predict the future causes of international conflict led to the ascendency of the "clash of civilizations" thesis (Huntington 1993). The terrorist attack on the USA on 11 September 2001 and the ensuing American invasions of Afghanistan and Iraq seemed to support the perspective. According to the "clash of civilizations" theory, cultural differences are permanent and fundamental. Culturally specific practices and behaviours can trigger conflict between countries with different cultural heritages.

The perception that Chinese culture may be culpable in animal cruelty is understandable. I am not surprised when foreign readers ask if Chinese people are culturally programmed to violence towards animals. China stands out for its extensive use of nonhuman animals for a variety of purposes. Unlike traditional healing practices in most other countries, traditional Chinese medicine has experienced a revival in the contemporary era. It justifies the use of over 1,800 animal species as ingredients. Foreign observers cannot help but wonder that the runaway poaching of rhinos, for example, is attributable to the Chinese belief in the alleged healing power of rhino horns. However, belief in the medicinal properties of animals is not limited to China. Most cultures have used animal parts as remedies for a wide range of illnesses.[6] A more pertinent question is perhaps why Chinese belief in

---

6   See for example Zhu Liudi's report "律师文革时举报母亲致其被枪决40年后申请母墓地为文物" (An attorney asked to make the tomb of his mother a "cultural relic" 40 years after his mother was executed because of his reporting on his mother to the authorities during the Cultural Revolution),

the healing power of animal parts has been getting stronger at a time when modern medicine has made so much progress. Are traditional beliefs themselves convincing the public of the so-called unparalleled healing power of rhino horns, tiger bones, or pangolin scales? Or are these beliefs recreated, promoted and perpetuated by business interests?

Chinese food culture is known for its diverse ingredients, elaborate preparation, and exquisite presentation. The richness of the ingredients in Chinese cooking and the willingness of some Chinese to try anything edible are summed up in a well-known saying: "The Chinese eat anything with wings except the airplane and anything with legs except the table." In Zhao Rongguang's *A History of Chinese Culinary Culture*, the author reveals that "the Chinese nation has not only consumed all that is edible but also all that is indigestible or should not have been consumed" (Zhao Rongguang 2006, 23).

Chinese culinary culture evolved in response to a harsh natural environment, limited productivity in ancient times, and perennial food shortages caused by natural disasters, warfare and the pressure of a growing population. Traditionally, however, people had a well-balanced diet. The same book points out that varieties of vegetables, fruits, beans and nuts were so abundant that meat consumption in China's past was never significant; admonitions against meat consumption because of religious considerations and compassion were loud and clear in China's dynastic past.

In East Asia, however, traditional medicine does mystify certain animal parts for their perceived properties as tonics, in nourishing the mind, or in preventing and curing disease. Exotic animals are believed to possess more of these alleged qualities. For example, the flesh of owls is believed to have the power to cure malaria (Li Shizhen 1994, 491–92). A folk belief in parts of China has it that owl meat has an unparalleled ability to restore or improve a patient's eyesight, in addition to curing headaches. The perceived curative properties of such ingredients are believed to be best preserved through particular preparation methods and unusual, often cruel, methods of slaughter, as well as particular

---

Xinjing News (新京报), 7 August 2013, http://politics.people.com.cn/n/2013/0807/c1001-22471729.html.

1 Animal cruelty in contemporary China: is culture to blame?

times for slaughter. Are these beliefs a legacy of a time when human knowledge of the natural world was limited, or are they elements of an evolving culture? Traditional fear of contaminated meat underlies the Chinese preference for meat from freshly slaughtered animals. Today the preference remains, but catering businesses seldom mention food safety considerations as the reason. Instead they claim that meat from freshly slaughtered animals tastes better. This explains the continuing existence of wet markets, where live or freshly slaughtered animals are sold, despite the availability of modern refrigeration technology.

China's thriving catering industry in the contemporary era has seen a revival of many allegedly traditional practices. In the late 1990s, some restaurants in southwest China served raw brains harvested from live monkeys to audacious eaters. The brutal act of cracking open the skull of the poor monkeys often took place in front of the customers.[7] How common this kind of cruel eating practice is, and to what extent it is truly traditional, remains a question for further study. In other cases, unborn lambs were taken from late-term pregnant sheep to prepare a special stew or soup. In south-eastern Jiangxi province, peasants used to love stewed puppy meat. Puppies born in wintertime were a delicacy that was believed to have a warming effect.[8] Puppy sales were particularly lucrative in the winter. This was a regional preference, rather than a practice found across the country. In China's Zhejiang province, sweet-sour carps with their mouths gasping for oxygen and their heads still alive used to be a proud local specialty served to guests from home and abroad.

---

[7] For the "criteria for producing successors of the proletarian revolutionary cause" or the "dignified socialist qualities," see for example Kenneth Lieberthal (2004), *Governing China: From Revolution Through Reform*, pp. 293–94. See also Harry Wu's *Bitter Winds: A Memoir of My Years in China's Gulag*, pp. 21–36, for the fate of someone in Mao's China who failed to meet the "dignified socialist qualities."

[8] While an overwhelming majority of Chinese people have never tasted or wanted to eat monkey brains, this rare "delicacy" does exist in southern China. A Google search in Chinese for "eating live monkey brains" produces 318,000 entries, many of which contain graphic images and video clips of brains being harvested from live monkeys.

In Shandong and southern provinces, restaurants allow customers to pick a live dog to be killed, de-haired, disembowelled, and chopped into pieces, all in front of other terrified dogs (Wu, Jun and Deng Yan 2004). In a cooking competition broadcast on China's national TV, fish and snakes are scaled and skinned alive. The twisting skinless snakes are then chopped into pieces and thrown into burning hot woks.[9] Shark-fin soup is a must-have dish at important events such as wedding banquets in Guangdong and Hong Kong. For Chinese New Year, tens of millions of sharks reportedly die a brutal death, their fins cut off and their mutilated bodies discarded back into the ocean (Kirby 2000). It calls for a serious academic study to find out if these controversial slaughter and food-preparation methods are truly traditional or if they are new practices created for profit.

Exotic eating has attracted controversial imports to the Chinese market. Members of the Canadian sealing industry openly expressed their jubilation when the provincial government of Newfoundland signed a memorandum on the export of seal meat with China. "The Chinese eat anything" was the reason underlying their optimism (Clark 2010). A Canadian journalist who defended the seal trade to China claimed that Chinese people viewed animals differently, and that this explained their habit of eating all kinds of animals (Murphy 2011). Similarly, an Icelandic company intended to market ten tons of minke whale meat to China (GJ Financial Consulting 2005). Activists also learned of the building of a plant in south-eastern China's Jiangxi Province for producing foie gras by force feeding geese.[10] In April 2011, two American companies announced a plan to stage rodeos at Beijing's Olympic Stadium. This proposed event, to be broadcast live to more than 2 billion viewers worldwide and with prize money of

---

9 Conversation in July 1991 with a former colleague who was a student of the professor.

10 Public trials and executions were first staged in 1951, when the Communist regime launched a campaign to suppress counter-revolutionaries. Mao Zedong was the mastermind of using public sentencing as a public education instrument. His police chief, General Luo Ruiqing, put the idea into practice and also suggested that public trials be staged before executions, to communicate to the public the various crimes of the counter-revolutionaries. See Yang Kuisong (2013).

1 Animal cruelty in contemporary China: is culture to blame?

$8 million, the biggest in rodeo history, was an audacious attempt to bring a controversial foreign "product" into China.[11] Like earlier plans by some foreign companies to introduce Spanish bullfighting to China (Magnier 2004), the aim of the two US companies was, in the words of a Chinese activist, to revive a cruel "sport" increasingly questioned by the public in their own countries.[12] In 2011, Australia was eyeing the Chinese market for its kangaroo meat exports (Siegel 2011). Efforts to open the Chinese market to kangaroo meat appeared to pay off. In 2015, it was reported that Australia was close to a deal with the Chinese authorities to supply Chinese consumers (Burton 2015). However, like the Canadian seal meat sales offensive, Australia's plans also failed thanks to the opposition of Chinese animal activists. Similarly, an Australian wildlife expert's suggestion that Australia slaughter cross-bred dingos and sell their meat to China also met resistance from animal activists in both countries (Samuels 2016).

Underlying foreign attempts to promote ethically questionable products and activities to China is a perception that nonhuman animals occupy a different position in Chinese culture. Does Chinese culture really sanction cruelty to nonhuman animals, as some foreigners and Chinese believe?

Culture as an explanation

A cultural perspective has long been used in China studies. In the 1950s and 1960s, scholars traced China's failure to modernise in the 19th and early 20th centuries to what they called "a static unchanging civilisation" (Cohen 1984, 59). The traditional values, norms, and institutions are construed as insurmountable barriers to Chinese efforts to modernise the Confucian state, its traditional economic system, and societal attitudes and behaviours. In other words, China's failure to modernise and catch up with the West is attributed to the strong

---

11 Interview with Chinese activists who conducted investigation of the foie gras project in North Jiangxi Province, 20 November 2011.
12 For details of the proposed rodeo program planned for Beijing's Olympic stadium, see the official site of the American sponsor at http://rodeochina.com.

influence of its cultural tradition (Cohen 1984, 57-96). Chinese culture was perceived as a roadblock to modernisation. The Chinese state was a pawn, controlled by the all-powerful culture.

Relevant to our study of animal cruelty is the cultural explanation of China's frequent use of violence against its own people and the perceived Chinese culture of cruelty. In a review of scholarly writing on this culture of cruelty, Andrew Nathan advanced an insightful analysis of the various scholarly arguments on Chinese politics of violence in the country's dynastic past (Nathan 1990, 30-35). To Nathan, Jonathan Spence's book *The Search for Modern China* (W.W. Norton, 1990) threw much light on Chinese history in the Ming and Qing dynasties as one of political repression, territorial conquest, and brutal violence. The underlying assumption of Spence's work is that a culture that gives prominence to the strong conquering the weak is unlikely to foster a compassionate national character. It was therefore not a surprise, in Spence's opinion, that a culture of violence emerged and was perpetuated in the Ming and Qing dynasties that included "burying alive, burning alive, slicing, strangulation, stabbing, drowning, poison gas inserted into tunnels, coerced suicide, exposure of severed heads, vengeful exhumation and dismemberment of corpses, arson, rapine, torture, corruption, epidemic, famine, forced migrations, wars, riots, strikes, rebellions, and piracy" (Nathan 1990, 30). The enormous human suffering in China's dynastic past prompted other scholars, such as Steven Harrell, to question the image Confucian China had projected to the outside world. In Nathan's view, the question Harrell raised was one many observers wanted to ask: "Why does a culture that condemns violence, that plays down the glory of military exploits, awards its highest prestige to literary, rather than martial figures, and seeks harmony over all other values, in fact display such frequency and variety of violent behaviour?" (Nathan 1990, 30).

Spence's answer to the question is that violence was embedded in the Chinese national character. The Chinese authorities did not have a monopoly on this violence: it was ubiquitous and permeated society. Violence against one another was as hideous as violence done to the people by authorities, with the poor squeezing each other to death. This culture of violence was passed down and shapes violent politics in the contemporary era. Spence's arguments on the ubiquitousness

1 Animal cruelty in contemporary China: is culture to blame?

of violence could indeed be supported by the many internal purges in contemporary China. Those of us who grew up in China in the 1970s are too familiar with Mao's concepts of "revolutionary violence" or "proletarian dictatorship," used unreservedly in high-level power struggles. Marshall Peng Dehuai (1898–1974), Vice Premier and Defence Minister, was humiliated at the 8th Plenum of the 8th Party Congress in Lushan for voicing opposition to Mao's Great Leap Forward. He was physically abused in 1966 and died of cancer in prison. Liu Shaoqi, Vice Chairman of the CCP and President of the People's Republic of China, was condemned as a "traitor" and "hidden enemy." He died in house arrest in 1968. Lin Biao, Vice Chairman and Defence Minister, died in a mysterious plane crash in 1971 after losing favour with the "Great Leader" barely three years after he was made Chairman Mao's "successor."

Professor Nathan also reviewed Bette Bao Lord's book *Legacies: A Chinese Mosaic* (Knopf, 1991). This book describes how the rank and file used Mao's mass political campaigns to settle personal grievances in the pre-reform era (1949–78). "They took their turns as victims and perpetrators in a cycle that left no one blameless and no one responsible," Lord writes (Nathan 1990, 34). Besides Lord's book, a number of works about Mao's China and political persecution document mass violence, state repression, and intramural conflicts at the top of the Chinese Communist leadership in the pre-reform era (Wu, Harry 1995; Wu Ningkun and Yikai Li 1994; Rittenberg Sr, Sidney and Amanda Bennett 2001). Memoirs published more recently by former high-ranking Chinese officials such as Qiu Huizuo and Li Zhuopeng add new evidence of the brutal political repression that befell the accused and their families (Qiu Huizuo 2011; Li Zhuopeng 2013).

Barend J. ter Haar, a Dutch scholar, has written a penetrating cultural analysis of the source of violence in China. His article "China's Inner Demons: The Political Impact of the Demonological Paradigm," argues that violence in Mao's years "was by no means an innovation of the Maoist era but had important roots in traditional Chinese religious culture" (ter Haar 2002, 27.). By looking at what he calls the "demonological paradigm and its messianic correlate," he sees Chinese religious culture as the source of the "cultural dimension of violence in contemporary China." Ter Haar argues that "extreme violence is viewed as legitimate in Chinese religious culture if it is used to fend off an attack by demons manifested as disease, fear, possession, barbarian invasions, flooding, famines, and so forth" (ter Haar 2002, 27-8). The dangers posed by these demons justify the use of brutal force to chase them away. Having identified culture as the root cause of the Chinese propensity for violence, ter Haar claims that the demonological paradigm has persisted in post-1949 China, and that it "contributed significantly to the specific cultural expression of mass political campaigns (including their extremely violent nature), both from the top down (party leadership) and from the bottom up (the local people)" (ter Haar 2002, 28).

Challenging the Chinese Communists' claim that China after 1949 had done away with traditional religious infrastructure, ter Haas argues that "the basic categories of the demonological paradigms were preserved." He believes that the Chinese authorities continue to "use the traditional religious discourse of viewing relationships between inside ('us') versus outside ('demons') in terms of violence and counter-violence" (Ter Haar 2002,28). In a television interview, Liu Binyan, a renowned Chinese dissident journalist, made a similar observation. According to Liu, "When a person was condemned as an anti-Party Rightist, he became a social outcast. Anyone could pick on him and humiliate him." In other words, "revolutionary violence" or "proletarian dictatorship" against the anti-Party elements, class enemies, or demons in ter Haar's characterisation, was justified in Mao's years because these "demons" were considered a threat to the "socialist state." The "demons" were therefore enemies of the entire society (Antelope 1993). In ter Haar's opinion, "the demonization of political enemies in contemporary Communist China, far from being a modern aberration, is continuous with Chinese tradition in that the demonisation of the Other has always been a fundamental element in Chinese religious culture" (Ter Haar 2002, 60).

In another article, "Rethinking 'Violence' in Chinese Culture," ter Haar advances the same theme that culture explains violence in contemporary China (Ter Haar 2000). In his words, "there is a much larger normative role for violence in Chinese culture, past and present, than is customarily acknowledged in most China research" (Ter Haar 2000 59). Ter Haar rejects the claim that China had already moved

1 Animal cruelty in contemporary China: is culture to blame?

away from "martial violence" before the founding of the Han dynasty in 202 BCE, and that the civilian ideal had triumphed over the military ideal during the Song dynasty (960–1276 CE). Instead, he argues, the cultural movement from "martial violence" to "refinement" was at best an ongoing process never fully completed. In fact, violence had always been used and justified despite the elite's stated intention to construct a nonviolent ideology. As a result, "Violence continued to be liberally used in the controlling of others," and "The persistence of violence as a form of cultural expression of power and moral values shows that the long-term trend away from violence was a highly modified one." The commonly held belief that China was a culture that condemned violence and awarded great prestige to literary achievements, according to ter Haar, is "solely an ideological construct." China's educated and social elites, in his opinion, "had no compunctions in using violence to maintain control" (Ter Haar, Barend J 2000, 131). Based on ter Haar's arguments, I wonder if a culture that endorses violence to humans will inevitably tolerate or sanction violence to nonhuman animals.

There have long been critical voices inside China questioning the merits of the country's cultural heritages. To these critics, China's traditional culture is one of repression and cruelty. China's "May 4th Movement" of 1919 was a milestone in the intellectual examination of China's traditional culture. Not only were Confucian classics, traditional medicine, and the imperial examination system challenged, the new generation of the literati class rejected traditional culture as a whole. Lu Xun (1881–1936), one of China's most celebrated writers, called the history of China's Confucian culture one of "cannibalism." In the contemporary era, critical views of Chinese culture come mostly from dissenting scholars who reject the authoritarian rule of the CCP. They see one-party dictatorship as a feudal state behind the facade of a modern Leninist party-state system. Nathan quotes a line from the Chinese TV serial *River Elegy*, broadcast on China's national television station (CCTV) in the late 1980s:

> What Confucian culture has given us over the past several thousand years is not a national spirit of enterprise, a system of law, or a mechanism of cultural renewal, but a fearsome

self-killing machine that, as it degenerated constantly, devoured its best and its brightest, its own vital elements. (Nathan 1990, 31)

This statement criticizing Confucian culture in name was in fact criticising the Chinese Communist regime for its continued repression in the reform era of independent-minded intellectuals and society at large. The thinly veiled criticism of *River Elegy* was not tolerated long. When Zhao Ziyang (1919–2005), Party Secretary General, was ousted on the eve of the Tiananmen Massacre in June 1989, the TV serial was banned. The Chinese government's suppression of the Tiananmen demonstration in 1989 helped to reinforce the scholarly view that state use of brutal force against the people was a continuation of the traditional Chinese culture of violence. To their critics, the Chinese Communist leaders were just as despotic, ruthless, and brutal as Chinese dynastic rulers.[13]

Zheng Yi, a Chinese scholar in exile, saw Mao Zedong and his comrades as devoted disciples of the politics of oriental despotism. Mao, in Zheng's opinion, had never hesitated to use brutal force against his opponents in the Party and class enemies in society. Worse still, he turned the entire society into a killing machine during the Cultural Revolution (Antelope 1993). Li Rui, a CCP veteran and a high-ranking official who was imprisoned by Mao for 20 years, held that Mao's love of the ancient Chinese classics may have shaped his preference for particular methods of governance in China's past (Li Rui 1996, 27–49). In 2007, Beijing writer Mei Sangyu published a sharp critique of the many TV dramas that were, in his opinion, eulogies to Chinese imperial rulers. He introduced readers to a long list of trickeries used by Chinese dynastic rulers to usurp and consolidate power. These violent trickeries, he argued, had been repeated for 5,000 years, and the legacy of autocratic violence continued in contemporary China. He warned:

> Although the last dynastic empire collapsed at the beginning of the 20th century, the spectre of dynastic nostalgia has remained … [The Emperor] has disappeared for nearly a century. Yet, the

---

13 Conversation with a Yulin official in the evening of 20 June 2016 in Yulin, Guangxi, China.

1 Animal cruelty in contemporary China: is culture to blame?

> autocratic despotism of imperial power has never ceased to leave a mark on the Chinese national character and on the mindset of the Chinese people. The "virus of despotism" still lives in the depth of the consciousness of some people. Carriers of the "virus" will seize every opportunity they can utilise to harm the nation and the people. (Mei 2007, 1)

China is still an authoritarian state. There is a considerable level of state control over the society. Open dissent and public opposition to the state and the ruling party are sure to be suppressed or violently silenced. There is no denial that China is a stand-alone civilization. Are we sure we are not giving too much credit to China's past for its perceived power in shaping Chinese attitude and behaviours in the contemporary era?

The limits of cultural explanation

As an explanation for contemporary Chinese attitudes and behaviours, "culture" has several problems. Its limitations are particularly obvious when Taiwan and Hong Kong, two other Chinese territories, are compared with mainland China. Can culture account for the progress made in animal protection in Taiwan and Hong Kong, two Chinese societies believed to be no less traditional than the mainland?[14] Chinese culture survived British rule in Hong Kong (1842–1997) and Japanese colonisation of Taiwan (1895–1945). Yet, relative to mainland China, Taiwan and Hong Kong have taken the lead in animal protection legislation in that there is legal protection for dogs and cats in Taiwan and wildlife is not defined as a "resource" in Hong Kong;[15] traditional culture has apparently failed to block humane progress in these two

---

14 Author's field investigation of the slaughterhouse in Jilin, Jilin province on 23 October 2019.
15 For information on the maintenance of traditional culture and practices in Hong Kong and Taiwan, see Cai Yirou's (蔡苡柔), 中西文化融會　香港保存了最好的中國? (The merge of Chinese and Western culture: isn't Hong Kong maintaining the best of China?) (香港01周報 HK01), 1 March 2019. See also 冯仑 (Feng Lun), 真实的台湾很中国, 很现代 (The Taiwan you see is both a traditional and modern society), a *China-Week* report of 30 November 2010, https://www.china-week.com/html/5807.htm.

Chinese societies, although much remains to be done in both places. In Mao's China, Confucius and "old culture" were in fact demonised and denounced. How can traditional culture maintain a tighter grip on the Chinese mainland, where several waves of state-orchestrated campaigns against tradition were launched in the pre-reform era, than in Taiwan and Hong Kong, where traditional culture that emphasizes order, respect for authority, humility, honesty and learning has been better preserved despite foreign administration and occupation?

The cultural explanation has other shortcomings. First, it tends to see non-Western cultures as lacking elements essential for modernisation, progress or compassion. In environmental studies, such cultural approaches may deny the existence of a legacy of environmental governance in traditional societies. Similarly, the cultural explanation sees Chinese culture as cruel to both humans and nonhuman animals. In other words, it supports the assumption, as China experts pointed out, that "the West embodied civilization and China barbarism" (Cohen 1984, 62). China's past "existed only to be overcome, destroyed, and left behind" (Cohen 1984, 83); there was no heritage in that culture that was worth preserving or that might contribute to humane progress in the contemporary era. This approach can easily lead to the view that China has no cultural legacy of environmental governance or animal protection.

Chinese culture does not have a monopoly on the values or behaviours sometimes attributed to it. Demonisation, for example, and a tendency to divide "us" from "them" transcend cultural and national borders. The 20th century provided us with many examples. Who demonised the Jews in the 1930s in Europe? Who demonised Japanese Americans in the early 1940s in the USA? The view that Chinese politics since time immemorial has been dominated by violence not only fails to see the strong influence of Confucianism, which promoted benevolence as a core value, but also reinforced a stereotypical view of Chinese people. Andrew Nathan sees such cultural explanations as intrinsically problematic. To him, the cultural explanation "makes the Chinese seem less our semblables and frères than mysterious others, sinister and cruel ... It offers a national stereotype instead of analysing the situations that can make people behave savagely" (Nathan 1990, 33).

1 Animal cruelty in contemporary China: is culture to blame?

Secondly, the cultural perspective takes a static view of non-Western cultures. It sees Chinese culture as unchanging and stagnant. China in the recent past was perceived as being mired in a state of eternal standstill: "There was no true historical progress but only a static unchanging civilisation" (Cohen 1984, 59). It was a backward society with nothing to offer either the Chinese people themselves or the outside world in the race for modernisation and progress. Such an obsolescent civilisation was "doomed to languish in the stagnant waters of barbarism" (Cohen 1984, 59–60). This view denies cultural evolution as a result of internal developments and external impact. It also denies a culture's own ability to rejuvenate itself. Since change from within was believed to be impossible, change would have to be imposed on China from outside. One obvious problem with this perception is its denial of the fact that for much of its history, China was not closed to the outside world. Chinese culture, despite regional variations and internal diversity, embodies time-tested social norms, belief systems, traditions, customs, values and institutions that have held the country and the people together. These norms, belief systems, traditions and institutions were results of internal evolution and adaptation to new ideas imported from foreign lands.

The cultural explanation also loses sight of the fact that modern states are not pawns controlled by cultural traditions. Modern states have a great capacity to shape culture and move society towards state-defined objectives. China's imperial courts and modern states were all active shapers of new culture and new social values. The People's Republic of China under the CCP has been most successful in crafting what was known as "socialist new culture" during the pre-reform era (1949–78) and "socialist spiritual civilisation" in the reform era.

The cultural perspective ignores cultural complexity and diversity within non-Western cultures. Chinese people are complex individuals just like their foreign counterparts. For example, Mao Zedong initiated a mass sparrow killing campaign in 1958 based on his view that sparrows consumed food grains, and he left behind a disastrous environmental mismanagement record. However, Mao also made sure that the horse he had ridden in the final years of the civil war was well taken care of for the rest of its life (Wang Hebing 2011, 273–74).

He was behind the yearly mass dog culls across China, yet "he asked how the cats I was taking care of were doing," said Professor Lu Di, who was Mao's assistant in Chinese classics.[16] China's vast expanse of territory and ethnic diversity has given rise to regional sub-cultures. Dog eating is a good example. For Han Chinese, who make up the majority of the population, dog eating happens among a small number of people though it is not a decent eating habit, whereas for Mongolians, Tibetans and other ethnic groups it does not exist. Similarly, while traditional Chinese medicine is now well-known for its use of animal ingredients, traditional prescriptions were composed primarily of herbs and minerals. Animal parts as medicinal ingredients were extremely rare. Some ancient traditional medicine practitioners even questioned the appropriateness of ending an animal's life for obtaining its body parts as medicine.[17]

Finally, relying on cultural explanations can divert attention from other more direct contributing factors to the problem under study. Hu Ping, a Chinese scholar, forcefully rejected cultural explanations for contemporary Chinese politics. In his opinion, blaming today's problems on China's past is unfair and unhelpful. It prevents us from identifying the root cause of many problems in contemporary China (Hu Ping 1988, 80). James D. Seymour, a Columbia University professor, said more directly that "contemporary Chinese attitudes have been influenced primarily by economic or political factors rather than cultural considerations" (Seymour 2005, 249). Chinese dynastic rulers were known to varying degrees to be despotic and arbitrary. Yet they never accomplished a level of watertight control even remotely comparable to that achieved by the Leninist party-state in Mao's era. Blaming the totalitarian politics of the Mao era on China's dynastic statesmanship misses the real target, i.e., the modern Leninist party-state. China's massive wildlife farming operations such as bear farming and fur animal farming in the contemporary era cannot be blamed on China's dynastic past. Industrialized wildlife breeding did

---

16 For information on the promotional activities of the Fan Kuai Dog Meat Processing Company, please visit their website at http://fk.vishang.cn/group_buy.php.

17 Conversation with Professor Lu Di, 6–12 July 2011.

1 Animal cruelty in contemporary China: is culture to blame?

not exist in ancient China. If we blame China's cultural tradition for the problems in today's China, we would fail to see the real cause of those problems. The political use of China's past is nowhere more apparent than in the Chinese authorities' own verdict on the causes of the many glaring errors committed by the CCP and Party leader Mao Zedong. The "national characteristic of feudalism" was blamed in the official Chinese historiography for Mao Zedong's errors in his later years and during the Cultural Revolution (1966–76) in particular (Nathan 1993, 283). This official version is obviously aimed at diverting critics' attention from the real problem so that no scrutiny is directed at the one-Party dictatorship and the Leninist Party-state. In Hu Ping's opinion, China's culture was used unfairly by the post-Mao regime as a scapegoat for the policy mistakes of the Party-state and Mao Zedong.

There is no denial that culture is relevant to any study of contemporary China. Yet the view that culture is the primary determinant of contemporary Chinese attitudes and behaviours is debatable. Scholars who challenge the link between the contemporary Leninist Party-state and China's traditional pattern of authority argue that political behaviour today derives primarily from the current Leninist political institutions (Walder 1986; Oi 1989). To understand the impact of contemporary politics on nonhuman animals, we cannot fixate our attention on China's past. There are more immediate and contemporary triggers that are perhaps more relevant to our understanding of the animal welfare crisis at the present time.

Economic reform and developmental states

During the 20th century China saw a dynastic collapse, revolutions, foreign invasions, civil wars, social upheavals, and political purges. In 1908 when Pu Yi (1906–67) was made China's last Emperor, the imperial empire that had lasted for more than 2,000 years was on the verge of an irreversible collapse. Eight years earlier, the anti-West Boxer Rebellion, encouraged and supported by the imperial court under Empress Dowager Cixi (1835–1908), who resented the Western position that constitutional monarchy should be established in China and the sidelined Emperor Guangxu be reinstated, led to the country's humiliating defeat by the "eight foreign powers."[18] The resulting indemnity of 450,000,000 haikwan taels paid to the foreign powers emptied the coffers of the collapsing empire.[19] In 1911, Sun Yatsen overthrew the Qing dynasty and established the Republic of China (ROC), Asia's first modern state. In the next 38 years, China experienced the chaos of competing warlords, Communist rebellion, Japanese invasion and civil war (1946–49). Between 1927 and 1949 the ROC government was preoccupied with military actions to achieve national reunification, resist Japanese invasion and to quell the Communist rebellion. Its attention to social and economic matters was scanty and intermittent. Despite this, the ROC government did experiment with a campaign for social transformation. Mme Chiang Kaishek, China's first lady, was behind a "New Life Movement" that encouraged the building of an animal protection association in Nanjing, the capital city of the ROC, and the adoption of an anti-cruelty policy. The ROC came to an end on the Chinese mainland in December 1949 when Chiang Kaishek, President and head of the ruling Nationalist Party of China, moved from Sichuan to Taiwan. The split of the country into the People's Republic of China (PRC) on the mainland and the Republic of China on Taiwan ushered in the rise of two competing political and social systems in the Greater China region.

The history of the PRC, since its founding in October 1949, can be divided into two eras. The years under Mao Zedong's rule (1949–76) are referred to as the pre-reform era. In this period, Mao supervised the building of a Leninist Party-state, a left-wing totalitarian regime. Marxism, Leninism, and Mao Zedong Thought were pronounced as the theoretical basis of China's socialist ideology. The society was segregated into two major groups based on class identity. The working class, consisting mostly of industrial workers and rural peasants, was the group to be relied on, while members of the overthrown propertied

---

18 See the Peixian Fan Kuai Dog Meat Processing Company website at http://www.fankuai.com/1/about.asp.

19 For a comprehensive account of the Boxer Rebellion, see Diana Preston's *The Boxer Rebellion: The Dramatic Story of China's War on Foreigners that Shook the World in the Summer of 1900* (New York: The Berkley Publishing Group, 2000).

1 Animal cruelty in contemporary China: is culture to blame?

class were to be reformed or suppressed. Throughout the 26 years of his rule, Mao launched one political campaign after another. These campaigns, such as the "Anti-rightist campaign" and the Cultural Revolution, were used to rid the society and Party of opposition voices and perceived hostile forces. In 1976, when Mao died, China was one of the most impoverished countries on earth. Beggary was widespread. Hunger threatened a majority of Chinese people. Towards of the end of Mao's rule, mass exodus to Hong Kong had never stopped.

In the Mao era, the party-state was determined to remove all ideological, political, and cultural obstacles that could derail socialist construction. Mao's "Patriotic Public Health Campaign," "the Great Leap Forward," and the "Mass Sparrow Extermination Campaign" were staged, among other reasons, to eliminate insects, parasites, pests, and dangerous wildlife such as tigers. In the Mao years, to speak publicly of a "love of animals" would have sounded bizarre. The term "love" was rarely heard in the Chinese media to refer to intimate feelings between two people. "Love" was more a synonym of "care deeply about somebody," "have a strong feeling of love for someone in position of power and authority out of respect and gratitude for what she or he has done for the public," or "show great affection for a young child." Besides caring for one's family members, the emotion of "love" could only go to Chairman Mao, the Communist Party, and the "People's Government" out of gratitude and respect. In these years, love, compassion or sympathy for a random person could be politically problematic. According to Mao Zedong, there was no abstract or classless "love" in the world. Such "love would be possible only when class was eliminated from human society (Mao 1991, 847–79). Until then, love should only be extended to "brothers and sisters of the same class," i.e., members of the working class. Love of pets, love of gardening, or other such passions were ideologically questionable, as they had been denounced as bourgeois hobbies. China under Mao had no place for concepts such as "animal protection," "animal welfare," or "animal rights."

In the reform era (since 1978), animal cruelty in China has caught much media attention thanks to the relaxation of government control over the media and the presence of Western journalists. Yet, it has failed to capture significant Western academic interest. The few works that do touch on animals in China mainly address perceptions of animals in China's ancient times, or the devastation of wildlife as a result of environmental destruction in the contemporary era. A comprehensive examination of the animal welfare crisis in the reform era and its causes is lacking. However, scholarly works on China's environmental mismanagement are an important source of information, since they see reform politics as a roadmap for understanding the side effects of the current development programs. Zheng Yi's *China's Ecological Winter* (2001) is a well-documented and comprehensive survey of China's environmental mismanagement in the reform era. Not only does Zheng reveal in great detail the shocking deforestation, soil erosion, desertification, loss of farmland, shrinkage of water resources, air pollution, and destruction of wetlands, he also devotes an entire chapter to exposing the survival crisis of a wide range of wildlife animals. Throughout the book, Zheng reminds readers that environmental crisis in China has accelerated in the reform era. The development-first outlook of many local leaders, in Zheng's view, is causing irreparable damage to the country's natural environment and sustainable growth.

The River Runs Black: The Environmental Challenge to China's Future (2004) by Elizabeth C. Economy is another major work on China's environmental mismanagement in the reform era. While denying that China had a cultural legacy of environmental protection, Economy focuses on the institutional, political and policy constraints of China's reforming state. The animal welfare crisis is not Economy's subject, but her elaboration of the survival crisis facing wildlife species such as the Tibetan antelopes on the Tibetan Plateau reveals an uncongenial and even hostile institutional and political environment that hinders the nation's environmental and wildlife conservation efforts. Through her examination of non-governmental efforts at protecting Tibetan antelopes, for example, readers can see several major obstacles to environmental management in China. These obstacles include the government's lukewarm interest in environmental protection in contrast to its enthusiasm for economic growth, the hardships faced by non-governmental groups in fighting for limited government resources and against the various interests sabotaging their work, and official suspicion of foreign participation in the environmental movement. Although Economy's claim that Chinese culture has no legacy of environmental protection is debatable, her

1 Animal cruelty in contemporary China: is culture to blame?

focus on contemporary politics to explain environmental problems is effective and insightful.

Admittedly, the question of animal cruelty is a controversial subject. What is considered animal cruelty in one country may be viewed differently in another. Passing judgement on a culturally or politically sanctioned behaviour in a foreign country can be construed as cultural imperialism. The 2011 debate in California about banning shark fin consumption was a good example (Joyce 2012): the issue of animal welfare is a minefield of potential controversies. In 2015, Deborah Cao published *Animals in China: Law and Society* (Palgrave MacMillan, 2015), a great work on the current state and challenges of legal protection for nonhuman animals in China. With her focus on laws, regulations and policies in the area of animal protection and management, Professor Cao brought attention to the political, social and economic backdrop against which the country is struggling to respond to the seemingly intractable and mounting number of cruelty cases and animal management issues. Her tackling of the controversial subject of animal protection in China is hugely commendable. It is my hope that more scholars shall step into this minefield. While recognising the cultural underpinnings of animal–human relations in any society, I believe culture is not necessarily the main determinant of a society's collective attitudes and behaviours at a particular point in time. While total cultural convergence may never happen, the gulf between cultures will narrow rather than widen in the 21st century, as we see an increasing and expanding transnational flow of capital, goods, services, personnel, and ideas.

In mainland China, animal cruelty has yet to attract political attention. Seventy-one years into its rule on the Chinese mainland, the CCP has yet to legislate against animal cruelty. Mainland China is today almost 200 years behind the industrialised nations in lawmaking for animal protection if we use the British *Cruel Treatment of Cattle Act* (1822) (sometimes called "Martin's Act") as the point of reference. Mainland China is more than half a century behind India in the same area of legislation. Yet Chinese culture did not prevent Hong Kong and Taiwan from legislating for animal protection. China in the reform era has not lacked legislative activism. The National People's Congress (NPC), the country's national legislature, has been unprecedentedly active in economic lawmaking (Ngok King-lun 2002, 23). The NPC has adopted laws related to animal management, animal disease control and prevention, and productive activities involving nonhuman animals. Laws solely for animal protection are yet to be made. The domination of economic matters in the legislative agenda serves the political objective of China's developmental state.

To animal protection professionals around the world, animal protection involves more than the conditions in which animals are raised, transported, kept, used and slaughtered. It also involves questions of food production, conservation, protection of biodiversity, public health and pandemic prevention, social morality, state–society relations and even international relations. Studies have linked poor animal welfare to substandard meat and dairy products (De Passille and Rushen 2005, 757–66). Exploitation of wildlife is not just a conservation problem. The connection between China's wildlife trade for the exotic food markets and pandemics (SARS in 2002 and COVID-19 in 2019) is not a secret (Guan et al. 2003, 276–78; Chen, Liu and Guo 2020, 418–23; Rodriguez-Morales et al. 2020, 3–5). Similarly, an outdated urban animal management policy can cause problems beyond animal welfare. Besides exposing the government's lack of competency in urban animal management, it can also undermine its responsibility to ensure public safety and public health (Zhou et al. 2016; Seimenis and Tabbaa 2014, 131–36). An outdated dog registration policy requiring exorbitant registration fees, designed to discourage and penalise pet ownership, for example, can encourage widespread resistance, leading to a low rate of dog registration in most urban areas (Liu Qin 2018). Unregistered dogs are also more likely to be intact and unvaccinated. China has yet to adopt a nationwide rabies prevention measure that is cost effective and meets the government's plan to make China rabies-free in 2025.[20] These and other issues related to animal protection and animal welfare, in the eyes of Professor Lu Di, founder of the China Small Animal Protection Association, a nationally registered animal advocacy NGO, cannot be ignored by the Chinese government any longer.[21]

---

20   Interview with Qin Xiaona, founder and director of the Beijing Capital Animal Welfare Association, 21 May 2016.

1 Animal cruelty in contemporary China: is culture to blame?

Given the enormity of China's animal welfare challenges and the problems with "culture" as an explanation, I would like to ask: what *is* the appropriate theoretical approach for interpreting China's animal welfare crisis in the reform era? This book acknowledges the relevance of Chinese culture to our understanding of human–animal relations in China, but it shall focus more on China's contemporary reform politics. I will consider how China's reform politics have influenced human–animal relations at a time when the country is experiencing breathtaking economic growth. To examine the source of a wide range of animal cruelty practices in contemporary China, I turn to the theory of developmental states for a roadmap.

Developmental states

A single-minded drive to achieve fast socio-economic growth is the first defining feature of developmental states. Efficiency and productivity become obsessions for governments that have adopted a state-led development strategy. Government policies are designed to achieve fast GDP growth, especially in the short-term. Because of this growth-oriented government economic policy, production expansion and growth rates take precedence over other considerations such as social and environmental justice. The rationale underlying this development model is a belief that economic growth and social justice cannot be achieved at the same time. One has to make way for the other, at least in the short-term, or until substantial economic growth is achieved. In almost all developmental states, growth is given first priority. Although the term "developmental state" is most frequently associated with contemporary East Asian states, they do not have a monopoly on this development-first outlook. It in fact mirrors the experience of Western industrialisation in the last 200 years. Charles Dickens' novels revealed the distortions created in British society during the Victorian era, when rapid industrialisation was relentlessly pursued at the expense of social justice and labour rights. The

---

21 Interview in Chengdu with Professor Tang Qing, senior researcher at the China Center of Disease Control, 20 October 2014.

development-first outlook calls for the removal of any institutional, political, societal or cultural obstacles to rapid development.

East Asian developmental states in the 20th century were highly motivated engines of growth. They often shared certain experiences: repressive poverty, economic collapse caused by civil or international war, foreign occupation, internal turmoil, and severe regime legitimacy crises. Governments in post-war Japan, South Korea and Taiwan were under pressures to push for rapid economic growth as a means to end economic crises, restore national pride, rebuild international credit, defuse political instability, and neutralise security threats from both within and without. Rapid economic development was therefore the immediate target of these states' economic policies. Like European states in the past and Japan in the Meiji era, economic backwardness was not necessarily an insurmountable obstacle to economic modernisation. It was both a primary motivation and, in fact, an advantage for initiating a catch-up industrialisation strategy (Gerschenkron 1962). Post-war Japan, despite its occupation by the USA – the world's champion of the free-market economy – chose to embrace state-led development as a quick-fix for its war-torn economy, and in order to rebuild national confidence following its devastating defeat. Japan's state-led reconstruction and the role played by the country's growth-conscious technocrats and economic bureaucrats were dissected by Chalmers A. Johnson in his ground-breaking 1982 study of the Japanese economic take-off. In the 1950s the Chinese Nationalist government in Taiwan faced twin threats of internal instability and invasion from the Communist mainland. In response, rapid economic growth was prioritised as a strategy to consolidate the ruling order on the island and to buttress its defences against the Communists. Topping the list of factors that explained Taiwan's economic miracle was official commitment to development (Gold 1986).

Developmental states are not liberal democracies. Therefore, post-socialist developmental states such as the PRC can fit into this category. The 20th century East Asian developmental states are all authoritarian. These states maintained competent bureaucracies dominated by technocrats trained in science, engineering and economics. These technocrats are generally insulated from society.

1 Animal cruelty in contemporary China: is culture to blame?

Through these technical administrators, the state "dictates not only the norms and rules of the social, political, and economic existence, but also the directions of development" (Bolesta 2007, 109). Developmental states are interventionist. They maintain an authoritarian institutional setting and a developmentalist ideology. Existing policies that hinder productivity and business adventures are quickly dismantled and replaced by policies that promote efficiency, competitiveness, maximum resource use, and quick adoption of new production models and technologies. Developmental states take a proactive approach to the construction of a favourable policy environment to achieve rapid growth.

Some central-planning socialist states have been known to sacrifice one sector, such as agriculture or consumer industries, in favour of heavy industry. Developmental states, in contrast, act more as regulators or facilitators; in Peter Evans' characterisation, the state acts as a "custodian," "demiurge" or "midwife" (Evans 1995, 14). Through government policies, developmental states regulate, assist and motivate the private sector, often targeting particular industries to encourage growth. The role of favourable government policies in stimulating growth is such that these policies themselves constitutes a comparative advantage. Flexible policy adjustments allow developmental states to remove obstacles to growth or to shield domestic industries from adverse outside impact. The adoption of favourable trade policies is indispensable for growth in countries that are integrated into the global division of labour (Krueger 1980).

Developmental states are in command of capitalist economies. While state sectors may exist, private production and other non-state sectors are the backbone of the economy. In East Asia, a developmentalist ideology fits nicely with the society's culturally ingrained entrepreneurial impulse, Confucian respect for authority, and "faith in the transformability and perfectibility of the human condition (Tu 1989). Entrepreneurs respond quickly to signals of state policy change. Unlike in centrally planned socialist economies, where the means of production are nationalised, developmental states protect and encourage private production.[22] Through policy instruments,

---

22 Telephone interview conducted 23 July 2013.

developmental states set the limits to permissible corporate behaviours, direct resources to sectors the state wishes to target, and encourage industry expansion and modernisation. Although most domestic production is done by privately owned enterprises, developmental states take the lead in introducing new technologies and production models to increase productivity. Knowing the importance of the private sector to economic growth, developmental states make efforts to shield private enterprises, particularly high-yielding and job-creating businesses, from pressures exerted by labour, consumer, environmental and animal protection groups. The profit drive of private businesses aligns with the state's short-term objective of quick economic results.

Developmental states do not have plans for democratisation. Their goal is not to build an open society with democratic institutions. In the initial stages of development, they use state power to suppress societal voices that are perceived to contradict development objectives. One perspective holds that East Asian developmental states should be construed as "bureaucratic-authoritarian industrialising regimes" (Cummings 1999, 70). In these countries, namely Japan in the 1950s, and Korea and Taiwan in the 1970s, labour, student, consumer and intellectual groups had a hard time making their concerns heard. Voices that challenged state-led capitalist development, or that were perceived to be obstructing or slowing growth, were silenced and penalised: "East Asia has meant industrialization without Enlightenment" (Cummings 1999, 70). The underdevelopment of civil society in developmental states is no accident. Governments use economic development, national security and domestic stability to justify policies that limit civil liberties and autonomous activities. To the bureaucrats of the developmental state, autonomous societal forces such as labour, environmental and consumer groups obstruct growth and should therefore be discouraged. Their interests are seen as parochial or myopic, and likely to get in the way of economic modernisation. Developmental states do not hesitate to stand with the business community against workers and other interest groups.

Developmental states are part of the capitalist world economy. They are especially attracted to advanced technology and production models. States that are late to industrialise "ardently desire modern technology; it is their passport to modernity, their membership card in the 20th

1 Animal cruelty in contemporary China: is culture to blame?

century" (Goulet 1995, 105–6). Productivity increase is the primary attraction of foreign advanced technology and production models. Unlike command economies of the former Soviet socialist camp, developmental states are open to the West. Participation in the capitalist world economy and in the global division of labour is pursued enthusiastically as a way to gain a foothold in the global market and to have access to the latest technologies for accelerated growth. The importance attached to foreign learning is reflected in the developmental authorities' educational policies and their emphasis on producing college-educated talents equipped with knowledge of advanced science and technology. This explains the enormous emphasis placed on science subjects in school education in East Asian nations in their initial stages of industrialisation.

While efficiency and productivity can be achieved through the adoption of foreign science and technology, progressive foreign and indigenous ideas related to social justice, labour rights, and nature conservation are generally brushed aside. To the technocratic elite in developmental states, the attraction of Western technology was irresistible, as Denis Goulet, a scholar who writes on development ethics, observes:

> Nothing is sacred to them: the earth, and nature itself, are there to be mastered – and altered in the process ... While Western technology promotes certain values of rationality, efficiency, and problem-solving, it also threatens or destroys other key values when "transferred" to Third World countries. (Goulet 1995, 108)

The Chinese government in the reform era fits well into the category of post-socialist developmental states. Economic growth or, in the words of Deng Xiaoping, "developing productivity," has been the primary objective of China's reforming government. Since December 1978, the post-Mao reformist leadership has pursued an aggressive development strategy aimed at rapid growth in the near term and national modernisation as the ultimate objective. It is important to note that China at the end of the 1970s was struggling to pull itself out of the quagmire of an economic crisis caused by Mao's extremist autarkic development model. By the end of Mao's rule in 1976, the crisis had sent the majority of China's 900 million peasants into a state of abject poverty, eking out a living on the verge of starvation. The mismanagement of the national economy from 1958 to 1962 had starved more than 30 million peasants to death (Yang Jisheng 2013; Edwin 1962, 1–11). Despite the fact that the Communist states had all sealed their borders against defectors, hundreds of thousands of Chinese peasants voted "no" to Mao's "tyranny of scarcity" by crossing into neighbouring countries and territories such as the Soviet Union, North Korea, Burma and British-ruled Hong Kong (Chen 2011; Yin 2005). Deng Xiaoping, the architect of China's economic modernisation program, warned his comrades who were hesitant to support his reform initiative that the Communist Party and the PRC would be overthrown if people continued to be mired in poverty (CCP Central Document Research Institute 2004, 380–381, 450–451). Ending the legitimacy crisis of the CCP in the late 1970s motivated the post-Mao regime to use economic growth to defuse the crisis.

After moving away from its Stalinist totalitarian past, mainland China entered an authoritarian era. Like Taiwan and South Korea between the late 1940s and mid-1980s, the PRC has continued one-party dictatorship. Yet the CCP has de-collectivised the economy, decriminalised private production, scaled down and eventually suspended centralised planning, and legalised private ownership. It also opened up the country to the capitalist West. The reforming state has become a powerful guardian of the nation's economic interests. Preferential policies and incentives in the form of tax breaks and reduced land-use fees have been given to investors. Local authorities have been known to put down protests directed at, for example, polluting enterprises. Despite economic liberalisation, the Chinese government has never loosened its grip on its society. It raised barriers to discourage the formation of NGOs, for example (Yan Dong 2007, 147–59). The limited number of registered NGOs and the hundreds of thousands of "underground" societies are under constant scrutiny by state agents. The Chinese government does not tolerate demands or protests that pose a threat to growth. Democratisation is not the goal of China's reforming state.

Even though the Chinese government has embraced the concept of a "socialist market economy," it is always ready to intervene through

1 Animal cruelty in contemporary China: is culture to blame?

its command of the nation's key resources and its policy-making power. In the early years of the economic reform, the Chinese government abolished a large number of policies made in the pre-reform era and adopted new policies aimed at "emancipating productivity." Target sectors were identified, and corresponding policy incentives were provided in an effort to elicit rapid growth. Food production and agriculture in general were the first sectors to be relieved from the shackles of the Maoist collective economy. The "household responsibility system," under which peasants were allowed to work on their land and make their own production decisions, unleashed enthusiasm among Chinese farmers. When grain production reached the highest level in Chinese history in 1984, the Chinese government, through new incentives, began to direct surplus rural labour to the production of cash crops and livestock. As in other East Asian developmental states, the authorities steered the direction of economic development.

Economic modernisation calls for proactive learning from other countries. China has adopted a highly selective approach to learning from the outside world, particularly from industrialised Europe, Japan and North America. This is also common among other East Asian developmental states. What China wants is advanced foreign know-how and production models, not ideas about democracy, autonomous society, environmental activism or animal welfare. The rationale underlying this selective learning is the belief that new technology and new production models contribute directly to efficiency and productivity. In the 1870s, Chinese scholar-officials of the Manchu dynasty sponsored the first massive introduction of Western technology in an effort to protect the existing ruling order, which was the most immediate concern of the rulers of the moribund Qing dynasty (1644–1912). The foreign concepts of parliamentary democracy and constitutional monarchy were rejected as having no practical application in China. What the imperial government needed was to quickly produce powerful weapons and strong gunboats like those sported by the British expedition forces to the Far East in the 1840s and 1860s.

Then and now, China's catch-up motive is reflected in its education policy, and in important aspects of Chinese society. Chinese youths were sent to Europe and North America to learn the tricks of gunboat production during the Manchu dynasty, and to study the latest engineering know-how in the reform era. The popular slogan "With an education in science subjects, one can earn a living anywhere under the heavens" is well received by the public. Science subjects receive more attention from school administrators than social sciences or liberal arts courses. To the Chinese governments of the late 19th century and of the contemporary era, the school system is a tool for achieving the objective of making China prosperous and powerful. School curricula serve the goal of modernisation. As in other East Asian developmental states, graduates from the nation's engineering schools have been favoured by government recruiters. Science graduates are prized because of their training in technology.[23] China in the reform era has many of the features of a devoted growth-oriented developmental technocracy. An explanation of China's animal welfare crisis cannot be achieved without looking at the prevailing politics of the reform era.

Cultural traditions occupy an important role in shaping a society's collective cognition and behavioural orientation. Yet the impact of culture can be enlarged or reduced by a culture-shaping modern state. China's contemporary Leninist party-state, in comparison with its predecessors, has a greater capacity to transform Chinese society so that it is in line with the party's ideology and political imperatives. To the Chinese government, culture is to be used to serve the party-state's objectives. Cultural traditions cannot in any way obstruct or define the party-state's course of action. In the pre-reform era, the Chinese government under Mao Zedong launched waves of anti-tradition campaigns in an effort to remove what it called the "residues" of feudal tradition, which it warned would become roadblocks to the achievement of the party's political ends.

In the reform era, the Communist Party is still promoted as the most progressive force, destined to chart the nation's future. It has adopted a utilitarian approach to traditional culture in its effort to consolidate the existing Leninist political system and safeguard state-led development (Lu Xiaobo and Jingping Lai 2011, 33–39). The

---

23 WeChat interview with Huan Yu, a police officer and an animal activist in a northwestern Chinese city, 2 October 2015.

1 Animal cruelty in contemporary China: is culture to blame?

determination of China's developmental state to guide Chinese society in its pre-determined direction has remained intact. The capacity of Chinese culture to derail that determination is marginal, if not completely non-existent.

2
Human–animal relations in Chinese history

As in most other cultures, nonhuman animals have played an important role in the evolution and growth of the Chinese nation. Archeological findings have confirmed the contributions of animal lives to the survival, nourishment, and growth of the ancient people of the land mass we call China today. The ancient Chinese used animals as objects of worship. Animal images were carved on jade, stones and other objects as far back as 5,000 and 8,000 BCE (Mang Ping 2009, 21–22). The Chinese people were one of the first domesticators of wild animals. As human knowledge of the natural world increased, their relations with nonhuman animals changed from awe and respect to assuming dominion. Animals have been eulogised, portrayed in arts and literature, mythologised, sacrificed in religious ceremonies, demonised in rituals, used for companionship, farming and hunting, and consumed as food, clothing and medicine. Many influences shaped people's view of nonhuman animals in ancient times. These included early folklores, customs, and native religious thoughts. The *Classics of Mountains and Rivers* (山海经), for example, compiled around 25 BCE, was a multi-volume collection that depicted, in addition to other elements of nature, hundreds of animals, some of whom were portrayed as sentient beings (Mang Ping 2009, 27–30).

The Chinese view of animals and of human–animal relations has never been static. It has evolved by absorbing ideas from foreign religions such as Buddhism. To understand Chinese cultural attitudes to animals and to human–animal relations, we must look at the Chinese core belief systems, i.e., the indigenous Daoism, Confucianism, and Chinese Buddhism. As renowned scholar Professor Ji Xianlin of Beijing University wrote, no understanding of Chinese culture can be achieved without a study of Chinese religious thought (Ji Xianlin 2009, 185–86). Let's therefore take a look at the three thought systems that have shaped Chinese worldviews, including their ideas about nature and human–nature relations, for more than 2,000 years.

Daoism (Taoism)

Daoism, called Daojiao in Chinese, is a native Chinese system of philosophical ideas and religious concepts. Originating in the Yin and Zhou eras (1600–500 BCE), Daoism was at first a primitive religion that developed into a folk belief worshipping heaven (nature), God, and ancestors. It can be construed as a religious thought system that prescribes the right or morally acceptable "way" for people to deal with one another, with the cosmos, and with fate. Daoist thought focuses on nature, the place of humans in nature, the interaction between humans and the cosmos, and other subjects such as longevity, wu wei (无为, freedom from desires and wants), immortality and spontaneity. The most fundamental belief of Daoism is that humans need to have a clear consciousness of their own place in the cosmos, and, equally importantly, of their own limitations vis-à-vis the other elements of nature. By holding the natural world in contempt and inflating their own importance and capacity, humans are sure to be disappointed.

Ancient Daoist thinkers saw "civilisation as the beginning of man's degeneration." Since Daoists saw the danger of human intelligence and the futility of human efforts, they were known to preach "Be Stupid!" to their followers. It was not a surprise that Daoism, in Yutang Lin's opinion, "taught also the wisdom of stupidity, the strength of weakness, the advantage of lying low, and the importance of camouflage." Whereas Daoism looked like a theory of ignorance and stupidity, "the theory itself was the result of the highest human intelligence" (Lin Yutang 1966, 116–17, 119).

2 Human–animal relations in Chinese history

Since its genesis, Daoism, through the numerous Daoist texts and folk Daoism, has shaped almost all aspects of Chinese culture, especially cuisine, arts and literature, traditional medicine, martial arts and qigong. The texts *Dao De Jing* (道德经) by Lao Zi and *Zhuang Zi* (庄子) by Zhuang Zhou are the main sources of Daoist ideas. Daoism's focus on withdrawal from earthly pursuits and on a simple life with the least impact on the natural world has made it the thought system believed by its adherents to be best for the nourishment of the human body (Zhou Chonglin 2004, 43–44). It is also believed by many to be the philosophy that is least threatening to the environment and ecology.

The unity of nature and humanity and the "three treasures"

The concept of "unity of nature and humanity" (天人合一) is an idea shared by Daoism and Confucianism. To Confucian scholar Ji Xianlin (1911–2009) of Beijing University, this concept is "the fundamental subject of Chinese philosophy." Referring to Zhuang Zhou's idea that humans and nature are interdependent, Professor Ji admitted that the Daoist concept was much more specific than the Confucian one (Ji Xialian 2009, 59–61). The Daoist "unity of nature and humanity" defines a reciprocal or interdependent relationship. To Daoists, humans are only one of the many members of the universe. It is therefore absurd to give humans a commanding or dominant position. Humans cannot be superior to animals, mountains, rivers or other elements of nature. This is what a contemporary scholar of philosophy in China calls the "Daoist idea of all lives being completely equal" (Zhang Songhui 2006). In Lao Zi's opinion, humans have no reason to consider themselves privileged creatures. Human intelligence, rather than an asset, is in fact a liability. It cannot be the basis of human claims to greatness. To Lao Zi, humans and nonhuman animals differed from each other only in physical characteristics; this difference did not give humans a privileged position or allow them to do whatever they wanted (Lao Zi 2009, 79–83).

Zhuang Zhou inherited this idea and reaffirmed the interdependent relations between humans and nature. He said that the ability of humans should never be exaggerated and that humans had no right to overpower nature. For Zhuang Zhou and Daoists, "the biggest harm comes from excessive wants while the biggest mistake emanates from desires" (Sun Jiang, He Li and Huang Zheng 2009, 182). Zhuang Zhou's view of "all lives being equal" was more vividly projected in his "age of perfect virtue," when "men lived in common with birds and beasts, and were on terms of equality with all creatures, as forming one family ..." (Zhuang Zhou 1990, 152–54). This Daoist conceptualisation of human–nature harmony and the equality of species allows no manipulative relations between humans and nature. The Daoist idea of the "unity of nature and humanity" is therefore praised by China's master historian Qian Mu (1895–1990) as "the biggest Chinese cultural contribution to humanity." Qian argued that this Chinese belief in the interdependence of humans and nature could offer a better solution to the problems brought about by modernisation and industrialisation than Western ideas (Ji Xianlin 2009, 65). At a time when humans have unprecedented power to conquer nature, Qian suggested, Daoist humility, if adopted to guide human behaviours, could mitigate or avoid destruction.

In later dynasties, Daoists continued to expound the idea of species equality. They classified all animals into five categories based on bodily features such as feathers, fur, scales and shells. Humans make up only one category and are not superior to the others (Zhang Songhui 2006). This Daoist view admonishes humans to lower their heads, abandon any belief in their own superiority, and learn to come to terms with being just one constituent part of the cosmos. The human sense of superiority, in the eyes of Zhuang Zhou, was the cause of human aggressiveness (Zhuang Zhou 1990, 283–286). This conception of the equality of species could be seen as one of the earliest arguments against speciesism.

The concepts of unity and equality underly the hailed Daoist "three treasures" of compassion, frugality and modesty. These virtues are particularly relevant to our discussion of Daoist attitudes to human–animal relations. Compassion (also translated as "mercy") in Daoism precludes killing, harming and exploiting animals. Killing is condemned in almost all Daoist texts. To Daoists, slaughtering animals, burning forests, hunting wildlife, and fishing are all sins. Human desires, when unchecked, drive aggression and bring forth humanity's destructive power (He Huaihong 2002, 52–54). Over-indulgence, extravagant consumption and exploitation of the natural world are all condemned (Chen Zhiye and Haihua Xie 2004). An extravagant lifestyle encourages arrogance and indifference, while frugality and modesty foster compassion and sensitivity to the feelings of others.

According to Lin Yutang (1895-1976), a celebrated Chinese writer and translator, Daoism "stands for the rural ideal of life, art and literature, and the worship of primitive simplicity." The "rural ideal of life" is believed to be the least threatening to the various forms of life that make up the natural world (Lin Yutang 1966, 117). One chapter of the *Zhuang Zi*, "The Normal Course for Rulers and Kings," states that efforts to transform nature in order to enrich human lives should be avoided, since they could be disastrous to nature and humans alike (Zhuang, Zhou 2009, 128-29). Instead, humans should try their best to leave the natural world the way it is. Rather than viewing the degradation of the natural world in a fatalistic manner, Daoism calls for people to proactively refrain from making excessive demands on nature.

Folk Daoism and anti-cruelty

Daoists do not simply condemn killing; they call for humans to rescue other animals from exploitation and danger. In many Daoist texts, acts such as kicking and whipping farm animals, capturing hibernating animals during winter, destroying nests, harvesting eggs, and harassing or terrorising animals are prohibited (Sun Jiang, He Li and Huang Zheng 2009, 182-84). In the *Zhuang Zi*, "Horses' Hoofs" explains that controlling horses through branding, hair clipping, hoof paring, bridling, confinement, denial of food and water, etc. is exploitative and cruel. How can horses not die en masse when they face "the evils of the bit and ornamented breast-bands," followed by "the terrors of the whip and switch," asks Zhuang Zhou (Zhuang Zhou 2009, 150-52). In another chapter, "The Floods of Autumn," Zhuang Zhou is appalled at nose-piercing of oxen and horses. He admonishes: "Do not by the human doing extinguish the heavenly constitution; do not for your human purpose extinguish the appointment of heaven; do not bury your proper fame in such a pursuit of it" (Zhuang Zhou 2009, 288-90).

Daoism exerted its greatest influence on the masses, however, through "folk Daoism." Daoist classics such as those by Lao Zi and Zhuang Zhou were incomprehensible to the general public. Folk Daoism, in contrast, addressed the practical and psychological needs of common folk (Kohn 2000, xi, xiv); its ethics were more pragmatic and actionable. Instead of calling on people to retreat completely from materialistic pursuits, it appealed to ordinary people to refrain from killing, extravagance and selfishness (Wang Ming 1960, 184). Three of the most important and widely circulated popular texts of Daoism, sometimes known as "Daoist bibles," could be found in the collections of the imperial court, the rich and powerful, and commoners alike. These texts called on humans to care for animals, respect their right to life, and extend compassion to them (Sun Jiang, He Li and Huang Zheng 2009, 184).

Two pillars of folk Daoism were a belief in karma and in a particular set of ethics. To be protected by the gods and to obtain happiness, believers were expected to act morally, which meant acting with kindness, mercy and compassion, and refraining from killing, excessive wants, and undesirable expectations. The *Treatise of the Exalted One on Response and Retribution*, a Daoist text from the 12th century CE, includes the following recommendations:

The right way leads forward; the wrong way backward.
Do not proceed on an evil path.
Do not sin in secret.
Accumulate virtue, increase merit.
With a compassionate heart turn towards all creatures.
Be faithful, filial, friendly, and brotherly.
First rectify thyself and then convert others.
Take pity on orphans, assist widows; respect the old, be kind to children.
Even the multifarious insects, herbs, and trees should not be injured.
Be grieved at the misfortune of others and rejoice at their good luck.
Assist those in need, and rescue those in danger. (Terebess Asia Online)

2 Human–animal relations in Chinese history

Many of the aphorisms in the *Treatise*, such as "accumulate virtue and increase merit," have become colloquial expressions in China.

Daoists opposed the use of animals for the entertainment of humans. They disapproved of keeping animals in captivity and denying them physical comfort. A Daoist doctor of the 7th century CE, Sun Simiao, recommended avoiding animal parts as ingredients in medicine. He believed that animals had the same desire for life and the same right to life as humans, and that killing them for medicinal use only made the task of saving human lives more difficult (Jiang Jinsong 2016).

Daoism thus includes a belief in animal rights and animal welfare, and Daoist texts contain some of the earliest expressions of these concepts.

Confucianism

Confucianism was not a religion, although it had "certain feelings towards life and the universe that bordered on the religious feeling" (Lin Yutang 1966, 105). It is one of the oldest Chinese philosophical systems and political ideologies and had perhaps the greatest impact on the formation of the social, political and moral values of traditional China. It was founded on the teachings of Confucius (or Kong Fuzi [孔夫子], 551–479 BCE) and his disciples and advocates such as Mencius (4th century BCE), Xunzi (3rd century BCE) and Dong Zhongshu (2nd century BCE). It was established as the state orthodoxy by the 1st century before Christ and for more than 2,000 years maintained its hegemonic position as a moral code, shaping institutions, attitudes and behaviours in China and in other East Asian states that were part or outside of the Chinese tributary system. Its power in cementing a Chinese national character is succinctly summarised in the following text:

> Many Chinese have professed themselves to be Taoists, Buddhists, even Christians, but seldom have they ceased at the same time to be Confucianists. For Confucianism since the time of its general acceptance has been more than a creed to be professed or rejected;

it has become an inseparable part of the society and thought of the nation as a whole, of what it means to be a Chinese, as the Confucian Classics are not the cannon of a particular sect but the literary heritage of a whole people. (De Bary, Chan and Watson 1960, 15)

The most important of Confucius' work is the *Analects*, a collection of his ideas about humanity, society, governance and nature. Other great Confucian works include *Great Learning, Doctrine of the Mean*, and the *Mencius*. The ideas contained in these books about nature, society and governance have been passed from generation to generation in China.

Anthropocentric or anthropocosmic?

Compared with Taoism, Confucianism is an anthropocentric ideology. Lin Yutang observes that Confucianism unapologetically puts humans at the centre of the universe, believing them to be the most precious of species (Lin Yutang 1966, 101–105). A core concept in Confucianism is *ren*. Although sometimes translated as the more general "benevolence," *ren* has also been interpreted as "love of people," suggesting the centrality of humans in the Confucian concept of the cosmos. Xun Zi (ca. 312–230 BCE), a celebrated Confucian master, affirmed that, of all the living creatures on earth, humans were the most important, thus assigning greater value to human lives than to those of nonhuman creatures. Dong Zhongshu (179–104 BCE), a Han Confucian master, wrote that humans were above all other creatures. In this worldview, animals existed for human use.

To Confucianists, there is nothing wrong with humans using nature. As a state ideology devoted primarily to solving human and social problems, Confucianism sanctioned the exploitation of nature so long as it served the interests of a benevolent government, a harmonious society, and cordial inter-personal relations. To Confucius, for example, animal sacrifice was acceptable if it was used to honour an established ritual (Bai Tongdong 2009, 85–99). Ritual – a euphemism for law and order – was more important than the lives of nonhuman animals.

2 Human–animal relations in Chinese history

The perceived anthropocentrism of Confucianism has in recent years been criticised by some Chinese activists and philosophers. Zhang Songhui, a contemporary Chinese scholar, is representative of these critiques:

> The Confucian scholars repeated their view that humans were supreme. However, this conclusion was arrived at by us humans. It was not the common opinion of all the life forms on earth. It is fair to say that early Confucians represented by Confucius were all anthropocentrists. Almost all their attention was cast on humans. In their opinion, only the life of humans had value. All other lives were valuable as instruments or tools. Nonhuman creatures exist for humans. And, without humans, nonhuman creatures would lose their value of existence. (Zhang Songhui 2006)

Despite its anthropocentrism, Confucianism did not endorse or sanction untrammeled violence or cruelty (Sun Jiang, He Li, Huang Zheng 2009, 177–78). The word ren (benevolence) appears more than 200 times in the *Analects* (Mang Ping 2009, 3). While Confucius believed humans had a right to use nonhuman animals, he advocated respect for other species. Xun Zi and Dong Zhongshu went further, arguing that benevolence should be extended to all living creatures. In their opinion, a truly benevolent person was one who did not limit compassion to humans. Zhang Zai (1020–77), a Song dynasty Confucian, affirmed that benevolence meant love of all of nature. Since humans were part of the natural world and shared common features with all other living creatures, benevolence and compassion should not be limited to humans (Sun Jiang, He Li, Huang Zheng 2009, 178).

Some modern scholars have challenged the idea that Confucianism is an anthropocentric ideology. Tu Weiming, one of the most renowned scholars of Confucianism, chose to call it instead "anthropocosmic." According to Tu, Confucianism did not necessarily see humans as the centre of the universe, but rather as a microcosm intimately linked with the rest of existence (Tu Weiming 1998, 2–21). Similarly, Le Aiguo, another Chinese scholar, has argued that Confucianism evolved during the Song dynasty (960–1279 CE) into a cosmos-oriented philosophical system that saw humans and nature as one body sealed by a common physical capability called *qi*, or the flow of energy (Le Aiguo 2013).

Many Confucian masters, from Confucius onwards, offered advice about how humans should treat nature and nonhuman animals. Mencius, the most famous Confucian after Confucius, saw pity as an additional virtue to the "four virtues" (i.e., benevolence, righteousness, rites and intelligence) (Sun Jiang, He Li, Huang Zheng 2009, 177–78). In his essay "The Doing of Huan of Qi and Wen of Jin," Mencius spoke highly of King Xuan, who pardoned an ox that was to be slaughtered as an offering in a ceremony. Mencius wrote:

> A gentleman who has seen a bird or beast alive cannot bear to see him die. If he has heard his voice, he cannot bear to eat his flesh. This is why a gentleman put the slaughterhouse and kitchen far away. (Wang Yuexi and Wang Enbao 1990, 121)

Mencius was using this story to illustrate a political point, arguing that a sovereign who had compassion for animals would make a better ruler than one who did not. Kindness to animals would support a sovereign's claim to magnanimity and benevolence, and thus to moral authority. Some Chinese scholars therefore argue that the Confucian concept of benevolence did not extend solely to humans (Mang Ping 2009, 72–76). According to these scholars, Confucianists acknowledged that animals had feelings similar to those of humans (Sun Jiang, He Li and Huang Zheng 2009, 180).

Wang Yangming (1472–1529 CE), a Confucian scholar during the Ming dynasty, advanced a more controversial, even revolutionary perspective on the relationship between humans and nonhuman animals (Liu Xing 2010, 82–85). His interpretation of the concept of *ren* or benevolence was partly captured in the following statement:

> Everything from ruler, minister, husband, wife, and friends to mountains, rivers, spiritual beings, birds, animals, and plants should be truly loved in order to realize my humanity that forms one body with them. (Wang Yangming 1998, 53–54)

The essence of Wang Yangming's argument is that humans should not be the only objects of compassion. Since humans and nature in general are inseparable, love and compassion should be extended to nonhuman lives and other parts of nature. Only in this way can the ideal of humanity be realised, and a more harmonious society be achieved. Wang Yangming's view of compassion for nonhuman animals was influenced by Zhang Zai (1020–1073), an earlier Confucian scholar. Seeing the world as a unity in which humans and nonhuman beings were linked by *qi* (the flow of energy), Zhang argued that there was no reason for humans and nature not to co-exist in harmony. He wrote:

> Yang (Heaven) is the father; yin (Earth) is the mother. And I, this tiny thing, dwell enfolded in them. Hence, what fills Heaven and Earth is my body, and what rules Heaven and Earth is my nature. The people are my siblings, and *all living things* are my companions. (Zhang Zai 1020–1077; italics added for emphasis)

Zhang Zai and Wang Yangming lived in transitional periods of their respective dynasties. Fear of unrest and disruption of the existing order was a dominant concern of the ruling class. Both Zhang and Wang were perhaps more concerned with the building of a harmonious order in their respective lifetimes. Building a public consensus on the relationship between humans and nature was not their ultimate objective. Their first priority was to consolidate the established hierarchical structure of authority. In calling for people to extend compassion to nonhuman animals, Wang was describing what he believed to be a virtuous trait required of people in positions of power. In his opinion, an official who had compassion for others beyond his immediate family was more qualified to hold office (Liu Xing 2010, 83). As Mencius had expressed many centuries earlier, if a ruler could care for nonhuman animals, he would have no difficulty in caring for the people.

In emphasising the unity of humanity and nature, however, Zhang and Wang stood out among members of the literati of their times. They are often referred to and quoted in studies of environmental ideas in ancient China.[1] In view of the environmental issues facing humanity in the 21st century, and at a time when humanity's ability to conquer and exploit nature has reached an unprecedented level, their ideas from almost 1000 years ago remain significant and thought-provoking.

Reasonable use and the doctrine of the golden mean

While Daoists were naturalists and warned against the exploitation of nature, Confucianists were pragmatists and advanced ideas about reasonable use. Confucius reportedly rejected using close nets, i.e., nets that can catch small and young fish, in fishing and other forms of indiscriminate hunting. He was also believed to oppose shooting birds who were nesting (Mang Ping 2009, 3). Mencius called for restraint in the use of natural resources, warning that people should stockpile materials in times of abundance in preparation for times of scarcity. He denounced excessive logging, uncontrolled fishing and indiscriminate hunting (Sun Jiang, He Li, Huang Zheng 2009, 179). The following paragraph from Mencius' "King Liang Hui I" highlights his opposition to reckless and excessive use of natural resources:

> If the seasons of husbandry are not interfered with, the grain will be more than can be eaten. If close nets are not allowed to enter the pools and ponds, the fishes and turtles will be more than can be consumed. If the axes and bills enter the hills and forests only at the proper time, the wood will be more than can be used. When the grain and fish and turtles are more than can be eaten, and there is more wood than can be used, this enables the people to nourish their living and mourn for their dead, without any feeling against any. (Mencius)

---

1 See for example Zhang Jing's essay "The thought of ecological civilization is an embodiment of Chinese traditional wisdom regarding ecology and environment" (生态文明思想蕴含中国传统生态智慧) published in the *Economic Daily*, 11 April 2019. Zhang traced Xi Jinping's "ecological civilization" thought to Confucian and Daoist views on the unity of humanity and nature in the Song and other dynasties. For scholarly work on Wang Yangming and his ecological thoughts, see also Jonathan Keir's 2017 "Pity for stones?: The new Confucian ecological turn and the global ethic project," *International Journal of Religion & Spirituality in Society* 7(2), pp. 25–34.

Admittedly, Mencius was concerned less about the lives of nonhuman creatures than about the need to conserve natural resources for sustainable human use (Zhang Songhui 2006). The Confucian concepts of reasonable and justified use of natural resources was based on the Confucian doctrine of the Golden Mean. This Doctrine calls for moderation and restraint in attitudes and behaviour. It cautions against extremism, excess and self-centredness. It has served to prevent the anthropocentric Confucian outlook from endorsing or tolerating an all-out assault on nature and was therefore inadvertently conducive to ecological conservation (Mang Ping 2009, 76–77).

In ancient China, the idea of moderation guided state lawmaking against excessive use of nature. During the Han dynasty (206 BCE–220 CE), the imperial government issued China's first law for protecting birds in 63 BCE. The law banned the killing of birds and the harvesting of bird eggs during spring and summer (Sun Jiang, He Li and Huang Zheng 2009, 72). The doctrine of reasonable, planned use informed policies relating to the use of wildlife resources in dynasties thereafter. To emphasise the importance of restraint, dynastic rulers went so far as to warn that indiscriminate killing and destruction of bird nests, for example, could bring bad luck and national crises. For example, Emperor Wu of Liang (464–549) wrote *On Abstaining from Wine and Meat*, issued as an edict to call on the society and the Buddhist monks to live a life free from animal suffering and excessive want. Emperor Wu not only promoted vegetarianism but practised it himself (Chen Zhiynan 2013, 98–126, 403–4).

Buddhism

Buddhism originated in South Asia around the 6th Century BCE. It was introduced to China between 58 and 75 CE. The success of this foreign religion in taking root and prospering in China was no accident. After its introduction, it evolved to become a nationwide religious movement. Why did Buddhism, a foreign religion, fit with Chinese psychological and political needs?

The Buddhist view of nature

Buddhism's success in China can partly be attributed to the similarities between the Buddhist view of nature and Chinese indigenous thought. According to Lily de Silva, a scholar on Buddhism, early Buddhism stood for a close relationship between human morality and the natural environment. This was stated systematically in the theory of the five natural laws (*pañca niyamadhamma*): physical laws, biological laws, psychological laws, moral laws and causal laws.

> This means that the physical environment of any given area conditions the growth and development of its biological component, i.e. flora and fauna. These in turn influence the thought pattern of the people interacting with them. Modes of thinking determine moral standards. The opposite process of interaction is also possible. The morals of man influence not only the psychological makeup of the people but the biological and physical environment of the area as well. Thus, the five laws demonstrate that man and nature are bound together in a reciprocal causal relationship with changes in one necessarily bringing about changes in the other. (de Silva 2011)

This reciprocal or interdependent relationship was, in the opinion of contemporary Chinese scholars, an integrated view of the cosmos. In Buddhism, humans and nature were an integrated whole inseparable from each other, very similar to the Daoist belief in the unity of nature and humanity. The passage by de Silva quoted above points to the fundamental Buddhist tenet that all elements of nature had life (Sun Jiang, He Li and Huang Zheng 2009, 185). In this integrated natural world, humans were only one component. In the natural world, the line of demarcation between humans and others was blurry at best. This Buddhist outlook was in line with the Daoist interpretation of human–animal relations.

Professor Ji Xianlin, a renowned scholar of oriental religions at Beijing University, confirms the similarity between Chinese and Indian beliefs about the relationship between humans and the rest of nature. In the opinion of Professor Ji, it was the ancient Hindu view of nature (Brahman) and humans (Atman) as a united entity that made

Buddhism easily accepted by the Chinese in the 1st century (Ji Xianlin 2009, 59). The idea of the unity of nature and humanity was influential and deep-rooted in the many thought systems in India, Professor Ji added. In China, nature is called "天" (heaven) while in India "brahman." The Chinese concept of "人" (humans) is referred to in India as "Atman." The Chinese belief in the unity of nature and humanity was similar to the Indian concept of "Brahmatmaikyam." Ji argues that China and India shared this fundamental idea that humans and the natural world at large were an integrated whole. Humans might be different from other members of the natural world, but they were expected to act morally towards the rest of the cosmos.

Both cultures advocated a worldview in which humans and nature are unified, not opposed. In this shared outlook, nature was not an object to be exploited. Importantly, the indigenous religious beliefs of both countries called on followers to practise vegetarianism and to reject killing (Ji Xianlin 2009, 59–71). The attraction of Buddhism to the Chinese and its ascendency as a state orthodoxy were achieved without much opposition compared with Christianity, an occidental belief system.

Like Daoism, Buddhism had a normative objective; i.e., it sought to define right actions and behaviours, including in human relations with nature. Buddhism warned against extravagance and wastefulness: "Man must learn to satisfy his needs and not feed his greed" (de Silva 2011). A simple life was considered the exemplary lifestyle.

Prohibition against killing

The essence of the Buddhist view of life is that all life forms are equal and all life is to be respected (Jiang Sun, He Li and Huang Zheng 2009, 185). The prohibition against killing includes any action that would result in the loss of life of humans or other living creatures. The five Buddhist precepts (pañca sila) contain the minimum code of ethics for Buddhists to follow. These precepts call for Buddhists to abstain from any act that would cause harm to life, and to cultivate compassion and sympathy for all living creatures. In Chinese Buddhism, killing is the biggest sin to be avoided, and respect for life is the most important requirement. Believers are advised not to engage in businesses that profit from animal slaughter (de Silva 2011).

The Buddhist prohibition against killing is reflected in two compassionate practices common among Chinese Buddhist believers, both of which will be addressed in greater detail later. The first is vegetarianism. In the Buddhist view, those who consume meat are as sinful as those who slaughter animals. When animals are killed for our consumption, how can we cultivate compassion? (Xu Changwen and Jing Xu 2007, 95–97). The second is mercy release, which is commonly practised by purchasing live animals from the marketplace and setting them free, back into the water, air or wilderness. If vegetarianism is a passive response to the prohibition against killing, mercy release is a proactive act of compassion when practised correctly. Some Chinese scholars have argued that the Buddhist prohibition against killing is as progressive as contemporary animal rights ideas (Xu Changwen and Jing Xu 2009).

The Buddhist idea of karma

The concept of karma also helped Buddhism to find acceptance in China. When Buddhism was first introduced, the Buddhist concept of karma was in direct conflict with indigenous Chinese ideas about karmic retribution. The Chinese concept of karma was based on secular moral values. The objects of karmic retribution were the individuals concerned and their offspring: whoever violated the prevailing moral code would be punished in this lifetime, and the punishment would also befall their children and grandchildren. Whatever is sowed in this life would be reaped in this life. The Buddhist concept of karma was more spiritual and fatalistic. The object of Buddhist karmic retribution was the individual only, and retribution would happen in future lives. This Buddhist notion of karma did not sit well with the Chinese, who were pragmatic and fundamentally more concerned with the present life, and with the wellbeing of their children and extended family (Chen Xiaofang 2004, 91–95). Chinese Buddhist masters reinterpreted the Buddhist idea of karma and modified it to satisfy the psychological needs of the Chinese. Since the early years of Buddhism in China, Chinese Buddhists have believed not only that moral behaviours would help them in the afterlife, but more importantly that they would improve the lot of their entire family in the present life (Chen Xiaofang 2004; Zhong Lianhai 2009, 17–21).

This revolutionary interpretation of Buddhism served to encourage followers to practise good deeds in anticipation of good fortune for themselves and their offspring in the present life, and to deter immoral acts that might invite misfortune to the family (Chen Xiaofang 2004, 91–95). Chinese Buddhists believed that those who committed killing, theft, slander, extravagance and other immoral acts would be condemned accordingly. Their punishment might be forthcoming in the present life, or they might be condemned to hell or to suffer as hungry ghosts.

Underlying the concept of karma was the idea that one's fate was the result of one's own acts. It was meant to encourage moral acts and deter immoral behaviour (Zhou Hongmin 2010, 155). Chinese Buddhists also believed that Buddhism helped to create a peaceful society. "[T]he true Buddhist follower is a kinder person, more pacific, more patient, and more philanthropic, than others," argued Lin Yutang. As regards animals, the belief that killing or cruelty would invite misfortune served as a warning against brutality to all living things. According to Lin Yutang, Buddhism did not necessarily teach the Chinese to befriend animals, but it did teach that killing and cruelty should be avoided (Lin Yutang 1966, 126–27).

Buddhism as state orthodoxy

Buddhism could not have prospered as it did in imperial China without official backing. Following its introduction in the first century, government officials were the first group of believers. Early Chinese Buddhists helped to reinterpret Buddhist ideas in light of native Chinese beliefs (Ji Xianlin 2009, 187–96). By the time Buddhism was introduced, China had already built a highly centralised administrative system that had the capacity to override any social or religious movements if it chose to. Buddhist monks therefore made special efforts to win believers among the upper classes. After a short period during which Buddhist ideas clashed with indigenous Chinese moral values, assimilation began. According to historical records, the earliest

Buddhists in China did not include commoners; rather, they were scholar-officials, aristocrats, members of the imperial households and the sovereign. In the Southern and Northern dynasties (420 CE-589 CE), the spread of Buddhism was further boosted thanks to the support of the ruling class (Zhong Hailian 2009).

By 166 CE, Buddhism had acquired equal status with Daoism among the Chinese ruling class (Ji Xianlin 2009, 190-192). Emperor Wu (464-549 CE) of the Liang dynasty and Empress Wu Zetian (624-705 CE) of the Tang dynasty were two of the most famous sovereigns who not only made Buddhism a national religion but were also themselves devoted believers. Admittedly, adopting Buddhism as a national religion was in part a politically motivated act. The Buddhist message of nonviolence, according to some Chinese scholars, served the political purposes of China's dynastic rulers. If followers practised restraint and adopted the right attitudes and behaviours, the established order would not be seriously challenged (Yu 2007, 42-43; Ji Xianlin 2009, 223). However, the success of Buddhism in converting the entire dynastic bureaucracy as well as the emperors suggests that the instrumental use of Buddhism for political purposes was only one of the reasons underlying its rapid spread. What should be pointed out is that Buddhism did serve the dynastic stability objective of the ruling elites. Buddhist followers were more peaceful, less aggressive, more compassionate, and less of a threat to the established ruling order.

State protection of animals in ancient China

In China's recorded history, edicts, laws and orders regulating human interactions with animals are numerous. As early as 4000 BCE, China's rulers issued orders banning logging and hunting in springtime so that forests and wildlife could multiply in the most fertile season of the year. Underlying this ban was an advanced knowledge of the lifecycle of plants and animals. This may be one of humanity's earliest animal protection and conservation policies. It suggests an awareness of the importance of planning and conservation to ensure the sustainable use of natural resources. In describing such rulings, ancient Chinese scholars stated clearly that nature conservation was the responsibility of the rulers (Sun Jiang, He Li and Huang Zheng 2009, 71).

Subsequent dynasties continued the policy of "planned" use of natural resources. According to the ancient *Book of History* (史记) and *Book of Past Dynasties* (尚书), in King Shun's time (2300 to 2200 BCE), special offices were created to manage forests, rivers and lakes, and wildlife. The *Rites of Zhou* (周礼), an official document on politics and economics written towards the end of the Xizhou (Western Zhou) dynasty (1122–770 BCE), entrusted the chief minister of public works with responsibility for the protection of plants and animals. The fact that conservation was included as a government responsibility in the *Rites of Zhou* was of particular importance. The *Rites* discussed important state affairs that were key to building a system of efficient and rule-based governance (Sun Jingtan 1997). King Wen of Zhou, the founder of the Xizhou dynasty, on his deathbed urged his successor to take good care of the nation's forests and wildlife.

Ancient Chinese rulers were among the first to promulgate policies for the planned use of natural resources out of a concern for the consolidation of the basis of their ruling order. Xizhou rulers issued one of the most draconian and perhaps the world's earliest environmental protection orders, *Fa Chong Ling* (伐崇令), banning the destruction of property and interference with forests, natural sources of drinking water, and wildlife. Convicted perpetrators could be condemned to death. During the Qin dynasty (221–207 BCE), cattle received much legal protection. If the death rate in cattle herds exceeded 33%, the officials in charge would be punished. This law was admittedly issued to protect cattle as an economic asset. Yet it still served to deter acts of cruelty or neglect that could cause cattle death. The Qin dynasty bans on logging, harvesting of wild plants, and hunting of animals during spring time were strictly enforced (Sun Jiang, He Li and Huang Zheng 2009, 72). The rulers of the Han dynasty (206 BCE–220 CE) continued the Qin dynasty's legal protection of animals.

It seems that from very early on, the Chinese acknowledged the need to place a brake on the excessive exploitation of natural resources. Similar bans were issued by emperors in succeeding dynasties outlawing the harvesting of eggs, the killing of migratory birds, and the capturing of eagles and other exotic birds during the spring and early summer. The Song (960-1127) and Yuan (1271–1368) dynasties required that hunters distinguish female animals from males, spare pregnant and young animals, and stop hunting altogether during winter and spring. Violators were strictly penalised (Sun Jiang, He Li and Huang Zheng 2009, 72-73).

Ancient Chinese laws banning the excessive and untimely use of animals served to advocate compassion for other living creatures. According to "Yue Ling" (月令) of the *Book of Rites* (礼记), it was against the law to destroy nests and to kill young birds or animals who were just learning to run or fly. This ban was not simply to preserve animal lives for human use; it also called on people to be gentle to the weak and disadvantaged. Knowing the inevitable suffering and death that awaited captured exotic birds, Emperor Gaozu of the Tang dynasty issued an edict in 618 banning the offering of exotic animals to the imperial family. In the 13th century, Genghis Khan passed what was known as the Genghis Khan Code containing very detailed articles on the care of farm animals. The code included articles, for example, punishing indecent and disrespectful acts towards livestock such as urinating on an animal who was resting on the ground (Sun Jiang, He Li and Huang Zheng 2009, 72-73). China's Yuan dynasty laws and policies were influenced immensely by the Genghis Khan Code.

Compassion in action

I will now look at three ancient Chinese practices that had a direct impact on human attitudes towards animals: vegetarianism, slaughter suspension, and mercy release. Vegetarianism existed in China long before the introduction of Buddhism.[2] While these practices were by

---

2   It was documented in the *Book of Rites* (73-49 BCE) that ancient Chinese started to practise vegetarianism on the first and fifteenth days of each lunar month during the Spring and Autumn Period (771-476 BCE). This ancient practice of abstention from meat or any animal food consumption two days a month was later adopted by the majority of Chinese Buddhist followers. For the text of the *Book of Rites* on the two-day vegetarian practice in ancient times, see 中国素食文化的起源和发展 (The origin and development of vegetarian diet in China) at http://fzzhxdwh.com/article/208.

no means exclusive to Chinese culture, their widespread acceptance in society, their practice by imperial rulers and their endorsement by the imperial government, were perhaps unparallelled in the world.

Vegetarianism

Vegetarianism as a conscious lifestyle choice was seen during the Spring and Autumn Warring States period (770–221 BCE). While meat-free meals dominated commoners' diets year-round, aristocrats, officials and the rich chose to go vegetarian during important festivals or ceremonies. Ancient classics such as the *History of the Former Han* (汉书), the *Book of Rites*, and the *Book of Mencius* (孟子) encouraged vegetarian meals, especially at times of natural disasters (Du Li 2008, 20). Jia Shixie, an agricultural expert during the North Wei dynasty (386–534 CE), wrote a 10-volume book, *Qimin Yaoshu* (齐民要术), on farming and agriculture. Volume 9 included a chapter devoted to vegetarian cooking and diet. It covered subjects ranging from the selection of vegetarian ingredients, types of vegetarian dishes, vegetarian meal preparation, the use of spices, and cooking methods (Du Li 2008, 20–23).

Daoism greatly influenced Chinese cooking and diet. Daoist priests believed that those who practised vegetarianism were healthier not only physically but also morally. This reinforced the belief that meat-free meals were a key to longevity, and a lifelong vegetarian diet was recommended for those who aspired to immortality. Compassion for nonhuman animals was another consideration in Daoist support for vegetarianism. As described above, Daoists argued that nonhuman creatures had the same right to life as humans (Zhou Chonglin 2004).

Although vegetarianism had a much older history in China, the introduction and spread of Buddhism made notable contributions to the rise of a meat-free culinary culture. Chinese Buddhists and Buddhist temples were the main force in the popularisation of vegetarian cuisine. Since Buddhist monks were required to be vegetarians, Buddhist temple kitchens produced a large variety of meat-free dishes made of seasonal and preserved ingredients. Legend has it that a temple chef in the era of Emperor Wu of Liang was capable of producing ten different dishes using one vegetable. During the Tang and Song dynasties, vegetable dishes became a distinctive cuisine. During the Song (960–1279), Ming (1368–1644) and Qing (1644–1911) dynasties, banquets of meticulously prepared vegetarian dishes, artistically presented and creatively named, helped to promote meat-free cooking. Despite the opposition of the Buddhist monks, chefs prepared vegetarian foods that were prepared to look like meat dishes. Imitation pork, fish, and sausages, for example, catered to the tastes of meat-eaters. These creative dishes were used to introduce vegetarian diet to the general public.

Importantly, vegetarianism was endorsed and practised by China's dynastic rulers. Early Buddhist monks in China were not all vegetarians. It was Emperor Wu of Liang (502–557 CE) who decreed, after extensive debate with the Buddhist establishment, that all monks and nuns adopt a meat-free lifestyle. In this imperial decree, titled "On Abstention from Wine and Meat," Emperor Wu reasoned that monks and nuns must pursue a vegetarian lifestyle on account of Buddhist moral codes, compassion for nonhuman lives, karmic retribution, and the fact that offerings in Buddhist ceremonies no longer included slaughtered animals. He warned that if the Buddhist establishment did not comply with the decree, the imperial government would have to enforce it (Xia Meida 2010, 86–92). Emperor Wu's decree was no doubt an extreme example of government interference in religious affairs. As Chinese scholars have pointed out, the emperor mostly resorted to persuasion to get the consent of the Buddhist establishment to his "On Abstention" decree. The emperor himself was a devout Buddhist, and the power of his example was unparalleled. He was even involved in editing and interpreting Buddhist texts, thus establishing his scholarly authority among the monks and nuns. The official endorsement of vegetarianism, combined with the emperor's moral leadership, boosted the popularity of vegetarian cuisine (Mang Ping 2009, 3–4). Even ceremonial offerings that formerly included meat were later prepared using imitation meat made from flour or other cereals. Historically, when imperial rulers themselves practised what they preached, their appeals to society to do the same carried powerful moral weight.

By the end of the Tang dynasty, the number of vegetarians had multiplied. To Chinese Buddhists, going vegetarian was a means both to end killing and to accumulate virtue. It was therefore a highly respectable course of action. A woman who practised vegetarianism for an extended period would bring honour to her entire family (Mang Ping 2009, chap. 4). Widows who went vegetarian were particularly celebrated in this period; their vegetarian lifestyle was often mentioned on their tombstones (Mang Ping 2009; Jiao Jie 2000, 95–99). The influence of these role models was strong and long-lasting.

However, Chinese people are intensely pragmatic. The majority of Chinese Buddhists were not strict vegetarians. Although meat and dairy products were very rare for most Chinese people anyway, food made of animal products was absolutely avoided on the first and the fifteenth days of the lunar calendar. Like mercy release, abstinence from meat two days a month was a symbolic gesture. Regardless of its largely self-serving intentions, however, it helped to create an atmosphere in which a small sacrifice on the part of humans preserved the lives of nonhuman animals. At the same time, it satisfied the spiritual needs of the Buddhists who observed it. Low productivity and food shortages also encouraged meat-free eating: during times of extreme shortages, some communities ate wildlife, but this was generally limited to a small number of people on the so-called "uncivilised" periphery of the Celestial Empire. Vegetarianism was a far more common response to times of scarcity.

The moral force of religion, state endorsement, the example of the Buddhist establishment and the sovereign, and economic necessity thus all contributed to the rise of vegetarian food culture in China. Daoism and Buddhism were its philosophical foundations, but it was state promotion that helped to create a vegetarian movement. Daoism and Buddhism were also the main contributors to the rise of three distinct vegetarian cooking styles: Buddhist temple dishes, imperial court dishes, and commoners' dishes (Mang Ping 2009, 139). Meat-free diets were so common that they were also adopted by other religious movements. During the Tang dynasty (618–907 CE), for example, Chinese followers of the Nestorian sect of Christianity adopted a vegetarian lifestyle.

Slaughter suspension

Compassion in action was also reflected in the unique Chinese practice of "slaughter suspension" (断屠), meaning no animals were to be slaughtered on certain days of the year. At the time of Emperor Wu of Liang (464–549 CE), slaughter was suspended on six days of every month. Slaughter suspension could last 108 days a year depending on the situation, resulting in the disappearance of meat and other animal products for food. Emperor Wen Xuan of Northern Qi (550–559 CE) went further and suspended slaughter for three months of every year. In 602, Emperor Wen of the Sui dynasty (589–618 CE) issued an order suspending slaughter for one day to celebrate his birthday. Suspension of slaughter as a state policy was officially started in the Sui dynasty (Zhang Ping 2002, 79–84).

It was under the Tang dynasty that suspension of slaughter was carried out most systematically and consistently. In 618, Emperor Gaozu established not only the Tang dynasty but also a system of fasting months. Buddhism was affirmed as the official religion. The purpose was to create a new era of political stability, benevolent government, and compassion for all living creatures after decades of war, turmoil and destruction. The emperor decreed that the nation should stop slaughter during the first, fifth and ninth months of the lunar calendar, and on the tenth day of every other month. In addition to those months when Buddhists were to be meat-free, the 1st, 8th, 13th, 15th, 18th, 23rd, 24th, 28th, 29th and 30th day of other months were designated fasting and slaughter-free days (Zhang Ping 2002, 79–84). Slaughter suspension was also carried out for three days in the 1st, 7th and 10th months. Slaughter was suspended during festivals, celebrations of a birth, times of mourning, and celebrations of the Tang emperors' birthdays. Together, these occasions could impose a meat-free diet for more than half the year. When Wu Zetian, a devout Buddhist, became empress, she suspended slaughter for two years (698–700 CE). In 709, Emperor Zhong Zong issued a decree listing the punishments that could be imposed on those who violated slaughter suspension (Zhang Ping 2002, 79–84).

Slaughter suspension was to be practised not only by professional butchers and the imperial court, but also by ordinary people. Master Lian Chi of the Ming Dynasty (1368–1644 CE) listed seven occasions

2 Human–animal relations in Chinese history

on which slaughter should be suspended. These were when a birthday was being celebrated; when a baby was born; when the deceased were being remembered; when a wedding was being held; before dinner parties for friends or family; when prayers were being said for restoration of health; and when a person could move to a different livelihood from a butcher's profession (Lian Chi 1535–1615). The argument was that killing at times of celebration ruined the festive atmosphere. Celebrations should be times to accumulate virtue rather than to create sorrow and unhappiness. The imperial court took the lead, suspending slaughter when the emperor held a major ceremony or marked a birthday, or when natural disaster struck (Mang Ping 2009, 105; Wei Lingxue 2015). This tradition continued in China until modern times. In 1933, when Wuhan in Central China was struck by major flooding, the city government forbade butchery for three days (Lin Yutang 1966, 126–27).

The state-ordered suspension of slaughter sent several messages. First, killing was repulsive and to be avoided when possible. This perhaps explains the traditionally low social status of butchers in Chinese society. Legend has it that Mencius' mother refused to move to a house next to a butcher's residence (Mang Ping 2009, 135). Second, while livestock slaughter could not be stopped completely, the intensity of slaughter and the number of animals killed could be reduced. Third, it encouraged the nation to be sensitive to animal suffering and to be thankful to animals for their sacrifice.

The Chinese practice of slaughter suspension was also adopted by neighbouring countries in the Chinese imperial tributary system. In August 1392, learning about the death of the crown prince of the Ming empire, Korean King Lee Seong-gye ordered the suspension of slaughter for three days, wedding ceremonies for one month, and all other celebrations and entertainments for 13 days (Yang Zhaoquan and He Tongmei 2001, 463). The Tang dynasty's practice of slaughter suspension was copied most religiously in Japan. In 718, 722, 737, 755 and 758, Japanese emperors issued edicts for slaughter suspension when the imperial court was handling natural disasters and imperial family crises or illnesses (Wei Lingxue 2015).

Mercy release

Mercy release, the setting free of captured animals, is a ritualistic and mostly symbolic act still exercised in contemporary China. Like vegetarianism, it can be traced back to a distant past in Chinese history. To the ancient Chinese, respect for life was the highest virtue, and freeing trapped or captured animals was an honourable act. One of the earliest recorded acts of mercy release was done by Zhao Jianzi (?–476 BCE), a high-ranking official of Jin in the Warring States era who also argued against hunting (Feng Jun 2010, 61–63).

The Buddhist admonition against killing and the endorsement by successive sovereigns helped to increase the popularity of the mercy release ritual. In the Sui, Tang, Ming and Qing dynasties, special pavilions, ponds and societies were established for the practice. In the Ming dynasty, famous Buddhist masters and men of letters wrote pamphlets, essays and collections of writings on the importance of exercising mercy, compassion and care for nonhuman animals. In the Tang dynasty, Master Yin Guang called on the people to stay away from cruelty and killing and to exercise mercy towards all living things.[3] In the Ming dynasty, Master Lian Chi authored a collection of essays titled "Prohibition of Killing and Mercy Release" (Lian Chi 1535–1615). Ming Dynasty playwright Tu Long wrote "On Abstinence from Killing and Mercy Release." Renowned translator Li Zhizao (1571–1630) published his "On Promoting Mercy Release Far and Wide." Qian Muzhai, a famous Ming poet, penned "On Mercy Release" (Feng Jun 2010, 62–63). These literary works influenced generations of Chinese scholars, officials, and the general public.

The ritual of mercy release could not have become a national custom without the endorsement, support and participation of the imperial rulers. Emperor Yuan of Liang (508–554) built mercy release pavilions in Jinzhou to encourage more people to put their Buddhist beliefs into practice. Emperor Suzong of the Tang Dynasty issued an imperial edict calling for the building of release ponds at every Buddhist temple (Feng Jun 2010, 62).

---

3 Master Yin Guang, "A commentary on the renewal of the mercy release pond at the Nanxun Jilei Temple", posted by Buddhist followers at https://www.douban.com/group/topic/63495032/, 29 September 2014.

2 Human–animal relations in Chinese history

Like slaughter suspension, mercy release was practised at celebrations such as the new year, birthdays, weddings, business openings, and other events (Mang Ping 2009, 102–105) marking or anticipating new beginnings, good fortune for the family, success in business, and prosperity. Mercy release, a gesture of kindness, was believed to be the most appropriate thing to do to enrich the fortune of the family. It was also traditionally conducted in times of natural disaster or great adversity. The act of mercy release was less a symbolic offering of live animals to the various gods than a ritual to show humans' sincerity of belief in the importance of kindness. The belief that people of compassion would be spared nature's assault and bad luck was deep-rooted among the Chinese. Mercy release was one expression of that belief.

Members of the country's literati class helped the spread of this ritual. Wang Anshi (1021–1086), a Song dynasty scholar-official, was known to buy fish for release in the rivers. Su Shi (1037–1101), one of China's most accomplished writers and calligraphers, and Lu You (1125–1210), a great poet, called for the release of wildlife animals that had been captured for human consumption. Legend had it that Su Shi once purchased the West Lake in Hangzhou for mercy release. Corresponding to the idea of exercising mercy to animals was a rejection of the use of animal parts as ingredients in traditional medicine. In the Tang dynasty, Buddhist master Lian Chi stood against the use of drugs containing animal parts. He argued that men of virtue should not encourage killing by using medicine made from animal parts, even if the ingredient could allegedly save human lives. Taking one life to save another was no solution to human illnesses (Mang Ping 2009, 103).

The practice of mercy release has continued. Religious groups in mainland China and Taiwan conducting mercy release have recently realised that care must be taken to release the animals in the right place, to ensure that the released animals survive (Wen Wu 2010, 50).

Compassion in literary works

Compassion for animals is a consistent theme in Chinese literature. In 2006, Guo Geng, a prolific writer on wildlife conservation, compiled a collection of Tang dynasty poems describing and celebrating various bird species, *Birds and Three Hundred Poems of the Tang Dynasty* (Guo Geng 2006). Bai Juyi (772–846), a Tang dynasty poet, wrote a touching poem on the need for humans to be sensitive and compassionate. In this poem that was about protecting animal lives, he wrote:

> Please do not say that animals have no emotions.
> They are just like you and me.
> Please do not shoot the bird resting on the tree branch.
> The young are awaiting the safe return of the mother bird
> (Mang Ping 2009, 236)

Du Mu (803–852), another great Tang dynasty poet, shamed hunters for insensitive killing of animals. He wrote:

> The two freshly shot eagles are still bleeding.
> Horses and cattle work for us as transportation and in the field.
> I ask you not to shoot migrant geese.
> They may be messengers carrying letters for families afar
> (Master of the Nebula 2012).

Other men of letters also used their pens to call for kindness. As a scholar-official, Su Shi stood for reforms that would improve the lives of people at the bottom of society. His concern for the underdog extended to animals. "Leave food if you care about mice. Stop using oil lamps if you care about the moths," he wrote (Mang Ping 2009, 106). Zhen Banqiao (1693–1765), a Qing dynasty scholar-official best known for his paintings and calligraphy, questioned the habit of keeping birds in cages. In a family letter on education, he wrote that keeping birds in cages pleased humans, but turned birds into prisoners. What justification did humans have for denying birds their freedom? "Isn't planting trees far better than keeping birds in cages?" he asked. While snakes might look fearsome, he argued, their looks were not their fault, and less a justification for humans to end their lives: "What we can do is to simply drive them away and avoid seeing them so we are not scared" (Zeng Fanchao 2018, 79). This letter, written for his family on the subject of the education of his young son, expressed

2 Human–animal relations in Chinese history

empathy for living creatures often sacrificed for use by humans as toys, tools, transportation or food. It also contained comments on animal welfare and ecological conservation as progressive as those found in the contemporary world.

Having been introduced to the ancient Chinese thought system, state policy of slaughter suspension, and the ancient Chinese practices of vegetarianism and mercy release, I wonder if people would still claim that Chinese traditional culture sanctions cruelty to animals. Are the Chinese culturally programmed to animal cruelty? There is no denying that China was as anthropocentric as the rest of the world in ancient times. Animal cruelty did happen in its dynastic past. But dog meat was called "dirty" meat in the Tang dynasty not because it was unsanitary but because it was morally "dirty." Dogs slaughtered for food in ancient China were mostly stolen from their owners. The meat was therefore "dirty" because it came from an illegal act, and killing a dog for food was considered cruel. Dogs were raised to guard homes. In fact, compassion and kindness towards the weak, the disadvantaged and nonhuman animals were part of China's core value system with roots in Daoism, Buddhism and Confucianism. To explain the massive scale of animal cruelty in contemporary China, we need to shift our attention from the country's cultural traditions to contemporary politics.

Animal protection in pre-1949 China

In 1911, the Qing dynasty collapsed. Monarchy, which had existed in China for more than 2,000 years, came to an end. Dr Sun Yat-sen, the founding father of the Republic of China, vowed to rebuild the Chinese state, society and culture according to his vision of what would be best for the country's revival. Until 1949, when the ROC was replaced by the People's Republic of China (PRC), the country had been thrown into a period of monarchical restoration, armed conflict among various warlords, Japanese invasion, and a civil war (1946–49) between the Nationalists and the Communists. Yet the ROC era on the mainland saw the rise of voices for animal protection. In fact, the Chinese government was behind the emerging civil society and social transformation campaign, which included animal protection.

Vegetarianism and its decline

In the early years of the ROC, vegetarianism was a topic of public discourse. Scholars, revolutionary utopians, anarchists, left-wing writers, and social activists in the 1910s and 1920s believed that vegetarianism would help China to modernise (Liang Qizhi 2017). These vegetarian advocates included Wu Tingfang, a diplomat, who considered meat unfit for the physiology of the Chinese. Li Shizeng, one of the founding members of the Chinese Nationalist Party, was another strong advocate of vegetarianism. He held that animal flesh contained toxins harmful to mental and physical health, and that a vegetarian lifestyle was more suited to China's level of economic development. The most influential advocate of a vegetarian lifestyle was Sun Yat-sen. As well as practising vegetarianism himself, he believed that vegetarianism should be the mainstream diet of the nation (Liang Qizhi 2019).

In the 1930s, a "Reforming Vegetarian China" campaign emerged, challenging the earlier vegetarian advocates. The challengers believed that a meatless diet was responsible for China's shorter life expectancy and higher infant mortality rate, and for the small physical stature of the Chinese. Societies were established for the study of the connection between nutrition and physique. Voices advocating for a vegetarian lifestyle died down in the 1930s, in part because of the growing national crisis. Facing Japanese aggression in northeast and northern China, the Chinese public were more likely to embrace calls to build a strong nation. The argument that a vegetarian diet for the majority of the population, i.e., the peasants, was not compatible with nation-building found support. Many believed that China should urgently reform the vegetarian dietary habits of its peasants. In 1945, the Chinese government set up a national diet reform committee in response to calls from scholars returned from the West for a culinary revolution. The ultimate purpose of the dietary reform was to achieve national power through the strengthening of the physique of the Chinese people (Liang Qizhi 2017).

2 Human–animal relations in Chinese history

The New Life Movement

In 1933, Chiang Kaishek announced the start of a "New Life Movement" to create a new Chinese culture. Kindness to animals was a component of this movement.

Discussions of animal welfare were not unfamiliar in 1930s China. In 1926, writer and animal lover Lu Bicheng had brought a civil lawsuit against Ping Jingya, publisher of a Shanghai newspaper. Ping's newspaper had published an article ridiculing Lu Bicheng for her lawsuit against a motorist who hurt her pet dog. In the article, Lu was described as a small-minded person who loved dogs more than her fellow human beings. Lu's lawsuit against Ping Jingya became known in the press as the "dog lawsuit" and attracted much public attention (Li Yizhi 2018). For Lu, the "dog lawsuit" was less about defending her own reputation than about arousing public awareness that it was time to be kind to animals. Lu had been educated in Britain, where she learned about the British Royal Society for the Prevention of Cruelty to Animals and witnessed its activities. In 1928 she proposed the establishment of a Chinese society for the prevention of cruelty to animals. Her proposal materialised six years later when the country's first animal protection association was established in Nanjing.

As capital of the country, Nanjing was at the forefront of the New Life Movement. In 1934 the city adopted "Implementation Measures" for the prevention of cruelty to animals. These measures were to be applied to horses, cattle, sheep, dogs, chicken, ducks and other animals. The same year, the Nanjing Society for the Prevention of Cruelty to Animals was founded and officially recognised. The mission of the society was to stop cruelty to all species, promote animal wellbeing, and spread knowledge of animal health and animal protection. As an officially registered organisation, the society could participate in lawmaking, law enforcement and supervision. Nanjing is situated in Jiangsu province, which led the country in adopting animal protection policies. The provincial legislature's *Jiangsu Provincial Tentative Rules Prohibiting the Transport and Slaughter of Draught Cattle* set an example for the rest of the provinces (Chang Jiwen 2010).

However, the New Life Movement and the associated social transformation programs were soon suspended with the escalation of the civil war between the Nationalists and the Zhu-Mao Communist guerrilla forces in southern Jiangxi, and Japanese aggression in northeast China. In December 1937, Nanjing fell to the invading Japanese forces. For the next 12 years the Nationalist government was preoccupied, first by resisting Japanese occupation and then by fighting the Chinese Communists (1946-49). Economic development and social transformation were only priorities if they served the military objectives of the Chinese government.

Human-animal relations in pre-reform China, 1949-78

The Communist Party of China (CCP) founded the PRC in 1949 after defeating the Chinese Nationalist regime. The new government represented a radical change to the course of modern Chinese history. The triumphant CCP, encouraged by its victory in the civil war, adopted an uncompromising stance on a host of policies. It allowed no room for much of the political, economic and social experimentation that had been orchestrated by the overthrown Nationalist Party of China (KMT). It allowed no political rights to members of the KMT, former government officials, or the propertied class in general. The Communist regime held no expectations of a working relationship with the capitalist West led by the USA. Western cultural, religious, philanthropic and political influences were to be eliminated. By the end of 1951 the People's Republic had succeeded in physically expelling most foreign staff members employed by Western institutions (Yang Kuisong 2010). Determined to build China into a strong and prosperous socialist country, the CCP launched an unprecedented nation-building effort. It viewed the shaping of a new Chinese culture as an important part of this effort. In this section I explore the possible link between the politics of the pre-reform era and human-animal relations in the People's Republic during that period.

People vs class enemies

Mao Zedong (1893-1976), the founder of the PRC, once wrote that distinguishing those who were for revolution and those who were against it was a question of the highest importance (Mao Zedong 1991,

2 Human–animal relations in Chinese history

3). When the PRC was established, one of the first policy measures implemented by the new regime was to divide the society into two groups. The class that was to have political rights included peasants, workers and other urban labourers. These were referred to as "the people" or "working-class people." They were considered supporters of the revolution and of socialism and were therefore trusted allies of the CCP. The opposite group included formerly rich peasants, landlords, capitalists, and anyone else who at the time of "liberation" had been a property owner or had worked for the overthrown nationalist government. These people were labelled members of the "exploiting class" and were allegedly enemies of socialist transformation. By the end of 1953, all of mainland Chinese society had been categorised into one of these two classes. One's economic status, family affiliation, social relationships and political views were used by the state to determine one's class status and political reliability.

The classification of society into two groups was an instrument of societal control. The working class, also referred to as the proletariat, was the majority. As "masters of socialist China," they were entitled to political and economic rights denied to members of the exploiting class. In a Western democracy, the majority and the minority are fluid: depending on the issues and politics involved, members of the majority may become the minority and vice versa. In the People's Republic and other Eurasian socialist countries, the minority, namely members of the exploiting class, could never join the majority, i.e., the working class. One's status as a member of the enemy class was for life, unchangeable and hereditary. However, a member of the majority (working) class could be condemned to join the minority (exploiting) class if he or she was found to hold ideas that were considered bourgeois, reactionary, anti-Party or counter-revolutionary.

These classifications were used to justify an openly discriminatory policy towards members of the exploiting class.[4] Mao said very clearly in his essay "On the people's democratic dictatorship" that members of

---

4   See for example Robert C. Tucker's exposition of Lenin's hard-line policy towards opposition in the newly built Soviet state in *Political Culture and Leadership in Soviet Russia: From Lenin to Gorbachev* (New York and London: W.W. Norton & Company, 1987), particularly chapters 2 and 3.

the overthrown class were the objects of "dictatorship" (Mao Zedong 1991c, 1468–82). The exploiting class must be suppressed or their resistance would undermine the socialist state. They would never reconcile with the reality that their former privileges had been dismantled; their hostility to the "people's government" would persist. Furthermore, despite their economic and political disenfranchisement, the exploiting class members were still a threat to the new society. They might be politically suppressed or even physically destroyed, but their bourgeois ideologies and lifestyles were a lasting source of contamination. This was why "continuous revolution," as Mao called it, was necessary in socialist China and suppression of class enemies important.

Discrimination against class enemies was therefore justified to protect the socialist society. This discrimination was extended to their families. Children of former KMT officials, for example, were prohibited from joining the Communist Party, the Communist Youth League and the Communist Pioneers. They were not eligible to work for the government, to join the army or to study overseas. On collective farms, class enemies were the last to receive compensation in kind. They received food rations that were qualitatively and quantitatively less than those given to working-class members. At school, the children of class enemies were not allowed to sit in the front rows. One's class label was hereditary and passed on to one's offspring (Yu Xiguang 1993, 1–34).

This discrimination against class enemies was unchallenged. Members of the enemy class who questioned these policies would be punished severely, while members of the working class who showed sympathy for the mistreated class enemies would be viewed as ideologically disloyal and politically untrustworthy. "Sympathy towards an enemy class member is tantamount to cruelty to the working-class people," commented one engineer who was condemned in 1958 as a "counter-revolutionary rightist" for being sympathetic to his rightist co-researchers.[5] This was not an isolated case. An individual's position on a given political issue defined his or her class status. Young people were encouraged to denounce or report their parents if they expressed

---

5   Conversation with a former colleague, 12 April 1984, Beijing.

anti-Party views. One's blood connection with his or her parents was secondary to political and ideological loyalty to the Party.[6]

What ensued in Mao's era was the rise of collective indifference to the suffering of others, in the interests of self-protection. You could not afford to act compassionately to a stranger in need without knowing their class label. An act of kindness was justified and laudable if it was directed at someone from the working class, but the same act would be ideologically questionable and politically costly if it was directed at a member of the enemy class. Mao once stated that love and compassionate were not abstract values. They had class connotations. He wrote:

> It is a basic Marxist concept that being determines consciousness, that the objective realities of class struggle and national struggle determine our thoughts and feelings. But some of our comrades turn this upside down and maintain that everything ought to start from "love." Now as for love, in a class society there can be only class love; but these comrades are seeking a love transcending classes, love in the abstract and also freedom in the abstract, truth in the abstract, human nature in the abstract, etc. (Mao Zedong 1991, 852)

Mao's class-based interpretation of love was powerfully influential. For the general public, it was safer to be indifferent to the disadvantaged than to lend a helping hand. This perhaps explains the shock felt by a Communist cadre when he saw a female CCP commander offer food to a begging grandchild of a landlord. The commander's unorthodox act ran counter to Mao's notion of class love. In her words, the child did nothing wrong. Why should he go hungry because of his grandparents' class status? (Huang Hua 2008, 76–77) Yet in the pre-reform era,

---

6 See for example Zhu Liudi's report "律师文革时举报母亲致其被枪决 40年后申请母墓地为文物" (An attorney asked to make the tomb of his mother a "cultural relic" 40 years after his mother was executed because of his reporting on his mother to the authorities during the Cultural Revolution), *Xinjing News* (新京报), 7 August 2013, http://politics.people.com.cn/n/2013/0807/c1001-22471729.html .

particularly in the 1960s, ideological fanaticism gathered momentum. Class awareness took precedence over humanitarianism. Human feelings of compassion, sympathy and pity became conditional and even stigmatised. These feelings could not be extended to members of the opposite class and not even extended to a family member if she or he expressed views against the Party.

"Dignified socialist qualities"

In China's pre-reform era, the Communist authorities came up with a set of criteria for political socialisation purposes. These criteria, also called "dignified socialist qualities" (社会主义高尚情操), were generally consistent in the different periods of the pre-reform era. These attitudes and behaviours were the opposite of those associated with the feudal past. "Dignified socialist qualities" included willingness to "serve the people whole-heartedly," "place public interest above an individual's private interest," namely the public interest defined by the Party, "work hard and resist extravagance" (艰苦朴素), and learn from the workers and peasants. These qualities downplayed individual pursuits and preferences and commanded individuals to concentrate their efforts on collective, state-directed objectives and to be firm against members of the exploiting class. In the most radical years of the Cultural Revolution, those who tried hard to pass the Party's political evaluation were more motivated to resort to violence against a class enemy or even their family members to demonstrate their trustworthiness.[7]

Looking back, "extravagance" in Mao's era is an oxymoron. When the majority of Chinese people were living on starvation rations, extravagance was only accessible for the country's top officials and their families. For most people, "resisting extravagance" really meant not seeking out non-essential items or pursuits such as cosmetics, fashion,

---

7   For the "criteria for producing successors of the proletarian revolutionary cause" or the "dignified socialist qualities," see for example Kenneth Lieberthal (2004), *Governing China: From Revolution Through Reform*, pp. 293–94. See also Harry Wu's *Bitter Winds: A Memoir of My Years in China's Gulag*, pp. 21–36, for the fate of someone in Mao's China who failed to meet the "dignified socialist qualities."

vacations, pets, or gardening. For the authorities, particularly local officials with limited education, personal hobbies such as gardening and pet keeping were luxuries, not relevant to the daily lives of working people and distractions at a time when concentrated efforts were needed to build a strong socialist economy. These so-called non-essential personal hobbies could create unreasonable demand on the state for resources, when the Stalinist economic system was already struggling to provide necessities to the people. Additionally, there was an ideological stigma associated with, for example, women who smoked, used make-up, wore high-heeled shoes or kept a pet dog, and this scared people into conformity. No one wanted to be judged a political outcast or a pursuer of a decadent bourgeois lifestyle, labels that could impact a person's employment, access to food rations, or urban residency status. In Chinese movies and literature produced in the pre-reform era, women who led a bourgeois lifestyle were portrayed as the wives of capitalists, KMT agents, or prostitutes. Because of the ideological bias against so-called bourgeois practices, pet owners as a group disappeared in Mao's China.

"Revolutionary violence"

To the ruling CCP in the pre-reform era, class struggle was the major form of conflict in socialist China. To neutralise and eliminate the perceived hostility of members of the exploiting class and of "capitalist roaders," namely officials who did not agree with Mao's policies in favour of a collective economy, Mao Zedong and his supporters resorted to mass violence against their perceived opponents. Such violence, carried out in the name of proletarian dictatorship, was even encouraged (Lieberthal 2004, 294). Violence reached an extreme in the last 10 years of Mao's rule. Class enemies were verbally humiliated, physically abused and publicly executed. The nation's young people, called Red Guards, witnessed and participated in these acts of mass violence.

Mao launched five major political persecution campaigns, each involving young students. During the Cultural Revolution, middle school and college students turned themselves into Red Guards who humiliated their teachers, abused their peers, brutalised and even reported on their own parents.[8] Their violent behaviour received the endorsement of the Great Leader. Violence was believed to be not only necessary to suppress the resistance of class enemies, but also commendable, since it would remove resistance to Mao's "continuous revolution" and help produce a new generation of "successors of the proletarian revolutionary cause." Abusing class enemies was a sign of political loyalty. The most fanatical Red Guards were also the most brutal. In 1966, the apartment of an English professor at a Beijing college was stormed by the school's Red Guards. To denounce the professor's alleged membership of the exploiting class, the leader of the Red Guards grabbed the condemned teacher's cat and smashed it to death on the wall in front of him.[9] Those who participated in physical violence during the Cultural Revolution represented a small minority of the Red Guards. But the majority of young people bore witness to brutality. They may have been desensitised and internalised violence against condemned class enemies and nonhuman animals as normal and unsurprising.

In Mao's China, public violence was often staged as a deterrent.[10] In the early 1950s, public trials were used to establish the authority of the new regime and to remove residual resistance from landlords and rich peasants. Later, during the Cultural Revolution, public denunciation meetings were held to punish class enemies. Public executions often drew huge crowds and were used by local authorities to send a strong message that crimes and dissent would not be tolerated (Ding Shu 2014). Public executions continued into the mid-1980s and early 1990s

---

8   For violence against teachers, condemned officials and class enemies, see Xu Youyu, *1966: Memories of Our Generation* (Beijing: China Association of Arts and Literature Press, 1998).

9   Conversation in July 1991 with a former colleague who was a student of the professor.

10 Public trials and executions were first staged in 1951, when the Communist regime launched a campaign to suppress counter-revolutionaries. Mao Zedong was the mastermind of using public sentencing as a public education instrument. His police chief, General Luo Ruiqing, put the idea into practice and also suggested that public trials be staged before executions, to communicate to the public the various crimes of the counter-revolutionaries. See Yang Kuisong (2013).

in some places. Studies are necessary in mainland China to determine the effect of exposure to public executions and other state-sanctioned violence on desensitisation and normalisation of violence and cruelty.

In the pre-reform era, violence against nature was also justified on ideological terms. In the early 1950s, massive land reclamation was carried out in the nation's mountainous and border regions. Environmental destruction, deforestation and wildlife devastation were not of concern to the new government, which was preoccupied with the restoration of the national economy. In 1958, Mao called on the entire nation to wipe out sparrows. He insisted, despite the disagreement of the scientific community, that sparrows should be killed because they consumed grain and caused food shortages for working-class people. Sparrows were a threat to public interest along with the other three pests identified by the state for extermination: mosquitoes, rats and flies. Animal control by brutal means happens in most countries, but in Mao's China it was common people, rather than professional animal-control experts, who were often mobilised to kill animals deemed to be pests. The mass killing of sparrows was ecologically and politically consequential. Without the birds, there was an exponential increase in insect populations, worsening the country's grain production and contributing to the Great Famine of 1959–61.

Perhaps most morally problematic was the involvement of the nation's youth in a killing spree that brutalised defenceless victims, sending young people the message that they could do anything to the weak as long as their acts were ideologically correct. Elementary and secondary school students joined adults in sparrow-killing contests, using brutal methods to dispatch the hapless birds (Li Xinlian 2013). Those who participated in sparrow killing destroyed the birds' nests, crushed their eggs, and broke their wings and legs. This indifference to animal suffering could not but shape young people's attitudes to fellow humans from the enemy class. The most disturbing consequence of Mao's sparrow killing campaign was perhaps the desensitisation of China's young people to violence and cruelty. Those who have been in positions of power and policy-making since 2012 are from the same generation as the youths who participated in or witnessed the sparrow killing.

Another event that may have desensitised participants to cruelty involved the nation's wildlife animals. In 1960 and 1961, the Great Famine threatened the lives of tens of millions of Chinese peasants. Urban residents saw their food rations drop precipitously. Starvation was widespread. To tide themselves over, people took to the mountains in search of edible plants and animals. The armed forces were mobilised to help with hunting, with the central government even sending hunting teams into the vast Gobi Desert in northern China, to supply game meat to top Communist leaders and their families (Huang Zhen 2006, 208-9). Indiscriminate hunting caused severe devastation to species such as Mongolian gazelle. Hunting for survival is less controversial than hunting for sport or entertainment, but these mass hunting expeditions may have served to reinforce societal indifference to animal suffering.

Pre-reform politics in summary

China in Mao's era (1949-78) did not have the ideological, political or material conditions necessary for the rise of an animal protection movement. Ideologically, society was divided into two opposing groups, much like the artificial divide between "super-men" and "sub-men" seen in other totalitarian regimes in the 20th century (Reichsfuhrer-SS Office 1942). While working-class people, Mao's version of the "super-men," were the "masters" of the socialist state, class enemies were villains to be reformed, humiliated and conquered. Love and compassion had class connotations and could not be expressed towards the enemy class. The party-state not only orchestrated psychological and physical assaults against class enemies, but also publicly staged these assaults as instruments of political socialisation. A host of so-called bourgeois practices, including pet keeping, were condemned (Red Guards of the School of Mao Zedong Thought 1966). Individual pursuits not conducive to the party's political objectives were suppressed, and personal hobbies that used material resources were rejected as extravagant. Pet keeping was condemned as a hobby of the propertied class members who lived on the sweat and blood of the working-class people. Keeping dogs as pets in urban China disappeared during Mao's years.[11]

The impact of Mao's politics on human–animal relations deserves a systematic study. Studies of abused children, children who have witnessed animal abuse, and children who grew up in abusive households have found that an abusive environment can have a negative impact on child development (Ascione 1998, 119–33; Ponder and Lockwood 2000, 1–5; Bell 2001, 223–34; and Boat 1999). Some abused children become desensitised to cruelty while others adopt "abuse reactive" behaviours triggered by memories of abuse or by the sight of an abusive situation. Some children who witness animal abuse may "suppress their own feelings of kindness and tenderness towards a pet because they can't bear the pain caused by their own empathy for the abused animal" (Siebert 2010). Hopefully, this study shall spark academic interest in the impact of "revolutionary violence" in Mao's China on the society's attitude towards nonhuman animals in post-Mao China.

Chinese culture: some conclusions

This introduction to Chinese culture has been exploratory rather than definitive. It is far from a complete review of Chinese attitudes and behaviours towards animals. However, some preliminary conclusions can be drawn about Chinese culture and human–animal relations in ancient China.

Anthropocentrism

China in the past was as anthropocentric as the rest of the world. The fact that Daoism and Buddhism emphasised respect for nature is indicative of the existence of a dominant human-centred society.

---

11 In Mao's China, pet dogs disappeared in urban areas. Those who could afford to keep a pet dog secretly had to give their dogs to relatives in rural area to avoid having their dogs killed by the government. See Ba Jin's 小狗包弟 (My dog Baodi), http://www.heepets.com/2246.html.

Daoist masters advocated the rural ideal of a simple life because this lifestyle was being abandoned in the society with breakthroughs in productive powers and in the increase in number of conflicts over resources. Similarly, Buddhist admonitions against killing and overindulgence were a response to such vices. Buddhist and Daoist emphasis on the equality of humans and nonhuman animals was also a response to a world that humans dominated. As state orthodoxy, Confucianism neutralised the impact of the idealistic Daoist and Buddhist teachings. China was no less anthropocentric than other societies. The need for the Chinese nation to survive natural and man-made crises also served to undercut the influence of the Daoist and Buddhist teachings. The Daoist and Buddhist admonition against killing, for example, has subsequently remained a lofty ideal.

As in other cultures, nonhuman life has instrumental significance to the Chinese. Since time immemorial, animals have been the objects of worship, literary works, sacrifice, and human consumption as meat, tonics and medicine. They were also used for transportation and labour. Chinese use of animals was no different from that in other cultures and civilisations either. Traditional Western medicine uses a wide range of animal parts as ingredients, as does traditional Chinese medicine (Venzmer 1968). Yet Chinese cultural traditions were against excessive use and exploitation of nature. As Chinese scholars have recently discovered, controlled use of natural resources was implemented more than 4,000 years ago when vast areas of China were sparsely populated and wildlife species were abundant (Sun Jiang, He Li and Huang Zheng 2009, 71). Strict laws had been promulgated for the protection of forests and wildlife animals. We cannot say that the ancient Chinese laws and practices limiting excessive hunting and fishing were implemented with a conscious desire to maintain an ecological balance or to protect animals for their own value independent of human interests. Yet they served to enculture the instrumental value of the natural world and the importance of reasonable use.

Counter-cultural ideas

This is an area where Chinese culture stands out in comparison with other countries. While there are historical examples of counter-cultural

2 Human–animal relations in Chinese history

voices on animal welfare in the West, such as St Francis of Assisi (1182–1226), counter-cultural practices such as vegetarianism, mercy release and slaughter suspension became national movements and even government policies in China. Official sanction helped Daoist and Buddhist ideas about species equality to penetrate Chinese society. Traditionally, Chinese culture was pulled in two opposite directions. On the one hand, Chinese people were expected to fulfill their earthly responsibilities by providing for their families, and to do so they could take what they needed from nature. On the other hand, refraining from excessive desires was believed to satisfy a person's spiritual needs and to bring good luck and fortune to their family. The result was a unique Chinese religious attitude that balanced pragmatism with the psychological need for spiritual fulfillment.

The tradition of temporary "slaughter suspension" is a good example of this: it was implemented to cater to the spiritual needs of the nation without really ending slaughter. Similarly, Chinese Buddhists made special efforts to avoid consuming meat on particular days and on special occasions, but could eat meat with peace of mind the rest of the month. This pragmatism perhaps explains why China, unlike India, has not maintained a large vegetarian population in the contemporary era (Lin Yutang 1966, 127–32). However, although vegetarians have never made up a majority of the population, meat was not traditionally consumed daily. As one Western scholar who studied Chinese cooking pointed out, the Chinese did prepare various kinds of sausages, smoked meats and dried meats for the long winter months in provinces such as Sichuan, but there was "nothing comparable to the riot of such products that one finds in Switzerland or Bavaria, for the Chinese ... are basically vegetable eaters" (Anderson 1988, 167).

Chinese pragmatism did not prevent compassion for animals. Daoist and Buddhist beliefs neutralised the influence of the anthropocentric Confucian outlook. In China's past, expressions of compassion for animals were pervasive. Literary expressions of kindness towards migrant geese and nursing mother birds were indicative of a universal pity for species who often succumb to human insensitivity and brutality. Nonhuman animals were depicted as having feelings just like humans, and the Chinese were among the first to acknowledge animals as sentient beings.

Remarks against keeping birds in cages and instead advocating tree planting were progressive statements against animal cruelty. Most importantly, the Confucian scholar-official who made the remarks not only criticised inappropriate behaviours, but also offered a constructive, humane and empathetic alternative for bird lovers. Such statements against cruelty were not simply emotional utterances by the few. They were moral appeals to Chinese society, from Daoist, Buddhist and Confucian masters and from the emperors themselves. So far, no historical records have been discovered from ancient China depicting mass acts of animal abuse for human entertainment comparable to those seen in Ancient Rome or in contemporary China.

The limits of cultural influence

China's recorded history, however, is not short of stories of suffering, repression and violence. Jonathan Spence's *The Search for Modern China* (1990), for example, documents brutal politics and widespread suffering during the Ming and Qing dynasties. The ancient monarchs who practised vegetarianism and mercy release were so much talked about because they were in the minority. Dynastic change in ancient times was often bloody and violent. Daoist and Buddhist admonitions of kindness were irrelevant in times of great political upheaval; Daoist frugality, Buddhist mercy for animals and Confucian moderation were often brushed aside by the rich and powerful (Liu Bo and Yang Liu 2011). The "retreat of the elephants" from vast areas of East Asian continent to the tip of Southern China, documented human exploitation of elephants when they were "useful" for the ancient Chinese and their sacrifice when they were in the way of human survival (Elvin 2004). Ancient China was no less anthropocentric than other countries. Kindness to nonhuman animals, honourable as it was, was secondary to the needs of humans. For ordinary people eking out a living on the verge of starvation, the lofty ideals of compassion and respect for nature were secondary to survival.

In adopting elements of Taoism, Buddhism and Confucianism, the Chinese have been remarkably pragmatic. Lin Yutang, one of modern China's great scholars of Chinese culture, observed that "There is no doubt that the Chinese are in love with life, in love with this earth, and will not forsake it for an invisible heaven" (Lin Yutang 1966, 10). Chinese culture does not sanction cruelty to nonhuman animals – but the Chinese would not sacrifice earthly needs to pursue a purely abstract religious or philosophical goal. As Lin Yutang pointed out, Chinese Buddhists are kind, pacific, patient and philanthropic – but when they practise philanthropy, they expect good fortune and future happiness in return.

All in all, Chinese culture does not sanction cruelty to nonhuman animals. For a better understanding of the triggers of animal welfare problems in contemporary China, this book focuses on the politics of economic modernisation. In the following chapter on the conflict over dogs, I hope to connect reform politics with the country's controversial dog meat trade. Is dog meat part of the mainstream Chinese food culture? Is the dog meat industry a traditional one that has been passed down from ancient China, as traders have claimed? Or does the controversy over dog meat originate in more recent developments?

3
China's "civil war" over dogs

Of the more than 660 sub-provincial cities in China, Yulin, in the Guangxi Zhuang Autonomous Region in the country's south, is arguably the best known internationally. Since 2010 this city has attracted worldwide attention for its Yulin Dog Meat Festival (YDMF), which was launched by local dog-meat traders. In June 2014, the festival became one of the most reported subjects in Chinese media, second only to the World Cup. Western journalists have also been attracted to Yulin. CNN, the BBC, the *New York Times*, the *Washington Post* and Channel News Asia, to name just a few, have all covered the festival. In 2016, US Congressman Alcee Hastings, a Democrat from the state of Florida, launched a Congressional Resolution (HR 752) specifically addressed to the Chinese government regarding the Yulin festival.[1] Congressman Hastings also appealed directly to the chairman of China's National People's Congress and to President Xi Jinping, urging them to stop the festival and to legislate a ban on the dog-meat trade.

The festival, held to coincide with the summer solstice (21 or 22 June in the northern hemisphere), has become a public relations crisis for the city, for Guangxi and for China. In the three years following the inception of the festival, traders began to slaughter and process a large

---

1   The resolution was renamed H. Resolution 30 in 2017.

number of dogs one week before the summer solstice in preparation for the festival, an occasion for local businesses to thank local and outside business partners. Promoted as a tourist attraction, the festival seemed to continue for several more days after the summer solstice until outside tourists and visitors left the city. As soon as it was launched in 2010, the YDMF drew criticism from Chinese animal activists, who condemned the event for two obvious reasons. First, although the YDMF was established by local dog-meat traders, it was endorsed by the Yulin authorities. The city's tourism bureau was particularly enthusiastic and saw the annual event as a way to boost tourism and attract outside investment. To the critics, the government's endorsement of a controversial eating habit showed that it was out of touch with the new reality, where millions of families keep dogs as companion animals. The official endorsement ran counter to the belief that governments should promote healthy lifestyles and social progress.

Second, to many people, the YDMF was ethically provocative and morally wrong. Thousands of dogs are slaughtered during the festival, in broad daylight and in public places, including in open markets, in front of other dogs, in residential areas, and in front of young children who may happen to be around. When dogs are abused, humans also feel the pain. The Chinese public in general were appalled that the mass slaughter of dogs was being celebrated as a "festival."

I have been to Yulin five times since 2014. At the city's live dog markets, I saw hundreds of dogs crammed into suffocatingly small cages to be sold to restaurant owners and slaughterhouses. The dogs displayed fear, fatigue, dehydration, food deprivation, pain and suffering. A majority had injuries such as open wounds, broken noses or broken limbs. Some were dying of unknown illnesses. At least 10% of the dogs I saw on 14 June 2014 had skin problems of varying degrees of severity. These dogs had been shipped to Yulin, some from nearby provinces and others from hundreds of kilometres away, from provinces in central or eastern China. The source of these dogs was suspicious. Since China does not have dog farms, a large number of the dogs shipped over great distances to Yulin are suspected to have been pet dogs or rural guard dogs who were stolen from outside their homes.

Slaughterhouses were scattered in different parts of the city, some in residential areas, and dogs were killed in front of other dogs waiting

3 China's "civil war" over dogs

for their turn. In April 2016, in a slaughterhouse inside a marketplace in the centre of Yulin, I witnessed terrified dogs huddling together and trembling behind a huge barrel. They had just witnessed the morning's intense killing spree and displayed signs of severe mental agony. Standing in a pool of blood left by the slaughtered dogs, they were silent and expressionless when we approached them, and tried to avoid eye contact with us (Li, Peter 2016a).

In the eyes of Chinese animal lovers, Yulin has become synonymous with insensitivity and brutality. Activists from local groups and nearby provinces were the first to respond to the festival. In June 2011, Du Yufeng, founder of the Guangyuan Baoai Animal Protection Center of nearby Sichuan, staged a protest in front of the dog meat traders at Yulin's Dongkou Market. In June 2012, artist Pian Shan Kong staged a one-man performance piece at Dongkou Market, kneeling in front of a pile of dog carcasses to apologise on behalf of humanity for its ungratefulness and cruelty (China Daily 2015). Days before the summer solstice of 2013, a petition led by Guangdong's Love First and Beijing's Capital Animal Welfare Association (CAWA) was signed by more than 60 Chinese animal protection groups urging the Yulin authorities to shut down the bloody event (China Animal Protection Network 2013).

Seeing no signs of change, animal protectionists launched a nationwide campaign against the festival. In 2013 and 2014, risking personal safety, Chen Mincai, director and founder of Chongqing Animal Protection Association and campaigners, artists Pian Shan Kong, animal rescuer Yang Yuhua and others converged in Yulin to call for an end to the festival. Celebrities from mainland China and the Greater China Region joined the nationwide campaign against the festival (Jiang Gewei 2014). Across the country, a candlelight vigil for Yulin dogs took place on the campuses of some 30 universities, organised by the Dalian Vshine Animal Protection Association (Vshine).[2] Letters of petition to the Yulin authorities, to the Guangxi Autonomous Region government, and to the national government were part of the continuing efforts to stop the slaughter. On 9 June 2016,

---

2   Telephone conversation with Dezhi Yu, program manager of the Vshine Animal Protection Association, 19 June 2014.

animal protectionists in the country's capital gathered in front of the Yulin Representative Office in Beijing and submitted a new petition to shut down the festival (Li Jing 2016).

A Google image search for Yulin brings up tens of thousands of graphic photos of dog slaughter, dog carcasses hanging in the air, and other bloody scenes. Ending the YDMF has become a global campaign. In 2013, more than 50,000 people around the world signed an online petition initiated by the US-based Humane Society International. In 2015, more than 130,000 signed a similar petition.[3] Globally, petitions to end the festival were signed by more than 3.8 million people in 2015 (ITV 2015). In 2016, more than 11 million people worldwide signed four petitions to end the Yulin Dog Meat Festival (Li Jing 2016). Chinese and foreign celebrities joined the call to shut down the event, and there were US Congressional appeals and a discussion in the British Parliament.

In response to mounting domestic and international criticism, Yulin authorities withdrew official endorsement of the festival in 2014, and warned government employees and their families not to patronise dog-meat restaurants. They have made some window-dressing efforts to discourage the trade, such as forcing dog-meat restaurants to cover the word "dog" in business signs. This change in the official position was revealed in an internal directive issued by the Yulin government to government employees. The directive was made public by a Yulin official who was reportedly an animal lover himself.[4] However, the YDMF, without the word "festival" in its title, and without official patronage, has continued.

What explains the resistance of Chinese authorities to worldwide appeals to shut down the YDMF and the dog meat trade? China's Foreign Ministry spokeswoman, Hua Chunying, assured foreign reporters that the event did not have official backing (Ministry of Foreign Affairs of China 2016). Obviously, both the Yulin authorities and the national government are aware of the controversy surrounding

---

[3] This was a petition organised by Humane Society International only and the result was not published.

[4] I was shown a copy of the directive when I was investigating Yulin's dog meat markets on 14 June 2014. The directive was issued in mid-May.

the event and the dog meat trade more generally. Why have they allowed it to continue? Does the Chinese government accept the argument that dog meat consumption is part of mainstream Chinese food culture? Or have economic considerations, such as the industry's contribution to local development and employment, stopped the authorities from taking a stand?

Dog meat consumption in Chinese history

Dog meat was part of mainstream Chinese food culture from at least 2255 BCE, the time of the legendary Emperor Yao in prehistoric China, and for the following 2,831 years, reaching a peak during the Han dynasty (206 BCE–220 CE), particularly among the rich and powerful. During the Sui dynasty (581â€"618 CE), however, the consumption of dog meat was increasingly questioned. By the Tang dynasty (618–907 CE), dog meat was considered ethically and legally "dirty" because it mostly came from stolen dogs. The educated elite stayed away from dog meat. Soon after Emperor Huizong of the Song dynasty ascended the throne in 1100 CE, he issued an edict banning the slaughter of dogs and the sale or consumption of dog meat. According to the edict, violators would be punished severely, while those who reported offenders would be rewarded. However, meat vendors found ways to get around the ban. They started to sell dog meat disguised as mutton, giving rise to the expression "selling dog meat under the hanging sheep head" (Xiang Sunan 2018).

During the succeeding dynasties, i.e., the Yuan, Ming and Qing dynasties, there was no opportunity for dog meat to return to the mainstream. The founders of the Yuan and Qing dynasties were descendants of nomadic Mongols and Manchus. The Mongols valued dogs as guards, herding helpers, and hunting buddies, more than as food. Before 1619 the use of dogs for food and furs was not unheard of among the Manchus, when they were largely confined to what is now northeastern China. Song dynasty scholar Xu Mengxin recorded in his *San Chao Bei Meng Hui Bian* (三朝北盟会编) (*A Collection of Historical Materials on War and Peace with Jin Under the Reign of Three Song Emperors*), completed in 1194, that dog meat was consumed by the

Manchus' ancestors, the Jurchens. The Jurchens consumed fresh dog blood mixed with rice, garlic and chives, and Jurchen healers believed that slaughtering a dog could drive away illness. Another historical record, the *Da Jin Guo Zhi* (*A Recorded History of the Great Jin Dynasty*), records that during the Jin dynasty (1115–1234 CE), dog fur was made into clothing, mostly for the poor. However, although dog meat was consumed during this period, it was not a commonplace food like pork or mutton (Kai Chen 2017). During the early Qing dynasty (1644–1912 CE), the Manchus stopped eating dog meat. Various theories have been advanced to explain the Manchus' rejection of dog meat and dog fur. These include speculation that the Manchus felt "indebted" to dogs, who protected and worked for their owners; that dogs came to be seen "as a Manchu god," to be worshiped, not slaughtered for food; that "superior people do not eat dog meat"; and that dog meat came to be considered unclean because dogs ate human waste (Kai Chen 2017).

Dog-meat consumption did continue among a small number of Han Chinese, but it was not part of mainstream Han Chinese food culture. Even when dog meat has been eaten in China, it has never been consumed with a frequency even remotely close to the consumption of fish, pork, chicken or mutton. When dog meat was eaten, it was often done in private, suggesting that it was not something to be proud of. In the dynasties before the Han dynasty, dog butchers existed and were a respected profession; after the Han dynasty, this trade no longer existed. From the Tang dynasty onwards, many people kept dogs as pets. During the Qing dynasty, pet dogs in the Forbidden City provided sex education for the young princes and princesses, who learned about sex by watching their pet dogs mate. Traditionally, as in contemporary China, sex was an embarrassing subject for Chinese parents.

Pet keeping is a taboo for China's Communist leaders. As of the writing of this book, I have not seen one photo of a Chinese Communist leader holding or walking with a pet dog. In contrast, ancient Chinese rulers did not hide their love of pet keeping. Emperor Jiajing (r. 1521–66) of the Ming dynasty was known to be a cat lover, while Emperor Yongzheng (r. 1722–35) of the Qing dynasty loved his many pet dogs (Ge Zhonge and Xu Xianjiang 2009, 171–72). Chiang Kaishek, President of the Republic of China and leader of the

3 China's "civil war" over dogs

Nationalist Party of China (Kuomintang), was seen with his dogs in movies and photos in the early 1940s in Chongqing and in the 1960s in Taipei. For Chinese Communist leaders from Mao Zedong to Deng Xiaoping and Xi Jinping, by contrast, pet keeping, including posing for pictures with their pet dogs, if they had any, would be a politically incorrect thing to do.

Dog-meat consumption today

Unlike in North Korea, where dog meat is on the menu of Pyongyang's state banquets (Zhang Zuoliang 1998, 86), dog meat consumption in China is a subculture. Like snakes, monkey brains, or fried maggots, dog meat is not eaten by the majority of Chinese people. The Animals Asia Foundation (AAF) conducted a four-year survey of dog meat consumption in China. The study divided China into two regions based on the level of dog meat consumption. In the provinces where dog meat consumption is relatively common, 48.8% of those surveyed had not eaten dog meat during the survey period (2010–12). In contrast, 78.45% of people in the rest of the country had not eaten dog meat in the same period (AAF 2015b). Among those who do eat dog, dog meat is consumed once or twice a year, or even once or twice in their lifetime, usually because of a special invitation or other trigger.

Two other surveys commissioned by the Humane Society International (HSI) confirmed the AAF's finding that dog eating was a minority habit. However, HSI's nationwide survey found that more urbanites ate dog meat than did rural residents; educated respondents were more likely than the less educated to eat dog meat; and dog meat was more popular in northern China than in the south. These findings confirmed that dog meat was not generally prepared at home, but rather was a commercialised product sold chiefly to urban consumers, particularly at special catering events. This result confirmed that dog meat traders targeted restaurant goers and office workers, who typically eat out for lunch or when meeting with clients and business partners. Contrary to the belief that South China was the main dog meat market, the HSI survey showed a downturn in dog meat consumption in the more developed southern provinces, particularly in Guangdong.[5] In the country's coastal regions, dog eating is disappearing (Sun, Celine 2018).

A third survey, conducted in November 2015 in Yanji, an ethnic Korean city in Northeast China, found that only 16% of the rural respondents reported that they often ate dog meat, where "often" was defined as more than 10 times a year. Dog meat was not a daily or weekly food on the dinner table. In urban Yanji, 58% of the respondents never ate dog meat while 42% ate it infrequently. Dalian in Northeast China's Liaoning Province is a predominantly Han Chinese city and one of the most urbanised in the region. Of the surveyed rural residents in Dalian, 93% never ate dog meat. In the urban area of Dalian, 82% of all urban residents (including office workers, service sector workers and government employees) never ate dog meat (Li, Peter, Sun Jiang and Dezhi Yu 2017, 1–20). Among office workers specifically, only 2% reported eating dog meat.

South China's Guangdong, Guangxi, Guizhou, Hunan, and Yunnan combined are the nation's biggest dog eating region in terms of the size of the dog meat market. The second major market is Northeast China's Jilin, Liaoning and Heilongjiang Provinces. The third biggest market includes northern Jiangsu, western Shandong, and eastern Henan. Peixian county in northern Jiangsu, the hometown of Fan Kuai, a legendary general of the Han dynasty (256–195 BCE) and a dog butcher before his military career, is China's centre of processed dog meat, including sausages, canned meat and salt-preserved meat.

There is no official count of the number of dogs slaughtered in China. In 2003, China was believed to consume most of the 13 to 16 million dogs eaten in Asia annually (Bartlett and Clifton 2003). More recently, a Guangdong activist estimated that 20 million dogs may be killed annually in China for food.[6] One commercial report estimated that China produced 97,500 tons of dog meat from an estimated 10 million slaughtered dogs in 2012 (ASKCI 2014). Since one third of each slaughtered dog (hair, internal organs and body fluids) is discarded, the remaining weight from the 10 million dogs, i.e., 97,500 tons, would provide about 700 grams of dog meat per person for 10% of the

5   HSI-CAWA survey of China's dog eating and attitude towards the Yulin Dog Meat Festival, June 2016, unpublished report.
6   Telephone conversation with Shan Dai, head of Kindness First, a Guangdong volunteer group, 14 June 2014.

population. In contrast, China produced more than 80 million tons of pork, beef, mutton, and broiler chicken in 2013.

Dog meat restaurants have made special efforts to target two main groups of consumers: urban, educated white-collar workers, and rural, older, less educated low-income consumers. The consumption of dog meat is most common in three major markets (South China, Northeast China and Central China), where dog meat is promoted openly as part of the local dietary subculture. However, even in these regions and among these groups of consumers, as I have shown, dog meat is not a mainstream food choice (Li, Peter, Sun Jiang and Dezhi Yu 2017).

Both in output and in terms of meeting people's nutritional needs, the Chinese dog meat industry is negligible. What makes this small trade so stubbornly persistent?

The dog meat industry

The dog meat trade is not a major industry in China. When it started in Guangdong in the early 1980s, it was a productive activity for peasants freshly freed from the shackles of Mao's People's Communes. Today, the industry is composed of dog collectors, transporters, slaughterhouse operators, dog meat processors and restaurant owners. It is also involved in making dog fur products, particularly in Northeast China. In the other dog meat markets, dog meat is usually eaten with the skin on, but in the northeast it is sometimes consumed without skin, meaning the fur can be used to make gloves, hats and jackets. However, the use of dog fur has gone down in this part of the country in recent years, as a result of the booming industry in furs from other animals.

Employment numbers

There are no authoritative statistics on the scale of the industry, the number of people employed in it, or the potential economic impact of its shutdown. Since restaurants specialising in dog meat do not account for a significant number of restaurants in any market, they do not constitute an independent business sector. Most restaurants that serve dog meat primarily serve other dishes. Dog meat is only one of the offerings on their menus, and often not the main one. Meanwhile dog collectors, many of whom are involved in stealing dogs, do not do this work on a full-time basis. It is a sideline job to make some quick additional money. Transport operators specialising in shipping live dogs are also very small in number. Most truckers transport dogs only when they are not moving livestock or other agricultural produce. Those who do specialise in dog transport are often also working as dog collectors. They buy live dogs from people who capture, often illegally, stray dogs, free-roaming rural dogs, and urban pet dogs. Dog collectors keep these animals in a holding facility until they have accumulated enough dogs – say 500 – to fill a truck.

In all markets, the dog meat production chain has mostly been operated by traders from rural backgrounds. Although they are small in number, many of those who rely on the dog meat trade for their livelihood are unskilled former peasants who might otherwise struggle to earn a living, and this is one reason for the government's reluctance to interfere with the trade. Just how many people are employed by the industry, in what roles, and what adverse social and public health impact their employment in the industry might be having on society seem to have been ignored by the local authorities. As long as the industry provides employment, local governments in the major dog meat markets will not care about anything else unless a public health crisis arises from the consumption of contaminated dog meat.

No official statistics are available on the number of people working in the dog meat trade. We failed to find any data for Yulin, Yanji, or Changchun, the target cities of our investigation. Most of the people working in the industry, whether as dog collectors, transporters, slaughterhouse owners or hospitality workers, do not working exclusively in the dog meat industry. There are thousands of dog collectors around the country, but most only moonlight in dog collection, buying surplus dogs and puppies, old and sick dogs from rural households, or dogs from failing breeding operations. Since the end of the 1990s, some have resorted to theft using poison-tainted arrows to steal owned dogs.

The catering industry as a whole employs no more than 5% of the 700 million people who make up China's labour force (Rush 2009). As we saw above, only a tiny fraction of these would be working in

3 China's "civil war" over dogs

dog meat restaurants. Changchun has the biggest number of dog meat restaurants in China. Most of these (70%) are small operations employing on average no more than seven people. If we use a generous estimate of 10 staff per restaurant, the 898 dog meat restaurants in Changchun would employ 8,980 workers. Yulin city proper had 46 dog meat restaurants, all small operations employing no more than 460 people in total.

According to an activist who has been involved in 15 dog rescue operations on Chinese highways, those involved in transporting dogs to the three major dog meat markets would not exceed 200 truckers. Nationwide, direct or indirect dog meat trade employment would not exceed half a million people.[7]

Restaurants and catering

To determine the volume of dog meat being traded in the three major markets, I searched, with the help of two research assistants, for the number of dog meat restaurants and for the sales revenue of dog meat in the local catering industry. Although South China's Guangdong was for many years the biggest market for dog and cat meat, the number of dog meat restaurants has been going down in recent years. With the help of a search on China's most popular online restaurant listing, Dianping.com, we found only 36 dog meat restaurants that mentioned "dog meat" in their restaurant names in Guangzhou in the summer of 2016. This suggests a drastic reduction in the dog meat trade in the city of some 13 million residents. Ten years earlier, there were numerous dog meat restaurants in areas of the city where migrant workers were concentrated.[8] In contrast, we found 14,110 restaurants serving Cantonese food and 4,365 serving Western food or Western desserts.[9] Contrary to perceptions that Guangzhou is the "capital" of

---

7 Interview with Mr Huang Ziyang, a Tianjin animal activist, 24 December 2015, Tianjin, China.
8 Interview in Shenzhen with Li Qiang, an electronic component trader in Guangzhou, 23 July, 2013.
9 Guangzhou restaurant numbers were pulled from http://www.dianping.com/ using search words "dog meat restaurants," "Cantonese food restaurants," and "Western food restaurants."

dog meat consumption, dog meat does not seem to be a popular food choice. These Dianpin.com search results may be fluid, since the catering business faces fierce competition and restaurants have a hard time staying in business. But the small number of restaurants serving dog meat relative to those serving other foods still suggests that dog meat is not a mainstream food in Guangzhou.

Yulin appears to have a sizable dog meat industry, as we are led to believe from its dog meat festival. But we failed to find any official statistics on the sales of dog meat in the city's catering industry. Yulin's official statistical report of economic and social development in 2015 covered all the major components of the local economy. For example, the report disclosed its slaughter of 6.13 million pigs, 219 million poultry, and other agricultural and industrial outputs (Yulin City Statistical Bureau 2016). Nowhere was dog meat mentioned.

Like in other cities where dog meat is consumed, dog meat sales in Yulin do not stand out. There is a trade in dog meat year round, with increased sales volume during the winter months and around the summer solstice in late June. Much of July, August, September and October constitute a slack season for dog meat sales. Importantly, dog meat consumption in Yulin happens mostly in the urban areas, where it is promoted by the traders.[10]

Like most other mainland Chinese cities, Yulin has a thriving hospitality industry. In 2014, the retail sales value of Yulin's catering industry reached 5.2 billion yuan, an increase of 16.33% over the previous year (Yulin Statistical Bureau 2015). When we searched for dog meat restaurants, we found 48 in the city proper and 122 in the wider metropolitan area. Most of these were small-scale operations with between 10 and 60 tables. There were more Sichuan restaurants (203 in total) and more Western food and fast food restaurants (147) than dog meat restaurants.

Peixian in northern Jiangsu, the country's third largest dog meat market, has the biggest dog meat processing operation. Yet its annual revenue stands at about 70 million yuan, a fraction of the city's GDP of

---

10 Conversation with five dog meat traders on 24 May 2015 and a meeting with a Yulin government researcher on 21 June 2016. Both meetings took place in Yulin when I was doing the field study.

60.5 billion yuan (Peixian Statistical Bureau 2016). Fankuai Dog Meat Processing Company is the biggest producer of processed dog meat. Built in 1994, the company claims to have developed from an 8 million yuan investment; it now has its own dog farms and slaughterhouses and a research and development team, and produces 300 tons of processed meat a year. The company reportedly employs about 100 workers to produce some 30 different packaged meat products (Peixian Fankuai Dog Meat Catering Management Corporation a). However, as in Guangzhou and Yulin, the dog meat trade is not mentioned in government reports as a contributor to the city's catering industry. The retail trade in dog meat in Peixian, a city of 200,000 people, also appears to be small. Of the more than 2,600 restaurants in the city, 72 were dog meat restaurants.

Northeast China's dog meat market remains robust compared with the other two markets. However, it appears that sales have hit their high point, with no room for further growth. Jilin is a province with 1.14 million ethnic Koreans, accounting for 60% of the 2 million ethnic Koreans in China (Central People's Government of China 2015). Jilin is the biggest dog meat market in Northeast China. Changchun, the provincial capital and a city with some 7.7 million people, had 897 dog meat restaurants based on a search of Dianpin.com in 2016.[11] However, there were more than 1,820 Sichuan restaurants and 25,802 fast food restaurants. In Haerbin, the provincial capital of Heilongjiang Province, there were 469 dog meat restaurants serving the city's almost 10 million people. There were more restaurants serving Sichuan food (1,830 in total) and fast food (32,224). Even in one of the country's strongest dog meat markets, dog meat was not an everyday food choice. A survey of 100 Harbin households in 2016 confirmed that dog meat was not an ingredient most people consumed at home. Only three households had cooked dog meat at home and none of the 100 households had ever stored dog meat in their refrigerators.[12] Yanji in Jilin is an ethnic

---

11 In a 2019 search on the same website, we failed to retrieve any entries when we searched for "dog meat." However, searching for "sweet meat," a term used by traders, we found 61 restaurants in Guangzhou, 287 in Changchun and 104 in Yulin that had dog meat on their menus. We have sent an enquiry to the management of Dianping.com about this.
12 In November 2016, a field study by Vshine Animal Protection Association was conducted in Harbin and Changchun. In Harbin, a randomly selected

Korean city of 430,000 people. People believe that this city must be full of dog meat eaters. The survey mentioned earlier confirmed that dog meat was not a mainstream food choice for the majority of the residents. There were 41 dog meat restaurants in 2016, compared to 275 Sichuan restaurants and 1,607 fast food outlets.

The dog meat industry is not a significant contributor to the Chinese economy. In 2015, China's GDP was $10.87 trillion (World Bank 2016). The catering industry achieved a record sales volume of 323 billion yuan ($47 billion), or 4.3% of the total GDP. In 2013, China's total meat output was 85 million tons (FAOSTAT 2014). Compared with these figures, the estimated total output of dogmeat, 97,500 tons, was a drop in the ocean. China produces more rabbit meat (727,000 tons in 2013), poultry (19 million tons), and mutton (2 million tons) (FAOSTAT 2014). Its pork production was 54 million tons in 2013, overshadowing the combined total of the world's next five top pork producers. In this context, putting an end to the dog meat trade, in the words of one Yulin official, would have "no impact on the local economy and the life of the Yulin people."[13]

The politics of dog meat

The dog meat industry exists as a result of the Chinese government's economic reform politics, and continues to have political significance today. In the pre-reform era, dog meat consumption was a sporadic private practice. Commercialised dog meat consumption activities did not exist in Mao's China. The number of dogs went down drastically between 1960 and 1976, the final years of Mao's rule, because of ideological bias against dog keeping and an oppressive food security crisis. There were no dog meat restaurants, no trans-provincial dog transport, and no mass slaughter of dogs for consumption. Private

---

100 households were interviewed on the frequency of their dog meat consumption and to see if dog meat was in the refrigerators of these households.

13 Conversation with a Yulin official in the evening of 20 June 2016 in Yulin, Guangxi, China.

3 China's "civil war" over dogs

production was outlawed. After 1978, economic liberalisation, the decriminalisation of private production, and the government's market economy reforms created a favourable policy environment for the dog meat trade.

Expanding meat production and consumption

China's economic reform was designed to end the food security crisis that had trapped the country's 900 million peasants in abject poverty. Agriculture was the sector most targeted for fast growth. Rural reforms were intended to stabilise the countryside by increasing food production. In the words of Deng Xiaoping, only when the countryside was stable would the country have political stability. For this purpose, the post-Mao regime enacted more than 3,000 new policies designed to boost rural production.

Decriminalising private production was one of these steps. At the 3rd Plenum of the CCP's 11th Congress in December 1978, the post-Mao leadership decided that peasants' autonomous production should be respected. Peasants should have the freedom to farm their chosen crops and to engage in "sideline production." The country's first dog meat traders went into the trade in this capacity. At the same plenum, the party leadership accepted Deng Xiaoping's proposal that the government should allow some people, through their hard work, to get rich first. Transporting dogs from rural Jiangxi and Hunan to Guangdong was one of the "get rich" modes of production conducted by the peasants. The mushrooming of dog meat restaurants in Guangdong, Guangxi and Northeast China in the early 1980s could not have happened without this change in the Party's economic policies. Like other private rural production activities, such as tobacco farming and livestock farming, dog transportation and dog meat sales are protected as an agent of poverty reduction.

The dog meat trade received a further boost in the early 1980s, when the post-Mao leadership abolished the defunct People's Communes, China's version of the Stalinist state farms. According to the policy notice Document 75, headed "Questions on Further Strengthening and Improving the Responsibility System in Rural Production," not only were the People's Communes abolished, farmland was also to be distributed among rural households. Peasants were encouraged to grow whatever they wanted as long as they repaid the state in fixed amounts of the produce, i.e. agricultural tax, under a contract responsibility system. Surplus was allowed to be sold at rural markets or used by the peasants themselves. The result of this ground-breaking policy change was a record increase in grain output. By 1984, the food security crisis that had oppressed Chinese peasants for the last three decades came to an end. With the food crisis over, the number of dogs in rural China began to increase.

Rural reform not only freed peasants from the land but also created surplus rural labour. Tens of millions of rural youth began to migrate to the coastal urban areas to work on assembly lines. Others went into the catering sector as transporters, retailers, slaughterhouse workers, and restaurant owners. Promoting meat and dairy production was part of the government's food security strategy. In the 1980s and 1990s, the Chinese government enacted a series of policies and adopted measures to support the country's animal husbandry industry. For example, in March 1981, the CCP Central Committee and State Council jointly endorsed the State Agriculture Commission's *Report on Actively Developing Diversified Production in the Rural Areas*. This report called for significantly more crops and land to be dedicated to meat production (China Animal Husbandry Industry Yearbook Compilation Committee 2000, 166). In 1988, the Agriculture Ministry issued *Implementation Measures for Carrying out the State Council Decision on the Key Points of Current Economic Policies*. These measures called for an increase in cattle and sheep farming in grain-producing provinces as a way to absorb surplus labour and fight soil erosion in the grasslands of the north and north-western provinces (China Animal Husbandry Industry Yearbook Compilation Committee, 2000, 172–73). This policy was reaffirmed in 1992 and 1998 by the State Council and the CCP Central Committee.

By the end of the 1990s, China had seen a steady increase in the production of beef and mutton, animal products not traditionally widely consumed by Han Chinese. At the same time, the government eliminated market restrictions and encouraged larger-scale production, adoption of modern farming techniques, and imports of foreign high-yield breeds. New animal products previously unknown to most Chinese people, such as ostrich meat and turkey, were introduced, and dairy production and consumption expanded. In 1999 the government initiated a "school milk" program to encourage milk drinking among elementary school students. Milk, an animal product that had previously been available to the rich and to political elites, was promoted as a daily food for the nation's young people in an effort to boost their nutrition (China Development Research Foundation 2019). This steady growth in livestock production encouraged a new culture of meat consumption, especially among those who had lived through the Maoist years of food scarcity. The dog meat trade is an outgrowth of this national drive for greater meat production and consumption.

Support from local government

While dog meat traders were aggressively promoting their business, more mainland Chinese families were keeping dogs as pets. Dog meat consumption became increasingly controversial. Nevertheless, local authorities in the country's major dog meat markets have protected the industry. Jilin is one of the few places where dog slaughter is regulated, on account of the local ethnic Korean subculture of dog eating. A major dog slaughterhouse in the city of Jilin displayed signs at the entrance that read "City Dragonhead Agribusiness" and "an enterprise receiving special protection." The owner of this slaughter operation hoped that these signs of official endorsement would silence critics.[14] The owner of Hanzhuang Dog Meat City, Jilin's biggest dog meat restaurant chain, was showered by local authorities with all kinds of honours. She was also made a deputy to the Provincial People's Congress. With official support, the restaurant chain publicly and unashamedly, in the eyes of animal protectionists, showcases a wide variety of dog meat dishes including "extraordinarily sweet dog meat prepared with secret recipes and ingredients," "dog meat with skins," "a dish of assorted dog meat," and "dog meat stir-fried with soybean sprouts," to name just a few of the offerings.[15]

---

14 Author's field investigation of the slaughterhouse in Jilin, Jilin province on 23 October 2019.
15 An investigation conducted by research assistants in China of Changchun's dog meat restaurants on 25 August 2019.

Fan Xian-tao, the owner of the Fankuai Dog Meat Processing Company in northern Jiangsu's Peixian and the self-proclaimed 77th descendant of Fan Kuai, the famous Han dynasty "dog meat general," was honoured as a local "successful businessman." The method for processing his dog meat products was recognised by the provincial government as "intangible cultural heritage" (Peixian Fankuai Dog Meat Catering Management Corporation b). With government support, Fankuai dog meat products are marketed locally and sold in markets in nearby provinces. The processed dog meat, sold in atractive packages, is advertised as a traditional food with many health benefits. To promote its products, the Fan Kuai company packages its meat products for specific customers. Discounts are offered to individual and group buyers during promotional sales.[16] Fan Xian-tao is the most fierce and vocal defender of his dog meat operation and of the industry as a whole. To Chinese animal protectionists, Fan's defiance of public opinion and "his nasty and shameless defense of his business of cruelty" are not surprising. "He was supported by the local and provincial authorities," Dezhi Yu, secretary-general of Beijing's Capital Animal Welfare Association, commented at an event in Beijing in the summer of 2019.[17]

Yulin's Dog Meat Festival was a direct result of government encouragement. In 2008, the government of the Guangxi Zhuang Autonomous Region sought to promote the regional catering industry. In 2010, they issued the *Guangxi Zhuang Autonomous People's Government Recommendation on Accelerating the Development of the Hospitality and Catering Industry*, or Guangxi Government Document 70. This policy stated that developing the catering industry was part of a wider effort to encourage domestic consumption, improve people's lives, absorb urban and rural surplus labour, and upgrade catering services. The creation of local specialties and local brands was promoted as a major responsibility of local authorities. At the top of the

---

16 For information on the promotional activities of the Fan Kuai Dog Meat Processing Company, please visit their website at http://fk.vishang.cn/group_buy.php.

17 Conversation with Dezhi Yu, secretary-general of Beijing's Capital Animal Welfare Association, 14 July 2019.

list of proposed tasks was "Using festivals to create markets," including a plan to develop "a festival of fine Guangxi-style foods" (Guangxi Zhuang Autonomous People's Government 2010). In June 2010, the Yulin Dog Meat Festival was launched as part of the second Yulin Medicine Expo, supported by the local authorities. This was what was called "using fine foods as a tool to promote business transactions," a business promotion measure adopted by local governments including that of Yulin (Yong Xinzhong and Zhang Wei 2014).

The Yulin authorities adopted this recommendation and in 2011 issued the *Yulin Government Recommendation on Accelerating the Development of the Hospitality and Catering Industry*, which proposed the development of three to five local specialty dishes and the creation of local gourmet festivals (Yulin City Government 2011). The Yulin city government's support for the local dog meat trade and the launch of the Dog Meat Festival was documented by the official local media. In the early 1990s, the Yulin government was contemplating building a gourmet street in response to an increase in the number of restaurants serving dog meat. Dog meat consumption was traditionally rare in summer time in Yulin.

It was in 1995 that a "Lychee and Dog Meat Festival" was first proposed by the local dog meat traders, to be staged on the gourmet street. The proposal did not get enough support and therefore the market did not materialise. In 2008, however, the *Guangxi Daily*, the provincial Party Committee's mouthpiece, reported that the "Lychee and Dog Meat Festival" and "Raw Fish Eating Festival" would be part of the gourmet festival of Yulin to showcase local "traditional fine foods."

A government project, the Collection on the Survey of Intangible Cultural Heritage, identified the "Lychee and Dog Meat Festival" as a local event to receive government support. Yulin local media reported that the local Office of Culture planned to enter the festival as an example of the intangible cultural heritage not only of the city, but of the province as well. Whether the festival was truly a traditional event or not was not important to Yulin officials, as long as it would generate tourism revenue and contribute to local employment.

Encouraged by government endorsement, Yulin's dog meat traders engaged in aggressive promotion, especially during the summer solstice and winter months. Dog meat, a hot food, has ironically been mystified by traders as a great food for fighting the summer heat. "Crispy skin dog meat," also the name of a restaurant, has been promoted as a local specialty. The owner of the restaurant even bragged of plans to open a subsidiary in nearby Guangdong province. In the first four years (2010–13) following the launch of the dog meat festival, the patronage of Yulin officials helped to promote dog meat consumption and the business interests of dog meat traders.

Official support for the dog meat business is manifested in awards and other official honours. The Fan Kuai Dog Meat Catering Management Corporation from Pexian displays 11 government "certificates" on its website, suggesting official endorsement of its operation. These include a certificate recognising Fan Xian-tao, the owner, as the "inheritor" of the so-called "turtle-sauced dog meat," allegedly a local specialty, and recognising Fan Kuai as a local "gold brand." The website promotes "turtle-sauced dog meat" and its preparation method as part of the "intangible cultural heritage" of Jiangsu Province.[18] In Jilin, Changchun's biggest dog meat restaurant, Hanzhuang Dog Meat City (a subsidiary of Changchun Hanzhuang Catering Company, founded in 1999), has been recognised as a "Jilin famous brand name." In 2009, it was listed as an "outstanding private business" and honoured for employing 500 jobseekers each year. Tang Hong, founder and owner of the company, has been recognised repeatedly as an "outstanding entrepreneur" (Baidu.com). "Despite the controversial nature of its operation, Hanzhuang Dog Meat City generates income to its employees," remarked a local industrial and commercial bureau official. "Since Jilin is an agriculture province, we attach great importance to businesses that can help alleviate the employment burden of the government."[19]

All three of the markets discussed above – Yulin, Peixian and Jilin – are trying to catch up with the rest of the country or with more developed neighbouring markets. In 2015, Yulin had an average per capita income of about $4,000, some $3,900 lower than the national

---

18 See the Peixian Fan Kuai Dog Meat Processing Company website at http://www.fankuai.com/1/about.asp.

19 Interview with a retired official of Jilin provincial industrial and commercial bureau, 2 July 2016.

average. It is situated in Guangxi Province, which was ranked 17th out of the 31 provinces in terms of GDP (Twenty-first Century Economic Report 2016). Peixian is situated in northern Jiangsu's Xuzhou city, which was ranked 5th in the provincial economic ranking, and in 2015 had a per capita GDP of $9,899, almost $1,000 above the national average. Compared with other cities in Jiangsu Province, however, Xuzhou has a gap to close: its per capita GDP may be high by national standards, but it is well below that of neighbouring Suzhou ($21,988), Wuxi ($21,048), Nanking ($18,995) and Changzhou ($18,028) (Shijiejingji.net 2016). Peixian is one of the less developed counties in Xuzhou, with a per capita GDP of about $4,000 in 2016 (Peixian Government 2016).

Jilin, meanwhile, ranked 22nd in GDP among the 31 provinces and municipalities. Its per capita GDP, ranked 24th, was $5,200, more than $3,000 below the national average in 2015 (Haojinggui.com 2016). Provincial authorities have been under pressure to catch up with the more developed southern and coastal provinces. For local officials in Yulin, Peixian and Jilin, there is a strong reason not to interrupt the local dog meat industry.

Criticism of the dog meat trade

With government support, the dog meat industry has aggressively promoted dog meat consumption. However, since April 2011, when activists intercepted a truck carrying dogs in Beijing, the industry has been the target of a nationwide campaign by animal welfare activists, who argue that the trade in dog meat is both illegal and immoral.[20] The 2011 highway rescue was the first of hundreds. Increased media attention has helped bring government attention to the controversy of the dog meat industry. To avoid falling into a seemingly fruitless debate on what constitutes acceptable meat for human consumption, animal protectionists have consistently called on the general public and the authorities to see the criminal, moral and social impact of the trade. The

---

20 Interview with Qin Xiaona, founder and director of the Beijing Capital Animal Welfare Association, 21 May 2016.

following section is devoted to an examination of these impacts as they have been highlighted in Chinese media and scholarly publications.

Dog theft

Dog theft for the meat trade is an open secret in China. It became a public issue towards the end of the 1990s. In the early 1990s, dog farms had experimented with cross-breeding St Bernards and indigenous Chinese dogs to produce muscular dogs for meat. Booklets on farming "meat dogs" were published and agricultural and animal husbandry websites included information about dog breeding. However, farming meat dogs was not cost-effective, and the experiments failed miserably. It takes on average eight months to raise a dog to 20 kilograms. This would cost the farmer at least 480 yuan per dog. Since a live dog only sells for about 16 yuan per kilogram when demand is high, and 10 yuan when demand is low, farming meat dogs does not make money (AAF 2015a; Shu Xiqiang 2015).

In December 2014, interviews with workers at seven so-called dog farms confirmed that none of these farms were raising dogs for food. Instead, they said that they had shifted to breeding pet dogs, which can be sold for higher prices. A national Agriculture Ministry official also acknowledged that many dog farms no longer sell dogs for food.[21] The owner of China's biggest dog-meat processing company has claimed that "23 dog farms" and "400 specialised dog farming households" raise a quarter of a million dogs for slaughter in Peixian (Peixian Fankuai Dog Meat Management Corporation c), but a report by *China Youth Daily* failed to find these farms or households (Shu Xiqiang 2015). My own studies in Yulin (2014, 2015, 2016, 2018), Yanji and Dalian (2015) did not find traces of dog farms either.

With the failure of dog farming, the meat trade has turned to theft as an alternative source of dogs. The AAF's investigative report *Lies, Illegality and Stolen Lives: A True Crime Story (2011–2014)* covered 21

---

21   Telephone conversation with an activist who participated in the petition on 26 December 2014 at the Ministry of Agriculture to close an illegal slaughter operation in Henan Province.

provinces and 700 news stories. The report confirmed rampant dog theft across vast areas of the country. Guo Peng of Shandong University found that 87% of the households in one Jinan suburban village reported dog thefts between 2007 and 2011 (Guo Peng 2012). Her study around Yulin suburbs also confirmed dog theft (Guo Peng 2013).

Further evidence of dog theft was exposed during the highway rescue on 15 April 2011 mentioned earlier. Animal welfare activists stopped a truck carrying 460 dogs of various breeds and sizes. Some of the dogs wore collars while others wore jackets. They displayed behaviours typical of household pets. "You just wonder what kind of dog farmers would put collars and jackets on the dogs to be sent off to the slaughterhouse," observed Mme Qin Xiaona, founder of Beijing's Capital Animal Welfare Association. "And who would raise and sell dogs for food that could fetch a higher price if sold as pets?"[22] In 2015, the British *Daily Mail* reported that two traders caught stealing dogs were brutalised for nine hours by angry villagers who had lost dogs over the years (Miller and Chow 2015).

Why has the nation's law enforcement failed to respond to dog thefts? We interviewed a policewoman identified as "Huan Yu," a dog-lover herself. She said that dog theft had become a "profession" because there was a reliable supply of unregistered dogs. In Shanxi, for example, almost all the rural dogs are unregistered and therefore not microchipped. The owners of unregistered dogs have no evidence of ownership. "One way to deter dog theft," Huan Yu said, "is registration and microchipping."[23] Most rural owners refuse to register their dogs, and dog registration has a bad reputation in China. Not too long ago, a number of cities imposed an exorbitant fee (6,000 yuan to 10,000 yuan) on dog registration, intending to discourage dog ownership in urban areas. Most dog owners resented and resisted the policy. In 2006, a massive protest against the policy and other restrictions placed on dogs took place in Beijing. Since then, most cities have reduced their registration fees.

---

22 Telephone interview conducted 23 July 2013.
23 WeChat interview with Huan Yu, a police officer and an animal activist in a northwestern Chinese city, 2 October 2015.

While dog registration has been increasing in cities, it lags behind in rural areas. Beijing reportedly has a 60% dog registration rate (with close to one million registered dogs in total) in the city proper. However, in the suburbs, where there are an additional one million dogs, dogs are still largely unregistered.[24] Nanjing has an estimated 100,000 pet dogs, less than 30% of which are registered, according to Ha Wenjin, director of the Nanjing Ping An A Fu Animal Protection Group. Chengdu is estimated to have 800,000 pet dogs. Yet according to Qiao Wei, director of the Chengdu Qiming Animal Protection Centre, dog registration rate is no more than 40%. The city with the highest registration rate is Dalian, where 90% of its 200,000 dogs are registered.[25]

Low dog registration rates make law enforcement difficult. A low registration rate also suggests low awareness among dog owners of the need to use the law for protection. One explanation for the low registration rates is government failure to use the money collected to provide services to dog owners. And although they have been drastically reduced, dog registration fees in most Chinese cities are still among the highest in the world.[26] Dog owners have been complaining that they have not got anything in return for the high fees they have paid to the government (Zhang Muhan 2007). "Where have the registration fees gone?" is a question raised by many owners who have registered their dogs.

Another contributing factor to the prevalence of dog theft is the surplus of rural labour. The reduced attraction of coastal jobs and social welfare polices biased towards urban areas have encouraged rural youths to look for other ways to make money. During our field study

24 Conversation with Beijing police officers in charge of pet dog management who attended the 5th China Dog Ownership Management Symposium held in Chengdu, Sichuan, 18 November 2014.
25 Interview on 18 October 2015 with Ha Wenjin, Qiao Wei and Yu Dezhi, heads of local animal protection groups in Nanjing, Chengdu and Dalian, groups that are involved in local police management of the government shelters.
26 For example, Beijing charges 1,000 yuan for dog registration in the city proper; Shanghai charges 2,000 yuan in the central parts of the city; and Dalian charges 500 yuan.

of Yulin's dog meat market in 2015, not only did we see dogs and cats wearing collars waiting to be slaughtered. We also saw advertisements openly selling guns, stolen vehicles, drugs, and forgery services on busy streets in downtown Yulin. This indicates an erosion of law and order and the inability of the local economy to absorb the surplus labour.[27] Although registration may be a deterrent to dog theft, when rural unemployment remains a challenge, jobless youths can still be lured to make fast money by stealing dogs, whether the animals are registered and microchipped or not. For local authorities, it is rural unemployment, not dog theft, that occupies their attention. Their superiors in Beijing are more likely to scrutinise their ability to reduce unemployment than to ask if they have stopped dog thefts.

Disease control

Critics of the dog trade also argue that it poses a public health risk. There is no evidence to suggest that rabies can be contracted by consuming cooked dog meat. However, rabies can be transmitted during dog handling, transportation or slaughter (Yan Jiaxin 2014). Dog meat traders, particularly those who slaughter a large number of dogs of unknown origin, have a higher risk of becoming infected through cuts or abrasions on their hands. This danger was identified in a 2009 study by British and Vietnamese scientists (Wertheim et al. 2009). Other studies have recorded rabies infections caused by handling infected carcasses (Wo et al. 1991, 1224). In 2014, senior researcher Professor Tang Qing from China's national Centre of Disease Control joined an appeal to the Chinese authorities to stop mass dog transportation and slaughter in Yulin (Tang Qing et al. 2014). Her participation in the joint letter was out of a concern for rabies prevention.

---

27 For Chinese scholarly discussion of rural surplus labour, problems and solutions, see for example Jiang Taicai and Jiang Chaoliang, "On the co-existence of the short supply of migrant workers and rural labour surplus: an analysis and recommendations," *Marketing Modernization* 34 (December 2010), pp. 203–5.

Scientists are not alarmists. Guangxi, Hunan, Guangdong and Guizhou, the major dog meat markets, accounted for 63.9% of all human rabies cases in the country between 2002 and 2012 (Miao, Song et al. 2014, 212–21). Guangxi had the most human rabies cases between 2007 and 2011 (Tang Qing 2013). Yulin, home of the dog meat festival, was the hardest-hit city in Guangxi (Zhang Ailin 2007), and in 2007 was one of the ten cities with the highest number of rabies cases (Ministry of Public Health 2007). Unsurprisingly, none of the dog meat traders and slaughterhouse workers I interviewed in Yulin in 2014 and 2015 were vaccinated against rabies. Most dog collectors (or dog thieves) and slaughterhouse workers are young, uneducated, unskilled, and uninformed about the importance of vaccination.

The Chinese authorities are aware of the rabies risk to traders. In 2011, the Agriculture Ministry issued *Procedures for Quarantine Inspection of Dogs at the Place of Origin*. According to this policy, dogs displaying symptoms of illness within 21 days of rabies vaccination cannot be transported out of their place of origin. A 2013 notice from the Agriculture Ministry restated the importance of verifying that every dog slated for trans-provincial shipment meets the health check requirements in the 2011 policy. Both of these policy documents, if enforced, would help to safeguard traders against rabies infection. Yet the 2011 policy was opposed by dog meat traders and their supporters as government action against the dog meat industry, allegedly made under the influence of activists and animal protection NGOs.[28]

The concentration of rabies cases in South China is mainly attributable to a low vaccination rate among rural dogs. The consensus among worldwide rabies experts is that vaccination of at least 70% of dogs is the best defence against rabies. In South China, where there are 10 to 15 dogs per 100 people in rural areas, the rabies vaccination rate is no more than 20%. This explains why 97% of human rabies infections happen in rural China (Tang Qing 2013). In the last three decades, China experienced two waves of rabies outbreaks. The average number of rabies deaths per year hit 5,537 in the 1980s. In 1981 alone, 7,037 people died of rabies. The second wave peaked in 2007, when rabies

---

28 Electronic communication with a dog eating supporter in Guangdong, July 2015.

3 China's "civil war" over dogs

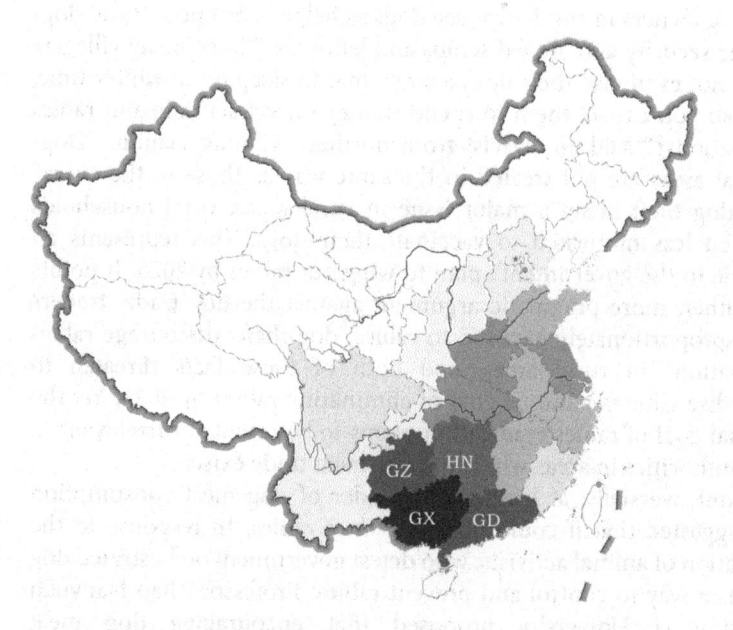

Figure 3.1 Geographical distribution of rabies in China, 2005–2014. GZ= Guizhou; GX=Guangxi (where Yulin is located); GD=Guangdong; HN=Hunan. This map was used by Professor Tang Qing (2014), a senior researcher at the China Center of Disease Control, in her presentation 中国狂犬病监测与防控 (The monitoring, prevention and control of rabies in China), delivered at the Chengdu China Dog Ownership Management Symposium.

killed 3,300 people (Ministry of Public Health 2009). To control rabies, the authorities resorted to mass dog culls, provoking strong reactions from the Chinese public, particularly animal activists. In view of the greater cost of post-exposure treatment per person, Chinese experts have proposed mass dog vaccination, which costs annually as little as 20 yuan ($3.20) per dog, as the only effective way to prevent rabies.[29] The Chinese government is yet to accept this proposal.

---

29 Interview with Professor Tang Qing of China Centre of Disease Control, 22 October 2014, Chengdu, China.

Dog owners in rural areas see dogs as helpers, not pets. Rural dogs provide security and are fed scraps and leftovers. "Since many villagers would not even give their dogs a straw mat to sleep on in winter time, how can you expect them to spend money on vet services and rabies vaccinations?" said an activist from northern China's Tianjin. "Dogs in rural areas are not treated in the same way as those in the cities." With dog theft being a major issue in rural areas, rural households are even less motivated to vaccinate their dogs. This represents an obstacle to the government's plan to wipe out rabies by 2025. It points to another, more pragmatic argument against the dog trade: traders are disproportionately exposed to rabies; dog thefts discourage rabies vaccinations in rural areas; and both of these facts threaten to jeopardise China's national goal of eliminating rabies by 2025. Yet the national goal of rabies eradication seems to be remote or irrelevant to local authorities in areas where the dog meat trade exists.

Controversially, at least one defender of dog meat consumption has suggested that it could help to *reduce* rabies. In response to the frustration of animal activists, who detest government orchestrated dog culls as a way to control and prevent rabies, Professor Zhao Nanyuan of Tsinghua University proposed that encouraging dog meat consumption, particularly the consumption of stray and abandoned dogs, could effectively reduce rabies. Killing stray dogs for food, in his opinion, would be a win–win for dog meat lovers and for public health officials (Tencent 2014). However, this argument was so provocative that it drew immediate criticism not only from animal activists, but also from the China Centre for Disease Control.[30]

Food safety

The dog meat industry has a lot to explain as to the source of dogs that are slaughtered and processed for food. In the Food Safety Law of the People's Republic of China (2015), Item 7 of Article 34, and Item 3 of Article 123, ban the production and sale of meats and processed

---

30 Interview with Qin Xiaona, director and founder of Beijing's Capital Animal Welfare Association, 23 July 2017; conversation with Professor Tang Qing of China Center for Disease Control in October 2014.

products from livestock, wildlife animals and aquatic species that have died of illness, poison or unknown causes. Item 8 of Article 34 also bans the production and sale of meat products that have not been inspected, that have been inspected without following procedure, and that have failed inspection (National People's Congress 2015). However, dogs are not livestock, and so are not subject to the food safety inspection procedures that are mandated for livestock animals. A dilemma has therefore arisen: while the state does not explicitly ban dog meat, selling unregulated dog meat poses safety risks to consumers.

The 460 dogs rescued on 15 April 2011 reportedly displayed symptoms of various illnesses. None of the 40 randomly selected samples from the dogs were found to have the rabies antibody (An Xiang 2012), suggesting that they had not been vaccinated against rabies, and had likely not been vaccinated against other common canine illnesses either.

As well as illnesses, captive dogs are subjected to a range of stressors: trans-provincial transportation, food and water deprivation, injuries, mental stress, rough handling, and internal organ damage caused by poisons. Open wounds from fighting in crowded conditions lead to infections and allow disease to spread like wildfire. Mass deaths often ensue soon after the dogs arrive at their destination.[31] Stray dogs with skin problems and other health issues are also common. When China bans the sale of products from livestock that have died from illness or poison, why are dogs with serious health issues considered safe food?

An unambiguous threat to food safety comes from poisoned dogs. In May 2006, 50 villagers in Guangxi were poisoned by eating dog meat (Zhao Min 2006). In December, 2012, a family's New Year's Eve dinner almost turned fatal when all seven members of the family became sick from eating dog meat (Yu Shoujun 2012). In December 2014, a father and son in Jiangsu province were almost killed after eating processed dog meat (Yu Suyun and Xue Mayi 2014, 9). Police action in Hunan and Zhejiang in 2013 and 2014 uncovered 27 tons of poisonous dog meat and resulted in the prosecution of some 30 traders. The poisons

---

31 Interview, 16 February 2015, with a Beijing veterinarian who was involved in the post-rescue care of rescued dogs in 2014.

used were suxamethonium chloride and cyanide (Zhang Liutao 2014). About one third of dog meat on the market is believed to come from poisoned dogs. According to a *China Youth Daily* investigaton, 95% of the dead dogs supplied by traders are believed to have been poisoned. Dead dogs cost a third of the price of live dogs, making them very tempting for meat processing companies. "Almost all the packaged dog meat sold on the supermarkets in Peixian was processed from dead dogs," one dog meat trader told the investigator. "Very rarely are live dogs killed to make processed dog meat" (Shu Xiqiang 2015). Could China's existing food safety regulations be applied to dog meat? The government is being pulled in opposite directions. While the dog meat industry would prefer to continue to operate outside the state's regulatory mechanism, critics have urged the government to outlaw the trade. The presence of poisonous dog meat is no secret to the Chinese authorities.

In the absence of a ban on dog meat, one temporary measure that could curb dog poisoning is strict enforcement of State Council Order 344, the *Regulation on the Safety Management of Toxic Chemicals*. Articles 38, 39, 40 and 84 regulate the sale of toxic chemicals (State Council of the PRC 2011). Currently, despite the government ban, online sale of the chemicals is out of control. Controlled chemicals such as potassium aurous cyanide, dimethylnitrosamine, mercury perchloride and others are reportedly available from online retailers or directly from producers (Chen Ruo 2014; Zhang Xuebing and Pan Lina 2013).

Whether the Chinese authorities will tackle the online sale of poisons remains to be seen. The Chinese government has been known to respond decisively to political threats to the ruling order. Compared with labour rights activists and advocates for religious freedom, the illegal sale of substances that are used to kill or immobilise dogs is not an immediate threat to the regime. Local governments seem to be even less motivated to do anything. "To the local authorities, those who are 'employed' in dog thefts are at least not asking for employment assistance from the authorities," said Mme Qin of the Capital Animal Welfare Association. Besides, the Chinese authorities are facing a bigger food safety problem, in the form of tainted meats and other products, that impacts a greater number of people. In 2014, China had 4,694 reported food safety violation cases, an increase of 157.2% from the previous year (Yan Chunxiang 2015, 5). Since these food safety scares potentially affect the entire population, they are more likely to attract government attention and resources.

Public slaughter, desensitisation, and child abuse

Lastly, activists opposed to the dog meat trade argue that it exposes citizens to animal cruelty and that this has consequences for public morality. Cruelty to animals, be it abusive acts by individuals or institutionalised practices, can have serious social consequences. Animal abuse or cruelty to animals can desensitise both the participants and the witnesses (Ascione 2001; Gullone 2011, 144–60). Institutionalised practices such as factory farming, slaughter, animal testing and wildlife breeding can be even more desensitising since they are routine, widespread, and considered socially acceptable (Berne 2004, 39–65). Focused studies have tried to show the connection between institutionalised cruelty and anti-social behaviour (Fitzgerald, Kalof and Dietz 2009, 158–84; Broadway, Michael 1990, 321–44). The psychological impact of public slaughter and other institutionalised practices on youth development is yet to draw the attention of the Chinese authorities, but activists have drawn attention to the problematic practice of public slaughter.

To Qin Xiaona, director and founder of Beijing's Capital Animal Welfare Association, public slaughter is the single most controversial practice of the dog meat industry. Dogs are slaughtered next to elementary schools, in rural markets, on the streets, and in residential areas, often in full view of pedestrians and young children. "I have asked this question again and again: 'how can the dog meat traders not see the frightened looks of the other dogs waiting for their turn and how can the traders not see the frightened looks of the young children who happen to see the slaughter?'"

The traders' lack of sensitivity to the trauma suffered by bystanders, particularly young children, is shocking to Chinese animal lovers. What can explain it? The pervasive public slaughter of livestock in rural China desensitises rural residents more than urbanites. "Why do you target dog slaughter?" asked a dog meat trader in Yulin. "You only need to visit any rural marketplace here in our city and you'll not miss chicken slaughter or even cattle slaughter in the open. Most rural kids grow up watching pig slaughter."[32] He was right. Most rural communities, sub-provincial cities, and suburban towns have a "wet market" where residents get their daily groceries, including fresh meat.

In the major cities and most urban centers, consumers are more shielded from livestock slaughter. They are perhaps less desensitised than their rural counterparts. Mega supermarkets selling frozen meats and other animal products are common in China's urban centres, and have increased their presence in provincial and sub-provincial cities. Since 2005, smaller supermarket chains have invaded rural townships and remote suburban areas. Perhaps unique to China, fresh food (vegetables, frozen meats and dairy products) account for 30% of the shelf space in these supermarkets. The result is an accelerating decline of rural wet markets. Heightened awareness of food safety and booming e-commerce also pulls some shoppers away from the traditional wet markets.

To urban animal lovers, dog meat traders are "heartless scoundrels" who care nothing for the suffering of dogs or the psychological trauma they inflict on minors. The slaughterhouse workers I interviewed in Yulin were in fact no different from livestock farmers or pig slaughterhouse workers. They were certainly more desensitised to animal suffering than the majority of people in society. Having lived in the countryside and routinely witnessed slaughter for most of their lives, they didn't see dog slaughter as innately cruel. They said that they would move to other jobs if they had the skills. Many of the dog slaughterhouse workers who were killing dogs in public places had been exposed to animal slaughter in their home villages at a young age, and so did not see it as a form of child abuse, or as psychologically damaging. China's animal activists, however, have called on the government to recognise the effects that witnessing slaughter can have on children.

---

32 Conversation with five dog meat traders in Yulin on 26 May 2015.

3 China's "civil war" over dogs

The public debate: a tug-of-war over dogs

In the face of all of the objections listed above, defenders of dog meat consumption and the dog meat industry seem to have won over Chinese officials. What arguments have they used, and why have they been successful?

Appeals to nationalism

As we have seen, dog meat traders and their supporters argue that consuming dog meat is a tradition, part of the Chinese folk diet, and part of Chinese food culture. Zhao Nanyuan, a Tsinghua University professor, has been the country's most vocal defender of dog eating as a cultural tradition. If Westerners can raise cattle for beef, why can't the Chinese raise dogs for food? "No one animal is morally superior to others," he has argued (Zhao Nanyuan 2010). Supporting Zhao, others proclaimed that the Chinese had eaten dog meat since ancient times and that this Chinese eating habit deserved respect just like beef eating in the West (Tencent Commentary 2016). Of course, as pointed out by Sun Jiang, an animal law professor at Northwest China University of Politics and Law, the argument that dogs are not morally different from other animals killed for food could lead to a different conclusion: i.e., that humans should not be exploiting any of these species.[33]

Commenting on the cultural defence of dog meat consumption, an official from Henan, which is the main supplier of dogs for Northeast and Southwest China, said that "Interfering with [dog eating] would encourage calls to end other traditional but controversial practices in our country" and that "the government has to consider [this] in its decision-making."[34] Knowing that dog eating is controversial, its defenders argue that it is perfectly fine for some people to love their pet dogs and for others to eat their meat dogs. They deny that the dogs slaughtered for food include stolen pet dogs and call for "peaceful co-existence" between dog eaters and pet lovers.

---

33   Interview with Sun Jiang, Professor of Law of Northwest China University of Law and Politics, 12 September 2014, Houston, Texas.
34   Interview with a Luohe official, 14 June 2014, Luohe, Henan.

Defenders of dog meat consumption have also approached the issue from a public policy angle. Zhao Chali admitted that dog lovers had the moral high-ground in the debate, but that their extreme tactics would only encourage authorities to take drastic measures to end the conflict. Only by incorporating the opinions of both sides into public policy, Zhao Chali has argued, will the conflict be effectively managed (Zhao Chali 2014). Zhao did not advance specific proposals to achieve this.

Supporters of dog meat consumption have resorted to nationalism to defend the controversial eating habit. They see ulterior motives behind those who criticise the practice. Zhao Nanyuan has alleged that the controversy over dog meat was created by hostile foreign forces with the aim of demonising China (Tencent.com 2014). He argues that Chinese critics of dog meat consumption have a lot to learn from the South Koreans, who rejected Western ethnocentrism and defended Korean cultural traditions when they were criticised for eating dog meat during the 2002 FIFA World Cup, which they co-hosted with Japan. Worse still, Chinese animal activists, including those who oppose dog meat consumption, "are providing weapons of information to the new imperialists in their cultural and military aggression" towards China, and "have acted consciously or unconsciously as the 5th column of the neo-imperialist countries" (Zhao Nanyuan 2012). Foreigners who condemn China's dog meat consumption are members of "hostile forces" with ulterior motives. Samuel Huntington has described what he called a "clash of civilisations" between the non-Western and Western countries (Huntington 1993, 22–49). Professor Zhao argued that the controversy over dog meat is an example of this clash:

> Huntington's "clash of civilizations" describes global conflicts in the future to happen around the clashes among Christianity, Islam, Hinduism, Buddhism and others. In recent years, "neo-imperialism" has described the clash of civilizations as a conflict between civilization and barbarism. In the eyes of the neo-imperialists, the world will inevitably head for Western Christian civilization and accept its values promoted by developed Western nations. For the so-called barbaric countries,

there are two options: accept Western values and be assimilated into Western civilization or reject assimilation and stay in the state of barbarism. For countries that choose the latter option, the Western countries can use any coercive measures to destabilize their regimes, support new regimes that surrender to Western standards of civilization, and to start cultural integration in these countries. (Zhao Nanyuan 2012)

Professor Zhao paints a bleak picture of Western intentions in China. What Professor Zhao did not realise or refused to admit is that banning dog meat consumption was first proposed by the Chinese themselves in ancient times. Song dynasty Emperor Huizong (1082–1135) even issued a decree against using dog meat in ritual sacrificial events, in response to the rise of a mainstream food culture that detested dog meat consumption (Huot 2015, 608–9). Today, Chinese social media is full of fanatical statements about the perceived sinister designs of Westerners who criticise the eating of dog meat. Although these do not allow us to determine a collective Chinese attitude, they are indicative of the intensity of the conflict over dog meat consumption. One blogger, "Befly2000," combined nationalistic feelings with a Marxist analysis of the unravelling conflict. He began his analysis with a colloquial expression to the effect that "the trustworthy are always those who butcher dogs while the dishonest are the literati class." In other words, those self-proclaimed moral leaders, members of the upper social class, are in fact less honest than those at the bottom of society. He defined the conflict as a "class struggle" instigated by "Western forces" and carried out by Chinese elites (Befly2000 2014). He seemed to suggest that this class struggle was aimed at marginalising the country's working class people and giving the elites an exclusive role in defining the society's moral values.

"Befly2000" proposed three options for the authorities. His least-preferred option was government inaction in the face of continuing conflict between supporters and opponents of dog meat consumption. He argued that this approach would amplify government negligence and allow foreign forces to destabilise society. A second option was to legislate against dog and cat meat consumption. This approach, he argued, would be a violation of the rights of ethnic minorities and undermine national unity. The only acceptable option, he argued, would be to formally regulate dog meat consumption by drafting legislation to cover slaughter and quarantine inspection of "meat dogs," and by regulating the dog meat industry. Government should also encourage meat dog farming and provide subsidies to dog farmers to ensure a steady supply of dog meat (Befly 2014). In this "class struggle," he urged, the authorities must stand with dog meat traders and protect their livelihood.

"Befly2000" is just one of an unknown number of like-minded nationalistic bloggers who see the eating of dog and cat meat as a dutiful "continuation of the great Chinese national and time-tested traditional culture" and "an act of great patriotism" by which to show "one's love of the Chinese nation." Such supporters claim that eating dog and cat meat is the best counter-attack against hostile Western forces and their Chinese agents (Gou Rou Hao Hao Chi).

Some commentators have added an environmental dimension to the nationalistic arguments in defence of dog meat. Zhu Wei-yi, a Columbia University–educated legal expert, wrote in a Shanghai weekly publication: "Isn't it time to eat dog meat?" In this essay, Professor Zhu held that the keeping of pet dogs, like cars, had been introduced to China by Westerners, and that both practices contributed to global warming. Citing a Western scholar, Professor Zhu argued that dog keeping was a luxurious hobby that only relatively affluent families could afford (Zhu Weiyi 2010).

Zhu's argument that dog keeping contributes to higher carbon emissions was not too far-fetched. However, arguing that dog keeping was a foreign import and somehow un-Chinese showed that he was new to the subject. He went on to argue that eating dogs was better environmentally than keeping them as pets. This argument ignores the fact that many environmentally impacting resources are required to farm dogs for food. These resources include disease prevention and control supplies, sanitation equipment, water, waste management, and other facilities needed to support meat dog farming. The provision of these resources for dog farming can also generate carbon dioxide emissions and cause environmental problems.

3 China's "civil war" over dogs

Jobs, growth and political stability

Policy-making in China has never been solely based on culture or tradition. Since its establishment in 1949, the PRC has outlawed many traditional practices, including arranged marriages and polygamy. What prevented the Chinese government from responding to calls to shut down the dog meat trade?

In June 2014, I sat down with two officials in Central China's Henan province, a major source of stolen dogs for the country's dog meat markets. Both officials agreed that dog meat consumption as a culinary subculture had no future. Yet they explained that for local governments, cultural projects received government support only if they also brought immediate economic results or contributed to local employment. "In this city of ours, meeting people's livelihood needs, particularly the need to create more jobs, is a top priority," they said. "Without employment, there would be no GDP growth and no social stability."

Employment is a major challenge for the Chinese authorities. In a special report on China's population and labour, researchers from the Chinese Social Sciences Academy, a state-run think tank, found that unemployment was a problem faced particularly by rural migrant workers, college graduates, and rural youth. Nationally, labour supply will continue to outnumber job openings through 2020. On a yearly basis, the Chinese authorities are tackling the employment problem for some 12 million new job seekers. Employment is a top priority for governments at various levels (Hu Yinbing 2016). Structural changes in the Chinese economy, rising labour costs, the closure of labour-intensive and polluting plants, and other industrial adjustments have worsened the employment pressure on the government. In 2008, a senior scholar with the Central Party School in Beijing warned that joblessness could invite massive social unrest, rocking political stability. He called on the authorities to face the fact that the country's actual unemployment could be 12% or 14%, rather than the official figure of 4% (BBC 2008).

Provinces in Northeast China have been among the hardest hit. In the late 1990s, many workers were laid off in the provinces of Liaoning, Jilin and Heilongjiang, where there was a concentration of malfunctioning state-owned plants. Of the 12.1 million jobless people who had been laid off from their loss-making state enterprises in 1997, for example, 2.4 million were in Northeast China, representing almost 20% of the national total (Tan Youlin 1999, 48–55). Provincial authorities in Northeast China used policy measures to promote employment, and these are the regions where the dog meat industry has received strong government support. In 2005, Liaoning and Heilongjiang authorities issued provincial policies designed to assist the jobless to re-enter the job market through government assistance and training programs (China.com 2006). As recently as 2016, the municipal government of Changchun, China's new "capital of dog meat consumption," launched a program called "Warm Currents" to help raise the income of the city's six most disadvantaged groups (Wang Xiaoye 2016).

In Yulin, where the Dog Meat Festival aroused worldwide criticism, local authorities launched an "Employment First for Poverty Reduction" project, targeting poor families and assisting them to acquire stable employment (Guangxi Zhuang Autonomous Region Department of Human Resources and Social Security 2016). In Yulin, more than 400,000 people reportedly live in poverty. It was the city's objective to lift 110,000 of them out of poverty by the end of 2016 (Tang Jingmei 2016). Similarly, the county government of Peixian, the country's dog meat processing centre, has been tasked with reducing poverty through basic skills training programs, job fairs and encouraging employment (Peixian Information Centre 2010).

In this context, provincial and local authorities are not motivated to stop the dog meat trade. Although the trade is not a major contributor to employment, it employs some of the least skilled and most disadvantaged workers. Yulin has no more than 500 people employed directly or indirectly in the city's dog meat industry. To the local government, however, this means 500 people who are no longer a burden on the authorities. In Changchun, the capital city of Jilin, about 8,000 people are thought to be employed in the city's 800 restaurants serving dog meat. This may be a small figure in a city of several million people, but "Those who are involved in dog slaughter, dog transportation, and the restaurant business are the most vulnerable in the workforce," said a local official. They include former peasants who have lost their farmlands and laid-off urban workers; both groups lack the skills and education to compete on the job market. To the authorities, it is not the size of the dog meat industry but the concentration of the most vulnerable of the labourers that matters.

Employment shall remain a major challenge to the Chinese authorities. Zhou Tianyong, the Central Party School researcher, recommended that "employment creation through business ventures" should be elevated as the "highest national strategy" (Zhou Tianyong 2009). To local authorities, the dog meat trade is one such business venture. Chinese Premier Li Keqiang said in May 2016 that "employment is the foundation of livelihood." "We cannot emphasize enough the importance of job creation," he added. Ending the dog meat trade would remove the "foundation of livelihood" of some of the country's most vulnerable labourers, potentially threatening political stability.

Conclusions

Dog meat consumption is a hugely controversial eating habit among a small number of people in China today. It is not a daily household food and is not part of China's mainstream food tradition. However, it has been promoted by dog meat traders and supported and tolerated by some local governments. The Yulin Dog Meat Festival is a prime example. It was launched in the name of glorifying an alleged local food culture, and Yulin's local officials were as enthusiastic as the traders when the event began. They saw the festival as a way to boost tourism and attract investment, at a time when the city was under pressure to eliminate poverty and to catch up with the rest of the country in economic growth. Although China has joined the ranks of middle-income nations, it is still fighting to eradicate poverty and to provide employment for all its citizens in an increasingly urbanised society.

Employment, rather than food safety or animal welfare, is the key concern for Chinese authorities, as an issue with the potential to destabilise the political status quo. Although many public defenders of dog meat have focused on its alleged cultural importance, in reality the political objectives of poverty reduction, job creation and local growth explain the existence and continued operation of this trade that has been sustained by various resunlawful activities. Although the dog meat trade violates existing laws and regulations governing property protection, disease control, food safety, controlled substance use, and the protection of minors, its perceived economic significance has protected it from law enforcement.

Mao Shoulong, a public affairs professor at the prestigious Remin University of Beijing, admitted that the ideal policy would be an end to the transportation, slaughter, sale and consumption of dog meat, but that this is not achievable at present. Nor is peaceful co-existence of dog lovers and dog meat eaters likely: dog lovers will not accept this compromise and the conflict will continue. The only realistic approach, he concluded, was to place the dog meat market under government regulation (Mao Shoulong 2016). However, this would mean officially legalising the trade, and would be strongly resisted by the country's animal activists.

Indeed, professor Mao's suggestion is no solution. Mme Qin Xiaona, founder of Beijing's Capital Animal Welfare Association, when asked if government regulation of the dog meat trade would be an acceptable option, replied that "the dog meat trade should be abolished since it damages the public interest of the majority of the Chinese people while serving the selfish business interest of the very small number of the traders."[35] Mme Qin and her fellow activists believe that time is on their side. With China's continuing urbanisation and the expansion of the animal loving community, the "civil war" will end in favour of dogs.

---

35 Conversation with Mme Qin Xiaona, 29 November 2019.

4
Wildlife as a resource: the controversy of bear farming

In 2012, Guizhentang, a bear farm in China's Fujian Province became the target of international criticism. On 1 February, the company was reportedly among 220 companies awaiting approval by the Growth Enterprise Board of the country's Securities Regulator Commission for their applications to trade on the Shenzhen Stock Exchange, one of the top three stock markets (with Shanghai and Hong Kong) in the country. The report confirmed the speculation of some three years that Guizhentang, the biggest bear farm in southeastern China, was preparing to go public in an attempt to expand its operations. The bid for the initial public offering (IPO), if successful, could allegedly help the company raise up to $19 million for its business expansion plan. By the end of 2011, Guizhentang had 400 bears on its farm and a breeding program that produced 100 bear cubs each year. With a successful IPO, Guizhentang hoped to raise 800 more bears, increase its annual breeding capacity to 200 bear cubs, and produce 4,000 kilograms of bear bile powder a year (China.com.cn 2012).

The news was a bombshell. Standing at the forefront of the campaign to block Guizhentang's IPO bid was the Animals Asia Foundation (AAF), whose flagship campaign called for an end to the country's bear farming industry. One year earlier, AAF had appealed to the Fujian Securities Regulator Commission, urging the provincial agency to block Guizhentang's IPO plan and pointing out that

Guizhentang's business was not sustainable and that the company could face a huge drug safety risk, thus causing loss to investors. Following the lead of AAF, Beijing's Ta Foundation, deputies to the National People's Congress (NPC) and to the Chinese People's Political Consultative Conference, celebrities, and 3.2 million netizens formed a coalition calling on the State Securities Regulator Commission to remove Guizhentang's IPO from consideration.

Situated in Huian, Fujian Province, Guizhentang is a business with two major components: bear farming and the production of drugs used in traditional Chinese medicine. As a company worth 60 million yuan, it is considered a huge success story for Huian, a small agricultural county. Its founder, Qiu Shuhua, a former peasant with little education, was admiringly referred to in a 2003 media report as a loving "Bear Mother" for her donation of half of a million yuan's worth of drugs derived from bear bile to fight the SARS epidemic. Whether bear bile is a cure for SARS or not, the donation earned Mme Qiu national recognition. To wildlife and public health experts, the donation of drugs derived from bear bile, when SARS was a new epidemic whose cure was unknown, was foolhardy and unsophisticated to say the least (Kang Jianghai 2003). To some critics, the ridiculousness and unscrupulousness of her taking advantage of the public health crisis to promote bear drugs as "life saving" was matched only by her recklessness in incarcerating hundreds of live bears for bile extraction.[1]

In April 2020, Mme Qiu once again used the COVID-19 pandemic to donate her bear bile drug to Hubei for use to cure COVID-19 patients. The act was ripped on the Chinese social media as a shameful act of product advertisement in the name of helping the country fight the pandemic (Ai Ta 2020). Yet, the authorities did not seem to be concerned. Qiu was honoured with a seat at the local and provincial people's congresses. She was praised as a "successful businesswoman" for her contribution to local growth and rural employment.

Bear farming is not illegal in China, and Guizhentang is not the only bear-farm operator. Bear bile is considered a valuable and

---

[1] Conversation with Sun Jiang, director of the Animal Law Research Center of Northwestern China University of Law and Politics, 19 October 2012, Dalian, China.

4 Wildlife as a resource: the controversy of bear farming

"life-saving" ingredient in a variety of traditional Chinese medicines. China's Wildlife Protection Law (WPL), enforced since 1989 and revised in 2016, supports wildlife farming and other uses of wildlife for human benefit. Guizhentang's bear farming operation therefore does not violate the the law. However, Guizhentang's IPO drew international and domestic criticism. Why was Guizhentang's IPO so provocative?

A controversial farming operation

The 1989 WPL helped to create a formidable wildlife use industry. Nationally, although 54 wildlife species were officially permitted in 2003 by the State Forestry Bureau to be farmed and traded for food, Chinese wildlife protectionists believed that a far greater number of wildlife species have been farmed and on a different scale. By 2003, there were 42,000 wildlife farms across the country generating a revenue of 56.9 billion yuan (0.5% of China's GDP of 1.1 trillion yuan) (State Forestry Bureau 2004). Since 2004, the Chinese government has stopped producing national wildlife production statistics. In 2017, a team of scholars and researchers led by Ma Jianzhang, China's top wildlife expert, academician of the National Academy of Engineering, and the so-called "Father of Wildlife Utilization," as he has been referred to in recognition of his support of wildlife use for human benefit, published a comprehensive report titled *A Research Report on the Sustainable Development Strategy of China's Wildlife Farming Industry* (Ma Jianzhang et al. 2017). According to this 305-page report, China has the world's biggest wildlife captive breeding operation, raising the greatest number of animals for fur, for exotic food markets, for Traditional Chinese Medicine, for display and for use in laboratories. China also dominates the world in the captive breeding of amphibians, reptiles and wild geese.

This is a gigantic commercial operation, producing in 2016 a total revenue of 520.6 billion yuan ($77 billion), more than the GDPs of many small countries. The research team also found that the industry hired 14.09 million people. Fur farming and processing was the biggest sector of the wildlife industry, generating a revenue of 389.4 billion yuan ($58 billion). In 2014, there were 169,120 fur farms raising hundreds of millions of minks, racoon dogs and foxes. There were also 240,000 farms raising rabbits and sheep. Captive breeding for the exotic food market is the second biggest sector of China's wildlife farming industry. In 2016, it produced a revenue of 125 billion yuan ($19.5 billion) and employed 6.26 million people. Captive breeding for traditional Chinese medicine accounted for 5 billion yuan; breeding for display and the pet markets generated a revenue of 652 million yuan; and breeding of primates for laboratory use produced a revenue of 400 million yuan (Ma Jianzhang et al. 2017, 102–15).

Expanding and intensifying wildlife breeding was a policy of the Chinese government at the turn of the century. In December 1999, a national wildlife management conference was held in Beijing. The conference introduced five major tasks for the 10th Five-Year Plan Period (2001–5). These were nature reserve construction, wildlife habitat preservation, wetland protection, wildlife industry development, and the construction of scientific and technological support systems for conservation purposes (Li Diqiang 2000, 207). In June 2001, the State Forestry Bureau submitted to the State Planning Commission a long-term and comprehensive plan for wildlife protection and nature reserve construction that included detailed action points and budget estimates for wildlife farming in three different phases (2001–5; 2006–10; and 2011–30) (State Forestry Bureau 2001). This plan was arguably great news for the wildlife business interests. Captive breeding of wild animals was identified as a new area of accelerated growth for the rural economy.

Encouraged by the new policy and protected by the Wildlife Protection Law, local governments have been enthusiastic in supporting the expansion of their wildlife industries. For example, Xinyu in Jiangxi province planned to achieve a wildlife production revenue of 500 million yuan by 2020 (Gao Lang 2017). Hainan's wildlife farming was already a 1 billion yuan industry in 2006, with 23,000 farming units (Xinhuanet 2006). The bear farming industry is arguably the biggest single wildlife farming sector. It was estimated that its annual revenue was around 10 billion yuan ($1.4 billion) (Ma Jianzhang et al. 2017, 116). It exists in 11 provinces and employs directly and indirectly tens of thousands of people. The bear farming industry has been one of the most vocal defenders of the 1989 WPL. In 2015 and

4 Wildlife as a resource: the controversy of bear farming

2016, when the WPL was being revised, the wildlife farming industry had a strong presence at internal meetings sponsored by the NPC and other official agencies. The industry seized the opportunity to support retaining the WPL's "utilisation" objective, and to promote the bear farming industry as conservation-friendly, "life-saving," economically sustainable, socially beneficial and politically important.[2]

Bear farming began in China in 1984, using techniques introduced from North Korea. Bear-farming operations hinge on practices that are profit-driven and widely condemned for their negative welfare implications for the bears. These include solitary confinement, the use of iron cages, infliction of bodily injury and internal organ damage, denial of adequate and proper foods, daily bile extraction and psychological trauma. Before starting their lifelong incarceration, each bear goes through a surgical procedure to insert a metal or latex catheter into its body, which connects the gallbladder with an open wound on the stomach, through which bile is extracted. This method was later replaced by the creation of an artificial fistula, which uses the bear's own tissue for bile extraction. Bile is drawn once or twice a day through the exit site (Loeffler, Robinson and Cochrane 2007). Bears were also seen wearing iron corsets to prevent them from scratching at the bile exit site. Although it is illegal to use catheters and corsets for bile extraction according to a new policy of the Chinese government, these two banned implements were still found in recent farm visits by animal activists.[3]

The first Chinese bear farms were built in northeastern Jilin and Heilongjiang provinces. In the late 1980s, bear farming started to spread to other parts of the country such as Sichuan and Guangdong. By the mid-1990s, China had seen the rise of hundreds of backyard peasant bear farms with anywhere from one to 20 bears per household.

---

2   Representatives of the country's wildlife farming and wildlife use industries attended a forum on the revision of the Wildlife Protection Law sponsored by the National People's Congress and the State Council Research Centre of Environmental and Economic Development in Beijing in February 2016.
3   Conversation on 19 August 2015 with a leading member of the Ta Foundation on catheter and corset use on farms in Northeast China.

As a component of China's wildlife farming industry, bear farming received strong government support throughout the 1980s and was aggressively advertised by the industry. For the Chinese authorities, bear farming served several important purposes. Not only did it supply traditional medicine practitioners and pharmaceutical companies with what the farmers claimed was a "life-saving ingredient," thus purportedly meeting a public health need; it was also perceived to be of conservation value. The authorities believed that the amount of bile collected from one farmed bear was equal to the amount of bile collected from 40 to 200 bears killed in the wild, and thus by encouraging farming they were protecting the wild bear population (*Beijing Review* 1994, 34).

In the late 1980s and early 1990s, state media and entertainment programs glowingly promoted bear farming as a means to fight poverty, a top priority of the reforming state. Slogans like "get rich, have fewer kids but raise more bears" were painted on walls in the countryside in Northeast and Southwest China. Bear farms were even promoted as tourist attractions. However, government efforts to showcase bear farming to tourists as a "get-rich-quick" or "poverty reduction" activity backfired. Jill Robinson, founder of Animals Asia Foundation, exposed Chinas bear farms to the outside world following her visit as a tourist to two bear farms in Guangdong in 1993. Contrary to the expectation of local authorities, some tourists were not at all impressed by bear farming.

China's wildlife farming industry betrays clear evidence of government involvement. Bear farming is no exception. It was part of the rural production diversification program, in line with the reform politics promulgated at the 3rd Plenum of the 11th Party Central Committee in 1978. Provincial governments were particularly motivated to promote wildlife farming. Some provincial authorities adopted regulations to ensure the "healthy" development of wildlife farming. In 1988, for example, the Forestry Bureau of Jiangxi Province approved the building of a breeding farm for civet cats, porcupine, wild boar and other species (Liu Shahe 2016, 24–25). The same year, China's Public Health Ministry issued a "Notice on the Tentative Measures for Managing the Use of 'Extracted Bear Bile.'" The notice had two purposes. First, it officially certified that bile extracted from live bears

4 Wildlife as a resource: the controversy of bear farming

contained the same properties as bile collected from bears killed in the wild. Extracted bear bile was therefore permitted for use in traditional Chinese medicine prescriptions. The notice was read by bear farmers and animal protectionists alike as official endorsement of bear farming. Second, the notice acknowledged that bear farming called for professional and technical expertise and that farmers must abide by the state's law on medicine production and the "registration procedures for new drug approval" if they intended to make traditional medicines containing the ingredient (Ministry of Public Health 1988).

In 1989, bear farming got a major boost from the Chinese government. In March, China put into effect its first ever animal protection law, the *Wildlife Protection Law of the People's Republic of China* (WPL). The law stated unequivocally that the Chinese government supported wildlife farming for economic development purposes. No one in the fledging industry or in the community of wildlife researchers had any idea that the industry would soon be challenged on moral grounds.

During the following four years (1989-93), wildlife farming expanded across the country. Two or more farms raising bears for bile extraction opened in Guangdong right after the implementation of the WPL. Since Asiatic black bears were listed as a category II protected species in the WPL, in 1990 farms in Sichuan began a systematic program of artificial bear breeding (Yang and Li 1991, 41). As a result, Sichuan saw a sudden increase, with 50 bear farms soon operating in 26 cities. By 1995, Sichuan had 2,100 bears kept for bile extraction, accounting for 25% of the total number of farmed bears in the country. In 1995 Sichuan produced 1,700 kilograms of bear bile powder, 30% of the total national output (Yang and Li 1995, 137-38). By the end of 1992, bear farming was being praised as a technological breakthrough, a conservation miracle, and an effective poverty reduction strategy. From Northeast China, bear farming had spread to north-western, northern, south-western and southern China. By 2015, 11 Chinese provinces were home to about 20,000 bears for bile extraction (Ma et al. 2017, 117; Chang 2016).

In 1993, China's bear farms were exposed to the world for the first time. During the next four years, under international pressure, the Chinese government was forced to pay attention to conditions on bear farms. Jill Robinson, CEO of the Animals Asia Foundation, deserves recognition for her efforts to bring China's bear farming cruelty to the attention of the Chinese public, the Chinese wildlife research community, and the Chinese government. Government support for the bear farming industry took a seemingly substantial turn. In 1993, the Chinese government issued *An Urgent Notice on Rectifying and Streamlining Bear Farms*. This notice restated the ban on capturing wild bears, proposed a moratorium on issuing new licences for bear farming, prohibited practices that were against laws and regulations, and warned against cruelty to bears. It also set out to close farms that did not have farming permits. To protect the industry from negative publicity and media criticism, the authorities called for a shutdown of tourism programs that included tours of bear farms.

In 1996, the Ministry of Forestry sponsored a conference on bear farm management. At the event, the government called on the industry to phase out the use of catheters and shift to "free-dripping," a supposedly "humane" extraction technique, in return for government support. A set of new guidelines was soon communicated to the industry in a policy directive called *A Notice on Strengthening the Management Work of Bear Farming* (Li Bo et al. 2011, 233–36). Efforts to streamline bear farming took place. In 1997 the Chinese government adopted the *Tentative Regulation on the Management of the Black Bear Utilisation Technology*, known as the Ministry of Forestry Document 56 (Ministry of Forestry 1997). The Regulation banned the use of catheters and corsets, regulated the source, age and weight of bears allowed to be used for bile extraction, and set out requirements relating to cage size, the duration of caging, the care of bears and management of farms, and the use of "free-dripping" to replace catheters. The *Tentative Regulation* was the state's most authoritative regulation of the industry and was important at a time when the Chinese public started to question the morality of the industry. Small operations with extremely poor conditions were forced to close or to be incorporated into bigger farms. After this consolidation, which took about 10 years, it was believed that by 2005 there were 68 bear farms in China with a total of 7,000 to 10,000 bears.

In 2005–6, China's official data revealed that the country's traditional Chinese medicine industry could absorb between 3,000 and

4 Wildlife as a resource: the controversy of bear farming

4,000 kilograms of bear bile powder a year. Using 3 to 5 kilograms of bile production per bear as the basis of their calculations, critics of the industry believed that 1,000 bears should be enough to satisfy this nationwide demand (Wang Weijia 2016). By 2011, however, an unpublished investigation found that the industry may have expanded to 98 farms holding 10,262 bears. An unpublished report submitted to government agencies for policymaking reference estimated that the total number of bears on both legal farms (of which there were 68) and illegal farms was more than 20,000. Ten of these farms had more than 500 bears each (Chang Jiwen 2016).

In 2015, bear farms were scattered across 11 provinces. Jilin Province in Northeast China had the most bears in farms, with a total of 6,376 animals. This was followed by more than 3,700 bears in Heilongjiang, 3,000 in Sichuan, 2,000 in Fujian, and 1,080 in Yunnan. Liaoning in Northeast China is a new member of the bear farming club. In 2011, it had no bear farms. In 2014, 696 bears were being farmed for bile in the province, to the shock of animal protectionists who have been working to end the practice in China.[4]

The Chinese government continued to provide policy support to the bear farming industry in the new century despite a change in public opinion, which was increasingly critical of the industry. In 2004, a joint notice by the State Forestry Bureau, the State Industrial and Commercial Administration, the State Food and Drug Administration, and the State Traditional Chinese Medicine Administration called for stronger labelling requirements for "bear resources" used in medicine. Products containing bear bile must now bear a "Designated Trade Mark for Wildlife Business and Wildlife Use Management" label. In 2008, the State Forestry Bureau promulgated the long-overdue industry standard *The Technical Standards of Black Bear Farming*, intended to assist the industry to standardise operations, improve quality control and upgrade farm conditions.

The government's protection of the industry is also reflected in the many honours and awards bear farms and their owners have received.

---

4   Interview with a senior manager of a Beijing-based NGO that has been working in collaboration with other Chinese groups on the bear farm issue for years, 16 January 2017.

Guizhentang proudly listed the public "honours" it had received over the years from national, provincial and local governments. In 2001, its bear bile powder was reportedly included in a research project as part of the "National Spark Program," a state-funded research and development project. In 2008, its "research on the standard farming technology for bear bile extraction" was made a key project by the Fujian Provincial Bureau of Science and Technology. From 2006 to 2009, Guizhentang was named a "leading forestry business" by the Fujian Provincial Bureau of Forestry. The year 2009 was one of great celebration for Guizhentang: its proposed research was listed as a major regional project; its "ecological bear farming base" was included as a construction and implementation project of the "National Research Base (Fujian) of TCM Modernisation" program; and Guizhentang was recognised as a "high-tech enterprise" and "credible trade mark" of Fujian Province. In 2010, the Fujian Provincial Bureau of Industry and Commerce recognised Guizhentang as a "trustworthy local brand name" (Baike.com).

Guizhentang understands the influence of the wildlife experts who support the use of wildlife and shape wildlife policymaking in China. In 2010, to the shock of China's animal protectionists, Guizhentang took on an educational role when it was made a "post-doctoral research centre" by the National Ministry of Human Resources and Social Security. In the same year, the Fujian Provincial Communist Party Committee Organisation Department and the provincial government approved the creation of a research centre at Guizhentang, in collaboration with academics from the Chinese Academy of Sciences and the Chinese Academy of Engineering. Qiu Shuhua, founder of Guizhentang, was made a member of the 8th Political Consultative Conference of Fujian Province, a provincial legislative body.

In northeastern China, the Heibao bear farm in Heilongjiang Province is arguably the world's biggest bear farm. It covers an area of more than one million square metres and holds more than 2,000 bears, producing 2,000 kilograms of bear bile powder a year, with seven state-approved traditional Chinese medicine drugs containing bear bile. Heibao has 21 sales offices in 14 provinces and municipalities. Besides the seven approved drugs, it also sells bear-bile wine and bear oil. Like Guizhentang, Heibao had been preparing to go public,

4 Wildlife as a resource: the controversy of bear farming

although public opposition may have undercut Heibao's confidence in its IPO plan.

Also like Guizhentang, Heibao has been showered with honours by the government. Its bear farm, ironically called "Bear Paradise," was a designated tourist attraction, in contravention of earlier State Forestry Bureau policy. In August 2004, I spent four hours as a tourist inside this "Paradise." All the caged bears displayed neurotic behaviours of different degrees, which is typical of incarcerated and farm bears. The "Heibao Ms Bear Acrobatic Show" featured breathtakingly dangerous performances by the bears and unprotected mid-air stunts by young trainer-acrobats. A single misstep by the young acrobats would have crashed their bodies to the concrete floor below.

In 2002, Heibao was listed as a "famous provincial brand." Three years later, the provincial industrial and commercial authorities named Heibao a "trustworthy trademark" of Heilongjiang. The Ministry of Science and Technology commended Heibao in 2007 for its participation in the national "Spark Program." It has been named one of the province's "dragon-head enterprises," recognised as a law-abiding and trustworthy enterprise, won first prize for "progress in science and technology," and was acknowledged as a "high-tech and innovative enterprise" (Heibao Pharmaceutical Company). When I visited Heibao in 2004, I saw photographs of the provincial and national leaders who had visited the farm prominently displayed in the exhibition hall.

Perhaps most importantly, Liu Jide, the founder of Heibao, was appointed as a deputy to the Provincial People's Congress (Heilongjiang Provincial People's Congress 2002). Mr. Liu seized the opportunity of attending the annual session of the congress to promote bear farming and wildlife farming. He urged the provincial government to increase support for what he called the "bear economy" and "bear culture" including the extraction of bear bile, the "gold of traditional medicine" (Gao Changli 2005).

The makeup of the Chinese legislature has always mirrored the political priorities of the ruling Communist Party. In Mao's era, the NPC was dominated by urban workers, rural peasants and soldiers. The late Chairman saw the working-class members as the most loyal defenders of his version of China's socialist revolution. In the last two decades, both the NPC and CPPCC have seen a disproportionate number of business elites. Entrepreneurs accounted for 20.54% and 13.83% of all the members of the 9th and 10th Congresses (Zhao Xiaoli 2013). Of the 2,270 members of the 18th Communist Party National Congress held in 2012, 145 were entrepreneurs, making up 6.3% of the delegates (Guo Fang et al. 2012). In provincial people's congresses, entrepreneurs have disproportionately greater representation. Of the 636 delegates in the 10th Provincial People's Congress of Zhejiang, for example, 163, or 25.6%, were business people (Yan Ge 2007). This high business representation in the provincial congresses was indicative of the importance of the business community in helping the Party to fulfil its objective of economic growth.

To the authorities, Guizhentang and Heibao are such development agents. The high percentage of business representation in the national and local legislatures ensures that policy-making will not divert from the Party's mission of economic development. It is unlikely that Mr Liu of Heibao would vote for legislation against cruelty to captive wildlife animals.

The challenge

The shift in public opinion about bear farming began in the summer of 1993. Two bear farms in South China's Guangdong were designated tourist attractions. Jill Robinson, then China Director of the International Fund for Animal Welfare, joined a tourist group and visited the farms. Her eye-witness experience caused a big stir when it was reported by the international media. For the first time, the international community got a glimpse of what was going on behind the high walls of Asia's bear farms. This was also the first time that the Chinese authorities were forced to face the fact that, besides the alleged public health and economic benefits of the farming operation, there was an ethical question that they should look into. The reputation of bear farming began to crumble.

Ms Robinson went on to meet Chinese officials in Beijing about the need for China to shut down the operation. She later founded the Animals Asia Foundation in Hong Kong, launched the China Bear Rescue campaign, and started an international effort to end bear

4 Wildlife as a resource: the controversy of bear farming

farming in Asia. In the decades since, Chinese public opinion has experienced a sea change. In 1998, a nationwide survey confirmed that the majority of respondents saw the industry as ethically unacceptable (IFAW 1998). A 2016 survey of public attitudes showed that 97.4% of respondents rejected bear farming and 83.9% believed that the industry should be outlawed (Xin Wen 2016). The public reaction to Guizhentang's IPO bid in 2012 revealed the extent of this shift.

In 1998, an article by Hu Zhanfen, a Shanghai writer, brought the reality of bear farming to the attention of the Chinese public. As a member of a tour group, Hu visited a bear farm in Jilin's Changbaishan area. What he saw were individually caged bears, each wearing a metal corset. The iron jacket was placed on the bears to prevent them from scratching the exit site and pulling out the metal catheter. The cages were so small that the bears could barely stand up. They were weaving, biting the iron bars, licking and displaying signs of neurotic disorder. One bear tore apart the corset and pulled out its own gallbladder. The farm staff responded by overpowering the bear and chopping off its paws while the bear was still alive (Hu Zhanfen 1998). Hu Zhanfen's account of these conditions shocked millions of Chinese readers. Through Hu's account, the Chinese public learned for the first time about the use of metal corsets, catheters and crush cages, and heard about neurotic bears and the festering open wounds on their stomachs. It was from Hu's article that I first learned about this industry.

Since 1998 I have followed AAF's China Bear Rescue campaign, visited two bear farms and met several bear farmers, studied rescued bears for a week at AAF's Chengdu Bear Rescue Centre, and communicated extensively with Jill Robinson, Gail M. Cochrane (AAF's chief veterinarian), Toby Zhang of the Ta Foundation in Beijing. These are the people who have first-hand information about the conditions of China's bear farms, farming practices, welfare problems, and the conditions of rescued bears. These communications, and my own field trips to bear farms, have confirmed the conditions described by Hu Zhanfen in 1998. My six trips to the AAF's Chengdu Bear Rescue Centre and my observation of a surgery performed on a rescued farm bear with a gigantic liver cancer shed additional light on the welfare problems of China's bear farming.

My first visit to a bear farm took place in February 2004 as part of my field studies of China's bear farming. This was a small operation in the suburbs of Tianjin in northern China. There were two Asiatic brown bears in two iron, rusty cages inside a shed of some six square metres. They had been caged for nine years. Both bears looked ill, neurotic, undernourished, and miserable to say the least. What was shocking was that they each wore a metal corset around their stomach. The metal cases around their bellies were rusty, wet, dirty, and offensive in smell. Strong leather straps held the metal cases tightly to their bodies, making it impossible for them to pull the cases off. Bile was extracted twice a day through a latex tube that had been surgically inserted into their gallbladders. The shed in which the two bears were housed was windowless. It would be hot like a steamer during the summer. When I walked into the shed, the bears were eating carrots.

My 2004 field trips resulted in the publication of two articles on China's bear farming (Li, Peter 2004a, 71–81 and 2004b, 4–15). These articles were completed after visits to two bear farms, hours of interviews with bear-rescue campaigners (Jill Robinson in particular), days of observation of rescued farm bears, and meetings with former bear farmers and bear-farm workers. The animal welfare problems I revealed and discussed in those two papers are still present in the legal and unknown number of illegal bear farms. These problems are as follows.

Bile extraction methods

Originally, all bear farms used latex or stainless-steel catheters surgically inserted into the gallbladder for bile extraction. These catheters are between 10 cm and 20 cm in length, with a metal disc at each end. One disc is surgically inserted into the gallbladder and secured with a purse-string suture. The second lies within the abdominal cavity, supported by the abdominal muscle. An open wound is cut in the bear's stomach. The surgery and the insertion of the catheter are known to cause multiple complications, perennial irritation at the exit site, infection from blood and pus, and death.

In 1997, the Chinese government banned the use of catheters and required the adoption of a "free-dripping" method for bile extraction.

4 Wildlife as a resource: the controversy of bear farming

"Free-dripping" required the creation of an artificial fistula between the gallbladder and the abdominal wall. To create this, an opening is cut in the gallbladder so that it is stitched to a corresponding hole in the bear's abdominal wall. Or, a tube made of the abdominal mesentery is created to link the opening in the gallbladder to an open wound cut in the bear's stomach. Through this open wound, farmers insert a tube into the fistula once or twice a day to extract bile. "Free-dripping" is considered "humane" by the industry and the Chinese authorities. Yet veterinary inspection and posthumous examination of deceased bears tells a different story. Even if the surgery to create a fistula were done in completely sterile conditions, the open wound in the bear's abdomen allows bacteria to directly invade the body either from the environment or via the extraction tube during the bile extraction procedure.

Other more serious problems were also linked to "free-dripping" such as cholecystitis, polyp formations, abscesses at the connection of the gallbladder to the abdominal wall, gallstone formation, lesions on the inner surface of the gallbladder wall, and partial herniation of the gallbladder into the subcutaneous area. The "free-dripping" bears have to rely on antibiotics to fight infections at the open wound.

While the Chinese government claims that metal corsets and catheters are no longer used, a research report of 2016 admitted that at least some 1,000 bears were still wearing the corset and having catheters inserted into their stomach (Chang Jiwen 2016).

Farming conditions

Bear farming is unnatural. The ultimate purpose of all bear farming is bile extraction, and this cannot be achieved without pinning the bears down inside the cage. Getting the "liquid gold," as bear bile is called in the industry, is the top priority. How bears are caged, restrained, fed and raised is secondary. Farming practices have thus developed without any consideration for the wellbeing of the bears. Cages are designed with dimensions ranging from 2 x 1.5 x 1.5 metres to 1.5 x 0.7 x 0.7 metres. This is barely bigger than the size of an average bear. Earlier, crush cages were common. These were cages with a movable side on top that came down on the bear to press it against the bottom of the cage for easier bile extraction. Metal corsets were a common sight on bear farms in the 1980s and 1990s. Because of the popularisation of the "free-dripping" technique, metal corsets are seldom used today. However, unlicensed bear farms still use them (Chang Jiwen 2016). This device is used to prevent bears from taking out the foreign objects inserted into their bodies, scratching the bile exit site when it becomes irritated, and self-mutilating in response to pain and inflammation at the open wound.

De-clawing and cutting back teeth are two other practices commonly conducted on the bear farms. The third phalanx of each front digit is often removed to prevent them from harming the farmers and from self-mutilation. Similarly, their teeth are cut back to take away their defences. Food deprivation is also commonly practised on small bear farms. The rationale, according to bear farmers, is that high-protein, nutrient-dense foods require more bile for digestion. To extract more bile, farmers believe that bears should not be fed too well. Their daily diet is therefore composed of corn porridge and vegetables.

Physical abuse is only one side of the coin. Signs of mental torture are equally pronounced. Pacing, weaving, bar biting and self-mutilation, as described by journalist Hu Zhanfen, were disturbingly noticeable on the farm I visited in the summer of 2004 and were still common on farms recently investigated by Chinese activists. Years of incarceration without adequate space, food or freedom, and the daily physical torture of bile extraction, have conquered the bears psychologically as well as physically.

The condition of rescued farm bears reflects the physical and mental problems they have suffered on the farm. Since the launch of the China Bear Rescue campaign, AAF has rescued and helped hundreds of bears in China. The information below summarises the conditions of the bears that were accepted to AAF's Chengdu bear sanctuary:

> The bears we receive at the China sanctuary are in a terrible condition – suffering from abdominal tumors and infections and often some form of heart or liver disease. Up to 90 % also have one or more of the following physical removed impairments: missing limbs, amputated paws, diseased and deformed paw pads, claws, extracted or sawn off canine teeth and blindness. On top of this, many have deformity and joint and mobility problems caused by

4 Wildlife as a resource: the controversy of bear farming

spending years immobile in cages sometimes no bigger than their own bodies.[5]

Since the exposure of the welfare problems on bear farms, the perception that bear farmers are heartless souls and that they reflect a Chinese propensity for cruelty to animals has often been heard in Chinese and Western media.[6] The bear farmers I interviewed were in fact no different from most other Chinese people. "We were in the business to make a living," they said. "We took no delight in torturing the bears. We did not feed bears what they loved to eat not because those foods were expensive, but because the foods would draw bile for digestion."

They did not lie. Bear farmers were business people. By denying the bears access to space, outdoor enclosures, proper food, and physical and mental comfort, the farmers were after profits, not fun. Sichuan, for example, has an ample supply of a variety of fruits, nuts and leafy vegetables. These products are not expensive in the province. The food deprivation evident in bear farms is dictated by a desire to maximise bile production and so maximise profits. It is the profit motive that has given rise to this model of bear farming, and it is the profit motive that has made bear farming intrinsically and irreparably cruel.

The *Tentative Regulation* issued in 1997 by the Ministry of Forestry was the government's attempt to put an end to some of the most shocking practices on the farm. The regulation banned the use of young bears and bears weighing less than 100 kilograms for bile extraction. It banned the use of metal corsets and banned caging bears when they are not being milked for bile. As of the end of 2016, these requirements have all been violated. My visit to China's biggest bear farm in 2004 and a follow-up visit in 2008 by two student investigators confirmed that the

---

5 Conversation with Jill Robinson, 15 May 2015, Shenzhen, China.
6 For example a bear farmer was called "heartless" in a report for forcing two bears to wear a metal corset; see "跨省行动解救取胆熊" (A trans-provincial rescue of bears from a farm), *Huaxi Metropolitan News*, 12 February 2004, accessible at https://tinyurl.com/y6ymjo2q. For public condemnation of bear farming and bear farmers, see the comments written by participants of the petition "Stop Guizhentang's attempt to go public" at https://tinyurl.com/y64cbzzj.

1997 policy was ignored. For example, the outdoor enclosure was never used. Bears were caged all day long and they were not allowed to access the open enclosure, where the grass was intact. "We don't let the bears out because the open wounds on their stomachs could be exposed to harmful bacteria," said one worker when I asked if the bears were ever allowed to enjoy the sunshine in the outdoor enclosure. Allowing the bears to play outside the cages could increase the chance of infection at the bile exit site. Illnesses add costs and cut profits.

The industry defence

Since the end of the 1990s, and particularly since Hu Zhanfan's 1998 report, the reputation of the bear farming industry has plummeted. "I could not sleep in the evening and I still had in my mind that poor bear whose paws were chopped off while he was still alive," wrote one Beijing reader of Hu's article.[7] Animals Asia's massive public education programs and bear rescue campaign raised awareness of the controversy. At the 19th International Conference of Zoology held in Beijing in August 2004, the welfare problems of bear farming were the subject of a special panel. At this conference, international animal welfare experts, including Jill Robinson and her veterinarians (who had performed corrective surgeries on many rescued bears), sat down before an international audience with a consortium of officials who were supportive of wildlife farming and representatives from the bear farming industry. On this panel, the bear-farming industry was in a defensive position but used the occasion to promote its narrative that their operation contributed to conservation, public health and poverty reduction.

The following year, the European Parliament passed a resolution demanding that China shut down its bear-farming operations (Johnson and Ridder 2006). The Chinese government was under pressure. After consultation with the bear farming industry and accepting the industry's narrative, the State Forestry Bureau defended the industry

---

7   Conversation with Professor Li Xiaoxi of the Air Force Academy in Beijing, 27 March 2008.

4 Wildlife as a resource: the controversy of bear farming

as "humane" and "conservation-friendly." Its spokesman rejected the international calls to end bear farming and said that China had no plan to phase out the farming operation (Southern Metropolitan News 2006). He warned the international community against efforts to link China's bear farming with the 2008 Beijing Olympics (Guo 2006).

The controversy surrounding Guizhentang's IPO bid in 2012, however, highlighted the ongoing divide over bear farming. The strongest support for the industry came from the official All China Association of Traditional Chinese Medicine (ACATCM). In a briefing released to the press in February 2012, ACATCM stated that breeding wildlife for medicinal purposes was a humane business because it had phased out the use of metal corsets and catheters. The briefing then zeroed in on AAF in the most accusatory terms. The ACATCM alleged that AAF, purportedly with the support of Western pharmaceutical interests and using animal protection as a pretext, had for years engaged in actions against China's bear farming and traditional medicine industries. "The purpose of AAF's anti-bear-farming campaigns was to put pressure on China for the purpose of ending bear farming, stopping the use of bear bile in traditional Chinese medicine, weakening the competitiveness of traditional Chinese medicine, and creating conditions for Western pharmaceutical interests to have a monopolistic market share of drugs that contained synthetic bear bile ingredients," the briefing charged (Twenty-first Century Economic Report 2012).

At a press conference on 16 February, Fang Shuting, head of the ACATCM, proclaimed that bear bile was irreplaceable. According to Fang, "Traditional Chinese medicine is an industry in which China has exclusive intellectual property rights." "Since bear bile is a valuable ingredient of traditional Chinese medicine," Mr Fang said, "bear farming should be supported for the purpose of promoting the development of traditional Chinese medicine." Fang's remark that bile extraction was painless elicited an immediate reaction from the Chinese media. "The process of bile extraction is like turning on the faucet for tap water: simple, direct and painless," he said. "After bile extraction, the bears go outdoors and play happily. The bears do not show anything unusual, but [show] complete comfort." He argued that "bear farming is the best way to protect the bears" (Southern Metropolitan News 2012). Earlier, ACATCM accused AAF of colluding with Western pharmaceutical interests to undermine traditional Chinese medicine (Sheng Wei 2012).

The most "authoritative" defender of the bear farming industry is Li Lianda, a specialist in traditional Chinese medicine and an academician of the Chinese Academy of Engineering. In Li's opinion, the swing of Chinese public opinion against bear farming was the result of AAF's campaigning. Li called AAF a "riot leader" that had launched a campaign not just against bear farming but against China and the Chinese government, a charge that was tantamount to calling on the Chinese government to end AAF's work in mainland China. At a conference, Li said publicly that AAF "has pointed its gun at China and the Chinese government since the very first day of its establishment." He compared it to the eight Western powers that occupied Beijing in 1900, referring to an incident during the Boxer Rebellion that is widely accepted as a Western military occupation of China's capital. In Li Lianda's view, Jill Robinson and the AAF were using the issue as a means to "invade China" (Zhang Yan 2012).

Zhou Junsheng, an economist, suggested that the conflict between animal protectionists and the bear farming industry over Guizhentang's IPO bid should be resolved by the market. Accepting the claim that bear bile was "an irreplaceable lifesaving medicine," he argued that the stock market should not be turned into a moral battleground. "As long as Guizhentang is a legal business, it has the right to apply for IPO," he stated. In his opinion, animal protectionists had no right to oppose Guizhentang's IPO bid. If investors were concerned by accusations of animal cruelty, they would reject Guizhentang's stocks (Jinghua Times 2012a).

Unfailingly, support also came from Zhao Nanyuan, professor of popular science at Tsinghua University. Professor Zhao has been the most vocal critic of China's animal protection movement and animal activists. In 2002, he became nationally well known for his opposition to calls for animal protection legislation. In an article on the public outcry over Guizhentang's IPO bid, Zhao embarked on a biting tirade against animal protectionists. The following paragraph best summarises his main arguments:

4 Wildlife as a resource: the controversy of bear farming

> I am in full support of bear farming. This position of mine has nothing to do with traditional Chinese medicine. It is not concerned either with the question of whether bear bile can be substituted or not. I support bear farming because it contributes to the protection of bear populations in the wild and the protection of biodiversity. (Zhao Nanyuan 2012a)

Zhao apparently accepted wholesale the arguments of the bear farming industry and the traditional Chinese medicine community. "Developing new uses for wildlife products helps population growth of wildlife animals for sustained human use," he pointed out. "Although bear paws may not taste as good as pork feet, the fact that bear paws are hard to come by adds to their value as an income source." Because of the market value of bears, their population has increased. Utilisation by humans was therefore key to wildlife protection, as well as to economic development, Zhao stated. To Zhao, the extinction of South China Tigers, a unique Chinese subspecies of the tiger family, could be attributed to polices that discouraged humans from using tigers. Similarly, bajituan, or Chinese river dolphins, which are believed to have been extinguished in the Yangtze River, would have survived if they had been farmed and used for entertainment or other purposes, Zhao said. To him, the criticism that bear farming was cruel was groundless. "Bear farming is a tool for achieving profits," he said. The more bears are milked for bile, the more money can be made. "When animal welfare receives attention, the objective of animal breeding and use cannot be achieved." Bears in the wild would face a greater danger of extinction if bear farming were outlawed, he concluded (Zhao Nanyuan 2012a).

Other scholars also defended bear farming by referring to its perceived conservation and public health benefits. Some of these scholars agreed that the use of catheters and metal corsets should be phased out (Li Bo et al. 2011, 233–36). Zhou Ronghan, a professor at the University of Traditional Chinese Medicine, agreed that traditional Chinese medicine needed bear bile, and that bear farming contributed to conservation efforts. Li Ming, of the Zoological Research Institute under the Chinese Academy of Sciences, claimed that the "free-dripping" technique caused no harm to bears. He held that synthetic bile did not have the same properties as bear bile powder. Jia Qian, head of the Research Team of TCM Development Strategy under the Ministry of Science and Technology, claimed that the continued use of bear bile had caused the bear populations in the wild to grow steadily, from 10,000 to 20,000 (People's Daily 2012).

The bear farming industry did not sit still. The most controversial rebuttal came from Qiu Shuhua, founder of Guizhentang. In response to the growing opposition to Guizhentang's IPO bid, Qiu rejected charges of animal cruelty and illegal operations. She said that since 1993, Guizhentang had been a state-designated demonstration farm. "We have achieved ecological farming of bears, [and made] a huge contribution to bear conservation," she said. Bears at Guizhentang were perfectly healthy and successful in breeding, she added. "They are living a life of great comfort and are more comfortable than those of us who created the company." She announced that Guizhentang was a legal business. Its operation was approved by the State Forestry Bureau and its production of bear bile powder had been approved by the Ministry of Public Health in 1995. Qui went on to argue that "It is reasonable to say that opposing Guizhentang was tantamount to opposition to the government." Qiu called on Guizhentang's critics to stop their criticism and to leave it to the government to determine the future of Guizhentang's IPO. "Let's wait for the government to make the determination," she proclaimed (Voice of China.com.cn 2012).

Zhang Zhiyun, an investor and board member of Guizhentang, defended the bear farming industry as a line of production with great growth and market potential. He stood by his investment in Guizhentang by referring to the estimated market value of 20 to 30 billion yuan of bear bile products. Of the "four celebrated TCM drugs," namely tiger bones, musk, rhino horns and bear bile, bear bile has been used most extensively and featured in 123 traditional Chinese medicine prescriptions, Zhang said. "Bear farming is the most impressive and established production chain with great growth potentials," he added. He revealed that Guizhentang's Board of Directors had decided to "open 600 branch stores within three years with the aim of achieving a sales revenue of one billion yuan a year in five years" (Beijing Morning News 2013). While he rejected criticisms of animal cruelty, he admitted that bile extraction could not be completely painless. He echoed the

4 Wildlife as a resource: the controversy of bear farming

conservation claim and said that, following the expansion of the bear farming industry in the previous three decades, wild bear populations had risen from 8,000 to 48,000 at the end of 2002 (Fiance.ifeng,com 2012a). When there was a conflict between animal welfare and human interest, he argued, human needs should take precedence (Money.163.com 2012). He complained that some forces just did not want Guizhentang to succeed, but wanted to undermine traditional Chinese medicine and to turn China into an open market for Western pharmaceutical companies that intended to sell synthetic bear bile (Finance, ifeng.com 2012b). With regard to the claim that Guizhentang produced and sold products without state authorisation, Zhang said that the company had only produced two over-the-counter products, namely bear bile capsules and bear bile powder. "Never has Guizhentang violated state laws by producing health supplements with bear bile powder," Zhang told a reporter (Finance.ifeng.com 2012c).

Support for bear farming also came from 30 deputies of the NPC and the CPPCC. These deputies, mostly medical and public health professionals in traditional Chinese medicine, submitted a legislative proposal stating the indispensability and irreplaceability of bear bile as an ingredient in "lifesaving traditional Chinese medicine drugs." The proposal called for the government to actively support wildlife breeding and farming in accordance with Chinese law (Liu Xia 2012). As expected, the proposal did not go anywhere legislatively, although it was forwarded to the State Forestry Bureau, China's national administrative agency for matters related to wildlife conservation and wildlife use. Since the State Forestry Bureau is responsible for drafting and enforcing standards for wildlife farming, the controversy regarding Guizhentang's IPO bid presented a challenge for the Bureau. In response to an enquiry from a journalist, the director of the Department of Wildlife Conservation within the State Forestry Bureau claimed that Guizhentang had the right to go public as long as the application proceeded in accordance with the law (Zhang Ke 2012).

Opposing voices

In fact, illegal operation was one of the three main claims made by the opponents of Guizhentang's IPO bid. A coalition of forces came into being following the report on Guizhentang's plans. AAF was the leading campaigner. In a 2011 statement sent to the Fujian stock supervisory authorities, the AAF called for Guizhentang's application to be blocked on account of animal cruelty, the safety of bile products, and the profitability of the bear farming industry in the long run (Xie Xiaoting 2012). The Beijing-based Ta Foundation, established by some of the country's famous media personalities, initiated a joint petition to the State Securities Regulator Commission, signed by 72 celebrities, urging the state regulatory body to reject Guizhentang's IPO application.

The petition listed three reasons for disqualifying Guizhentang's application. First, Guizhentang's bear-bile business ran counter to the state's business policy: in 2001, the Ministry of Public Health decided that no health supplements containing bear bile would receive government approval. Besides, it was state policy to reduce and phase out the use of wildlife animal parts in traditional Chinese medicine: the 2010 edition of *The Pharmacopoeia of the PRC*, the official compendium of drugs, ingredients, doses and other information, contained no new ingredients from endangered species. The *Pharmacopoeia* no long included tiger bones, rhino horns, bear bile or other endangered animal parts for medicinal use. Guizhentang's efforts to expand bear-bile production by attracting investment on the stock market thus ran counter to state policies.

Second, the operation environment of bear farming had experienced a major change. Bear farming had progressively lost public support. In surveys conducted by Sina.com and Tencent.com, China's biggest internet portals, some 90% of citizens voiced opposition to Guizhentang's IPO application. They also rejected bear-bile products. In another survey, 3.2 million people voiced opposition to bear farming. Such overwhelming public opposition could force the government to consider a major policy change, leading to regulatory measures unfavourable to the operation of bear farming businesses. Also important to note was that after three decades of research by a team of scientists at Shenyang Medicine College, synthetic bear bile was

4 Wildlife as a resource: the controversy of bear farming

at the stage of state evaluation. If synthetic bear bile was approved, the entire bear-farming industry would be affected, causing further loss to investors.

Finally, in the previous three years, Guizhentang had violated state laws. State policies issued in 2001 and 2004 stated that bear bile powder could only be used in drugs with exclusive healing effects, in drugs that are indispensable for certain illnesses, and by designated hospitals. However, Guizhentang had sold bear bile tea without state approval, which violated state policy.

The petition from the Ta Foundation warned the Commission that a favourable decision on Guizhentang's IPO application would result in a strong public reaction, and that this could undermine the power and credibility of the government's supervisory bodies (Ta Foundation 2012). Following its first petition of 14 February 2012, which was co-signed by 70 celebrities, the Ta Foundation sent a second petition with 28 more signatories including Yao Ming, Sun Li, Yang Lan, Zhang Kangkang, Deng Chao and other nationally renowned celebrities (Zhang Ke 2014).

Critics of bear farming also had allies in the NPC and the Chinese People's Political Consultative Conference (CPPCC). Feng Jicai, Han Meilin and other members of the CPPCC submitted a legislative proposal calling for the government to outlaw bear farming. Han Meilin, a well-known artist, called bear farming "a national disgrace" and "a disgrace of the Chinese legal system" (Jing Jing 2012).

The tug-of-war between the two camps came to an end one year later. In June 2013, Guizhentang withdrew its IPO application and terminated the bid. It said, however, that it would consider making another IPO application in the future (China Daily 2013).

The politics of development

Wildlife farming was one component of China's rural reform. It was part of a push to diversify rural production that was initiated by China's post-socialist developmental state. As discussed earlier, the reform was intended to end the country's food security crisis and to lift the rural population out of poverty. For this purpose, the party leadership dismantled policies that had criminalised private ownership and discouraged private economic activities. The 1979 *Draft Decision on the Several Questions on Accelerating Agricultural Development* was a landmark policy directive. It eliminated restrictions on autonomous peasant farming activities. Deng Xiaoping argued that the government should encourage some people, through honest hard labour, to "get rich first" (Chinese Communist Central Documentary Research Institute 2004, 1091). For the first time since 1957, Chinese peasants were allowed to farm what they wanted and to raise what they chose to satisfy their family's needs, the state's procurement requirements, and market demand. Animal farming was one of the first areas stimulated by this change. Additionally, peasants were encouraged to explore types of farming that had been denied them in the pre-reform era. Wildlife farming had previously been solely owned and operated by the state. The more audacious peasants ventured into this production that had been denied to them in the pre-reform era. Liu Jide, CEO and founder of Heibao, was one of the scores of farmers who began their wildlife farming experiments in the mid-1980s. Qiu Shuhua, the founder of Guizhentang, reportedly started her career doing construction work in Southwest China, far away from her hometown in eastern Fujian Province, before entering bear farming.

The fact that local authorities support and protect bear farming is not surprising. Bear farming is part of the economic catch-up strategy of their respective provinces. As a province that has been lagging behind most coastal provinces, Heilongjiang is under pressure to accelerate economic development. In the national race for growth, Heilongjiang has seen its ranking steadily sliding down. In 1978, Heilongjiang's per capita GDP was $335, as opposed to the national average of $225. It had the fifth highest per capita GDP of the 31 provinces and municipalities. Since 1978, Heilongjiang has seen a steady increase in the per capita GDP, reaching $6,318 in 2015. But in the same period, its ranking has slipped from fifth place in 1978 to 21st in 2015. Heilongjiang's 2015 per capita GDP was below the national average of $7,990. The increase in Heilongjiang's per capita income between 1978 and 2015 was impressive, at 18.85 times. However, the per capita GDP of Zhejiang in 2015 was a breathtaking 63.67 times that of 1978. Given comparisons like this, since the end of the 1990s,

4 Wildlife as a resource: the controversy of bear farming

provincial leaders have been motivated to push for faster growth. The urge for faster development was reflected in the inclusion of Liu Jide and other peasant entrepreneurs in the Provincial People's Congress and provincial Political Consultative Conference, two "chambers" of the provincial legislature.

In Fujian Province, local priorities are similar to those in Heilongjiang. Facing Taiwan on the west side of the Taiwan Straits, Fujian has long been a strategic location for war preparations. Economic development was not a priority during the pre-reform era. But since 1978, Fujian has seen an exponential expansion of its economy. In 1978, Fujian's per capita GDP was the 23rd of the 31 mainland provinces. Its ranking went up to 12th place in 1995 thanks to Deng Xiaoping's call in 1992 to open up the coastal regions to investment from foreign countries and from Hong Kong, Taiwan and Macau. In 2015, Fujian's per capita GDP reached $10,953, or 67.61 times its 1978 per capita GDP, and was ranked seventh among the 31 provinces.

However, as a coastal province with a regional subculture similar to that of Taiwan, Fujian believed it had advantages that had not been tapped. In a 2015 article, a researcher from Fujian's provincial economic and foreign trade institute noted that Fujian was believed to lag behind other coastal provinces in GDP; that traditional, labour- and resource-intensive industries continued to dominate the provincial economy and foreign trade; and that geographic proximity had failed to forge closer ties between Fujian and Taiwan. Fujian was under great pressure in the race for faster growth at a time when Guangdong and the Greater Shanghai regions were both moving into value-added, capital-intensive and technologically innovative industries.

Fujian's per capita GDP in 2014, though more than 60 times greater than it was in 1978, was only 54% of that in the Greater Shanghai Region, 45% of the Greater Guangzhou Region, and 29% of Taiwan (Li Jinxiu 2015, 88–89). To upgrade the provincial industrial structure, the provincial authorities have pushed for the launch of an "Economic Zone of the West Coast of the Taiwan Straits" since 2009. In 2011, the Fujian provincial government set out to implement the Development Plan of the Economic Zone of the West Coast of the Taiwan Straits; the Comprehensive Development Plan of the Pingtan Experimental

Zone; the Xiamen Experimental Plan for Deepening the Cross-Straits Economic Exchanges; the Overall Plan of Fujian Straits Blue Economic Experimental Zone; and a financial experimental zone at Quanzhou. The priority of the provincial government was economic growth. Guizhentang's several "innovative" and "research-based" productions served the economic objectives of the province. The many awards and honours given to Guizhentang by the provincial authorities suggest that the company's operations also serve the political objectives of the provincial government.

However, the contribution of bear farming to the Chinese economy as a whole is a myth. No credible statistics on the size of the industry have ever been published by the State Forestry Bureau, the national government agency in charge of the country's wildlife industry. It was not even mentioned in the internal report by the State Council Research Centre of Development. By the end of 2016, bear farming reached a revenue of 1 billion yuan. Some 20,000 bears were farmed mostly in Jilin, Sichuan and Heilongjiang (Ma Jianzhang et al. 2017, 116). In 2012, according to an industry investor, the operation was supplying bear bile to 183 pharmaceutical companies in 27 provinces, as an ingredient for 153 drugs used in traditional Chinese medicine. He predicted that the total revenue from bear farming and the production of bile-containing drugs would reach RMB 20 or 30 billion (Liu Xiaotong and Zhang Xinpei 2012). "It is difficult to verify these numbers," commented Sun Jiang, professor of law at Northwest China University of Law and Politics. "We cannot rule out the possibility that the industry needs to inflate the numbers to support their claim that bear farming contributes to economic growth and to poverty reduction."[8] Professor Sun's comments were illuminating and rejected the so-called "conservative estimate" advanced by the industry insider.

Conclusions

On 14 December 2015, Guizhentang tried for the second time to go public on the Chinese stock market. After the defeat of its first IPO

---

8   Conversation with Professor Sun Jiang, Washington, DC, 19 August 2015.

4 Wildlife as a resource: the controversy of bear farming

bid in 2012, the business had continued to expand its operations, with a view to going public. By the end of August 2015, Guizhentang had reportedly raised 899 bears, and an additional 400 bears or so had been acquired for bile extraction. Nationwide, according to Toby Zhang, secretary-general of the Ta Foundation, there could be more than 30,000 bears being kept for bile extraction as of December 2015.[9] China's domestic market can absorb no more than 4,000 kilograms of bear bile powder for use in traditional Chinese medicine. This demand could be satisfied by 1,000 bears. The surplus bear bile may be illegally sold overseas, processed as supplements, and/or distributed as gifts in violation of state policy.

Guizhentang's second IPO bid also met strong opposition. In a report filed to the Stock Exchange Company against this second bid, the Ta Foundation pointed out that Guizhentang had committed three unlawful acts that should disqualify its IPO application. First, Guizhentang violated the country's Law on the Management of Drugs and Medicines and other policies related to the use of special marks for captive bred wildlife products produced by businesses with legal authorisation. Second, Guizhentang produced and sold bear-bile powder without approved product marks and with illegal packaging. Third, Guizhentang made exaggerated claims of bear bile's medicinal and tonic properties, in violation of appropriate Chinese laws and regulations.[10]

Guizhentang failed in its second IPO bid. However, wildlife farming and bear farming have continued to receive government support. The WPL enforced in 1989 was revised in 2015–16 (I discuss this process in chapter 6 of this book). In both the 1989 and 2016 WPL, wildlife is treated as a resource that can be used for human purposes. Rather than protecting wildlife animals, the WPL is designed to endorse, promote and protect the country's wildlife industries, and to serve the state's economic objectives. To local authorities in regions with wildlife-related industries, these businesses contribute to

---

9   Conversation with Toby Zhang, executive director of the Ta Foundation, 18 December 2015.
10 Ta Foundation, *Report to the State Stock Exchange Company*, copy obtained from the Ta Foundation, 2 November 2016.

employment, poverty reduction, and local growth, which are the main goals of the local leaders. Animal welfare and conservation are not a concern. In fact, the lack of concern for the wellbeing of farmed wildlife animals is not unique. As the next chapter attempts to show, China's massive animal agriculture, the world's biggest concentrated animal feeding operation, is reproducing welfare problems on a much bigger scale and impacting a staggering number of nonhuman animals.

5
Animal agriculture

In 1991, China overtook the United States and became the world's biggest livestock producer (FAOSTAT 2013). It has occupied that position ever since. In 2017, China slaughtered a staggering 48 million beef cattle, 302 million sheep and goats, 508 million rabbits, 717 million pigs, 2.2 billion ducks and 9.4 billion chickens (FAOSTAT 2019). The country's livestock industry as a whole produced in the same year 30 million tons of eggs, 86 million tons of meat and 30 million tons of cow milk. China's meat output was almost double that of the United States (46 million tons) (FAOSTAT 2019). Meat production, particularly pork, has significance beyond the dinner tables of the 1.3 billion mainland Chinese.

Pork is a strategic product that has remarkable political implications. In China, eating meat generally means eating pork. Vicissitude in pork supply can shake consumer confidence in the government's ability to ensure food security. Unsurprisingly, China has the world's only "strategic meat reserve" system, by which the government aims to stabilise pork supply to the country's increasingly affluent citizens. Livestock production is therefore no ordinary economic activity to be left to producers, but a crucial sector with implications for political stability. Despite privatisation in rural production, the Chinese government has never disowned the rural economy.

Exponential growth

China's animal agriculture underwent breathtaking expansion between 1979 and 2015, and this was reflected on household dinner tables and in changes to height and BMI.[1] An increase in meat output and the number of livestock slaughtered, changes to the scale and structure of production, and the adoption of Western farming models are all indicators of the expanding industry.

Meat production

Chinese peasants are known to respond to government policy changes. In 1979, 12.1 million tons of meat were produced, an increase of 21% over the previous year. As a percentage of world meat production, China's meat output rose from 7.9% in 1978 to 9.2% in 1979. This was a direct result of the reform program initiated in December 1978. During the following two decades there were fluctuations in the growth rate, but the upward trend was maintained. On average, between 1979 and 2013 the country's meat output grew by 6% each year, twice the average global annual growth rate of 3% per year. The table below shows a steady expansion of the country's meat production and its share in the global total during this period.

This increase in meat output has contributed to a stable supply of meat products on the market. Towards the end of the 1980s, meat rations for urban residents were phased out and per capita meat consumption began to rise. In 2012, China's 1.3 billion people consumed 62 kilograms of meat per person (FAOSTAT 2013). At the same time, the country's marine capture fisheries produced 13.9 million tons, making China the world's top marine fishing nation. China also had the world's biggest aquaculture, producing 43 million tons of farmed fish, 62% of the global output (UN Food and Agriculture Organisation 2013). Although livestock is not the only source of animal protein for

---

[1] For the changes in Chinese height and BMI, see Lucy Hornby and Ian Bott, "China's economic reform: 40 years of change," *Financial Times*, 4 December 2018, https://on.ft.com/3mCcqfJ.

5 Animal agriculture

Table 5.1: Meat Output: Annual Growth Rate and as % of the World's Total Output 1978–2017. Source: FAOSTAT 2009 and 2018.

Year	China total (millions of tons)	Growth over previous year (%)	World total (millions of tons)	As % of the world total
1978	10.05		127.50	7.9
1979	12.16	21.00	132.73	9.2
1980	13.65	12.25	136.74	10.0
1981	14.26	4.47	139.36	10.2
1982	15.21	6.66	140.66	10.8
1983	15.77	3.68	145.31	10.9
984	17.20	9.07	149.44	11.5
1985	19.44	13.02	154.49	12.6
1986	20.54	5.66	159.15	12.9
1987	22.38	8.96	164.89	13.6
1988	24.82	10.90	171.09	14.5
1989	26.19	5.52	173.67	15.1
1990	28.11	7.33	179.42	15.7

Animal Welfare in China

Year	China total (millions of tons)	Growth over previous year (%)	World total (millions of tons)	As % of the world total
1991	30.67	9.11	183.50	16.7
1992	33.32	8.64	187.02	17.8
1993	36.39	9.21	190.77	19.1
1994	39.74	9.21	196.72	20.2
1995	43.00	8.20	202.51	21.2
1996	43.62	1.44	204.98	21.3
1997	47.15	8.10	210.28	22.4
1998	51.00	8.17	218.09	23.4
1999	52.49	2.92	223.82	23.5
2000	56.04	6.76	229.94	24.4
2001	56.43	0.70	232.16	24.3
2002	57.92	2.64	239.24	24.2
2003	60.85	5.06	244.84	24.9
2004	61.96	1.82	249.70	24.8

5 Animal agriculture

Year	China total (millions of tons)	Growth over previous year (%)	World total (millions of tons)	As % of the world total
2005	64.55	4.18	255.77	25.2
2006	66.84	3.55	262.92	25.4
2007	68.70	2.78	273.37	25.1
2008	71.47	4.03	280.96	25.4
2009	76.56	7.12	286.11	26.8
2010	79.38	3.70	293.48	27.0
2011	79.74	0.45	297.48	26.8
2014	87.79	2.4	317.85	27.3
2016	89.98	0.86	329.8	27.2
2017	86.52	-3.8	334.2	26.0

mainland Chinese people, the authorities and the industry continue to see animal husbandry as the sector with the most potential for further expansion.

Meat consumption in China is uneven. Urban residents consume more meat and dairy products than their rural counterparts. In a study of the actual consumption of meat (at home and outside the home) among urban and rural residents in 2012, the per capita consumption at home for urban residents was 35.7 kilograms and 20.9 kilograms for rural residents (Cheng Guangyan et al. 2015, 76–82). Urban and rural residents also consumed different types of animal products: in a

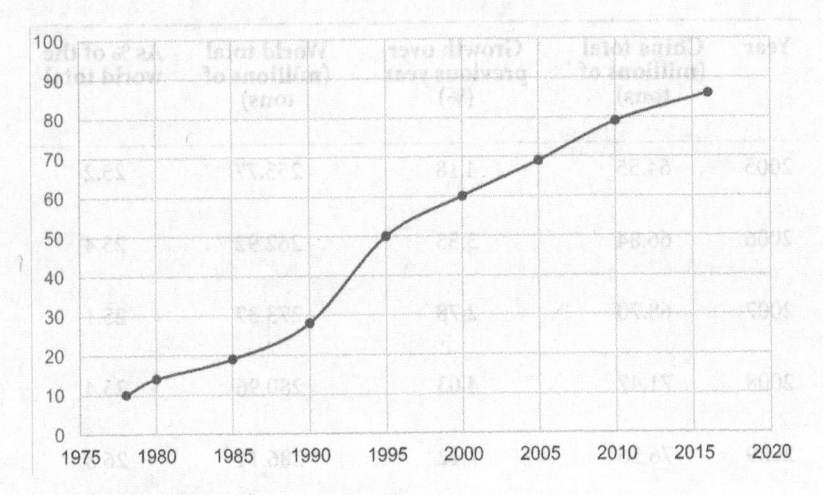

Figure 5.1 Meat production (tons), 1978–2016.

2007 study, Chinese scholars found that meat consumed by urbanites accounted for a smaller proportion of their animal protein intake, whereas meat made up a bigger percentage of the animal products consumed by rural residents. In other words, rural residents consumed more meat (73.2%) than their urban counterparts (53.2%). In a 2005 survey, more urban residents reported consuming eggs (17.9%, compared with 16.5% of rural residents) and dairy products (29%, compared with 10%) than rural residents (Li, Qin and Ding 2007, 664–67). The Chinese government's 2014 policy statement on promoting the expansion of livestock production aim to narrow the gap between rural and urban consumption (State Council of the PRC 2014).

The expansion of animal agriculture has contributed to a phenomenal growth in meat output. China seems to have consolidated its lead in world livestock production. In 2013, it produced 54 million tons of pork, accounting for 50.6% of the global total. The 717 million pigs slaughtered in that year were handled by 4,585 government-designated slaughterhouses (accounting for 31% of slaughter operations) and 10,135 small slaughterhouses (69%) across the country (Chinameat.org 2015).

5 Animal agriculture

Dairy production

The expansion of milk production has been similarly breathtaking. Milk was not traditionally part of the Han Chinese diet. In fact, most East Asians are believed to be lactose intolerant. In the USA, approximately one quarter of Americans, including most Asian Americans, are believed to be vulnerable to health issues caused by low levels of the enzyme lactase, which is needed to digest dairy products (Wiley 2004, 506–17). However, this does not seem to have dampened Chinese enthusiasm for milk production and for promoting milk consumption. In the pre-reform era (1949–78), the overwhelming majority of Chinese people rarely saw milk. In 1978, China's total milk production was 1.8 million tons, an average of 3 kilograms per person per year. This accounted for an insignificant 0.24% of the world's total output. In the 1990s and the first decade of the 21st century, milk production took off. Between 2000 and 2004 the average annual growth rate hit 25.23%, and in 2004 the country's milk production reached 23 million tons, or 18 kilograms per capita, accounting for more than 4% of the world's total. According to a report published on a Chinese government website, by 2007 China was the world's third largest milk producing nation, after India and the USA. In that year, China had 14.7 million dairy cows and produced 36.5 million tons of milk, an increase of 7.8% over the output of 2006 (Zhang Yi 2008).

This rapid expansion turned out to be a curse in disguise. The dairy industry experienced a catastrophic blow in 2008–9 when melamine-contaminated milk produced by San Lu, one of the country's biggest milk processing companies, poisoned more than 300,000 infants and young children from mostly poor and rural families (Ramzy and Ling 2008). The chart below shows a sudden drop in production in 2011 and 2012 following the scandal, which was the result of the government's regulatory failure. After hitting 37.43 million tons in 2013, the country's milk production has since levelled off.

Encouraged by the meteoric rise in production at the start of the new century, the Chinese government set higher goals for the industry. Per capita milk consumption in China is way below that in countries in North America, Oceania and Europe. In 2007, an average Chinese person consumed 28.7 kilograms of milk and dairy products per year. In North America, Oceania and Europe, it was 224.1 kilograms. Even

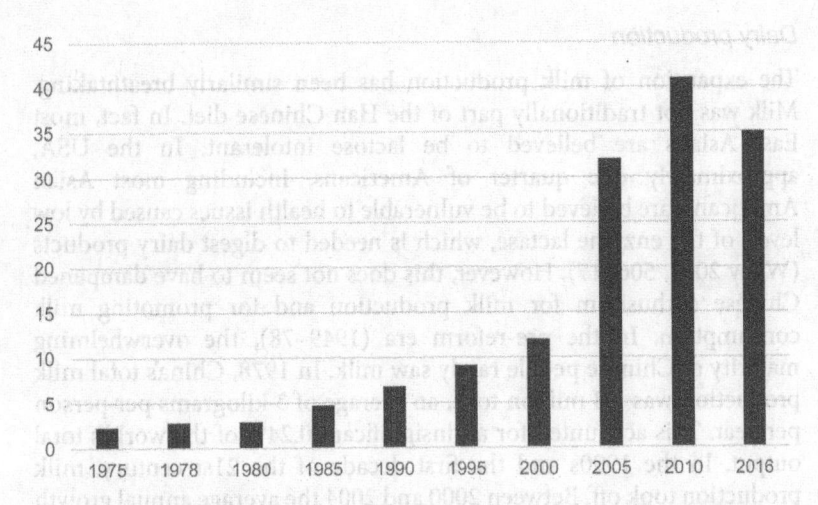

Figure 5.2 China's milk production, 1975–2016. Data Source: FAOSTAT 2017.

in India, a country with similar food security challenges to China's, an average person consumed more than 68.7 kilograms per year (FAOSTAT 2008). By 2012, per capita milk consumption in North America and the European Union had risen to 292 kilograms and 297 kilograms respectively, while in China it was only slightly higher than the 2007 level.

The Chinese government has taken various steps to encourage increased milk consumption. In November 2000, seven national government ministries jointly launched the "Student Milk" program on a trial basis, supplying milk to elementary school students. Prime Minister Wen Jiabao wrote in 2006 that his dream was for every Chinese person, particularly young children, to have a daily cup of milk (*Journal of Chinese Dairy Industry* 2006, 1). One year later, the government officially promoted the student milk program in its "State Council Document 31" (State Council 2007). In this policy document, which focused on making Chinese youth healthier and physically stronger, the State Council revealed its political objective in promoting the program. It called on the bureaucracy to appreciate the strategic importance of the healthy development of the dairy industry. Dairy production, the document said, was an integral part of modern agriculture and a source of income for peasants. It contributed to improved diet and stronger physiques. In order to achieve sustained and healthy development of the industry, according to the document, dairy farming operations should be standardised and intensified. The message was clear: milk was good for the economy and for building a strong nation.

The industry responded and, by 2014, recorded an output of 42 million tons, 15.6 times that of 1978 (2.7 million tons) (FAOSTAT 2005). By the end of 2014, 21 million of China's more than 100 million elementary students were being provided with daily milk (Xinhuanet.com 2015). Although the program does not yet cover the majority of students, the government's determination to expand the industry by cultivating a milk-drinking habit among young children is unambiguous.

Eggs

Like most food products, eggs were rarely seen in Chinese markets for much of Mao's era. In 1976, the country produced 2.3 million tons of eggs for its 900 million people, or an average of 2.5 kilograms per person annually. Most urban residents never received eggs in their monthly food rations. Eggs were sold only in major cities and were strictly rationed. In the reform era, egg production soared. In 1990, China's egg output reached 7.9 million tons, and this expansion has continued. In 2010, it reached 27.6 million tons. By 2014, China produced 29 million tons of eggs, or a per capita annual consumption of 19 kilograms (FAOSTAT 2015). These figures include chicken eggs; additionally, in 2013, China produced a 4.3 million tons of eggs from ducks and quails. The short supply of eggs is history.

China's accomplishment in ending the country's food security crisis in three decades has impressed the international community. The United Nations acknowledged China's poverty reduction results in a 2010 report. In June, 2014, China was awarded a prize by the UN Food and Agriculture Organisation for achieving the first Millennium Development Goal (MDG-1) of halving the number of its citizens experiencing extreme hunger, as compared with the 1990–91 figures.

Table 5.2 Milk output: China and the world compared, 1978–2017

Year	China's output (millions of tons)	World total (millions of tons)	China's output as % of world total
1978	1.1	411	.24%
1979	0.8	417	.19%
1980	1.14	422	.27%
1985	2.4	458	.52%
1990	4.2	480	.87%
1995	5.7	466	1.2%
2000	8.3	492	1.6%
2001	10.2	499	2.0%
2002	12.9	511	2.5%
2003	17.4	519	3.3%
2004	22.6	529	4.3%
2005	27.5	546	5.0%
2006	31.9	562	5.7%
2007	35.2	575	6.1%

5 Animal agriculture

Year	China's output (millions of tons)	World total (millions of tons)	China's output as % of world total
2008	35.5	587	6.0%
2009	35.1	591	5.9%
2010	35.7	602	5.9%
2011	36.5	612	5.9%
2012	37.4	625	5.9%
2013	39.8	767	5.2%
2014	41.8	794	5.3%
2017	34.4	828	4.2%

Government support for agriculture and the resulting increase in food production were identified as the two pillars of China's astounding accomplishment (Liu, Yu and Ge 2014). The UN Development Program also praised China's anti-poverty record as a model for other countries (UNDP 2015). "Food security success could not have been achieved without the growth of livestock production," a Chinese official from the Ministry of Agriculture commented.[2] International recognition of its development model has encouraged Chinese authorities to push for further expansion of livestock production.

---
2   Telephone interview with a national government official in Beijing, October 2016.

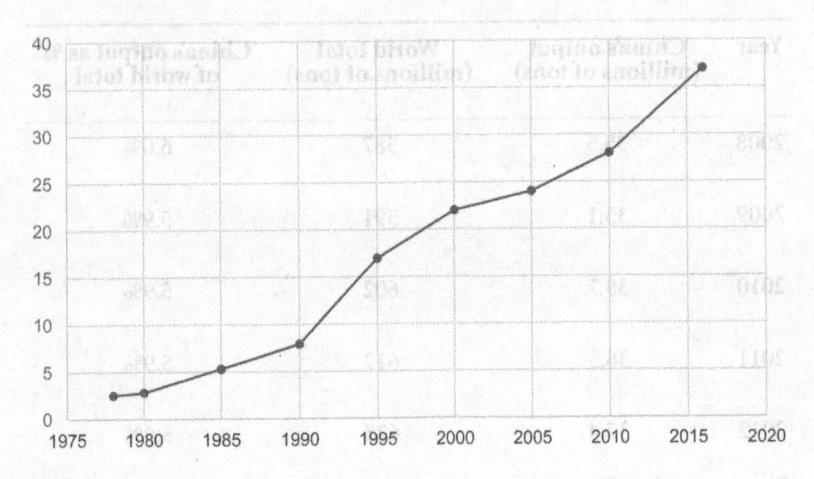

Figure 5.3 China's egg production, 1978–2016. Source: FAOSTAT (2017).

Explaining the phenomenal growth

What explains the phenomenal expansion of the country's livestock production in the span of three decades? What has been the government's role in the transformation of the livestock industry?

Intensification of production

In the pre-reform era, each rural household was a livestock farming operation. An average rural household in Jiangxi and Hunan in southeastern and southern China raised on average one pig, a few laying hens, and 10 to 20 ducks, geese, rabbits or chickens each year. Raising these animals required the intensive labour of at least four family members, outside their time spent labouring in collective farm work. Hunan and Jiangxi were China's grain producing provinces, with a natural environment that provided rich vegetation and agricultural by-products such as rice straws and vegetables from permitted household sideline productions. At least one third of China's 31 provinces and municipalities were not as well endowed. Rural households in parts of Shaanxi and Gansu were known to struggle and

5 Animal agriculture

could hardly raise one pig a year. Maoist collective rural production led to stagnation in food grain output. Livestock animals were mostly fed grain by-products and vegetables. In parts of Hebei province, however, food grains were barely enough for the peasants. Pigsties were typically built under the rural toilet, so that human waste could be used as pig feed. This ancient practice continued until surprisingly recently.[3]

In 1976, the last year of the Mao era, China produced 9.2 million tons of meat. This was the fruit of the labour of almost every peasant household (FAOSTAT 2015). A majority of the 192 million households in rural areas in 1976 were the producers.[4] The productivity of this enormous number of farming units was undeniably unimpressive. The per capita meat output in 1976 was less than 10 kilograms. Intensification of production with Western farming models was the decision of China's developmental state for the purpose of accelerating livestock production.

In the 1990s, intensification of production gathered pace with strong government support. A large number of rural households have since stopped livestock production and diversified their production into other agricultural products. By the end of the 1990s, more than one third of rural households had stopped pig farming. In 2003, there were still 108 million pig farms in the country. Small-scale operations (between 1 and 49 pigs) of peasant households accounted for 99% (107 million farming units) of all farms (China Animal Husbandry Yearbook Compilation Committee 2005, 225). China at the turn of the century had a population of 1.2 billion, 774 million (60%) of whom were rural residents. The intensification of pig farming has continued, with a drop in the total number of pig farms to 54.7 million in 2012 and 51 million in 2013 (China Animal Husbandry Yearbook Compilation Committee 2014, 186; 2015, 184).

---

[3] My investigation of peasant pig farming in Shijiazhuang region, Hebei province, as part of my study of China's animal agriculture conducted in 2005–6.

[4] The estimate of 192 million rural households is based on an aerage household size of four people. In 1976, the total population of China was 930 million, 17.44% of whom lived in urban areas.

Animal Welfare in China

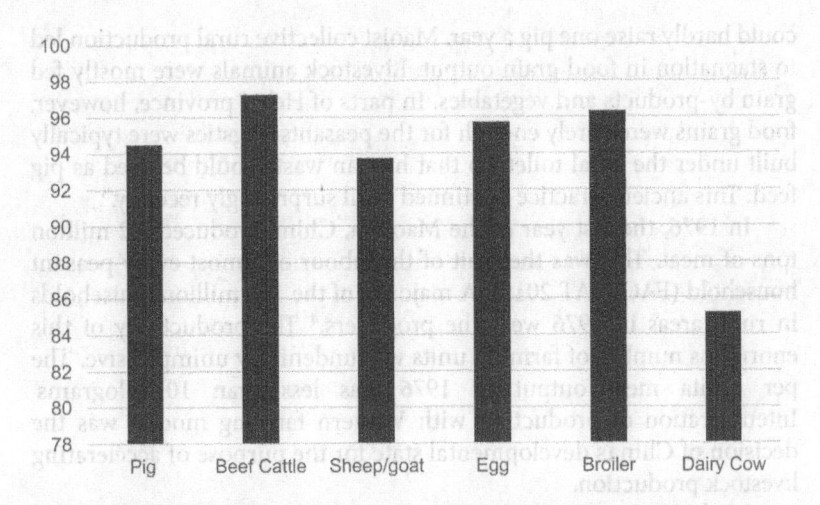

Figure 5.4 Peasant household farms as a percentage of the total number of farms in 2003, by type of farm. Data source: China Animal Husbandry Industry Yearbook 2004.

Despite the dominance of peasant household operations in terms of farm numbers, the small farms have been losing ground in production quantity. The 107 million peasant household operations (producing 1 to 49 pigs each) in 2003 contributed a disproportionate share (71%) of the total pork output. Some 29% of the pork output in that year was produced by 1.1% of the farms that raised 50 to more than 50,000 pig a year (China Animal Husbandry Yearbook Compilation Committee, 2005, 225–26). By 2013, the 4,769 farms that raised 10,000 or more pigs were producing a disproportionate amount of pork relative to small household-based peasant farms (China Animal Husbandry and Veterinary Science Yearbook Compilation Committee 2015, 184). This situation was also reflected in other livestock farms. The most intensified sector was broiler chicken farming. In 2003 there were more than 50 million small broiler farms (96.3% of all broiler farms), but these produced only 17% of the total chicken meat output (China Animal Husbandry Yearbook Compilation Committee 2004, 222–37). By 2014, there were only 23 million small broiler farms (i.e.

5 Animal agriculture

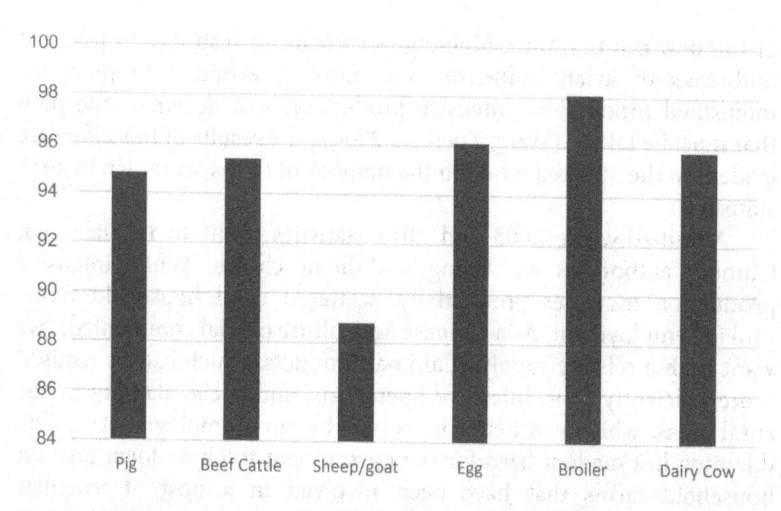

Figure 5.5 Peasant household farms as a percentage of total number of farms in 2013, by type of farm. Data source: China Animal Husbandry and Veterinary Science Yearbook 2015.

farms raising fewer than 2,000 chickens); these accounted for 98.1% of broiler farms but large, intensive farms (i.e. farms raising more than 10,000 chickens) produced far more meat for the markets (China Animal Husbandry and Veterinary Science Yearbook Compilation Committee 2015, 186). The reduction in the number of small household farms has come with an increase in the number of farms of scale.

The Chinese government has encouraged this intensification of production as part of its efforts to promote productivity and efficiency. In speeches by agricultural officials, the chief of the Agriculture Ministry and successive Chinese prime ministers, the authorities have made it clear that the future of China's animal farming industry is in more intense production. To the government, scattered peasant household-based farming operations keep productivity low and make disease control difficult.[5] Since the early 1990s, agriculture bureaus at the county and city levels have made efforts to assist the formation of centralised farming quarters or farming zones. In the first few years of the new century, the Chinese government, in response to frequent outbreaks of avian influenza, was more determined to push for intensified production. Intensive production was declared "the path that must be taken" (Wang Xuejiang 2004). The results of this effort are evident in the 50% reduction in the number of farms, as shown in 2013 statistics.

Admittedly, the 2003 and 2013 statistics point to the fact that Chinese authorities are facing a difficult choice. While intensive production increases productivity, scattered rural household farms provide employment. As a Chinese agriculture official commented, "we want both a reliable supply of animal products, which can be realised more efficiently from intensive operations, and social stability in the rural areas, which can better be served by rural employment ... The dilemma has made it hard for the government to close down peasant household farms that have been involved in a host of irregular practices, as long as no consumers are killed by consuming the problem products."[6] In China's post-socialist developmental state, rural employment and its impact on social stability weighs as much on the minds of officials as efficiency of production.

The Western farming model

One of the reform measures strongly supported by the Chinese government was the adoption of new production models and technologies. In Deng Xiaoping's words, it doesn't matter whether a cat is white or black, it is a good one as long as it catches mice. In other words, a production model is a good one if it achieves the desired economic results. In livestock farming, feed efficiency and productivity are the objectives. By the end of 2006, the Western factory farming model had penetrated some of the most remote regions of China, far beyond the country's more developed coastal regions, where foreign

---

5 See, for example, the speech by Qi Jingfa, deputy minister of agriculture, at the 1997 National Agricultural Work Conference, *China Animal Husbandry Yearbook 1999*. Beijing: China Agriculture Press, 2000, pp. 7–9.
6 Interview with a Northeast China official in charge of animal agriculture, 15 December 2014.

5 Animal agriculture

impact is more pronounced. Factory farming and its practices, tools and management methods, albeit in modified forms, had been adopted by farms in the inland and less developed regions.

The attraction of Western factory farming is not its scale of production, but the productivity and efficiency that can be achieved via other farming methods associated with the Western model. In pig farming, for example, there were still more than 50 million small farming operations, but they had all adopted factory farming practices to some degree in order to increase productivity. Despite rapid urbanisation, China has a huge surplus of rural labour. To the Chinese authorities, large-scale production may increase productivity and make animal disease control easier, but it does not serve the government's employment objective in rural areas. However, other Western factory farming practices and instruments have been adopted enthusiastically in China, as the following pages demonstrate.

Battery cages

While battery cages were being phased out in the European Union, Chinese enthusiasm for them was rising. The Chinese love of battery cages can be attributed to a belief in the "proven" advantages of the instrument: efficient use of space; reduced exposure to environmental and social hazards; reduced injurious pecking and bird mortality; easier monitoring of farming conditions; and lower biosecurity risks. These so-called advantages do contribute to productivity and efficiency defined in monetary terms, without considering the social, public health, environmental, and animal welfare costs. The Chinese industry and government departments who enthusiastically supported the wholesale introduction of this model admitted that they paid little, if any, attention to the animal welfare consequences of battery cage use, or to the restrictions battery cages place on birds' natural behaviour. To them, cage-related injuries such as wire-damaged claws were acceptable side effects.

Mutual pecking is acknowledged as a problem in battery cages, but it is largely dealt with by the modern farming practice of beak trimming. The seriously compromised health of laying hens, and the effects of drug additives in their feed, is not a concern for farmers.

It was not until recent years, thanks to rising consumer awareness, that Chinese agricultural agencies started to look more attentively at these issues. A series of food safety scandals involving the abuse of antibiotics, growth hormones and other controlled or banned substances triggered this attention. The health of consumers, not of farm animals, was the overriding concern of the country's regulators.

The farms I visited in Northeast China's Liaoning Province in December 2014 were typical layer farms. They each had five buildings, each housing 20,000 hens. Inside each building were four layers of battery cages stacked one over another on five rows of raised steel racks. Two hens were crammed into each cage, about 850 to 900 square centimetres in size. The farmers described battery cages as efficient and noted that "everybody is using them." Disease prevention was a major priority for these farmers, as it affects productivity and profit, and drug additives were routinely used. The discomfort of the hens, including self-mutilation and pecking injuries, was not considered an issue. No hen received individual attention and the same drugs were administered to all birds. On that trip in 2014, we also visited a new broiler farm under construction. What surprised us was that the owner planned to use battery cages to raise meat chickens.

One characteristic of China's animal agriculture is that Western farming practices are adapted to Chinese conditions. Battery cages are installed in makeshift sheds, in deserted factory workshops, and in farmhouses with poor ventilation and poor climate control capabilities. Stocking density varies. The most common practice is to fit two hens into one cage, with a space of less than 624 cm^2 per bird. De-beaking is used to avoid injuries caused by mutual pecking. Mortality can be as high as 10% or more, depending on the conditions and timeliness of drug intervention. One of the most common diseases on these intensified egg farms is cage-layer osteoporosis (CLO). As a solution to CLO, two Chinese scholars suggested opening the cages and allowing the hens to have access to open space (Zhu Xing and Hou Jiafa 2007, 27–28). Their recommendation has fallen on deaf ears. It is not a coincidence that this disease has been identified as a major health issue impacting Chinese egg farms in the last decade or so; the use of battery cages has swept across the entire industry in the same period.

5 Animal agriculture

Gestation and furrowing crates

Gestation and furrowing crates are Western inventions that ensure pregnancy and survival of piglets on breeding farms. Their attractiveness to the Chinese farm industry is obvious: they increase productivity, allow easy monitoring of the sows' and piglets' physical condition, allow more efficient use of space, and create a bigger profit margin (Gong Shaoqian and Bian Lizhen 2014, 4). Gestation and furrowing crates have been embraced by breeding farms across the country. In 2005, when I stepped into a breeding farm in a remote Jiangxi village, I faced rows of gestation crates waiting for their first occupants in a few weeks' time. Like battery cages, crates have been installed in breeding farms of all sizes and conditions. They were originally created for large-scale farming operations, but they have been adopted by backyard breeding operations with just a few sows. In modern breeding facilities, gestation and furrowing crates are standard equipment, with remote monitors watching the pregnant and breeding sows. They can be locked up in gestation and furrowing crates for up to 150 days. Because of their better "quality control" and productivity, the use of gestation and furrowing crates was strongly promoted by agriculture officials as part of the drive to adopt "modern" technology and production methods.

The use of battery cages and sow crates is a good example of the Chinese enthusiasm for Western factory farming methods. Again, agricultural production on the scale associated with Western factory farming is not currently attractive to authorities, because of the employment pressures faced in rural areas. Instead, it is the use of Western factory farming tools, technologies and production methods, albeit at a smaller scale, that makes livestock production "intensive."

Mutilation and early weaning

Mutilation is not new to Chinese farmers. Castration of male piglets and roosters used to be a common practice, to allow faster growth and growth beyond oestrus, rather than to eliminate boar taint or the like. Yet mass mutilation for productivity purposes is a Western invention and was introduced to China in the 1980s. Three of the most common types of mass mutilation, which traditionally did not exist in

China, now take place on Chinese farms. These are beak trimming, teeth cutting and tail docking, practised to reduce injuries caused by fighting in crowded conditions. In other words, these procedures are necessary to preclude or control what the industry calls the "vices." These procedures were unnecessary in traditional farming, where a peasant household raised only one or two pigs and a few free-roaming chickens. (My investigations have confirmed that tail docking is less widely practised in China than beak trimming. Pig tails can fetch a high price in China, like pork livers and pork stomach, as they are favoured by Chinese consumers.)

Early weaning is another pervasive practice in modern livestock farming, also for productivity purposes. Weaning of piglets in China now generally takes places on the 21st day after birth, one or two weeks earlier than in traditional breeding operations. Weaning of dairy cow calves – which was not part of the traditional farming operation in China's dynastic past – is introduced even earlier, a practice introduced from the West. Some can be separated from their mothers as soon as two or three days after birth to allow the mother cows to return to a new birth cycle. Early weaning is stressful physically and psychologically (Weary and Chua 2000, 177–88). China has over 14 million dairy cows, suggesting a staggering number of cows and newly born calves going through mental agony caused by early weaning (FAOSTAT 2015).

Drug use

China faces a serious food safety problem. A 2015 study of China's food safety scandals presented a gruesome picture. Between 2005 and 2014, select Chinese media reported 227,386 major food safety incidents. Despite the 2008 melamine-contaminated milk scandal, by 2011 there were 38,000 food safety violations. Meat and dairy products had the biggest share of violations, accounting for 9% of cases. The majority of violations (60.61%) happened in the course of food production (China Food Industry 2015, 12–14). Many of these scandals, such as the Shuanghui case of pork laced with clenbuterol (a banned synthetic steroid used to increase lean meat), implicated tens of thousands of small producers (Jiang, Jessie 2011). In 2013, 18 kinds of antibiotics were detected in chicken raised in Shandong and served in KFC outlets

5 Animal agriculture

(China Economic Information Net 2012). It was no secret that irregular drug use was rife among the 700,000 intensive operations in Shandong province (China Animal Husbandry and Veterinary Yearbook Compilation Committee 2014, 74). Nationally, China used four times the volume of antibiotics used in the USA in 2007, although its meat output was only 65% higher (68.7 million tons vs 41.6 million tons) (Zhu et al. 2013, 3435–40).[7] Sun Jungong, spokesperson for China's Supreme Court, revealed that the country's food safety situation was extremely grim. Across the country, cases involving the production and sale of products in violation of food safety standards increased by 179.8% between 2011 and 2012. Cases involving the production and sale of toxic and harmful food products grew by 224.6% in the same period (Zhao Xiaona 2013).

In January 2017 it was found that MCR-1, a gene detected by Chinese scientists in 15% of raw meat samples and 21% of pigs under study in 2015, is spreading around the world. MCR-1 positive bacterium can fend off colistin, a last resort of antibiotics (Liu Yu-yun et al. 2016, 161–68; Zhang, Sarah 2017).

The inappropriate use and abuse of industrial chemicals, human drugs, banned chemical compounds and antibiotics in farm animal feed are no secret in China. The Chinese authorities, agriculture experts, and the general public have expressed concerns over the food safety implications of meat from heavily dosed farm animals (Agriculture Ministry 2002; Li Zheng and Wang Yunjian 2009, 55–57). Clenbuterol was banned in 2002 by the Chinese government but has been used by pig farmers regardless. This so-called "muscle creator" or "magic potion" can reportedly cause pigs to gain up to 100 kilograms in a month. The primary objective in using such substances is increased productivity and/or feed efficiency through reduced growth times.

None of these methods are part of the traditional Chinese farming practice. The use of chemical compounds is an imported method. Factory farms in the West have long relied on a wide variety of growth-promoting substances. In the USA, for example, lactam antibiotics, including penicillins, lincosamides and macrolides including erythromycin and

---

7   China's much higher use of antibiotics could suggest two things: the abuse of antibiotics, or the greater need for them due to poor farming conditions.

tetracyclines are used in the pig industry. These antibiotics and their combinations are also used to treat infections in humans (Hughes and Heritage 2004, 129-52).

Drug abuse and public health implications

Landmark research, conducted by a nationally funded project team associated with the Guangzhou Geochemical Research Institute of the Chinese Academy of Sciences, produced some shocking findings. According to the scientists involved in the project, China in 2013 used 162,000 tons of all kinds of antibiotics, accounting for half of the total amount that was used in the entire world that year. Of the 162,000 tons of antibiotics, 52% was used to prevent and control livestock diseases. A considerable amount was also used more specifically to promote growth.

My 2005-6 investigation of Chinese farms in the country's major livestock farming regions confirmed that all used antibiotics "when necessary" in animal feed for disease prevention (Li, Peter 2009, 217-40). Antibiotic abuse has caused serious pollution in the areas of the Hai He River and Pearl River. In another study, mainland Chinese researchers detected the presence of antibiotics in animal waste and animal feed on every Chinese livestock farm they studied. The most shocking finding was that various kinds of antibiotics were found in a single livestock feed (Hu Mingqi 2015). The same study, based on a different total tonnage of antibiotics, i.e., 92,700 tons in 2013 as opposed to 84,240 tons in the same year of the Guangzhou Geochemical Research Institute project, focussed on 36 kinds of the most common antibiotics including amoxicillin and florfenicol. Of the 92,700 tons of these common antibiotics used in animal agriculture in 2013, 53,800 tons entered the water system in the form of urine and excrement. The regions or river basins with high antibiotic concentrations were those provinces with a higher level of livestock production (Zhang Qian-qian et al. 2015, 6772-82). China's overuse of antibiotics has caused international concern. The World Health Organisation warned of antibiotic overuse and launched the first World Antibiotic Awareness week in November 2015 (Shan, Juan 2015).

By the end of 2012, Chinese consumers had come to believe that quality control was better in Western fast food chains such as McDonald's and KFC. In 2012, China's national CCTV broadcast a series of reports on the broiler farms supplying KFCs in China. These farms were found to be using antibiotics meant for humans and other banned drugs to accelerate weight gain in broiler chickens. Ribavirin, an antibiotic used mostly in human hospitals, was found on farms in Shandong. According to China's regulations on animal drug use, human drugs cannot be used in livestock production. A broiler farm was also found to be using amantadine hydrochloride, a veterinary drug banned in 2005 by China's Agriculture Ministry. Use of dexamethasone as a growth promoter was common. This drug is used to boost feed intake and increase broiler weight by 500 grams within three to five days (Jinghua Times 2012b).

Physical wellbeing and disease control

The preceding section does not pretend to cover all aspects of China's animal farming industry. It attempts to show that Chinese enthusiasm for the new farming model has contributed to the rapid expansion of the industry. What average Chinese consumers do not know are the welfare implications of the new model and its new practices. Both scattered household farms and large-scale operations in China have displayed animal welfare problems common in concentrated animal feeding operations around the world (D'Silva 2006, 53–58; Li, Peter 2009, 217–40). Outbreaks of epidemics on farms is an animal welfare issue, and Chinese researchers have identified several prominent health issues affecting the country's livestock production.

Poultry farming and avian influenza

In a study in southeast China's Zhejiang province, researchers found that broiler farms suffered from a high rate of illness, multiple infections, appearance of new and uncommon infectious diseases, increasing cases of viral infections and parasitic diseases, and cases of illnesses from unknown or a combination of triggers. The causes of these patterns of illness were poor farming conditions, poor management, arbitrary use of drugs, failure to follow vaccination procedures, lack of technical training for farm workers, and shoddy drugs and vaccines (Jin Junjie et al. 2012, 10–12). These problems are not confined to the farms in Zhejiang. They are common across the country. On 9 August 2013, the "7th summit of healthy livestock farming forum and new broiler farming technology" was held in China's biggest broiler farming province, Shandong. This national conference was held in response to the media exposure of "fast-growth chickens" and chicken meat containing high levels of drug residue, and the outbreak of H7N9. Epidemic control on Chinese farms was identified as a major challenge for the industry. On average, between 1.5 and 1.7 yuan is spent on drugs for each broiler chicken in China. In contrast, the cost of drugs per chicken in the USA was believed to be only 0.5 yuan (Zhu Xuesong 2013, 32–41). While the Chinese researchers identified farm conditions (high density, poor ventilation, poor humidity and poor climate control) and questionable farming practices (incorrect administration of drugs, overdose of antibiotics, incorrect use or use of faulty vaccines) as contributing factors, one of their recommendations for controlling and preventing illness among farm animals was further intensification of livestock production. Apparently, the researchers blamed the problem on the farmers rather than on the production model.

Lameness is another problem caused as much by the modern factory farming technique of selective breeding as by poor farming conditions. On Chinese farms, lameness can affect up to 20% of broilers, according to industry insiders. Some 20% of the total value of broiler production is lost to illness and related causes, and lameness is one of the major contributors. It is no secret to animal welfare experts that growth promoters and antibiotics accelerate weight gain, resulting in crushing pressure on the legs and feet (D'Silva 2006, 53–58). This pressure becomes greater as slaughter time approaches. Abnormalities in gait, skeletal abnormalities, and diseased joints are all symptoms of poor welfare conditions and unhealthy breed selection practices, which are common on Chinese poultry farms. Other illnesses such as ascites and cardiovascular problems can be attributed to the production model and associated technology.

5 Animal agriculture

Chinese layer and broiler farms are dominated by operations with less than 10,000 and 30,000 animals respectively. Due to limited financial capabilities, small producers in China are more motivated to maximise profits through the exploitative use of existing farming spaces. Farmers are under pressure to pay off loans or investments as soon as they can. Western farming technologies and practices provide them with a way to achieve these goals faster. There are farmers who would not hesitate to bend the rules. They admit using drugs arbitrarily and administering doses five times greater than recommended when frantically fighting to control diseases. Shandong chicken farmers have been known to use some 20 different drugs, including 18 different antibiotics (China Economic Information Net 2012). The misuse of veterinary drugs has been such that drug-resistant bacteria and viruses have become a major concern (Liu Yu-yun et al. 2016, 161–68).

The outbreak of H5N1 illustrates the extent of the welfare crisis on Chinese chicken farms. According to a study by Chinese researchers, there were more than 100 incidents of H5N1 between 2004 and 2013. More than 80 cases were recorded in 2004 and 2005 alone. The destructiveness of H5N1 was such that it forced the Chinese authorities and the industry to take the disease seriously (Zhang et al. 2014, 497–503). The frequency of disease outbreaks including H5N1 and others on Chinese chicken farms has increased in number. Between 2010 and 2015, for example, there were 113 major epidemic outbreaks affecting the chicken farming industry (Agriculture Ministry of China 2016). The real number may have been even higher, as not all outbreaks were necessarily reported to authorities.

The first reported outbreak of H5N1 occurred on poultry farms in Hong Kong in 1997. In February 2004, H5N1 hit farms in 16 provinces on the Chinese mainland. Nine million poultry were reportedly culled. In August 2005 and October 2006, further outbreaks were reported in multiple provinces. There have long been suspicions that H5N1 had in fact broken out earlier on the mainland, sometime between 1996 and 2004, and that this information was suppressed by local governments. According to the World Health Organisation, three Hong Kong residents were infected with H5N1 in February 2003 after travelling to Fujian on the mainland, although Beijing did not report an outbreak of H5N1 in 2003 (World Health Organisation 2012). "Farm animal disease outbreaks are a hugely sensitive subject that local officials would not want to make public," one provincial agriculture official told me, on condition of anonymity. "No local officials want to see their animal products rejected on the market."

In 2008, six cases of H5N1 outbreaks were reported on Chinese farms, and in 2009 there were a further three (World Health Organisation 2012). Chinese scientists also identified other variants of the avian influenza such as H7N9, H5N8, H10N8, H5N3, and H5N6. This massive outbreak is not surprising if we take into account the trajectory of poultry production between 1978 and 2013. The high frequency of avian influenza outbreaks on chicken farms in 2008 correlated with exponential increases in production. Broiler production had accelerated at the turn of the century and by the end of 2003 there were over 65 million egg farms and 50 million small-scale chicken farms in China. The outbreaks of H5N1 have woken up Chinese authorities to the need for more careful disease control. However, the official consensus was that scattered or small peasant household farms were more vulnerable to the transmission of the avian influenza from wild birds, and that further intensification of poultry production was the only solution (Wang Xuejiang 2004).

"Wild birds have taken much of the blame for the spread of H5N1 across the world," according to a report by Compassion in World Farming. However, the charity pointed out, there was "evidence showing that the development of highly pathogenic strains of bird flu lies at the door of factory farming." The report, titled "The Role of the Intensive Poultry Production Industry in the Spread of Avian Influenza," showed that "an intensive poultry farm provides the optimum conditions for viral mutation and transmission," and that breed selection has "left birds' immune system less able to cope with infections and there is a high degree of genetic uniformity in the population, making spread of the virus all the more easy." The report warned that "intensive farming is creating highly virulent avian 'flu strains'" and that the global trade routes for shipping live poultry and poultry products across national borders were replacing birds' migratory routes as the primary pathways of bird flu transmission (Compassion in World Farming 2007). At the time of this chapter's writing, the Chinese poultry industry and agricultural agencies had failed to acknowledge the connection between intensive farming and the outbreak of bird flu.

Pig farming

Pig breeding farms, both big and small, use sow crates enthusiastically. The EU has banned the use of sow crates, but Chinese industry and agriculture experts do not believe China is ready for a similar move, citing concerns that it would decrease productivity. Leg problems are common on breeding farms. In one of my visits to a small breeding farm in southeast China, 20 of the 101 sows could barely stand up due to hoof damage. During a field trip in 2014 to a medium-sized breeding farm in a Northeast Chinese city, I found that bar biting occurred among 10 to 20% of the sows on that farm. "Sows that are used to the crates are generally lethargic or sleepy, while first-time occupants are always restless," one farm technician told me. Sanitation and sterilisation of the environment are two challenges for most breeding facilities in China. "Traditionally, Chinese peasants raised one or two pigs in squalid sheds in their backyards," the technician continued. "Most pig farm owners come from a peasant background and have low awareness of the importance of following the sterilisation protocol."

Hoof damages were known to trigger other illnesses among the sows. Poor farming conditions often exacerbated the welfare problems on the farms. According to Chinese evaluations, an increasing number of sows on most breeding farms are culled because of foot diseases (Wu et al 2011, 44). Culling was adopted not so much to end suffering as to reduce economic losses. One breeding farm owner admitted that on his farm of 1,500 breeding sows, crates did a lot of harm. Most sows weighed between 200 and 250 kilograms. On average, their crates were 50 to 60 centimetres wide and just long enough for an adult sow to take two steps forward and two steps backward. Lack of exercise and the crushing weight on their hind legs caused a high percentage of sows to experience foot and hoof problems. As well as restricting the animals' movement, confinement prevented them from displaying natural behaviours, and caused stress that led to the deterioration of their immune system. "As soon as a sow is impregnated, her 'imprisonment' starts,'" the farm owner admitted (Gong Shaoqian 2014, 4).

Fattening farms, or "growing farms," account for the largest share of pig-farming output in China. In 2012, there were 55 million small pig farms, each raising between 1 and 999 pigs (China Animal Husbandry Yearbook Compilation Committee 2014, 191). These small farming operations are no less intensive in terms of their use of factory farming practices. Sterilisation is carried out intermittently. Flies were out of control on all the farms we visited in the summer of 2014. Environmental barrenness was another prominent problem: straw beddings, which can reduce boredom, reduce stress on pigs' feet, and provide comfort, were absent at all the farms I visited in 2005, 2006 and 2014. Tail-biting and chewing of pen-mates were common.

Sanitation issues have also long troubled peasant pig-farming operations. On average, China loses 25 million pigs a year to disease. In 2012, the World Organisation for Animal Health confirmed that foot and mouth disease had hit a farm in north China's Hebei province (Perkins 2012). The outbreak that most shocked the world was the emergence of a new epidemic that hit 26 Chinese provinces in 2007: the mysterious blue-ear pig disease, a highly infectious and highly fatal reproductive and respiratory illness. Nationwide, more than 2 million pigs were infected and 400,000 of them died. In many places, entire farms were wiped out. By September 2007, it had reportedly swept across over half of the Chinese provinces, causing a pork supply crisis and pork price hikes of nearly 87% (Cha 2007). As mentioned earlier, the most shocking discovery by Chinese scientists in 2015 was MCR-1 that can reportedly fend off colistin, human's last resort of antibiotics (Liu Yu-yun et al. 2016, 161–68; Zhang, Sarah 2017).

Live transport

China covers a territory of 9.6 million square kilometres. The distance between Urumqi in Northwest China and Shanghai on the east coast (3,275 kilometres) is greater than that between Moscow and London (2,509 kilometres). China also has world's biggest population, with 1.3 billion people. This vast territory contains some of the world's longest

5 Animal agriculture

transport routes, connecting regions of production with centres of consumption. In the 1970s and 1980s, a train loaded with live cattle from Inner Mongolia could travel for two days nonstop before reaching the border between mainland China and Hong Kong. As the livestock industry has expanded, farming operations have become more concentrated in the country's grain-producing regions. Rapid urbanisation has also pushed animal farming further from urban centres. Chinese consumers have traditionally preferred fresh meat or "warm meat" to frozen, and this culinary preference has continued, though largely among the elders. Meat from freshly slaughtered animals is considered not only tastier, but also safer. The result is an elaborate live transport system that ships millions of animals daily, by water and by land, to the various centres of consumption. Figure 5.6 shows four major consumption centres with some 300 million consumers, and the source provinces of live transport (Appleby et al. 2008, 290–91). The Pearl River delta (Guangzhou–Shenzhen–Hong Kong) in South China is arguably one of the world's biggest consumption centres of animal products, with close to 40 million people. Live animals come from as far west as Sichuan and as far north as Heilongjiang, near Russian Siberia.

Within China, farm animals are transported live to three main destinations: wet markets (where animals are sold live and are often slaughtered on request for customers), slaughterhouses, and the trans-provincial trade. Despite the inroads being made by supermarkets, wet markets remain important in sub-provincial regions of the country. Slaughterhouses, meanwhile, have been increasingly centralised, as part of an attempt by the authorities to improve disease control and prevention. Traditional slaughtering practices, whereby butchers slaughtered animals in farmers' backyards, are rare today. Centralised slaughter operations can potentially improve animal welfare if proper measures such as electric stunning were strictly implemented. A major drawback of modern slaughter operations, however, is welfare problems during transportation. As farms near the major metropolitan centres are closed or have been moved further away, the transport time between farms and slaughterhouses is extended. This increases time spent by animals in cramped conditions, increases the risk of accident, and worsens the wellbeing of the animals. In February 2016, a fire on a sheep transport truck in Guangxi burned

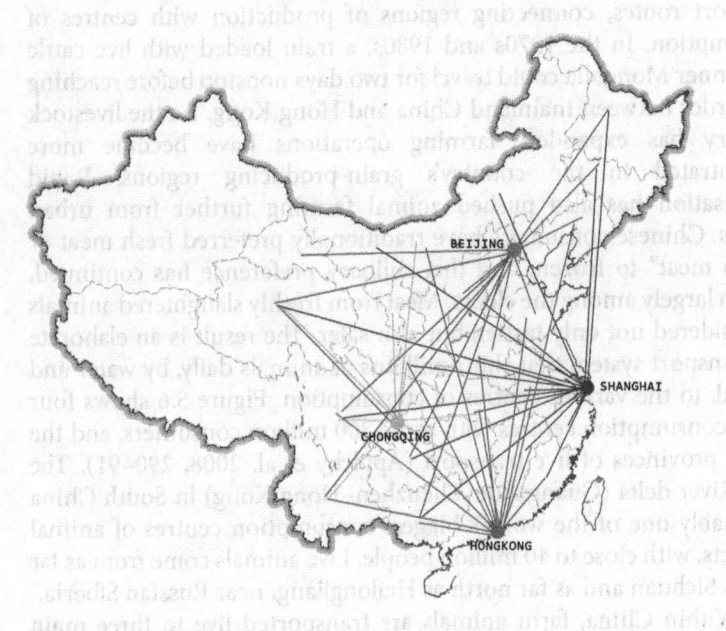

Figure 5.6 Transport Routes to the Four Major Consumption Centres

300 sheep alive (Xinhuanet 2016). Each year, road accidents send thousands of pigs to agonising deaths from injuries such as broken limbs and backs.

The trans-provincial livestock trade centres around wholesale livestock markets for producers who fatten, breed, transport or slaughter farm animals. Such markets also attract traders from surrounding provinces. For example, Zhangbei Livestock Trading Centre in Hebei province used to be the biggest livestock trading venue in north China, drawing traders from 18 provinces. All animals intended for local wet markets were first transported there. Although many animals are slaughtered at the market in front of customers, some are sold live or shipped to other places. These animals endure long journeys before reaching their final destinations.

There are four major livestock consumption centres in the country. These are the Hong Kong/Greater Pearl Delta Region, the Shanghai/

5 Animal agriculture

Nanjing Region, Beijing/Tianjin Region and the Chongqing Region. Each of these is a mega market for animal products. Take the Hong Kong/Greater Pearl Delta Region as an example. Hong Kong alone receives millions of live farm animals from the inland provinces. In 1952, the Chinese government started Express Train 751, a special rail service to transport live animals from Wuhan to Hong Kong, a distance of 919 kilometres. Later two more special trains were added: the 753 and 755, originating in Henan and Shanghai, covering 1,393 kilometres and 1,232 kilometres respectively. Beef cattle, pigs, sheep and other livestock animals could have been shipped over 500 miles from the farming regions to Wuhan, Henan and Shanghai before embarking on the final train ride to Hong Kong. By 2006, when express train 751 was suspended, Wuhan had shipped on average 250,000 live pigs a year to Hong Kong (Jiang Yuebo and Wu Zhiyuan 2006). These train services have now been replaced by trans-provincial highway truck transport. The majority of the 1.5 million pigs slaughtered annually in Hong Kong are supplied via the inter-provincial highways. Pigs raised as far north as Henan, and as far west as Sichuan, endure excruciatingly long journeys before reaching Hong Kong.

One of the longest transport routes links Tongliao in Inner Mongolia with Hong Kong. This route covers 2,500 kilometres. Up until 2013, Tongliao had shipped over 10,000 live cattle to Hong Kong on a yearly basis, accounting for half of the live cattle transported to Hong Kong from the mainland each year. A combination of factors such as reduced profit margins, increased consumption on the mainland, and the high death rate of cattle during the long journey, caused this number to drop by half in 2013 (Niu Tianjia 2013, 2). While shipments from the mainland of frozen beef and mutton have increased to make up the short-fall, Hong Kong has been looking at other potential sources of live cattle, such as Southeast Asian countries.

Urbanisation and environmental concerns are driving livestock production further away from China's other major consumption centres. The Greater Shanghai Region is the country's second largest manufacturing centre, with a population of more than 24 million. Inner Mongolia is the most distant supplier, while Jiangsu is the closest. In 2005, Shanghai accelerated efforts to phase out livestock farming to nearby Anhui, Zhejiang and Jiangsu provinces. This suggests that more livestock would be transported over greater distances to centralised slaughterhouses near the city. Broilers transported by truck come from as far as Hebei and Shandong provinces in North China (an average distance of 1,085 kilometres or more), while sheep and cattle come from Inner Mongolia (an average distance of 1,770 km).

Beijing-Tianjin is the third major livestock consumption centre. Beijing, a metropolis of more than 21 million people, slaughtered 12 million pigs in 2014. Yet the suburban areas were able to supply only 2.9 million pigs to local slaughterhouses (Zhou Ke 2016). Pigs from the nearby Hebei province filled the gap. At the turn of the century, Hebei's live animal sales to Beijing accounted for more than half of its total outbound sales of farm animal products. Slaughter operations in Hebei and Shandong also supply the Beijing market. Pigs were shipped to these facilities from different parts of the two and other provinces.

Live transport has animal welfare implications. In order to cut down the time spent on the road, drivers resort to uninterrupted travel, without stops to feed or water the animals. Lack of awareness of animal welfare, indifference to animal suffering, and widespread violation of related government regulations have led to the prevalence of cruel practices, such as forcing cattle or pigs to jump off trucks without a ramp. The most shocking cruelty is the illegal practice of forced watering, whereby pigs and cattle are forced to drink large quantities of water to make up the weight loss caused during transport. Some traders go so far as to pump mud through a hose into the stomach of the pigs awaiting slaughter in an attempt to add additional weight to the animals. In a campaign to eliminate such brutal and illegal practices, the Agriculture Ministry called on local agricultural departments to take punitive actions against the perpetrators (Lin Hui 2016).

China's geography and demographics pose further challenges to welfare improvements for farm animals. Accelerating urbanisation will stimulate both the growth of animal agriculture and live transport. People aged 55 and above are "ferocious" meat eaters. These are the people born during the Mao era and who lived through the Maoist "tyranny of scarcity." Food deprivation and hunger are fresh in their collective memory. Many from this age group are consuming meat and dairy products in a "compensatory fashion." In my 2009 article on China's livestock industry, I referred to this consumption mindset as revenge meat consumption. The sheer number of these consumers, who care more about the quantity of meat they consume than the quality, make animal welfare campaigns by NGOs, as well as government nutritional recommendations to eat less meat, difficult; both can look out of touch with the country's reality.

Live animal exports and imports

Besides domestic live transport, China imports a massive number of live animals. In the pre-reform era, China imported a very small number of live farm animals for breeding purposes. Today, it is one of the top importers of foreign pedigree breeds to replace its existing and degenerating stock. In 2003, for example, 1,797 pigs, 1.2 million hens and 45,000 dairy cows were imported for breeding purposes. Between 2009 and 2011, more than 240,000 dairy cows were imported to replace the existing low-yielding stock. Between 1978 and 2013, China imported 775,317 cattle and buffalo. In the same period, it imported 37,642 sheep, 15,694 goats, 203,139 pigs, and 55 million chickens (FAOSTAT 2014). In its spending on importing livestock for breeding purposes, China dwarfs most other countries. For example, in 2010 China spent $117 million US dollars on the import of live cattle and sheep. In 2016, spending went up to $173 million US dollars. China was the biggest destination for Australian cattle (94,000) and sheep (6,400) for breeding purposes (Australian Financial News 2017).

Export of China's meat and dairy products is insignificant. These products are mainly for domestic consumption. Despite efforts to export live sheep to the Middle East, the death of sheep in the course of transportation during the 1990s caused huge damage to the reputation of Chinese sheep farmers (CCTV 2005). Sheep exports peaked in 1993, when China exported 320,518 sheep, mostly to the Middle East. The export trade then plummeted to 1,183 sheep in 1999, rebounded to 145,269 in 2004, and decreased again in 2012 to 576 (FAOSTAT 2014). In 2013, China announced that it had signed an export agreement with Jordan, Kuwait and other Middle Eastern countries for the export of 200,000 live sheep (Zhang Wei 2013). Live farm animals sold to the Middle East are reared in China's remote inland provinces, more than

700 kilometres from the coast. This compounds the animal welfare issues involved, as they are transported long distances by road before beginning another long journey on the high seas.

The footprints of the state

The expansion of China's animal agriculture is not an accident. It has all the hallmarks of deliberate government policy. Agriculture was the first target sector of the government's reform program. Ending hunger by encouraging rural development was a top priority for the party, and the reforming state adopted thousands of new policies designed to create a favourable policy environment for the expansion of livestock production. It is not an exaggeration to say that China has a national obsession with food security.

Since time immemorial, food availability has been the top concern of the Chinese people. While Westerners greet each other by saying "How are you?" the Chinese traditionally greet each other by asking "Have you eaten?" The meanest insult in China is to condemn someone to be a "hungry ghost," the equivalent of "going to hell" in the West. This collective fear of hunger perhaps reflects the long history of famine in China. Between the founding of the Western Han dynasty in 206 BCE and the collapse of the Qing dynasty in 1911, there were 2,073 recorded famines. Of the 2,117 years during this period, 826, or 39%, experienced famine (Teng, Su and Fang 2014, 26–32). For much of the 20th century, China failed to escape hunger. Understandably, the Chinese obsession with food security has been a determinant of food-related policymaking. This obsession may also explain a higher level of awareness among the Chinese of the need to save money for contingencies like famine, job losses, natural disasters and other events beyond human control.

The Chinese government's obsession with food security was also a reaction to the food security crisis it had created between 1949 and 1978. Between 1959 and 1962, a policy-induced famine claimed the lives of more than 30 million peasants (Yang Jisheng 2013; Becker 1998). Peasants accounted for more than 80% of the Chinese population. Rural poverty was such that the post-Mao leadership feared a mass peasant revolt. Hunger in the Maoist era had driven millions to Hong Kong and the Soviet Union (Liu Huoxiong 2010; Xinjiang Academy of Social Sciences 2013). Peasants from some of the most devastated regions, such as Anhui and Henan, spent much of the slack seasons begging across the country (Zhang Guangyou 1995, 154–61). In the pre-reform era, compulsory state procurement of rural products at prices set by the state destroyed peasants' enthusiasm for production: "Hunger breeds discontent." The post-Mao leaders feared that the party's legitimacy would erode further if they did not put an end to rural poverty (CCP Central Document Research Institute 2004, 238, 380, 381, 450–51). Regime stability was therefore a strong motivator for the rural reform program. With agriculture identified as the key target sector for the reform program, livestock farming received much attention from China's post-socialist developmental state.

Future growth and challenges

The Chinese government sees animal agriculture as a new frontier for future rural growth. Rural meat and dairy consumption are still below the national average. In the view of the Chinese authorities, animal agriculture should increase to make up 50% or more of the rural economy. They agree that China may never catch up with North America, Western Europe and Oceania in per capita meat and dairy consumption, but it could certainly be higher, for example, than the 63 kilograms per capita consumption recorded in 2013.

Politics is behind China's animal farming industry. Rural employment and stability are important drivers for the sustained growth of animal agriculture. In 2003, 50% of the income growth of Shannxi peasants came from livestock production. The contribution of animal agriculture to peasants' income in the province has continued since then (Zheng Shaozhong 2003). Anhui, a major livestock producer, had six million people working directly and indirectly in the industry in 2015. Animal farming accounted for 12.3% of the average household income. In some areas, 50% of the household income comes from livestock production (Anhui Agriculture Commission 2006). Since Anhui lags behind most provinces in per capita GDP, the provincial government is particularly motivated to protect and expand the industry, a source of income for the peasants.

Similarly, Henan is China's biggest animal farming province. Livestock production has grown from 20.9% as a percentage of the total provincial agricultural output in 1991, to 24.4% in 1993 and 32% in 2016 (Zhang Xingjun 2017). Henan is also China's most populous province, with a population of 100 million in 2010. Among the 31 provinces, it ranked fifth in total GDP in 2015. Yet its per capita GDP ($5,297) ranked 22nd, lower than the national per capita GDP of $7,943, and considerably lower than the top two provinces ($14,142 for Jiangsu and $12,501 for Zhejiang). Henan leaders saw animal agriculture as a means to fuel rural growth and catch up with the rest of the country. The provincial leaders expected livestock production to increase to 40% of Henan's total rural agricultural output.

Nationally, 123 million rural households were "employed" in animal agriculture in 2013.[8] This means that about 246 million people, half of the rural population, depended on livestock production for their livelihoods. The importance of livestock production to rural employment and rural stability is undeniably clear to the Chinese authorities.

Conclusions

Food security is an obsession of China's reformist state for good reason, and this explains why the state has proactively shaped and assisted the country's livestock production. China's post-Mao developmental state needed food security to defuse social unrest. Since 1978 the Chinese government has dismantled old production systems, abolished policies that suffocated peasant enthusiasm, and adopted new policies to encourage autonomous and diversified production.

Animal agriculture is no ordinary industry. It is a strategic industry that serves the party's political objective of rebuilding its legitimacy.

---

8   For the number of households involved in livestock production, see *China Livestock Industry and Veterinary Science Yearbook 2014*. Beijing: China Agriculture Press, 2015, pp. 184–89.

5 Animal agriculture

And the industry's political importance has allowed the adoption of Western farming models and practices that enhance productivity with huge animal welfare consequences. Productivity has been the sole criterion to determine the usefulness of the Western farming model and its practices. The use and abuse of drugs and other substances have reached unprecedented levels. Intensification of animal agriculture is continuing in China. The Chinese authorities have not yet realised that pandemics are more likely in concentrated animal feeding operations that place a large number of animals in crowded conditions. China has stepped out of a food security crisis, only to find itself facing a burgeoning food safety, environmental, and public health challenge.

China's animal agriculture has political importance. It is a top employer in the rural economy, and has thus served the state's political objective of stabilising the countryside, traditionally where revolts toppled dynasties of the past, and where the Communist revolution began. The livestock industry is a source of income for half of the rural labour force. It is key to sustained growth and to decreasing the divide between the rural and urban people, which is another source of social conflict. The ruling CCP has held that the peasantry's problems are the whole country's problems. Rural stability is the foundation of regime stability. Since animal agriculture serves the regime's objective of political stability, problems such as animal welfare concerns, environmental pollution and the risk of pandemic have been secondary. The outbreak of COVID-19 should have served as a warning to the Chinese authorities that neglecting such problems could also have an impact on the stability of the regime.

6
Protection or utilisation: revising the wildlife protection law

The Wildlife Protection Law (WPL) of the People's Republic of China, adopted in 1989, was supposedly the country's first national legislation for animal protection. Its adoption towards the end of the 1980s was not an accident. Deng Xiaoping's economic reform set rural labour free, sanctioning production activities that peasants never could have dreamed of in the pre-reform era. The most entrepreneurial and audacious of this labour force ventured into wildlife farming. This new industry soon called for state policy support and regulation. The 1962 State Council *Directive on the Reasonable Use and Protection of Wildlife Resources*, an executive order to curb unbridled hunting activities from 1959–62, was not designed to manage the wildlife farming industry. During the 1980s, hunting and illegal capture of state-protected rare and endangered species got out of control. As the trustee of the country's wildlife resources, the Chinese government felt the need to curb poaching activities and to legalise state support for wildlife farming, a commercial operation that was useful to the state's political objective of fighting poverty and providing rural employment.

To add to the grim situation facing China's wildlife, a decline in arrow bamboo, a staple food of the iconic giant pandas, in northwestern Sichuan, threatened an entire population of this breathtakingly beautiful species. In the early 1980s, international collaboration and foreign financial input were attractive to China's financially strapped wildlife management agencies. One way to access international resources was to join the Convention on International Trade in Endangered Species of Wild Fauna and Flora (CITES). As a full member of the organisation, China was obligated to adopt a domestic wildlife protection law. This domestic law was also needed to regulate wildlife farming and to curb unbridled hunting. China's National People's Congress (NPC) therefore adopted the *Wildlife Protection Law of the PRC* (WPL) in 1988, the country's first ever national law purportedly for animal protection. The law went into effect in March 1989.

The 1989 WPL was by and large a wildlife utilisation management law. It was concerned with managing and protecting a fledging industry. How wildlife animals were raised and what conditions they were farmed in were not on the minds of the people involved in drafting the law. As a result, the 1989 WPL closely reflected the government's economic objectives The law sanctioned farming operations that have since been the target of domestic and international criticism. In the 1980s, expertise in captive wildlife behaviour and captive breeding was limited to a small number of scholars and wildlife experts, who believed that conservation or wildlife protection would be meaningless if protected wildlife were not utilised for human benefits (Ma Jianzhang, Chao Liancheng and Luo Zexun 1985, 70–78). These experts have since the mid-1980s become the main source of intellectual support for the government's wildlife policy.

In the early 1980s, the Chinese government and society at large were preoccupied with ending the country's oppressive food shortage crisis. Environmental protection, wildlife protection, and even questions of justice for Chinese migrant workers, women, minorities and religious groups could barely attract the attention of policy-makers or the public. Concern for the wellbeing of captive wildlife and for ecological balance could not have been a consideration for the NPC when the WPL was being drafted in 1988. Very few people in China were familiar with the concept of "animal welfare" at the time.

6 Protection or utilisation: revising the wildlife protection law

A worsening crisis

Contrary to the expectations of the country's wildlife management authorities and of the public, China's wildlife crisis has worsened since 1989. A wide range of wild animal species have since faced unprecedented threats from illegal poaching and other activities. The Chinese sturgeon, a native and endangered species on the Yangtze River, saw a drastic drop from some 10,000 individuals in the late 1970s to 263 in 2000 to fewer than 100 in 2017 (Fan Chunxu 2014; Hong Kong on.cc 2017). Wildlife eating, a culinary subculture of South China's Guangdong and Guangxi and a consumption promoted by wildlife breeders, traders and the exotic food catering businesses, became a nationwide "passion" at the turn of the century. The outbreak of SARS in South China's Guangdong in 2002-3 led to an exposé of the country's wildlife wet markets, where wild-caught and captive-bred wild animals were openly sold for food, slaughtered, disembowelled, skinned, dehaired and chopped into pieces (Epstein 2003). Wildlife eating was such that snakes, owls, and eagles were rarely seen in the wild, but mice were out of control (Li, Peter 2007).

Having depleted wildlife from China's mountains and valleys, Chinese wildlife traders went abroad for live animals, animal parts and by-products such as bears and bear paws, pangolins, monitors, sea turtles and even North American turtles (Bond 2013; RT.com 2016). Chinese tourists have even crossed the borders to neighbouring countries to eat wildlife (Mong La 2016), hunt for trophies (Yang Siqi 2016) and smuggle high-priced wildlife products or raw materials into China (Thornycroft 2013). Of the 2,062 marine turtles confiscated internationally between 2000 and 2008, mainland China was implicated in 2,017 of them, accounting for 98% of the whole specimen trade (Lam et al. 2012). Between 2010 and 2014, China was the biggest buyer of Canadian polar bear hides, importing 42% of the total Canadian export (Weber 2015). China has been the main destination for transcontinental ivory trafficking since 2008. Between 2010 and 2012, more than 100,000 African elephants were killed (Maisels et al. 2013). Some 50% to 70% of the illegal ivory was believed to have been shipped to China (Gettleman 2016). As a newcomer to trophy hunting, China was the second largest destination for African rhino horns between 2009 and 2018 (CITES Trade Database 2019).

In May 2015, to mark International Biodiversity Day, China's Ministry of Environmental Protection and the Chinese Academy of Sciences jointly released the *China Biodiversity Red List*. Created by 213 experts and scientists working in five teams, the list evaluated 4,357 vertebrates (673 species of mammal, 1,372 species of bird, 461 species of reptile, 408 species of amphibian, and 1,443 species of inland fish). It found that the trend of decline in China's biodiversity had not been curbed. A lot needed to be done, and urgently, to rectify this. Of the 4,357 vertebrate species (excluding marine fish) that were appraised by the Chinese scientific team, 17 were listed as extinct, extinct in the wild, or regionally extinct. Nine hundred and thirty-two species were listed as critically endangered, endangered, or vulnerable, accounting for 21.4%. Of the 4,357 species, 1,598 are endemic to China. A little over one third of these are threatened (Ministry of Environmental Protection and Chinese Academy of Sciences 2015).

The Chinese public is aware of the crisis. Wildlife use has been losing public support. In 1998, a public opinion survey conducted by the International Fund for Animal Welfare found that a majority of the respondants opposed bear farming (IFAW 1998). A 2016 survey on bear farming confirmed that there was a public consensus on the need to end the practice. Among the respondents, only 10% were loyal consumers of bear bile products, while 70% had never used these products. Of the 70% who had never used bear bile products, 90.2% said that they would not purchase the products in the future. More than 97% of respondents believed that bear farming was cruel and 83.9% thought the industry should be outlawed. Only 2.4% of respondents believed that bear bile was irreplaceable (Diao 2016).

In May 2016, results of a survey of public attitudes to the use of pangolins were released at a press event in Beijing. More than 80% of the respondents agreed that consumption of pangolin meat and the use of pangolin scales in traditional Chinese medicine should be outlawed and 90% said that they were willing to participate in pangolin protection activities (SWChina.org 2016). Earlier, a study of Chinese attitudes towards rhino use, rhino poaching and rhino protection found that there had been a 23.5% reduction in the belief that rhino horns had a medicinal effect, and that 95% of the respondents who did not consume rhino horn supported stricter government action against rhino use. Among those who did consume rhino horn products, 87% believed stricter regulations were needed (WildAid and African Wildlife Foundation 2015).

By the end of 2013, there was a consensus among concerned parties and the public that the 1989 WPL should be revised. The outbreak of SARS in 2002–3 triggered a new wave of public and scholarly discussion of the failure of the WPL. In 2007, I joined the Chinese conversation (Li, Peter 2007, 71–108). In 2013, Chinese authorities began efforts to revise the 1989 WPL. When the first draft of the revised WPL was released for public comments on 1 January 2016, legal scholars, wildlife experts, animal protectionists and wildlife business interests alike reacted enthusiastically (Chang Jiwen et al. 2015). An unspoken competition between two camps – groups against wildlife utilisation and the wildlife business interests – ensued and lasted until mid-2016, when the National People's Congress (NPC) Standing Committee voted in favour of the final version of the revised law.

To get a better understanding of the revised WPL, let's first take a look at the 1989 WPL.

The 1989 Wildlife Protection Law

As the first animal protection legislation, the 1989 WPL attracted an unusual amount of public attention and criticism. The criticism came from both the opponents of wildlife exploitation and representatives of wildlife business interests. By mid-2016, Chinese scholars and activists had focused on several important areas they believed made the law ineffective. Neither were wildlife business interests satisfied with the 1989 WPL. They saw the law as a hindrance to productivity. There was frustration among the wildlife industry that the law had failed to protect and advance their interests. Underlying all of these criticisms was a consensus among critics and industry that the law was outdated, had failed in its mission, was a roadblock to achieving their respective objectives and must be revised.

The purpose of the law

The purpose of the 1989 WPL was most criticised. The law had three objectives: protection of rare and endangered species, promotion of reasonable or rational use of wildlife resources, and protection of ecological balance. Critics of the law focused on the idea of "reasonable use of wildlife resources." Tian Song, a Beijing scholar, argued that as an objective, "reasonable use" was fundamentally flawed. In his view, the 1989 WPL prioritised human conquest of nature over conservation of the natural environment. It was therefore a "wildlife utilisation law," not a wildlife protection law. He explained as follows:

> The 1989 WPL was enacted on the basis of the ideology of industrial civilisation and of anthropocentricism. Wildlife was designated only as a resource to be protected in the interest of humanity or to be protected for advancing the interest of the Chinese nation. There are many controversial articles in the law for using wildlife. In actual implementation, the WPL has in fact turned into a "wildlife utilisation law." Furthermore, the WPL has failed in many ways to protect wildlife animal species. As a result of its endorsement of and legal support for wildlife use, the WPL has helped endanger those species that were defined as having "utilisation value" … In the past centuries of industrial civilisation, the biosphere has come to the brink of collapse. Humanity must walk away from industrial civilisation and embrace ecological civilisation … Let's walk out of anthropocentrism and recognise the value of nature as a subject.
> (Tian Song 2016, 47–49)

Tian Song's criticism of this "utilisation" objective was shared by others. They argued that "utilisation" should not have been included in the objectives of the law. Chang Jiwen et al. argued: "First, utilisation cannot be the objective of protection. The principal purpose of wildlife protection is the maintenance of ecological balance and biodiversity … Second, the biggest threat wildlife is facing comes most directly from human use of wildlife. And third, the so-called 'reasonable use' can never be defined accurately. What has happened is that 'utilisation' has taken precedence over 'protection.'" (Chang Jiwen et al. 2015). To He

6 Protection or utilisation: revising the wildlife protection law

Hairen, a senior legal researcher at the Law Institute of the Chinese Academy of Social Sciences, utilisation, if it is to be included in the legislation, should be expressly limited to non-profit purposes (He Hairen 2016).

Business interests and their supporters were on the opposite side of the debate. They held that "protection cannot be achieved without utilisation." This has become the standard line used by businesses and ironically some officials from the State Forestry and Grassland Bureau (SFGB) when the utilisation objective is questioned. "Protection in the abstract does not exist," one provincial wildlife management agency official said emphatically in a meeting to discuss WPL revision. "Wildlife utilisation can serve the purpose of protection." This argument was also the official position of the SFGB, the national government agency for wildlife protection and management.

There are two other critical points regarding the objective of "reasonable utilisation" in the WPL. The first is that, instead of being designated as an objective, "wildlife utilisation," if it has to be included in the law, should have been in provisions about wildlife management. Specifically, "wildlife utilisation" is not an objective of the law but rather a productive activity that should fall under the articles related to state management and regulation of the wildlife industry. The second point is that there is a rising awareness of the irreplaceable ecological functions of wildlife and the need for humans to change their utilitarian attitudes towards wildlife. The inclusion of wildlife utilisation as an objective in the 1989 WPL ran counter to global progressive change (Chang Jiwen et al. 2015).

When animal protectionists sarcastically call the WPL the "wildlife utilisation law," they are not exaggerating. Of the 42 articles of the 1989 WPL, only eight address "protection" while 17 relate to the management of wildlife use. The word "protection" appears 48 times. However, words denoting human use of wildlife animals, such as domestication, breeding, wildlife resources, and utilisation, appear more than 90 times. Most glaringly, "ecological balance," one of the three purported objectives of the 1989 WPL, is mentioned only once in the document. The WPL's critics believe that the contradicting objectives of the law make it self-defeating (Li Xiaoxi 2003), that domestication is erroneously equated with wildlife protection (Zhang

Endi 2002), and that the law reinforces a utilitarian attitude towards wildlife (Mang Ping 1999, 174). The consequences of this utilitarian outlook, supported by the WPL, are disheartening for the critics. The population of musk deer, for example, dropped from 1,665 in 1985 to 100 in 1996 (Hu Tianhua and Li Tao 2003, 4–5). Other wildlife species that have become critically endangered include the long-armed black gorilla (from 2,000 in the 1970s to 19 in 2000) and baiji, the Yangtze River dolphin (from 187 in 1985–87 to 5 in 1999) (Mei Zhiqiang 2003, 24; Hu Benzhen 2003, 28–30). In 2006, Chinese scientists feared that baiji may already have become extinct (Lovgren, 2006).

The scope of protection

The limited and questionable protection scope of the 1989 WPL is another issue. The 1989 law listed 410 nationally and provincially protected species under Category I (109) and category II (301).[1] These lists have been criticised as too limited in number. Rare, endangered, and other species of economic and scientific value were protected under Article 2 of the WPL. To the critics, this designation created problems of adverse impact. Species were included under state protection so that they could be used. Further, the use of population size or endangered status as the basis for protection ignored the fact that all the animal species in nature were part of an ecological community. In other words, endangered species or other vulnerable species should be protected not because of their value to humans but because of their value to the health of the ecological system.

Protecting some species while excluding most others could harm the completeness and unity of the ecological system. It created a group of privileged species, protecting the so-called "beneficial" while neglecting others. Critics of the law argued that the notion of "beneficial" species was seriously flawed. The emphasis on human benefit and the economic value of wildlife animals should be replaced

---

1 For a complete list of the protected species under the Chinese Wildlife Protection Law, see "Appendix I: List of State-protected Wildlife Species" in Hua Huilun and Yin Jingwen, ed., *Protected Animals in China* (Shanghai: Shanghai Science and Technology Press, 1992): 565–77.

6 Protection or utilisation: revising the wildlife protection law

by a recognition of the ecological value of these species (Chang Jiwen et al. 2015). Besides the need to redefine "wildlife animal species," the critics proposed that changes should be made to the scope of protection. More species should be placed under state protection, and inclusion should be determined not by their value to humans but by their ecological function in nature. These protection lists should be updated periodically. Importantly, wild animals should be left alone in their natural habitats. Captive breeding of wild animals should be limited to the level needed to save and protect the population in the wild. No commercial breeding of wild animals should be allowed.

Other critics feared that including a species in the protection lists could even speed up its extinction. In the last 40 years, wildlife consumption has spiralled out of control across the country. This is a new type of consumption that did not previously exist at the same scale. The claim that such wildlife consumption is traditional, that it can be traced back to ancient China, and that there is a demand for wild animal meats is misinformation spread and perpetuated by the country's wildlife breeders and owners of exotic food restaurants. I have studied China's wildlife farming and restaurant industry for the last two decades. Never have I found evidence to support the claim that China had a tradition of widespread wildlife consumption. Wildlife eating did exist in ancient China, particularly in the peripheral regions of the Chinese empire in times of hunger, and among some people on a more regular basis. There was no difference between ancient Chinese eating wild animals such as frogs, turtles and (more rarely) snakes and people eating game meat in other parts of the world. Wildlife eating in ancient China was rare, limited to specific regions and situations. Its existence in the past on a limited scale should not be surprising. As an occasional practice, wildlife consumption should not be interpreted as part of mainstream Chinese food culture. It was more an emergency measure for the poor to survive times of extreme food deprivation. By claiming that China has a tradition of eating wildlife, traders can risk violating laws in their efforts to encourage the consumption of protected species.

In the last 5,000 years of China's recorded history, there is no evidence in ancient records or classic literature of wildlife breeding on a scale even remotely resembling what is happening in contemporary China. China's massive wildlife farming operations and related businesses such as the production of wildlife feed, trans-provincial transport of live captive-bred and hunted animals, production of veterinary drugs, and the hundreds of thousands of exotic food restaurants are part of a business empire that has arisen in the last 40 years. Attributing this wildlife-exploiting empire to traditional Chinese culture, and thereby suggesting that it is something to be proud of, is a tactic designed by businesses to shut up the critics.

To promote the consumption of wild animal meats, the industry has in the last four decades gone out of its way to connect wildlife consumption with a wide range of alleged benefits. Wild animal meats have been promoted as good for health, for longevity, for fertility, for sex, and for fighting and preventing diseases. In their aggressive and rather bold promotional efforts, the industry has been known to use national public health crises to advertise questionable and controversial traditional medicines. In 2003, Guizhentang donated bear bile to Beijing's Xiaotangshan Hospital for use on SARS patients. In April 2020, it once again donated the controversial "drug," purportedly to fight the COVID-19 pandemic. In April 2020, Chinese and international media reported that China's national public health authorities had included tanrenqing, a traditional Chinese medicine injection containing bear bile, as one of the government-recommended drugs for treating COVID-19 patients (Nguyen 2020).

In April 2020, we conducted a survey in 50 cities across 22 Chinese provinces to confirm whether wildlife consumption is part of the mainstream food culture in China. Of the 211 households that participated in the survey, none kept snake or scorpions, or meat from deer, civet cat, bamboo rat, porcupines or other wild animals available at the market in their home refrigerators. If such foods are not eaten in typical Chinese households on a regular basis, can they be called traditional or mainstream parts of Chinese food culture? There is generally speaking no consumer demand for wild animal meats in China. The "demand" has been created and promoted by wildlife business interests. In 2003, China imposed a ban on the trade and consumption of wildlife in order to contain SARS. It was the wildlife industry, not Chinese consumers, that engaged in active lobbying to have the ban lifted. China has the world's only "Strategic Meat Reserve," a national food emergency response mechanism in case of a sudden

6 Protection or utilisation: revising the wildlife protection law

drop in meat supply caused by natural disasters or man-made situations. The "Reserve" stores livestock products such as pork, beef, mutton, chicken, egg and dairy products to be delivered to the markets to balance supply and demand. Wild animal meat is not part of the Reserve. In China, if pork supply were adversely affected by production shortages or other factors, people would demand that the government address it. The Chinese government can rest assured that mainstream Chinese consumers will not protest if the supply of snake meat or porcupine is disrupted.

Instead, the exotic food business has its eyes on a particular group of consumers: those who are rich and powerful. To this small number of socially irresponsible diners, eating the most rare and endangered animals is not shameful or unlawful. It is considered a status symbol (Baker 2014). Chinese officials, including some of those responsible for protecting the country's wildlife, have taken part in wildlife consumption. In 2012, Jiangxi local forestry bureau officials were implicated in the illegal killing of protected monkeys sold to local restaurants for official catering events (CCTV 2012). A more recent case involved officials in Guangxi who used endangered pangolin to cater official diners from Hong Kong on official duties to the Interiors (Soho 2017).

The issue of animal welfare

The welfare of wild animals is not generally addressed in the WPL. China does not have anti-cruelty legislation that might deter and penalise cruelty to animals in zoos, breeding facilities and other venues where wild animals are displayed or raised. The State Forestry and Grassland Bureau (SFGB) does not consider the welfare of captive wildlife its responsibility. Critics of the WPL disagreed with the SFGB and have complained that the Bureau has the responsibility for the wellbeing of wildlife animals in captivity, since China does not have comprehensive anti-cruelty legislation. They also believe that the SFGB, which is in charge of wildlife animals captured for captive breeding, should have responsibility for ensuring the wellbeing of captive wildlife.[2] In fact, the SFGB did take the lead in 1997 in laying down the basic standards for managing bear farms. The tentative regulation banned the use of catheters, corsets and young bears for bile extraction. To the critics, including provisions on the wellbeing of wild animals in captivity was not an excessive demand.

Compensation

The question of compensation to farmers for damage caused by protected species has also attracted criticism. The 1989 WPL (Article 14 of chapter two) stipulated that "local governments shall provide compensation for damage to agricultural producers or for any other damage caused by protecting the state or locally protected species." This article was particularly controversial for several reasons. First, it did not specify which local government – provincial, sub-provincial or county – was responsible for compensation. Most provincial governments did not come up with compensation measures. As a result, township authorities engaged in a tug-of-war with county and city governments to avoid paying compensation (Chang Jiwen et al. 2015).

Second, regions where wildlife protection was most needed were also the least developed areas of the country. Local authorities were financially strapped. Their unwillingness to compensate victims of wildlife damage was well known and to some extent understandable (Li Shizhen 1994, 3–4). Should the level of compensation be lower in less developed regions (Chang Jiwen et al. 2015)? While local authorities were unwilling to compensate farmers for damage done by wildlife, they have never hesitated to use local wildlife "resources" to "raise funds," which allegedly go towards wildlife protection. In the northwestern provinces, for example, hunting grounds were created for foreign hunters. Fees collected were reportedly used to protect the animals (BBC 2006).

Third, the 1989 WPL did not specify the source of the compensation funding. Critics suggested that the national and provincial governments should create a special "state compensation mechanism" so that the national government could subsidise nature reserves and provide compensation for damages and human casualties caused by protected

---

2   Interview with Mme Qin Xiaona, director of Beijing Capital Animal Welfare Association, 12 March 2016.

6 Protection or utilisation: revising the wildlife protection law

species (Chang Jiwen et al. 2015). They believed that wildlife protection could not be "downgraded" as a local government responsibility. The national government, with its command of greater resources, should not shirk its responsibility as the trustee of the nation's wildlife. If the national government created nature reserves, it must invest in them. Correspondingly, the national government should earmark special funds to fight wildlife crimes (Mang Ping 1999, 155–59; Ma and Chen 2003, 52–53).

Fourth, the scope and standards of compensation were absent in the 1989 WPL. Critics believe that losses from protecting wildlife species should be divided into two categories: primary and collateral damages. They asked if compensation for collateral damage was even covered by the law. Article 14 did not address damage to human life, human health and other related property damage. The 1989 WPL did not specify if compensation was symbolic. It did not say if compensation was to be determined by local economic conditions or if there would be one set of compensation standards for all localities, regardless of the local level of development. Shouldn't compensation be paid in full and in line with the actual cost of the loss (Chang Jiwen et al. 2015)? These were important questions not addressed in the 1989 WPL.

The compensation for damage caused by the protected Asiatic elephants in Yunnan was a classic case of the state's failure to compensate the affected farmers in full. In Yunnan's Nanpin alone, in the second half of the 1990s elephants caused damage of 1.6 million yuan, a staggering amount to the farmers still mired in poverty. Yet the local and provincial authorities only paid 14,000 yuan in compensation.[3] Critics suggested that full compensation, not symbolic compensation, should be implemented, so that wildlife protection would not be undermined (Chang Jiwen et al. 2015). As to the scope of damage compensation, they propose including personal loss, property loss (including primary and collateral damages), and compensation for mental injuries. With regard to the level of compensation, they believe in full compensation in line with the actual loss regardless of the level

---

3 Personal conversation with Dr Zhang Li in September 2003. See also Li Yumin (1994).

of economic development of the regions concerned. Compensation amounts should also be adjusted periodically (Chang Jiwen et al. 2015).

Critics believe the national government should be responsible for compensation, and that this should be stated unequivocally in the law. The state has a civil responsibility, not just an administrative responsibility, to pay compensation. County governments and administrative units in charge of nature reserves are responsible for delivering compensation payments, but national and provincial governments should budget special subsidies to be provided to provincial and sub-provincial governments. The WPL should also specify the level of financial contribution to be made by different levels of government and how it should be shared between them. Donations from society for compensation purposes should be permitted (Chang Jiwen et al. 2015).

Nature reserves

Nature reserves did not receive adequate attention in the 1989 WPL. Only three articles addressed them: Article 10, stating the importance of establishing nature reserves for protected species; Article 20, prohibiting unauthorised hunting in the reserves; and Article 34 on the legal responsibilities for damages to nature reserves. In the years following the adoption of the 1989 WPL, conflicts between the management of nature reserves and land-use rights have become prominent. According to the state Land Management Law, state-owned or collective-owned land can be contracted for business purposes. When a nature reserve is established, land-use rights in the area are unavoidably impacted. Land users' freedom of operation are restricted or reduced. The state, as the custodian of the country's wildlife "resources," has the legal responsibility to compensate land users for resulting losses.

The creation of nature reserves has to be scientific and reasonable. The law calls for consideration that balances the interest of ecology and the interests of the various stakeholders. Once a nature reserve is created, government reacquisition of land and government compensation for losses should be implemented to ensure wildlife protection (Chang Jiwen at al. 2015). By the end of 2014, violations in nature reserves had become rampant. Inadequate state financial input and failure to compensate farmers were the major contributing factors. Unsurprisingly, provincial and national nature reserves have been shrinking in size to allow development projects to proceed (Nanfang Zhoumo 2011).

Wildlife farming

Wildlife farming, a most controversial example of wildlife use, has drawn intense criticism since the commercial enterprise took off in the 1990s. In addition to animal welfare problems, questionable conservation claims and illegal restocking from the wild, wildlife farms have been conducting illegal wildlife activities under the disguise of legal farming operations (Tang Yifang 2014). Legal experts believe that farming operations conducted for profits should be distinguished from those for scientific and population recovery purposes: "All measures must be taken to stop commercial breeding of tigers, lions, bears and other endangered species. Businesses that breed tigers, bears and other rare and endangered species must be resolutely banned." They proposed government takeovers or buyouts as an approach to closing down problem farms. The government should draft a "phase-out plan" for wildlife farming or set up a "phase-out mechanism." Equally important, the authorities should promote alternative research and production when revoking the use of bear bile and other wildlife ingredients. Carcasses and body parts from protected species should not be allowed to be traded and should be used for scientific research purposes only (Chang Jiwen et al. 2015).

Noticeably absent was any discussion of the public health consequences of China's massive captive breeding operations. The neglect of this problem by the Chinese legal and wildlife experts at the time of the WPL revision was not surprising. By the end of 2015, China had not seen a SARS-like pandemic in 11 years. The Chinese public and the authorities seemed to have forgotten that SARS was connected to the country's wildlife trade. In March 2010, Zhong Nanshan, China's top medical scientist, warned that the risk of a pandemic was still there unless the country's wildlife breeding and trade were suspended. Using his opportunity to attend the National People's Congress at the time, Professor Zhong revealed to the media that scientists had not too long ago found coronavirus in wild animals sold in Hong Kong and Wuhan

(Wang Pu, Sun Xuan and Yu Ying 2010). His warning did not cause a stir. Professor Zhong could not have been consulted by the National People's Congress in the course of the WPL revision.

Hunting

Hunting is another divisive issue. In regions where wildlife animals are abundant, some experts propose to ban leisure hunting, commercial hunting and trophy hunting. Hunting can be permitted only if it serves the objective of reducing the pressure of overpopulation. Supporters of hunting, however, argue that a ban would result in price hikes for products sourced from hunting, creating conditions for illegal hunting activities to flourish, and thus accelerating the extinction of target species. Besides, a hunting ban would jeopardise the livelihood of hunters if a compensation mechanism were not in place. To opponents of such bans, hunting can be conditionally permitted for livelihood, for the control of wild populations, and for the public interest. As to leisure hunting, hunting rights for domestic and foreign hunters can be granted on condition that ecological balance is achieved and when the wildlife population has surpassed the level needed for population recovery. Commercial hunting should be strictly restricted and eventually banned. Hunting purely for fun and for showing off should be banned (Chang Jiwen et al. 2015).

Wildlife eating

Consumption of wildlife for food is closely connected with wildlife farming and trade. It is therefore a matter that should be addressed by the WPL. The consumption of wildlife meat has been blamed for the survival crisis facing wildlife species. In the last three decades, wildlife eating, once a habit of a small number of people in South China, has spread across the country and become a status symbol. The authorities have encouraged this habit among the rich and powerful by endorsing the farming, trade, slaughter and sale of wildlife animals. In August 2003, soon after the end of SARS, the State Forestry Bureau announced that 54 species of wildlife animal had been successfully domesticated

(State Forestry Bureau 2003). These animals were allowed to be traded, slaughtered and prepared as food.

In China, there are three discernible positions on the issue of wildlife consumption. Animal protectionists argue that the eating of wildlife animals should be banned, and that the 1989 WPL should be revised to arrest the country's runaway wildlife consumption. Apart from those wildlife animals used in traditional Chinese medicine, most, whether bred in captivity or caught in the wild, end up in exotic food restaurants and other catering businesses. Animal protectionists blame the 1989 WPL and its endorsement of wildlife use for the spread of wildlife eating. Others, including wildlife farming business interests, defend wildlife eating as part of Chinese food culture. They cite the State Forestry Bureau's endorsement of the 54 domesticated wildlife animals to support wildlife eating and their business operation. Their defence of wildlife eating is effective when they argue that the farming operation also serves the state's objective of poverty reduction.

A 2017 report on China's wildlife industry claimed that as many as 6.2 million farmers were employed in 2016 in wildlife farming to supply the country's exotic food market (Ma Zianzhang et al. 2017, 104). Some legal scholars, meanwhile, take a middle ground, arguing that wildlife consumption will gradually reduce as the economy develops, and as environmental protection awareness among consumers increases (Chang Jiwen et al. 2015).

Conservation challenge

Protection of wildlife, particularly of endangered and rare species, was the first objective of the 1989 Wildlife Protection Law (Article 1 of Chapter 1). Conservation should have been the top priority of the government's wildlife management. However, the 1989 WPL treated conservation as an instrument, not an objective. The mission of the WPL was in fact economic modernisation to be fulfilled through wildlife protection or conservation. This is why the law explicitly promotes commercial activities that utilise wildlife "resources" as a state-sanctioned approach to conservation, endorsing the commercial interests of the country's wildlife businesses. Wildlife breeders and traders have been the loudest defenders of the industry for its alleged role in conservation.

Both the Chinese authorities and businesses with an interest in wildlife farming have claimed that wildlife farming helps conservation (Yang Wenming 2017). They argue that the amount of bile collected from one farm bear in a year is equal to that collected from 220 bears killed in the wild. Defenders of the bear farming industry claim that the wild bear population has increased from 30,000 to 60,000 individuals thanks to bear farming.[4] Critics have long questioned the industry's conservation claims, and recent studies contradict the argument that wildlife farming is aiding conservation.

In China, Asiatic black bears are a Category II state protected species. China is estimated to have no more than 20,000 bears in the wild. Despite the large number of bears bred in captivity, bear cubs captured from the wild are a cheaper way for farms to replace unproductive old bears. A team of researchers under Professor Piao Zhengji of the Changbaishan Academy of Science in Jilin found that between 1986 and 2010, Asiatic black bear and Asiatic brown bear populations in the Changbaishan nature reserves had gone down by 93.4% and 38.8% respectively. This drastic decline coincided with a booming bear farming industry in that part of the country. Professor Piao and his collaborators argued that the decline of the bears' natural habitat and poaching were the two major contributing factors (Diao 2016; Piao et al 2012, 66–72).

Illegally captured wild bears have been used to re-stock bear farms. Moreover, bile from bears caught in the wild is considered to be more potent and valuable than that extracted from farm bears. To its critics, wildlife farming has failed its alleged conservation mission, and this failure can be attributed to the government's support of wildlife farming, going back to the 1989 Wildlife Protection Law.

---

4 Remarks made by an owner of a bear farm from an unpublished transcript of the speeches made by representatives of China's wildlife farming and use industry at an internal meeting on the revision of the Wildlife Protection Law sponsored by the State Council Economic and Development Research Institute, p. 14.

6 Protection or utilisation: revising the wildlife protection law

State and business interests

The failure of the 1989 WPL has other, more formidable contributing factors. Besides the flaws of the legislation itself, the Leninist party-state, the power dynamic between local and national authorities, and an alliance between the state and business interests have also undermined the authority of the law.

Institutional obstacles

The Chinese government is a complex bureaucratic web with horizontal and vertical power relationships (Lieberthal 2004, 186–88). Politically, provincial authorities must abide by political directives from the Party Central Committee. While provincial governments hold budgetary and personal powers over all the functional departments and bureaus, these provincial departments and bureaus receive professional directives and orders from the corresponding ministries in the national government. The side effect of this power relationship allows more power to the provincial authorities because of their control over budgets and the officials' career advancement. Provincial departments and bureaus are therefore more compelled to respond to the demands of the local authorities than to the directions of the national government ministries (Mertha 2005, 791–810).

In wildlife management, the Wildlife Protection Department of the State Forestry and Grassland Bureau (SFGB), formerly the State Bureau of Forestry, is the functional administrative agency of the national government. Provincial wildlife protection agencies report to the SFGB in Beijing on professional matters related to nature reserves, wildlife management, and wildlife trade. However, provincial wildlife agencies are also dependent on the provincial authorities that control their budgets and personnel decisions. In practice, provincial wildlife agencies defer more to local governments than to their national superiors. The result is that local objectives take precedence over the objectives of the national functional departments. Since failures in wildlife protection are not a threat to the regime's stability, the national government has tolerated local non-compliance.

Local forestry officials and their national counterparts are both working in an environment that gives priority to wildlife utilisation. They have no ideological conflict over the designation of wildlife as a natural resource to be used for human benefit. However, national government objectives in wildlife management do not always line up with local interests, and calls to enforce the WPL have often been met with local resistance. As a result, concessions are often made to local authorities. The shrinking of nature reserves in many parts of China is an example of a national conservation goal giving way to local development. One scholar has argued that wildlife protection should be considered a matter of public interest, and that private property should not be protected if it conflicts with the public interest of wildlife protection (Wang Xiaogang 2003, 4–5). In practice, private interests have been known to sabotage the objectives of wildlife protection when they feel they have not been properly compensated (Yeh 2014). Moreover, some private interests appear to attract more government sympathy than others: larger businesses and development projects seem to have more success in securing compensation than individual farmers.

Sichuan farmers have long complained about the difficulty of getting any compensation from the government for damages to crops and other property by protected bears, wild boars, egret and weasels (Wu Hao 2016, 11). In Anhui, farmers could hardly get any compensation for crop damages by protected Reeves's pheasants (Li Tiezhu 2020). While individual farmers who suffer losses caused by protected species often struggle to secure compensation, local governments are more likely to assist businesses and projects that could cause damage to wildlife. To local authorities, such industries and enterprises, although environmentally and ecologically harmful, create jobs and contribute revenue to local state coffers, and so serve the political objective of the local government. Because of their obsession with economic growth, local authorities are more likely to modify nature reserves to allow development projects to proceed. The controversial adjustment of the spotted seal reservation in Liaoning allowed a major development project to take place inside the original nature reserve for the endangered species.[5]

The most criticised nature reserve adjustment happened in Xinjiang. The Kashan Nature Reserve was adjusted six times between 2005 and 2015, reducing from the original size of 18,908 square kilometres to 12,825 square kilometres. This nature reserve is home to 14 species in China's Category I protection list and 39 Category II protected species. Yet the local government's plans to build a gold mine, a coal mine, and a quarry for high-grade granite led to the shrinkage and fragmentation of the habitat of these protected species (Shi Yi 2015). This drastic reduction was so controversial and so widely criticised that the environmental bureau of Xinjiang autonomous region announced in 2017 that no further nature reserve adjustments would be approved in the next five years (Jiang Xuejiao 2017).

Funding shortages

A shortage of funding has been another challenge facing the country's wildlife protection agencies at the grassroots level and has further undercut the institutional standing of the wildlife management authorities. The county-level authorities, who have the most wildlife protection and anti-poaching responsibilities, are the least funded. They fall outside provincial budgets and rely chiefly on fees and fines to fund their daily operations (Ma Jianhua and Chen Chunji 2003, 52–53). Complicating the problem of funding shortages is corruption. Wildlife officials often allow wildlife-related crimes to happen under their noses, causing suspicion of officials providing protection to poachers and hunters (Jinghua Times 2012). In 2004, China had 2,194 nature reserves covering 148 million hectares of land, 14% of China's territory (SFB 2006). By the end of 2014, it had seen the rise of 2,729 nature reserves. To manage these massive areas of protected land, only 28,392 people were employed. China's biggest nature reserve, Xingjiang's Aerjin Mountain Nature Reserve, built in 1985, covers 45,000 square kilometres, an area 9,000 square kilometres bigger than Taiwan, and

---

5   See for example the notice issued by China's General Administration of Environmental Protection on adjusting the nature reserves in Ordos of Inner Mongolia and other region issued on 22 June 2007 at https://bit.ly/3ay1ygJ.

was for many years supervised by a wife and husband team (Shen Lin 1999, 5, 42–43).

It was not until 2009 that the Chinese government began to invest more in the reserve. The national government funded 12 million yuan to build new infrastructure, including five inspection stations with 1,250 square metres of office space, a wildlife rescue centre, and an animal hospital. Two vehicles were provided to serve four mobile stations in the vast area of the reserve (Sun Tingwen 2010). As critics pointed out, this one-off investment of 12 million yuan, although commendable, fell far short of the ongoing funding needs of a nature reserve of this size.[6] Nature reserves and wildlife protection stations are generally located in mountainous or remote regions of the country. Lack of adequate and consistent government funding, harsh conditions, and unattractive wages have made it hard for the authorities to attract college graduates and people with wildlife and conservation expertise (Li Yuanbing 2016).

While wildlife protection work has always been short of funding, the State Forestry Bureau has seen a steady increase in its budget since 2001, when its long-term plan for wildlife protection was approved by the then State Planning Commission. What followed was a steady bureaucratic expansion of the State Forestry Bureau, purportedly in order to better manage the anticipated intensification of wildlife farming operations, the construction of nature reserves, and wildlife conservation. Indicative of this bureaucratic expansion was a steady increase in the bureau's annual budget. Between 2001 and 2009, the bureau's budget increased 409%. In 2000, the bureau's annual budget was 636 million yuan. It went up to 3.2 billion yuan in 2009, an increase of 260 million yuan per year since 2001. The increased budget allowed the State Forestry Bureau to fully fund all existing programs that had been under-funded as well as new areas of its responsibility, including wildlife resource conservation and captive breeding (State Forestry Bureau 2009). In 2019, the total budget of the State Forestry and Grassland Bureau (renamed in 2018) reached 8.5 billion yuan (State Forestry and Grassland Bureau 2019).

---

6   Interview with Qin Xiaona, director of Beijing's Capital Animal Welfare Association, 12 February 2016.

6 Protection or utilisation: revising the wildlife protection law

Judicial weakness

China's judicial system is a political instrument in the hands of the ruling Communist Party. Whether a court is harsh or toothless often depends on the nature of the offence. Courts have not hesitated to give long prison terms to those who have called for an end to one-party rule, for open and competitive elections, or for religious rights, for example. But the Chinese court system has failed to punish crimes that do not immediately threaten the established ruling order. Rampant food-safety violations, for example, would not have continued if the judiciary had been able to handle food-safety cases free from political interference. Offences under the 1989 WPL have been subject to similar interference. In my previous study of the 1989 WPL, I wrote the following on the failure of China's judicial system to punish crimes against protected species:

> Government interference in judicial decisions is by no means hearsay in wildlife related cases. China's court system is not an independent branch of the Chinese government. It depends on the executive arm of the government for budget and personnel, thus allowing the latter to sway its decisions. In China, 70% of the cases involving WPL violations by the catering businesses happened in Guangdong before the SARS outbreak. Yet, as of 1999, only 5 people had been condemned to death while 10 others sentenced to imprisonment. In 1999, 236 trafficking cases involving protected species were handled by China's courts. Forty-two of them were serious and extremely serious cases. However, the courts only detained 15 suspects. Of the 15 detainees, 11 received light sentences while four others were set free. (Li, Peter 2007, 87)

China's judicial system is expected to fulfil its political obligation, i.e., to ensure the smooth progression of the country's reform program. Growth is the top priority of the post-Mao developmental state. The performance of local leaders is judged by local growth, job creation and social stability (Bo Zhiyue 1996, 135–55). In Sichuan, Jilin and Heilongjiang, bear farming contributes to revenue and provides jobs, and so is zealously protected by the local authorities. Veterinary reports prepared by AAF have confirmed the presence of wild-caught bears on bear farms and the widespread violation of the WPL, since Asiatic black bears are a Category II protected species under the legislation. Yet those who catch bears illegally have largely escaped prosecution. Local authorities are not motivated to prosecute them. Similarly, the unauthorised marketing of bear bile products has rarely been confronted by law enforcement officials. On the contrary, Guizhentang, the biggest bear farm in eastern China, has been accused of marketing bear bile powder illegally, yet announced publicly in 2012 its intention to go public on China's stock market.[7] Instead of being investigated by the provincial law enforcement or punished by the judiciary, Guizhentang projected itself as a model business. To the judiciary, the Wildlife Protection Law would be the basis of judicial decisions only if the decisions served the country's economic development objectives.

Business interests

China's wildlife industry is composed of four business groups. The country's wildlife farming industry is arguably the most formidable in terms of its size. Next comes the Traditional Chinese Medicine (TCM) pharmaceutical companies. In 2017, there were 482,000 TCM doctors in China. More than 1,700 TCM drug makers, with a combined revenue of 860 billion yuan ($130 billion), supplied the TCM doctors with traditional remedies containing herb, mineral or animal ingredients. The output of TCM drugs represented one third of the total medicines produced in 2017 (China Daily 2017).

The TCM community is a powerful lobby. In the Chinese government, the State Administration of Traditional Chinese Medicine (SATCM) is the highest state authority in charge of the country's TCM industry and TCM health services. The SATCM is not only a government regulatory body equal in standing as the National Commission of Public Health and Family Planning, but also a spokesperson for the TCM industry. In Beijing, the China Association of Traditional Chinese Medicine has been a fierce defender of TCM

---

7   For the controversy of Guizhentang's IPO bid, see the collection of issues and views at http://stock.hexun.com/2012/gztsh/.

6 Protection or utilisation: revising the wildlife protection law

theories and TCM drugs containing wildlife parts. In 2016, wildlife breeding for use in TCM produced revenue of 5 billion yuan (Ma Jianzhang et al. 2017, 104). Although the TCM community has been involved in an incessant battle with its critics and sceptics since the beginning of the 20th century, it has managed to hold a position seemingly on a par with the Western medicine community in China. At the entrance to the main office building of China's National Health and Family Planning Commission (NHFPC), the name of the NHFPC is displayed alongside that of the State Administration of Traditional Chinese Medicine. The TCM community has used appeals to nationalism and "tradition" to reject criticism from the critics and sceptics.

The wildlife industry also includes entertainment businesses. In 2016, China's animal display and entertainment industry generated revenue of 9.2 billion yuan ($1.4 billion). Of this, 6.5 billion yuan was produced by some 200 zoos (Ma Jianzhang et al. 2017, 113, 215). In the last three decades, China has also seen a great increase in the number of aquariums built across the country. In 2018, China had 72 aquariums attracting 81 million visitors visiting 112 million times. Aquariums generated revenue of 7.2 billion yuan ($1.1 billion) in 2018 (chyxx.com 2019). China also had more than 100 travelling circuses by the end of 2016, generating a revenue of 200 million yuan a year. Big circuses such as Guangdong's Chimlong, Xiamen's Lingling and others had an annual revenue of more than 1 billion yuan (Ma Jianzhang et al. 2017, 114).

Wildlife farming businesses are another powerful member of the wildlife industry. This massive farming operation has five components: breeding for fur, for the exotic food market, for traditional Chinese medicine, for display, and for sale as pets and laboratory animals. Fur animal farming is the biggest sector, producing revenue of 389 billion yuan ($61 billion) in 2016. The second biggest sector is farming and trading for the exotic food market. Its annual revenue in the same year was 125 billion yuan ($20 billion). Wildlife breeding for traditional medicine, briefly mentioned earlier, generated revenue of 5 billion yuan ($781 million). The last two sectors – breeding for display (a category that includes pets) and laboratory animals – produced a combined annual revenue of a little over 1 billion yuan ($150 million). The power of the wildlife farming industry as a whole comes both from the value of its production and its contribution to the rural economy. The industry reportedly employed 14 million workers, 1.4% of China's 900 million labour force, in 2016 (Ma Jianzhang et al. 2017, 103). Although many of these 14 million workers were employed part-time or seasonally and paid by the hour, most of them are rural workers, the target of the government's poverty reduction programs.

The wildlife industry also has another powerful member: wildlife experts and scholars. These are academics who support the use of wildlife for economic purposes. In fact, until very recently, almost all Chinese academics teaching, researching and publishing on wildlife issues were "utilisation" scholars. Ma Jianzhang, China's top wildlife expert and an Academician of the National Academy of Engineering, has since the early 1980s advised and participated in major policy-making changes related to wildlife. Called the "father of China's wildlife utilisation," Professor Ma provides academic support to the Chinese government's wildlife commercialisation proposals. He has chaired expert committees to evaluate and approve projects such as granting hunting rights to foreigners, experiments with rhino farming, and other wildlife exploitation projects.

As the academic voice for wildlife utilisation, Professor Ma has consistently argued since the early 1980s that wildlife protection would be meaningless if it were not pursued for human benefit (Ma Jianzhang et al. 1985). Ma founded the Wildlife Resource College at the Northeast China University of Forestry, and his former students now work in wildlife management positions at the national, provincial and county levels. Ma is such an influential academic that he was invited to build a research station inside the Guizhentang bear farm in Fujian province (Guizhentang 2017). To his critics, Professor Ma, as the country's top wildlife scientist, has undermined his authority and objectivity through his close relations with wildlife business interests (Jiang, Jessie 2011; Zhang Jianfeng 2011).

A second group of academics, the "culture defenders," has also become part of the wildlife business lobby. The representative figure of this group is the late Li Lianda, a traditional Chinese medicine researcher and academic at the National Academy of Engineering. Unlike the "utilisation" scholars who advocate for the wildlife industry in policymaking, the "culture defenders" work to clear the way for wild animal use, particularly in traditional medicine, by attacking its critics. They see foreign criticism as an assault on Chinese culture and argue that China should stand firm in defending its "national industry" against criticism from domestic and foreign NGOs. They call foreign animal protection groups "anti-China organisations" and claim that foreign criticism of Chinese wildlife farms is a sign of Western cultural imperialism, and foreign animal advocates agents of Western invasion (Yicai 2012). Some believe that criticism of wildlife farming is intended to shut down the industry in order to open the Chinese market to American wildlife products such as pheasant, ostrich and deer meat, and to other foreign wildlife products. They have even suggested that critics of China's wildlife operations were radical environmentalists and human rights activists who should be cracked down on by the authorities (Ran Jingcheng 2020a). To these "culture defenders," defending the trade and consumption of wildlife meant defending Chinese pride, tradition and national interest. Scholars in this group see nothing wrong with using endangered species. In their view, ingredients derived from wildlife have unique properties and are irreplaceable (Jia Qian et al. 2003).

The bureaucratic interests of the national and local forestry bureaus are intimately connected with the interests of the wildlife industries. The regulatory responsibilities of the authorities cannot but be undercut as a result of the conflict of interest. The continuous existence and expansion of the wildlife farming industry serves the bureaucratic interests of the state and provincial forestry bureaus. In June 2001, the State Forestry Bureau's long-term plan for wildlife protection with a component for wildlife farming was approved by the then State Planning Commission. What followed was a steady bureaucratic expansion of the State Forestry Bureau, an expansion purportedly designed to enable better management of the anticipated intensification of wildlife farming operations. Indicative of this bureaucratic expansion was a steady budget increase in the following years.

This bureaucratic expansion has also taken place at the provincial level. By the end of 2017, 1,751 "Wild Animal and Plant Management Stations" had been created in 33 provinces and provincial regions (China Statistical Bureau 2017). Ironically the provinces with the most wildlife management stations are also the ones with the greatest number of wildlife crimes. A group of young volunteers conducted a study of 1,552 wildlife crimes and found that Hunan, Jiangxi, Shanxi and Hubei, provinces with more "stations," had the highest number of cases of illegal hunting of endangered species. Most of these provinces, including Xinjiang and Heilongjiang, also accounted for the biggest number of cases of illegal hunting in general (Shanshui Nature Protection Center 2020a). The "Wild Animal and Plant Management Stations" were set up with two purposes: to stop illegal hunting and to manage captive breeding. In practice, they have been more motivated to help whitewash breaches of the law committed by breeders than to help them comply with regulations. Officials working in these stations have been known to defend farming operations even when the government is dropping support for captive breeding for the exotic food markets (Ran Jingcheng 2020b).

Unsurprisingly, provinces with more wildlife management stations had more active captive breeding programs. Jiangxi, an inland province with 212 stations, had by the end of 2018 produced a wildlife farming revenue of 10 billion yuan (Tan Hong 2019). Hubei, with 105 stations, had 500 wildlife breeding farms under the supervision of the forestry officials, generating an annual revenue of 300 million yuan in 2016 (Wang Tong 2017). Heilongjiang, a province bordering Russian Siberia, had 157 wildlife stations that produced a wildlife farming revenue of 2.5 billion yuan in 2013 (Mu Jingjung 2014). The sustainability of the increased budgets for local forestry bureaus seem to depend on the sustainability and expansion of wildlife breeding operations. "If wildlife breeding is closed, these wildlife stations have no reason to exist," said a local forestry official in Jiangxi. "It is the job of the forestry police, not of these stations, to crack down upon wildlife crimes," he added.[8]

The revised Wildlife Protection Law

In September 2013, the 12th NPC Standing Committee finally agreed to include revision of the 1989 Wildlife Protection Law (WPL) in the legislative agenda. This decision was the result of the joint proposal of

---

8   Interview with a deputy forestry bureau chief of Jiangxi, 29 September 2019.

130 NPC and the Chinese People's Political Consultative Conference delegates, who called on the national legislature to start the WPL revision process. The NPC's Environmental and Natural Resources Committee (ENRC) was entrusted by the NPC Standing Committee to lead the revision work. In December 2015, the first draft revision was approved at the 18th Standing Committee meeting of the 12th National People's Congress. The revised draft was released for public comments on 29 January 2016.

In a 2015 speech on the need to revise the law made 26 years earlier, Wang Hongju, the deputy chief of the ENRC, made known official recognition of the crisis faced by the country's wildlife. Mr Wang, a former mayor of Chongqing, listed six major threats to the nation's wildlife. These included, first, illegal hunting, poaching, and the sale of wildlife animals; second, the prevalence of excessive consumption of wildlife; third, trafficking and the illegal trade of wildlife and related products; fourth, destruction and illegal use of wildlife habitat; fifth, the appearance of new channels of wildlife sales such as online peddling of wildlife products; and sixth, the lack of clear supervisory mechanisms with regard to illegal wildlife related productions and the lack of clear penalty stipulations (Peng Bo and Zhang Yang 2015). The 1989 WPL had, by the end of 2015, failed to arrest the crisis facing the country's wildlife.

The call to revise the WPL could be traced back to 2003. Following the outbreak of SARS, Liang Congjie, founder and director of the Friends of Nature (FON), first proposed to the NPC for a revision to the 1989 WPL. Since then, Chinese scholars, legal experts, and animal activists have on various occasions urged the national legislature to revise the WPL. In 2004, to the shock of Mr Liang and like-minded scholars and experts, the NPC, at the request of business interests and the SFB, made the first ever revision to the 1989 WPL, which included an expended item on wildlife exploitation. Item 2 of Article 26 was revised to open hunting grounds to foreigners. Applications to hunt in China were to be handled by the national government wildlife administrative agency (NPC 2004). This revision was a great letdown to Mr Liang and to wildlife experts and conservationists who believed that allowing foreigners to hunt in China would send the wrong message to the society by suggesting misleadingly that wildlife protection was no longer needed. To the Chinese authorities, particularly the SFB, the 2004 revision closed a loophole in wildlife management while it allowed the local authorities in the hunting area access to revenues from the approved hunting activities (Meng Si 2011).

In May 2015, the first draft revision to the WPL was produced for internal discussion of a small circle of experts and officials. In August 2015, a drafting team member and other legal experts arrived in Washington, DC for the second US–China Animal Law Forum. At open sessions with American wildlife experts from the Humane Society International and officials from the US State Department and Department of Justice, they disclosed that the third draft revision was being finalised despite the huge gap in expectations between wildlife business interests and the rest of the stakeholders. What divided the two camps was the question of "wildlife utilisation." The revision was seized by both sides as a rare opportunity to have their positions reflected in the revised law. On 24 December, the fifth-draft revision was finished and deliberated the next day at the 18th Standing Committee meeting at the NPC. This draft revision was released on 1 January 2016 for public comment.

The draft revision received 6,205 comments from 1,640 people. In April 2016, the draft revision went through the second review process at meetings held by the Standing Committee of the NPC. Public comments and expert feedback were collected for the second review in June (Liang Zhiping 2016a). The further revised WPL was enlarged from the original 42 articles to 60 articles and to 58 in the final approved version. In July 2016, the final version of the revision was adopted by the NPC. It came into effect on 1 January 2017.

Changes to the WPL's objectives

The revised WPL aims to "protect wildlife animals, save rare and endangered species, maintain biodiversity and ecological balance, and promote the construction of ecological civilisation" (Article 1). The revised objectives obviously resulted from attempts to balance the concerns of different interests. "Wildlife utilisation" or "regulated utilisation" in the 1989 WPL were removed. They were replaced by "biodiversity" and "ecological balance," the new buzzwords in Chinese public discourse on environmental governance. In calling for the "construction of ecological civilisation," the legislators were following a directive from party leader Xi Jinping, who advanced the concept of "ecological civilisation" soon after he took over the highest leadership position in 2012. The new objectives in the revised WPL were indeed an improvement. In retrospect, however, what could have been included but was not was biosecurity, an issue that has received much attention in China following the outbreak of the COVID-19 pandemic in November 2019. To prevent the country's wildlife breeding operations from becoming a breeding ground for future pandemics, the Chinese government has embarked on another revision effort to amend the Wildlife Protection Law that had gone through the last revision in 2013–16.

In the revised 2017 WPL, Article 3 reaffirms state protection of wildlife breeding operations. "Rational utilisation," which appeared in Article 4 of the 1989 WPL, disappeared. It was replaced by "regulated utilisation" (Article 4), suggesting greater government regulation of the commercial use of wildlife. This addressed the concerns of critics of the 1989 WPL, but the new legislation still subtly endorsed wildlife "use." The focus of Chapter III of the new legislation is still on wildlife "use" and the use is protected by law. Tian Song raised a thought-provoking question:

> Who are the "users" of wildlife animals? Why do they need to "use" wildlife animals? Let me put it simply. The users of wildlife animals are none other than a small number of interest groups who "utilise" wildlife animals to achieve their own interests. Their "utilisation" of wildlife animals is neither for the protection of wildlife species nor to meet the so-called needs of the general public ... Who needs health products made of wildlife animal parts? Who needs wildlife for "food"? Who wants to see wildlife animal performance? Who want to domesticate wildlife animal species? Neither the general public nor the wildlife animals themselves want all these. What an irony that China's WPL has become a law for protecting the private interest of a small number of businesses. (Tian Song 2016)

Tian Song's challenge to the WPL's endorsement of wildlife use raises several important questions. We know that there is demand among Chinese consumers for rice, vegetables and animal products, particularly pork. Is there also "demand" for wildlife products such as snake meat, pangolin meat and bamboo rat meat? The answer to this question is no. There were no documented Chinese protests asking the government to ensure the supply of wild animal meat. Does wildlife use serve the general public interest or the interests of the farming industry? Whose interests would be jeopardised if the wildlife farming industry ceased to exist? Shouldn't a nation's laws serve the general public interest rather than the parochial interests of a small number of business owners?

Wildlife as a natural resource

To the disappointment of its critics, the revised WPL continues to treat wildlife as a natural resource (Article 3). Supporters of the new law countered that at the current stage of development in China, wildlife has to be designated as a natural resource, and that this designation does not amount to a government endorsement of reckless or unregulated exploitation of wildlife. If wildlife were not designated as a natural resource, then the legal basis of wildlife use for medicine, food, clothing and other activities would be gone. Article 3 of the revised WPL states that "wildlife resources are owned by the state." "The state safeguards the lawful rights and interests of units and individuals engaged in the protection of wildlife and related activities, including scientific research and captive breeding according to the law."

This Article reaffirms the state's position that wildlife is a natural resource to be used for human benefit. However, its use has to be lawful. Defenders of this position argue that businesses that use wildlife resources legally deserve the protection of the WPL. Critics argue that the designation of wildlife as a natural resource undermines other objectives of the WPL, especially the objective of maintaining ecological balance and biodiversity. Wildlife species, in the opinion of these critics, are important components of the natural world whose ecological value is independent of, and far exceeds, their use value to humans. Moreover, wild animals have important and irreplaceable ecological functions to perform in the wild. The WPL should protect wildlife species not because of their instrumental value as a resource for human exploitation, but because of the important ecological functions they play.[9]

Scope of protection

The 1989 WPL extended protection to species of terrestrial and aquatic wildlife that were rare or near extinction or of important *economic* or scientific value. The scope of this protection has long been questioned by critics of the WPL. The revised WPL reads: "The wildlife protected under this Law refers to the terrestrial and aquatic species which are rare or near extinction and the terrestrial species which are of important ecological, scientific and social value" (Article 2). The much-criticised term "economic value" was replaced by "social value," suggesting that the use of wildlife animals should benefit the entire society, not just businesses, and "ecological value," which was missing from the 1989 WPL. Despite the change in wording, some critics still point out that the revised WPL attaches greater importance to the interests of industry than to animal welfare (Tian Song 2016).

Article 9 of the 1989 WPL divided wildlife animals into two categories of protection: first class (nationally protected species) and second class (provincially protected species). The lists of nationally protected species were to be drawn up by the SFGB. The provincially protected species lists were to be produced by local wildlife administrative agencies and the species on these second-class lists would be placed under the protection of local governments. The 1989 WPL did not specify a timeframe for updating these lists. The revised WPL requires in Article 10 that the lists of wildlife under special state protection be evaluated and revised by the SFGB every five years, and that the lists be approved by the State Council. The lists of provincially protected species shall also be adjusted after scientific evaluation organised by the provincial authorities. However, no timeline is set out for the updating of these provincial lists. It is important to point

---

9   Telephone interview with Qin Xiaona, director of Capital Animal Welfare Association, 16 February 2016.

out that the revised WPL still keeps the provision that separate lists of terrestrial wildlife with important ecological, scientific and social value shall be drawn up and announced by the department of wildlife protection under the State Council. This means that wildlife species on the list of wildlife with important social values can be used for breeding, trading and other commercial purposes.

Habitat protection

The word "habitat" did not appear even once in the 1989 WPL. It is seen 17 times in the revised legislation, in Articles 2, 5, 6, 11, 12, and 13. To critics of the 1989 WPL, this is a commendable improvement. Including habitat protection in the revised legislation reflects the government's increased awareness of the connection between habitat protection and wildlife protection. Articles 5,6, 11 and 12 are specifically devoted to habitat protection. These four articles commit government funding for the protection of wildlife species in their natural habitats and call for public support for habitat and wildlife protection. Article 6 addresses illegal hunting and catching. Article 11 requires that departments of wildlife protection at the county level or above conduct or commission regular surveys to monitor and evaluate wildlife and their habitats. Robust records of wildlife and their habitats should be established. It should be pointed out that this article is also designed to serve the interests of the country's wildlife farming businesses.

Article 12 stipulates that a list of important wildlife habitats, based on results of surveying, monitoring and evaluation, should be drawn up and published. The purpose of listing wildlife habitats is for the national and provincial authorities to designate nature reserves, in order to prevent potential damage from human activities that would disturb or threaten wildlife such as cultivating monocultures, introducing non-native species, and excessive use of agricultural chemicals. Wildlife protection departments at the county level and above, according to Article 13, have the responsibility to ensure that wildlife and their habitats receive due consideration when exploitation and utilisation plans are being drafted to avoid or reduce adverse impacts that could result from the implementation of these plans. Wildlife protection departments are also required to produce environmental impact assessments. More significantly, Article 13 also requires avoiding nature reserves and other protected areas and wildlife migration routes in planning construction projects such as airports, railways, roads, irrigation and hydroelectricity projects, cofferdams, and land reclamation. This article requires the building of structures to allow for wildlife migration, such as tunnels and fish passes, to eliminate or reduce adverse impacts on wildlife, a requirement that was absent from the 1989 WPL.

However, critics have pointed out that, by requiring the building of infrastructures for migratory wildlife, the revised WPL still allows development projects to cut through nature reserves, a concession that could potentially make the wildlife protection departments powerless. In 1999, the State Environmental Protection Administration issued a *Notice on the Several Questions on Environmental Management Work of the Development Projects inside Nature Reserves* (State Environmental Bureau of China 1999). This administrative order allowed key transportation, irrigation and hydropower construction projects approved by the state to go through nature reserves, including the core areas and buffer zones, and required the relevant authorities to appropriately adjust the function, size and boundaries of the impacted reserves. In the revised WPL, Article 13 has elevated the 1999 administrative decision in the national law for development projects to legally cut through nature reserves. In conclusion, while the inclusion in the revised WPL of habitat protection is commendable, critics worry that the law will remain toothless.

Funding

The 1989 WPL did not address the issue of funding for wildlife protection. For example, Articles 11, 13 and 14 addressed the investigation of harm done to wildlife, rescue of wildlife in emergency situations, and compensations for damages caused by wildlife, but did not specify where the money for these tasks should come from. The revised WPL is more specific. Article 5 of the revised law stipulates that "the State protects wildlife and their habitats. People's governments at the county level or above shall draft protection plans and measures for the protection of wildlife and their habitats, and include the expenses for protection of wildlife in their budgets." Furthermore, the revised WPL encourages citizens, legal entities and other organisations to participate in wildlife protection activities and to support wildlife protection efforts through donations, subsidies, volunteer work, and other means.

Article 19 says that "If protection of wildlife stipulated by this law causes injury or death to staff, losses to crops or other loss of property, the local people's governments shall make compensation for them, which shall be formulated by the people's governments of provinces, autonomous regions and municipalities." And, "Relevant local people's governments may urge insurance agencies to carry out insurance services for compensating harms caused by wildlife." The revised WPL does not mention how much compensation should be paid, and does not mention compensation for collateral damages. What it does mention in Article 19 is that the national government will subsidise local governments' necessary expenses spent on preventing and controlling hazards created by wildlife under national protection.

Several questions can be raised about the two articles that deal with budgets. Critics have long argued that the financial burden on local governments explained the failure of local authorities to enforce the WPL. The regions where wildlife protection is most pressing are also the country's least developed areas. Funding for wildlife protection is pervasively believed to be a waste of resources in areas where they are needed most to develop the local economy. Article 5 of the revised WPL continues to place the financial burden on local authorities for wildlife habitat protection. Article 19 only requires the national government budget to cover measures for preventing and controlling harm caused by wildlife under special state protection. It is therefore not obligated to share the direct expenditure for maintaining, managing, and protecting wildlife species, under special state protection or otherwise, and their habitats.

The revised WPL, like the 1989 law, contains articles that place indirect financial responsibilities on the local governments. Article 13 of the 1989 WPL stated that "if natural disasters present threats to wildlife under special state or local protection, the local governments shall take timely measures to rescue them." Rescue operations, post-rescue accommodations and rehabilitation and other necessary actions all call for expertise, personnel and financial input. "Timely measures" cannot be implemented without financial commitment. Article 15 of the revised WPL reads that "Where wildlife under key national or local protection are threatened by emergencies such as natural disasters or major environmental pollution incidents, the local people's governments shall take emergency rescue measures in a timely manner." Additionally, local governments are required to rescue and shelter wildlife. Shelter construction, maintenance, and rescue operations all require expertise, staff, supplies and other inputs, all of which cost money.

Wildlife breeding

Wildlife farming, domestication and breeding are also major issues for critics of the 1989 law. The Chinese authorities have long felt proud of the country's successful domestication of 54 wildlife species. In the revised WPL, wildlife breeding continues to be supported by the state. In Article 3, the revised WPL proclaims state protection of breeding or utilisation of wildlife. Article 25 states that the state shall implement a licensing system for the captive breeding of wildlife under special state protection.

Unlike the 1989 WPL, the revised law requires wildlife operators to meet animal welfare conditions. Article 26 reads:

> Captive breeding of wildlife under special state protection shall benefit the protection of the species and scientific research, and may not damage wild populations. Anyone intending to breed wildlife under special state protection shall ensure that they have the necessary living space and conditions for the movement, reproduction, hygiene and health of the animal according to its habits and properties; that they are equipped with adequate premises, facilities and technology in line with the purpose, type and scale of the captive breeding operation; that they can satisfy relevant technical standards and disease prevention requirements; and that the wildlife is not abused.

To critics of the revised law, Article 26 exhibits either a lack of wildlife expertise or its purposeful neglect. In revising the WPL, the revision team failed to refer to scientific data on the positive impact, if any, of wildlife farming on wild population stabilisation. There has been no scientific data whatsoever to support the claim that wildlife farming or captive breeding help to conserve wildlife populations. No captive-bred tigers have been successfully introduced to the wild in China.

Second, Article 26 proceeds from an unnegotiated and anthropocentric position that wildlife exists for human benefit, and that this use is justified as long as some basic conditions are met. Finally, Article 26 fails to recognise the fact that no artificial farming environment can replicate the natural habitats of wildlife animals. Captive breeding of a large number of wild animals in close confinement with one another can be an ideal breeding ground for pandemic outbreaks. Bear farming is a good example of an intrinsically cruel business operation. Nothing can be done to improve a system that depends on cruelty to operate. The failure of the revised WPL to acknowledge this makes apparent the SFGB and NPC's lack of understanding of the animal welfare implications and public health risks of much of the country's wildlife farming industry. In revising the WPL, they prioritised employment and revenue generation rather than animal wellbeing, biosecurity and public health.

The revised law includes new management measures, some of which have already been adopted. Businesses that intend to sell, purchase or use wildlife under state protection, or related wildlife products, must obtain labels ("special markings") (Article 27, 39), which show that they have official authorisation. Such markings are not new. They were implemented in 2012 for ivory products, after China was criticised for its domestic ivory trade. The mechanism may have slightly curbed the runaway domestic ivory trade, but it did little to stop the trade as a whole. Widespread violation and fraudulent use of the markings were documented by an investigative report by the International Fund for Animal Welfare (IFAW 2006). The intention behind the inclusion of the special label mechanism in the revised WPL is commendable, but its effectiveness is doubtful. The IFAW investigation found that if authorities were not willing to tackle the problem at its roots, traders had countermeasures to get around measures such as the labelling system (International Fund for Animal Welfare 2006).

Penalties

One of the criticisms directed at the 1989 WPL was that it failed to provide specific penalties for WPL violations. For example, Article 34 of the 1989 law stipulated in general terms that fines would be imposed on perpetrators who were responsible for damages to wildlife in natural habitats or protected areas. The revised WPL defines specific penalties in Articles 42 through 57. These penalties include administrative and legal penalties for officials who fail to carry out their duties (Article 42); confiscation of and imposing of fines two to ten times the value on wildlife illegally acquired under the guise of wildlife shelter and rescue (Article 44); revoking of special hunting licences, imposition of a fine up to 200,000 yuan, and criminal prosecution if a crime is involved. Other penalties include the revoking of breeding licences, withdrawal of approved documents, cancellation of special markings, and responsibility for the cost of recapturing non-native species illegally released to the wild. Appendix 1 summarises the offences and punishments in the revised WPL.

Critics of the 1989 WPL have consistently called for the law to provide specific and heavier penalties. It remains to be seen if the penalties listed in the revised WPL are enforced, but critics have reason to be pessimistic. Internationally, China is the main destination for exports of live wild animals and wildlife products. It is also one of the countries most severely impacted by the introduction of non-native species. In 2013, China identified 544 such species, more than 100 of which were particularly injurious to the native ecology, causing billions of yuan in economic loss (Mu 2013). Article 53 of the revised WPL stipulates that perpetrators of illegal import of non-native species, if convicted, shall receive a fine of between 50,000 and 200,000 RMB. Stopping non-native species from entering the country is a new challenge and an area that the 1989 WPL did not address.

Remaining issues

The process of revising the WPL was a tug-of-war between two forces. Animal protectionists and wildlife experts were the first to call on the national legislature to revise the 1989 law. Wildlife business interests, however, used the revision as an opportunity to consolidate and advance their commercial interests. The final revised WPL incorporated suggestions from both groups, but it seemed to reflect the position of the wildlife industry more than that of animal protectionists.

From "economic" to "social" value

The decision to revise the 1989 Wildlife Protection Law was made by the Chinese Communist Party leadership. Delegates to the National People's Congress (NPC) and the Chinese People's Political Consultative Conference, scholars, journalists and other people of influence had urged the Chinese authorities to revise the 1989 law, which was toothless to wildlife crimes. The NPC was expected to produce a draft that would take into consideration the weaknesses and loopholes in the existing law. By looking at the final product adopted by the NPC, critics believe the revised WPL was a great work of window-dressing. In other words, the NPC cherry-picked suggestions from critics of the 1989 law, replaced outdated terms with vocabulary that gave the impression of a new policy stand, and hid the ongoing designation of wildlife as a resource behind stipulations that ostensibly gave the state greater regulatory powers.

The revised WPL did go through a kind of "plastic surgery," as one Beijing animal activist commented.[10] Terms that denoted wildlife exploitation were either removed or appeared less frequently. For example, the word "domestication" was removed in the revised WPL, whereas it appeared nine times in the 1989 WPL. In the revised law, wildlife are still designated as "wildlife resources" at the beginning of the revised law (Article 3). This designation appears only once in the revised law. In contract, "wildlife resources" was repeated 15 times in

---

10 An interview with a legal scholar in Beijing, 16 July 2019.

the 1989 WPL. Similarly, "utilisation of wildlife" appeared nine times in the 1989 law and nowhere in the revised WPL. While these changes are cosmetic in nature, they indicate that members of the legislature were more sensitive to the likely reactions of their critics.

The most creative and, to some, most deceptive change was to replace the phrase "wildlife of economic value" with "wildlife of social value." Grouping wild animals under the category of "wildlife of economic value" in a law supposed to protect wildlife had been the target of strong criticism over the years. "Social value" suggests benefits beyond economic interests, and so was a creative way to replace a phrase that smacked of commercial interests. The revised WPL, however, does not change the designation of wildlife as "resources." It talks about "prioritising protection" to disarm potential critics, before introducing the idea of "regulating utilisation" in Article 4.

Article 25 of the revised WPL still endorses wildlife breeding for commercial purposes. The article starts with government support for captive breeding of wildlife by scientific research institutions for the purposes of wildlife protection, then endorses wildlife breeding by individuals for commercial purposes on the condition that they have a breeding permit. In contrast, the 1989 WPL stood unapologetically and unreservedly for wildlife use. State support for wildlife use for commercial purposes was expressed in Articles 1, 2, 3, 4 and 6 of the old WPL. The drafting team of the 1989 WPL did not attempt to conceal the "utilisation" objective of the law. The drafters of the new law, in contrast, seem to have tried hard to avoid using terms and phrases that might draw criticism.

The revised law also adopted some progressive ideas and terms. Article 1, which outlines the objectives of the revised law, pays lip service to the ideals of "biodiversity" and "ecological civilisation." However, both terms appear only once. Article 4 addresses the need to promote "the harmonious development of man and nature" and the "cultivation of public awareness of protecting wildlife." Article 8 of the revised law states that the government "shall encourage and support autonomous grass-roots civil organisations, social organisations, businesses and volunteers in their efforts to develop and promote awareness of wildlife protection laws and regulations and understanding of wildlife protection." This shows the government's recognition that Chinese grass-roots civil organisations are not enemies of the state but an important source of help for social and environmental management. Notably, the revised WPL also makes the country's wildlife protection departments and officials accountable and sets out punishments for any dereliction of duties in Article 42.

Captive breeding and animal performance

The revised WPL includes several highly controversial provisions resulting from the influence wielded by wildlife business interests. Article 25 advances a new concept of "captive-bred offspring," meaning animals born in captivity whose parents were also born in captivity. In other words, a "captive-bred offspring" is not to be considered a wild animal but the equivalent of livestock. The new law states that "Anyone intending to breed wildlife under special state protection shall use captive-bred offspring as founder stock." This provision and the category "captive-bred offspring" could open a Pandora's box, by providing legal grounds for the use of hundreds of tigers and other endangered species on Chinese wildlife farms. For years, tiger breeders had claimed that their animals were no longer wild animals but rather "captive-bred offspring" that should be treated like livestock.

In an internal consultation session between the National People's Congress officials and representatives of China's wildlife business interests, the latter argued that farmed wildlife animals were not the same as members of the protected species in the wild. In other words, farmed tigers should not be treated as members of an endangered species.[11] They called for state permission to sell bear paws, bear meat, and bear fat, since farmed bears should not be considered a Category II protected species. The industry wanted permission to promote wildlife products not only for use in traditional Chinese medicine, but also as food products, with a view to wildlife ingredients such as bear meat being "used comprehensively" and becoming a regular meat on the market.[12]

---

11 A meeting minute of the Forum on the Revision of the Wildlife Protection Law, held in February 2016 in Beijing.
12 Ibid, p. 11.

6 Protection or utilisation: revising the wildlife protection law

When the revised WPL was adopted in mid-2016, its critics were alarmed to see the "captive-bred offspring" proposition. They feared that this could be the harbinger of the official lifting of the Chinese government's 1993 trade ban on tiger bones and rhino horns. This fear was not baseless. In October 2018, the Chinese government issued a State Council Notice allowing the use of tiger bones and rhino horns from captive-bred tigers and rhinos, thus ending the 1993 ban (Independent 2018). This was arguably a huge win for the wildlife industry, as confirmed by a senior official of the NPC Legislative Work Committee in the same internal consultation meeting. However, mounting pressures from within and outside China led to the Chinese government's decision to suspend the implementation of the Notice.

To critics of the new WPL, this explicit endorsement of the use of wild animals in performance and for medicinal purposes was a step backward. The inclusion of exhibition and performance as legitimate business operations in the new legislation (Article 27 and 34) represented another victory for business interests. These two articles could have rendered illegal two administrative orders (issued by the SFB in 2007 and the Ministry of Housing and Urban and Rural Development in 2010) that called for an end to animal performances (China News Network 2007; Ministry of Housing and Urban-Rural Development 2010). To its critics, the revised WPL, like its predecessor, remains a law for wildlife resource management rather than wildlife protection.

Wildlife for traditional Chinese medicine

The revised WPL showed that business interests had achieved their two main goals. First, the revised law is believed to have opened the gate for the legal use of tiger bones and rhino horns from captive-bred individuals for use in traditional Chinese medicine. To its critics, this was one of the most disappointing results of the WPL revision. Article 29 goes so far as to explicitly endorse the use of captive-bred wildlife animals in traditional Chinese medicine, which is referred to simply as "medicine" to avoid strong reactions from sceptics and critics of traditional medicine. An official from the legislative office of the NPC confirmed that Articles 28 and 29 actually legalised the use of parts from dead tigers that were artificially bred, which had been prohibited since 1993 when the Chinese government banned the use of tiger bones in traditional medicine (State Council 1993).

At a press conference following the release of the revised WPL, the official said that the use of bones from dead tigers should be publicly discussed. He believed that banning the use of tiger parts was not only a waste of resources, but also hampered the development of traditional Chinese medicine, and therefore affected the interests and wellbeing of the Chinese people. He claimed that "natural ingredients like tiger bones and bear bile make traditional Chinese medicine uniquely effective." The use of substitutes would therefore undercut the effectiveness of traditional medicine. In his view, if wildlife animal parts were replaced by synthetic ingredients, traditional Chinese medicine would become useless. This official also hinted that substitute ingredients would be Western imports, and that this would allow the Western pharmaceutical industry to make money out of China. This official's view was strikingly similar to those of business interests (Liang Zhiping 2016b). The tilting of the revised WPL towards the interests of wildlife businesses was also criticised by Zhou Ke, a law professor at China's Remin University in Beijing. In Professor Zhou's view, by endorsing the interests of the wildlife industry the revised WPL neglects the public interest of wildlife protection (Zhou Ke 2016).

The slogan "Zhi bing jiu ren" ("cure illnesses and save lives") is used by wildlife businesses and their supporters to defend their commercial interests and to convince the National People's Congress that wildlife farming for traditional medicine is indispensable. In China, anything that is capable of "saving lives" becomes sacrosanct, and anyone who challenges a lifesaving medicine is not only short-sighted but also morally wrong. Critics of wildlife farming have confronted the "life-saving" claim, arguing that nobody will die if bear bile is not available as a medicine. Synthetic ingredients are safer, cheaper and more humane. It is commercial interests, not the needs of patients, that the wildlife industry was fighting for during the revision of the WPL. By the end of 2016, wildlife breeding for traditional Chinese medicine had an annual revenue of 5 billion yuan in China ($769 million) (Ma et al. 2017, 103).

6 Protection or utilisation: revising the wildlife protection law

Exotic food and wet markets

The revised WPL has maintained legislative support for wildlife breeding for the exotic food market. Although the revised law purportedly requires the use of "captive-bred offspring" for farming purposes (Article 25), and stipulates that participants in the industry should have appropriate conditions and expertise (Article 26) and secure breeding, trading, and other permits (Article 28), these requirements have remained on paper only. They were designed to muzzle critics of the WPL but have failed to deter the existing farms from operating in violation of the WPL. Wildlife farms have continued to catch wild animals and sell them as captive-bred animals. For example, at exotic food restaurants in Guangdong and other provinces, investigative journalists found that diners could order both captive-bred and wild-caught mallards, bamboo rats, civet cats, wild geese, leopard cats, toads, sparrows, badgers, eagle-owls, and all kinds of birds and snakes captured illegally (Yi Weekly 2020).

To industry insiders, the licensed farms have been used as a cover for massive illegal wildlife crimes. The damage these farms do to the ecosystem is greater than that caused by hunters and poachers, who mostly go after adult animals, whereas wildlife farms catch both old and young wildlife. The demand for wild animals to replenish the captive farms has led to a thriving industry producing hunting tools. In a police action in She County of Anhui, the authorities dismantled more than 8,302 leg traps, snake traps, bird catching nets, and vocalisation equipment used to catch birds and other animals (Wang Zhengxuan and Cheng Haifeng 2020). In Tianjin, volunteers found and dismantled a 20,000-metre long bird-catching net used to capture migratory and other birds for the exotic food market. Despite the revised WPL, Taobao and other hubs of electronic commerce in China have bird-catching implements for sale (The Paper 2020). The illegally caught wildlife are sold as captive-bred animals to restaurants.

After the adoption of the revised WPL, China has seen an increase in the number of permits issued to wildlife breeders. Most of the newly licensed wildlife farms are engaged in breeding for the exotic food markets. Wildlife farming for food in Jiangxi was further boosted with the adoption of the revised WPL. Of the 2,344 licensed farms in the province, 2,289, or 98%, are breeding operations for wild animal meat for consumption as food (Jiangxi Provincial Government 2020). Guizhou has also seen a drastic increase in wildlife farms for the exotic food markets. By the time of the COVID-19 outbreak, Guizhou had licensed 1,900 farms breeding porcupines, bamboo rats, sika deer, civet cats, blue peacocks, ostriches, cobras and other species (Wu 2020). In Guangxi, wildlife farming also saw a drastic increase in the number of farms and their rate of production after the adoption of the revised WPL. In 2018, the Guangxi Provincial Poverty Reduction Office included the farming of bamboo rats as a "special farming" project to help end poverty. In 2019, farms in Guangxi raised 18 million bamboo rats, producing revenue of 2 billion yuan (Gu 2020).

In January 2020, when the Chinese government shut down the wildlife trade for the exotic food market, some 20,000 farms across the country were impacted. Between 2005 and 2013, forestry bureaus at the provincial level issued 3,725 breeding and operation licences. However, in the seven years between 2013 and 2020, an additional 15,000 licenses were issued, an increase of 2,142 farms per year (Standaert 2020). At least half of these 15,000 farms received their licences after the revised WPL went into effect in 2017. One wildlife breeding farm in Anhui in Central China was issued a licence to breed more than 106 species, including almost all the parrot species of the world (Anhui Forestry Bureau 2019). Across the country, government abuse of power in issuing breeding permits, trade licences, and transport permits in violation of the WPL and other policies has become worse since the revision of the WPL (Zhang 2020).

Perhaps most concerningly, legislative support for the wildlife breeding industry suggests government endorsement of wildlife consumption. In 2003, SARS was attributed to the trade, particularly in wet markets, of wild animals such as civet cats that were identified as the host of SARS coronavirus. In my conversation with NPC staff members and legal experts involved in the revision of the WPL, I did not hear any mention of the need for the new WPL to curb the outbreak of another pandemic. This neglect was inexcusable, particularly given China's top medical scientist, Zhong Nanshan, had alerted the National People's Congress in 2010 to the fact that in 2009 coronavirus was found in wild animals sold for food in Hong Kong and Wuhan (Wang, Sun and Yu 2010). As well as issuing breeding and trading permits

6 Protection or utilisation: revising the wildlife protection law

as mentioned above, local authorities, in order to encourage wildlife production, loosened and held in contempt other requirements that had been imposed on wildlife farming. For example, local authorities in Guizhou allowed the shipment to other provinces of live wild animals without proper health and quarantine certificates, a huge public health and food safety risk (Wu Caili 2020).

China's wildlife farming industry and exotic meat markets involve a lengthy production chain. The millions of captive-bred and wild-caught animals have to be shipped to the major markets in South, Central, Southwest and Southeast China. Civet cats, for example, are often crammed into wire cages and loaded onto long-distance lorries that also carry other animals. While the majority of the wild animals are delivered directly to restaurants, a small number are dispatched to the wildlife markets, also called wildlife wet markets, where wild animals that are still alive, often dying or terribly injured, are slaughtered. Most of the buyers at these markets run small catering businesses. In 2017, the world's biggest wildlife market was situated in Conghua, Guangdong. Some 200 traders collected wild-caught and captive-bred animals from as far away as Xingjiang in Northwest China and Heilongjiang, close to Russian Siberia. These wildlife traders only displayed a small number of wild animals in the marketplace. They kept most of their animals on nearby farms or in storage facilities, from which they can supply the restaurants and hotels of the Greater Pearl River Delta region of some 35 million people.

In 2017, the Conghua market was moved to Qingyuan, 62 miles north of Guangzhou. Like most other wildlife markets, the new market has largely been beyond the reach of Chinese laws. Reported illegal sales have rarely been prosecuted (Yi Weekly 2020; Shanshui Nature Protection Center 2020 B). The wildlife market inside Wuhan's Huanan Seafood Market, the reported ground-zero of the COVID-19 pandemic, was a shocking mockery of the country's new WPL (Humane Society International 2020 b, 2-3). The market, dirty, smelly and chaotic, sold some 75 different species of both captive-bred and wild-caught animals. Animals were slaughtered on site. The concentration of a large number of wild animals of different species who were dying of diseases, injuries and mental trauma was believed to have created an ideal breeding ground for the pandemic.

To do justice to the WPL revision efforts, we have to acknowledge that the revised WPL is a more complete and comprehensive document and covers issues that were absent from the 1989 law. Thanks largely to the efforts of critics of the 1989 law, wildlife use is no longer treated as an objective, and animal welfare is included. The new law addresses habitat protection and non-native species, and provides a more complex set of penalties for illegal activities. Instead of focusing solely on the economic value of wildlife, the new law considers their social and ecological value. Despite these changes, however, wildlife use is still endorsed. The revised WPL was the product of a balancing act orchestrated by the country's increasingly sensitive national legislature. Overall, it falls short of the expectations of its critics.

Bureaucratic interests

If the revised WPL sought to balance three interests – those of business, government, and the public – Liang Zhiping, a legal scholar from Beijing, believes that the revised law has prioritised the first two. It has failed to truly balance all three. He argues that the dominance of business and government interests prevented critics of the 1989 WPL from having a more meaningful impact on the legislative process. Liang has observed that while the legislature twice invited suggestions during the revision process, there was no way to gauge the impact of those suggestions (Liang Zhiping 2016a). The revision process remained a largely closed exercise, much like China's legislation process in general, which is neither open nor impartial.

Law-making in China has been used as a political instrument to fulfil the state's objectives (Wu Qianlang 2017). It is no secret that a significant portion of China's laws and regulations are the work of administrative agencies with strong ties to the business interests they are authorised to supervise and regulate. Because they control the legislative process related to specific legislation, either by drafting proposed legislation or as the main source of information for those who do, these administrative agencies make sure that the outcome of the process is enforceable and takes into consideration the interests of the businesses affected. The fact that these administrative agencies are responsible for enforcing laws that they have participated in making has long been criticised by Chinese legal scholars (Yan Mingshen 2006, 49–56; Tian Xiangbo 2008).

This domination of lawmaking by administrative agencies has led to "the concentration of policy-making power in the hands of administrative agencies that seize opportunities to pursue and to maximise their own departmental interest." The use of lawmaking to advance parochial interests is an open secret (Tian Xiangbo 2008). In 2004, a senior researcher with the NPC Legislative Work Committee wrote that the infiltration of lawmaking by the interests of administrative agencies was a major problem. One way to overcome this would be to insulate administrative agencies from direct involvement in the making of a law they will also be responsible for its enforcement (Wang Xuejiang 2004).

In the case of the WPL, the influence of the State Forestry Bureau on the revision process was unambiguously powerful. The decision to revise the WPL created an opportunity for business interests to forestall changes that might undercut their commercial interests. The business interests aimed to achieve two objectives: to ensure that "wildlife use" remained a state-supported business, and to achieve legal protection for the use of wildlife parts – particularly the frozen carcasses of captive wildlife animals such as tigers and rhinos – in traditional Chinese medicine. These two goals were in line with the bureaucratic interests of the State Forestry Bureau, whose budget allocation by the national government depended on the existence of a growing wildlife industry. As noted earlier, the State Forestry Bureau experienced a drastic budget increase, from some 636 million yuan in 2000 to 11.4 billion yuan in 2020 (State Forestry and Grassland Bureau 2020), an increase of 15.5% a year for 20 years.

Conclusions

The revised Wildlife Protection Law was a result of great concessions to wildlife business interests. The revised law does include more detailed provisions for the regulation of wildlife-related businesses, nature reserves and non-native species. However, the apparent shift in focus from wildlife's "economic value" to its "social value" is a great act of deception. The revised WPL pays lip service to "ecological civilisation," "biodiversity," and wildlife protection. Admittedly, the revised WPL recognised the role of non-governmental and civic groups and their participation in wildlife protection. But in the final analysis, the law remains a "wildlife business management law" rather than a law for the protection of wildlife. By introducing the concept of "captive-bred offspring," the revised law has been suspected of preparing the ground for lifting a 1993 State Council ban on the tiger and rhino trades. This suspicion was confirmed in October 2018 when the State Council announced, in a thinly veiled administrative order, that it would be reopening the tiger and rhino trades.

More generally, the revised WPL has served to boost the country's wildlife farming industry and exotic breeding operations in particular. In January 2018, the wildlife industry scored another huge victory when the Chinese Communist Party Central Committee for the first time announced its endorsement of wildlife breeding, animal performance and wildlife tourism (Chinese Communist Party Central Committee 2018). With the party's support, the country's wildlife farming entered a new era of expansion. It took the COVID-19 pandemic to wake the Chinese authorities up to the danger of the country's massive wildlife exploitation industry. On 24 February 2020, China's National People's Congress (NPC) decided to impose a complete ban on the consumption and trade of wildlife. At the same time, the NPC felt the need to restart the process of revising the Wildlife Protection Law.

7
China's animal protection NGOs

The rise of non-government organisations (NGOs) is a new development in China's reform era. In the last four decades, NGOs have emerged, taken root, and expanded in areas where the party-state's presence was weak. The fact that China has stuck with the Leninist party-state while allowing the operation of NGOs has attracted much academic attention (White and Shang 1996; Saich 2000, 124–41). These scholars have considered a wide range of NGOs in areas such as foster care (Shang 2002, 203–30; Shang and Wu 2003, 523–40), environmental protection (Ho, Peter 2001, 893–921), trade unions (Ho, Peter 2001, 187–209), HIV/AIDS prevention (Kaufman 2011, 1218–22), disaster relief, and others (Teets 2009, 330–47). What explains the spirited rise of animal protection NGOs in China at a time when the party-state retains a tight control over political power and its political process is yet to be more inclusive? This chapter attempts to review, first, the political opportunities that have allowed the revival of civil society in reform-era China; second, the policy environment in which animal protection NGOs have operated; and third, the characteristics of the animal protection groups and the challenges and obstacles they face.

Political change and civil society

In its pre-reform era (1949–78), the PRC was an omnipresent and all-powerful Leninist party-state. To ensure socialist industrialisation, the CCP built a Soviet-style political structure that exercised full control of, and intervened in, all areas of society. By the end of the 1950s, it had succeeded in penetrating the grassroots of Chinese society. Not only did the party-state monopolise political power, it also controlled the distribution of most of the society's resources. In the pre-reform era, the party-state was the only source of income for the Chinese people. The political and material conditions for autonomous activities did not exist. In 1950–51, the campaign to rid China of societal forces that were allegedly hostile to the newly built Communist state succeeded in ending the civil society that had expanded in the final years of the Republic of China (ROC) under the defeated pro-West Nationalist Party of China (KMT). To the ruling Communist Party, autonomous groups served no meaningful purpose in socialist China. On the contrary, they were roadblocks to the party-led efforts to build a unified society that was to be in unison with the party-state.

However, there were semi-official social organisations in Mao's years. These included the All China Federation of Women, the All China Trade Union, the Communist Youth League of China, and the China Federation of Literary and Artistic Circles, to name some of the most well known. These groups, organised and controlled by the government, had penetrated every corner of the mainland Chinese society. The chiefs of these organisations were appointed by the party-state. The first honorary chairman of the All China Trade Union was Liu Shaoqi, Vice Chairman of the CCP. The first two chairwomen of the All Chinese Federation of Women were both veteran revolutionaries who were also members of the CCP Central Committee. Little wonder that the All China Trade Union has never ever organised a strike. It was also not surprising that the All China Federation of Women never protested against the government's policies that were injurious to women's rights and interests. The official propaganda proclaimed that, in socialist China, private ownership and class exploitation were abolished. Therefore, there was no conflict of interest between the socialist state and the working-class people. Trade

7 China's animal protection NGOs

unions no longer needed to fight against capital and management on behalf of the workers.

In the 1950s, there were 44 national governmental organisations. This had risen to a total of 100 in 1965. In the provinces, there were about 6,000 smaller organisations. These national and provincial organisations in the pre-reform era were grouped into nine categories such as trade unions, the Communist Youth League, women's federations, science associations, commercial and industrial associations, and others (Feng Xiaoming 2004, 45–46). They were not autonomous actors in society.

Political changes often trigger changes in society (Meyer and Staggenborg 1996, 1628–60). In 1978, the post-Mao leadership launched the modernisation program of economic reform. What followed in the next decade was earth-shaking. The People's Communes, the Chinese version of Soviet state farms, were disbanded. Private economic activities were decriminalised. Ideological campaigns were ended to allow a national drive for economic development. Foreign capital, information, and experts were welcomed to serve China's modernisation purposes. The rise of private businesses and the increasing diversification of the society opened up areas of societal management that were new to the post-socialist developmental state. The revival of civil society in post-Mao China was inevitable.

Civil society can exist in a nondemocratic state, although "a vibrant civil society is most likely to thrive in a democracy and vice versa" (O'Connell 2000, 471–78). Despite the party-state's tight control over the Chinese society, the country's first group of NGOs emerged in the countryside, the first target of the economic reform. Production and farming technology-related organisations emerged (Deng Guosheng 2004). In 1992, Deng Xiaoping made his famous "South China tour speech" urging bolder economic reform and more openness to the outside world. By the end of 1993, some 90,000 rural agricultural technological service NGOs had been established (Deng Guosheng 2004). In 1997, there were more than 180,000 NGOs at the county level and above, 21,404 at the provincial level, and 1,848 at the national level. At least three million more social groups were not registered or were in the process of registration (Feng Xiaoming 2004, 46).

Environmental NGOs, in which animal protection groups are often included, have since the early 1990s appeared on the Chinese mainland. Environmental NGOs are also the most studied by Chinese and Western scholars (Zhan Xueyong and Tang Shuiyan 2013, 381–99). In 1978, China's first government NGO, the Chinese Society of Environmental Science, was established. It was not until 1991 that a truly non-governmental organisation was registered: Liaoning Panjin Chinese Black-headed Gull (Saunders's Gull) Protection Association, a wildlife conservation organisation. In 1994, Liang Congjie, a Chinese People's Political Consultative Conference delegate, founded the Friends of Nature (FON) as a comprehensive environmental protection organisation. By the end of 2005, 2,768 environmental NGOs had been established with 224,000 activists, volunteers and members. This however represented a small fraction of the 315,000 NGOs and 3 million activists in the country (Ministry of Environmental Protection 2006). Animal protection groups did not appear until 1992, when the China Small Animal Protection Association (CSAPA) was established in Beijing. By the end of 2016, some 200 registered and unregistered groups for protecting, rescuing, and advocating for animals had been founded across the country.[1]

State and society

State–society relations in the PRC in the pre-reform era were very similar to those in other Eurasian socialist states in the Cold War years (1946–91). While China remains a Leninist party-state despite the drastic economic change, it has diverged from other former socialist regimes in state–society relations in more recent years.

---

1   The 70 or so animal protection groups are the registered or affiliated associations and operations devoted to animal rescue. The number was based on an estimate reached by the Animals Asia Foundation (AAF) and the Humane Society International (HSI), two international animal protection organisationss that jointly held the China Companion Animal Symposium between 2007 and 2016.

7 China's animal protection NGOs

An era of hostility (1949–78)

The history of state–society relations in the People's Republic of China can be divided into three eras. In the first era (1949–78), the party-state adopted a hostile policy towards non-governmental and autonomous groups and activities. Although in 1950 the Chinese government issued *Tentative Measures for the Registration of Social Organisations*, the new regime's hostility towards groups, associations, and foundations left over from the Republic of China (1912–49 on the mainland) and partially or wholly foreign-funded groups served as a deterrent to anyone who intended to organise non-governmental groups. In the entire pre-reform era, there was not a government agency entrusted with the responsibility for managing NGOs (Yan Dong 2007, 147–59). In retrospect, there was really no need for the Chinese government to delegate this responsibility to any government office, since NGOs were banned.

An era of cautious acceptance

The second era (1978–89) witnessed a change in attitude to NGOs, from hostility to acceptance or tolerance. In 1980, a "Bee Keepers Association" was established in Pixian County, Sichuan, one of the first NGOs organised by the peasants. In the same year, a "Society for the Study of Crossbred Rice" was founded in Enping County of Guangdong Province. These were arguably mainland China's first autonomous NGOs, created by the peasants themselves to share production knowledge, farming skills, ideas for increasing output, and knowhow of disease prevention and control (Deng Guosheng 2004). With the deepening of the country's economic reform and further relaxed political atmosphere towards the end of the 1980s, NGOs appeared in greater numbers. In retrospect, the 1980s, despite episodes of tighter political control in 1983–84 and 1986–87, did break the ground for the rise of autonomous activities in the society.

In 1979 and 1980, alongside the party's internal struggle between the reformers and the conservatives over the legacy of Mao and his policies, China saw a sudden increase of autonomous societal activities and publications urging bolder political liberalisation. The so-called "Democracy Wall" in Beijing, a place where people pasted big-character posters voicing their grievances and criticising government policies, was an autonomous forum that was copied in other cities as a way to express unorthodox views. "The Wall" could not have emerged if reformers in the party had not won the upper hand in debates about ending the ultra-leftist policies of the Cultural Revolution. The wall however alarmed and empowered conservatives in the party to stage a comeback and put pressure on reformers to take a stand on the emerging voices. Those who were most active and most critical of the party's policies were arrested and the wall was shut down. Wei Jingsheng, the most prominent of the "Democracy Wall" activists, was arrested (Lieberthal 2004, 137).

In 1981, in response to the rise of unofficial publications, political gatherings, and youth societies, the CCP Central Committee issued a policy document urging authorities at all levels to crack down on unregistered groups and autonomous activities. In November 1984, the CCP Central Committee and the State Council issued a joint *Notice on Strictly Controlling the Establishment of National Organisations* in an effort to prevent the organisation of national NGOs under the sponsorship of central government agencies (Yan Dong 2007). The 1981 and 1984 policy statements, however, failed to prevent the continuous growth in the number of NGOs. As Professor Lieberthal pointed out in his book *Governing China* (2004), efforts to correct the wrongs of Mao's repressive policies through rehabilitation, the dismantling of Mao's economic policies, ending Mao's political purges, and the opening up of the country to technology, capital and even information from the capitalist West unleashed unexpected consequences, to the shock of senior leaders including Deng Xiaoping and his reformist associates (Lieberthal 2004, 131–37). Against this much-relaxed political atmosphere, for the first time in the history of the People's Republic of China, Chinese society enjoyed some breathing room.

Towards the end of the 1980s, the concern of conservatives within the party leadership about the spread of so-called "bourgeois liberalism" led to a tightening of political controls. In 1988, the Chinese government adopted the *Measures for Managing Foundations* in response to the growing activism of college students and educated elites. The appearance during the 1989 "Beijing Spring" of unofficial student and trade unions, together with the massive nationwide protest against the party-state, sent a shockwave through the octogenarian power holders under Deng Xiaoping and Chen Yun, leading figures of the reformist and conservative camps respectively. In 1989, the party-state promulgated the *Regulation for Managing the Registration of Social Organisations* and *Tentative Measures for Managing Foreign Chambers of Commerce*. These three policy documents were designed to standardise government supervision of the existing social organisations and to curb the rise of new groups.

Most noticeably, through the *Regulation for Managing the Registration of Social Organisations*, the party-state established a dual management mechanism. While the Civil Affairs Administration was to manage NGO registration, a government office was to serve as the supervisor of each NGO (State Council 1989). Registration applications would be rejected if an organisation intending to register did not have a government office willing to be its supervisor. By requiring a government office to supervise each NGO, the "dual management mechanism" aimed to ensure that any politically or socially dangerous act would be squashed in its infancy by the supervisor. The era of cautious acceptance of non-government activities came to an end with the suppression of the students' demonstration in June 1989. China entered a new era of more restrictions and greater government surveillance.'

An era of restrictions

The third era (1989 to the present) of NGO development was one of great state supervision and restriction. Convinced that autonomous social activities could threaten the established ruling order, the party-state began to clean up and re-register social organisations. As a result, the number of nationally registered NGOs had by the end of 1992 dropped to 1,200, a reduction of more than 400, and locally registered NGOs had reduced to 180,000, a decrease of more than 20,000 (Yan Dong 2007). Despite the restriction, Deng Xiaoping's 1992 "South China Tour" speech calling for bolder reform and more openness to the outside world not only revived economic activities but also led to a more relaxed political environment. Administrative decentralisation, economic privatisation, increasing pluralism, and greater concentration of resources in the hands of private individuals have neutralised the restraining force of the new policies. Social groups dedicated to issues that were not politically sensitive took shape. This revival of autonomous social activities did not escape the watchful eyes of the party-state. In response, the CCP Central Committee and the State Council issued in 1996 a *Notice on Strengthening the Work of Management over Social Organisations and Private Non-profit Enterprises*. The party-state wanted to make sure that NGOs were not being used as a tool by domestic or international forces to challenge China's socio-economic system and the legitimacy of the CCP. The main targets of the 1996 Notice were NGOs that advocated political reform, individual freedom, political participation, human rights, religious freedom, separation of powers or competitive elections (Yan Dong 2007).

In 1998, the State Council revised the 1989 *Regulation for Managing the Registration of Social Organisations*. Additionally, in October of the same year it promulgated the Tentative Measures for the Management of the Registration of the Private Non-profit Enterprises. Following massive protests by Falun Gong followers in 1998, the CCP Central Committee and the State Council issued in October 1999 a *Notice on Further Strengthening the Work of Management over NGOs*, targeting the so-called sabotage activities that were allegedly exploiting the grievances of the jobless, veterans, and migrant workers (Yan Dong 2007). The notice reaffirmed the "dual management" mechanism. The Civil Affairs Administration was to ensure that all NGO applicants met the requirements for registration, while the supervisory agency maintained daily supervision of the operation of the NGO concerned.

For all governments, civil society is a double-edged sword. The Chinese government did make efforts to standardise management of the NGOs, as discussed above. In 1999, the State Council also adopted a Charities Act to regulate the fundraising activities of NGOs. In addition, there are more than 50 rules and regulations issued by the Civil Affairs Administration, and even more similar regulations at the local level. The state realised that NGOs are useful in areas of social management where the state is absent, weak or incapable of making a direct and effective impact. However, a civil society that relies on private resources and activists does not always see eye to eye with the party-state and may even have interests and objectives that are at odds with those of the state. A tension would always exist between autonomous societal forces and the Chinese government. While NGOs are more narrowly focused and have specific concerns that appeal to particular groups in the population, the party-state has to respond to competing voices and take care of the general societal interest.

In the reform era, the Chinese government sees economic modernisation as a top priority whose success or failure has implications for the stability of the regime. Activities that challenge the party's policies, question its development projects, or demand changes to productive activities for the sake of environmental protection are seen as roadblocks to the government's political objectives. This tension between the government and societal forces can generate mutual mistrust and consequences often unfavourable to the NGOS. Animal protection advocacy is a new phenomenon. Animal protection NGOs are one of the youngest of Chinese civic groups. How have animal protection NGOs been able to rise, operate and expand since the 1990s, and what are the challenges facing Chinese NGOs and activists?

The rise of animal protection NGOs

Although animal protection groups are relatively new members of Chinese civil society, there were efforts to create societies for animal protection in the pre-Communist era. Lu Bicheng (1883–1943), a writer, women's rights and animal protection advocate, was arguably modern China's first pioneer of animal protection. Not only did she publish newspaper articles introducing Chinese readers to European animal protection ideas and practices, she also filed a high-profile lawsuit – later known as "the dog lawsuit" – with the aim of bringing public attention to the need for greater compassion for nonhuman animals. In 1928, she called for the formation of a "China Society for the Protection of Animals," modelled on the British Royal Society for the Prevention of Cruelty to Animals (Li Yizhi 2018). Although Lu's views on women's rights and on animal protection were considered a far cry from the reality of China at that time and she was ridiculed for "loving animals more than people," she was happy to see the establishment of the country's first animal protection association, the Nanjing Society for the Prevention of Cruelty to Animals (NSPCA), in 1934 in Nanjing, the capital of the Republic of China.

The NSPCA was registered with the Nanjing municipal police authorities on 18 July 1934. The society produced a charter agreed upon by all its members. Article 2 of the Charter called for an end to cruelty to livestock, the promotion of animal health, and the public dissemination of information about animal care. Since the society was strongly supported by Mme Chiang Kaishek, China's first lady, it had some impact on policy-making and was allowed to contribute to the drafting of rules and regulations and their enforcement (Chang, Michaels, Littlefair and Li 2010, 254-55).The establishment of the NSPCA was ground-breaking in that animal protection had not previously been made a priority given the economic reality of the majority of Chinese people in the early 1930s. However, progress was hampered by the escalating Sino-Japanese war during the next 11 years.

By the end of 1949, China had gone through a 14-year war with Japan (1931-45) and a three-year civil war. No other societies against animal cruelty had been established. China was on the verge of a fundamental transformation when the Chinese Communist Party replaced the Nationalist Party of China as the ruling group. Building a strong, prosperous, and socialist new nation was the political objective of the triumphant Communist Party. During the entire pre-reform era, the Chinese Communist leadership maintained tight control over most aspects of people's lives. Besides the lack of the necessary material conditions for the rise of autonomous activities, the authorities did not believe that society should be given more freedom for such activities.

In the 1980s, dogs and cats began to enter the homes of urban residents thanks to improved economic conditions as a result of the initial success of the reform program and a weakening of the ideological bias against pet-keeping. Animal lovers began to form rescue groups, set up shelters, and stage protests in response to incidents of animal cruelty. They acted as individuals or organised as volunteer groups for specific tasks such as feeding stray cats or rescuing dogs or cats from the streets. Such ad hoc and temporary actions lasted until the end of the 1980s.

7 China's animal protection NGOs

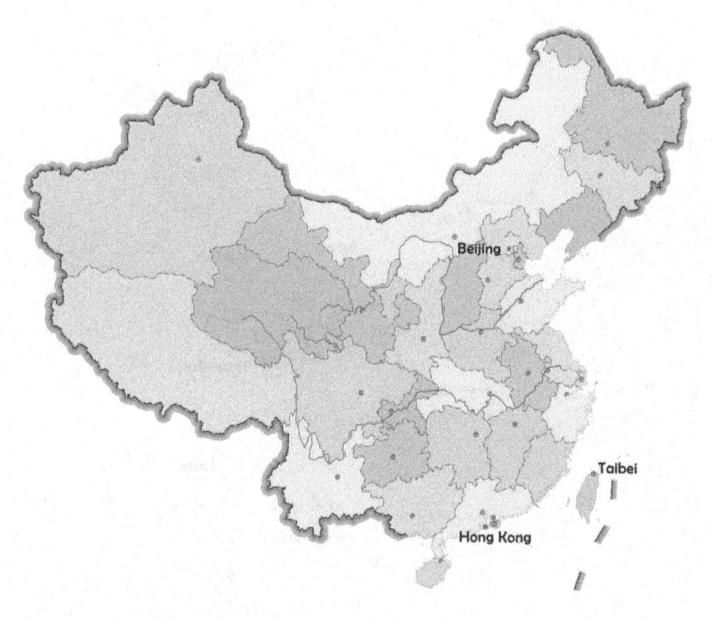

Figure 7.1 The animal protection movement in China, 1990.

In 1992, the China Small Animal Protection Association (CSAPA), the first national animal protection group, was established in Beijing. Since then, animal protection groups, societies, rescue operations, and shelters have multiplied across the country. The maps in figures 7.1, 7.2 and 7.3 illustrate the expansion of animal protection community in mainland China.

There is no national data on the total number of officially registered animal advocacy groups in the country. Unregistered groups for animal protection are believed to exist in all provinces and municipalities. The rise of animal protection groups has coincided with the expansion of NGO operations. Like NGO developments in other countries, the explosive expansion of autonomous activities happened at the turn of the century when the Chinese economy began a spirited take-off and when per capita income crossed the threshold of $1,000. In the early 1980s, when the International Crane Society and the World

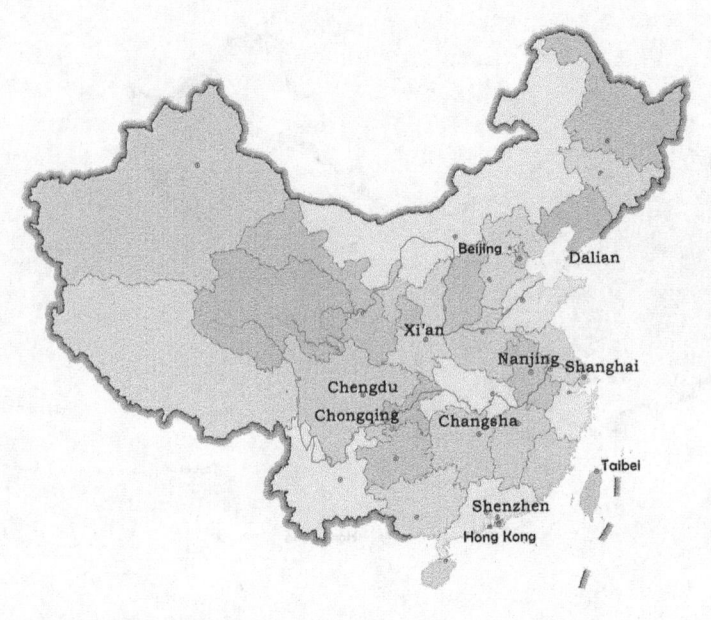

Figure 7.2 The animal protection movement in China, 2000.

Wildlife Fund started to operate in mainland China, animal lovers realised that they would be more effective under the umbrella of a social organisation for advancing animal protection. Following the establishment of the CSAPA, the Friends of Nature (FON) was created under the leadership of Liang Congjie, grandson of China's reformist scholar Liang Qichao (1873–1929). Although he was inspired by Greenpeace, a combative Western environmental organisation, Liang adopted a more conciliatory tone for FON.

FON aimed to assist and persuade the Chinese authorities to take into consideration the environmental consequences of their economic modernisation program. Through persuasion instead of confrontation, Mr Liang hoped to convince the Chinese government to tackle the environmental issues that he believed threatened China's long-term and sustainable growth. In this way, Mr Liang positioned FON as a collaborator of the government, not a troublemaker. In his opinion,

7 China's animal protection NGOs

Figure 7.3 The animal protection movement in China, 2013.

FON's interest in building an environmentally safe country did not contradict the long-term political objectives of the government.[2]

Wildlife is another area where nongovernmental activities increased in the 1990s. With the opening of the Chinese economy, the legalisation of private productive activities, and government support for the use of wildlife as a natural resource, China's wildlife has faced an unprecedented crisis. People who care about the country's wildlife have joined together to confront illegal hunters. For the early wildlife and environmental activists, China was a hugely dangerous terrain. The "Wild Yak" brigade operating in Kekexili on the Qinghai Plateau, more than 4,600 metres above sea level, was one such group that faced unimaginable difficulties, including the dangers posed by the much

---

2 Interview with Mme Qin Xiaona, founder of the Capital Animal Welfare Association, 16 July 2019.

better equipped poachers. The 60 brigade members consisted of local cadres, herdsmen, army veterans, and middle school graduates. They fought a bloody battle to protect Tibetan antelopes against poachers, who often outnumbered them and were armed with firearms (Zhang Tianfu 2017). Their heroism touched the hearts of many in China, particularly NGOs such as FON, CSAPA, and Green Pearl River, an environmental group in Guangzhou. Chinese celebrities and journalists joined the call for the Chinese government to step up efforts against poaching. The pressure paid off. In 1996, Kekexili was made a provincial nature reserve. One year later, it was elevated in protection and was made a national nature reserve. In 2000, some of the "Wild Yak" brigade members were employed by the Kekexili Nature Reserve Administration. It was reported that, since 2006, no gunshots had been heard on the reserve and the population of Tibetan antelopes grew from some 20,000 to more than 60,000 (Zhang Tianfu 2017).

Another major focus of animal protection groups has been rescue and sheltering operations. Starting in the mid-1990s, shelters for rescued dogs and cats began to emerge in Beijing, Chengdu, Chongqing, Shanghai, Wuhan, Dalian and other coastal cities. Many of these began as informal operations and later became registered NGOs. In April 2017, the China Companion Animal Protection Symposium held in Chengdu was attended by 154 activists representing 109 groups from 49 Chinese cities. It was estimated that 36 of these groups were officially registered NGOs.[3] Registration is the goal of most animal protection groups that have worked in rescue, animal care, emergency response, and sheltering. In 2013, the Qinhuangdao Small Animal Protection Association was officially registered after years of efforts to do so. The Kuitun Small Animal Protection Association of Xinjiang in northwestern China was finally issued a registration certificate in 2016 after helping to shelter and care for thousands of abandoned dogs collected off the streets by the city's animal control officers. More organisations however are still undergoing the tedious and time-consuming process of registration at the same time as they are overwhelmed with the daily operation of their facilities.

---

3   Interview on 22 November 2017 with Irene Feng, director of Companion Animal Protection Department, Animals Asia Foundation.

7 China's animal protection NGOs

Seeking legal status

Registration is important for NGOs, as it confers legal status. Additionally, successful registration helps to build an NGO's public trust and social acceptance, and its capacity to raise funds, recruit staff, and advocate for policy change. Although animal protection work is largely not politically sensitive, registration has been a headache for most animal protection organisations seeking to gain legal status. The government's registration policy can sometimes seem to be an insurmountable obstacle. According to Article 10, Chapter 3 of the 1989 *Regulation on the Management of Registration of Social Organisations*, an applicant must provide an application for registration, a consent form from a government office willing to act as its supervisor, a copy of the organisation's charter, contact information, information about the person in charge, and membership information. However, the new regulations adopted in 1998 made NGO registration requirements more specific and more stringent. For example, the applicant organisation must have full-time staff members (Item 4, Article 9, Chapter 3), and must provide proof that it has the right to use its premises (Item 3, Article 11, Chapter 3).

The 1998 Regulation also requires the applicant organisation to have at least 50 individual members or 30 member organisations (Item 1, Article 9, Chapter 3). Additionally, national organisations must have an operations fund of at least RMB 100,000 yuan, and local organisations a fund of RMB 30,000 yuan (Item 5, Article 9, Chapter three). However, it is the requirement that NGOs must find a government office willing to be their sponsor and supervisor that is the biggest hurdle. Whichever office agrees to be the supervisor of an NGO, it has the responsibility to make sure that the NGO "behaves itself" and does not make trouble, and the heads of the office concerned can be held accountable for activities perpetrated by the NGO. This is why government offices are not motivated to be sponsors or supervisors. While this hurdle has blocked the registration efforts of most of the NGOs wishing to acquire legal status, others have been able to surmount it.

"Registration is both difficult and achievable," said Wang Lisha, director of Zhuzhou Small Animal Protection Association. Below are examples of NGOs that have successfully registered and how these animal protection groups were able to achieve this.

China Small Animal Protection Association (CSAPA)

The CSAPA was the first nationally registered animal advocacy charity in China, and its name ensured its position as the national flagship organisation. CSAPA was founded in Beijing by Lu Di, a legendary retired college professor, Korean War veteran, and former special assistant of Chinese classics to the "great leader" Mao Zedong. With decades of rescue experience, in 1988 Professor Lu started the process of registering CSAPA with the Civil Affairs Ministry. The registration application was delayed when the 1989 student demonstrations ended in bloodshed, after which the Chinese government put a hold on all applications. It was not until Deng Xiaoping's "South China Tour" and his speech calling for accelerated development and greater openness that applications for NGO registration were reviewed and handled by the government. In December 1992, CSAPA was successfully registered. As a national NGO, CSAPA's mission is to promote respect for the lives of all creatures; to protect animals; to safeguard the right to life of animals; and to stand up for their right not to be abused.[4]

Achieving legal status for CSAPA was challenging. "Finding the appropriate government office to be our sponsor or supervisor, as required by the registration regulation, was not easy," said Professor Lu. Indeed, animal protection was a new policy area, and most officials did not know which government office would be the most appropriate supervisory agency. Professor Lu approached various national agencies. "We knew that there was legal responsibility on the part of the government office if it were willing to be our 'boss,'" said Professor Lu. Eventually, she was able to get the Ministry of Agriculture to be the supervisor for CSAPA thanks to her decade-long connections with senior officials in the national government. Commenting on CSAPA's

---

4 Interviews with Professor Lu Di in December 2009, November 2010, December 2010 and June 2011 in Beijing. See also China Small Animal Protection Association, "An introduction to China Small Animal Protection Association," at http://www.csapa.org/about.htm.

registration under the Agriculture Ministry, Mme Qin Xiaona, director of Capital Animal Welfare Association, believed that animal protection was not a politically sensitive matter and that Professor Lu Di was a member of the establishment. "The Agriculture Ministry had no reason to be afraid that CSAPA would be a troublemaker," said Mme Qin. "Her experience as Mao's assistant in Chinese classics was definitely an asset that had helped bring down the mental barriers among the officials in the Ministry."[5]

Kuitun Small Animal Protection Association

Unlike Professor Lu Di, Zhao Yixia, director and founder of Xinjiang's Kuitun Small Animal Protection Association, started her rescue work in direct confrontation with the local authorities. As in most Chinese cities, stray dogs used to be handled brutally by local authorities. For years, Kuitun authorities beat stray dogs to death on the streets, rounded them up and deserted them in the mountains, or buried them alive. There was no government facility to accommodate stray dogs. Zhao quit her own business when she started rescuing the stray dogs to prevent the brutal dog cull. By rescuing and sheltering the dogs, she aimed to show local authorities that there was an alternative approach. To get the local authorities to stop the dog culls, she reported to the provincial authorities in Urumuqi on the negligence and incompetence of the local officials in urban animal management. Under pressure from Urumuqi's Autonomous Region Government leaders, Kuitun senior officials sat down with Ms Zhao to listen to her criticism and suggestions. At the same time, "they sent low-ranking officials without my knowledge to spy on my sheltering operation, partly to see if my operation was involved in any shady or illegal activities," said Ms Zhao.[6]

The local authorities found nothing illegal or inappropriate that could be used against Zhao. "Although they did not say it, I could feel that most officials who went to see my facility were genuinely impressed with what I had been doing," she said. The local authorities realised that

---

5 Interview with Mme Qin Xiaona, founder of Capital Animal Welfare Association, 23 July 2017, Beijing.
6 Interview with Ms Zhao Yixia, 10 September 2017, WeChat.

what Zhao was doing was in fact what the local government should be doing. In 2015, the local authorities helped to secure a location as a shelter for Zhao's dogs. Knowing that her long-term operation was not sustainable without legal status, Zhao contacted the city government for registration assistance. Recommended by a deputy mayor, the Kuitun Agriculture, Animal Husbandry and Water Resource Bureau was designated as the overseeing agency for the Kuitun Small Animal Protection Association. Zhao received the registration papers on 31 March 2016.[7]

Ping An A Fu Animal Protection Association

Nanjing is the provincial capital of Jiangsu Province. It is also one of the fastest growing cities in the country. By the end of the 1990s, pet dogs had increased in number in the city. Conflicts over dogs and draconian police measures against stray and confiscated dogs had become a major public issue. In 2002, Ha Wenjin created a volunteer group, the Nanjing Small Animal Rescue Station. In a matter of a few months, the station was inundated with hundreds of rescued dogs. Ms Ha had no choice but to build an organisation that could act beyond responding to calls for help with stray and abandoned animals. At the same time, she realised that an end to the government's draconian dog cull and the adoption of a new urban animal control policy would be a better way to deal with conflict over dogs and dog ownership.

By the end of 2009, Ms Ha had involved her volunteers in a variety of police operations to rescue abandoned dogs and cats, confiscating dogs bound for the meat markets, getting dogs off the highways and out of cruel situations, and educating the public about responsible pet ownership. She attended hearings for revising the city's regulation on dog ownership. At the hearings, she opposed the use of a dog's height to determine its eligibility as a pet in the core regions of the city. She also suggested that Nanjing should avoid the mistake of imposing a high registration fee on dog owners. Importantly, since 2007, Ms Ha and her team have helped to operate and manage the dog shelter of the Nanjing police. In 2013, when Ms Ha decided to register her group as Ping An

---

7   Interview with Ms Zhao Yixia, 10 September 2017, WeChat.

7 China's animal protection NGOs

A Fu Animal Protection Association, the Nanjing Police Department agreed to be the supervisory agency.

As the biggest animal protection group in Nanjing, Ping An A Fu has become, in the words of Ms Ha, a "dumping site" for unwanted dogs and cats. "We cannot say no to these animals left at our doorstep," said Ms Ha. The result was a crushingly huge number of dogs and cats at Ping An shelter. Ping An A Fu had in May 2019 more than 9,000 dogs and 300 cats under its care. Feeding this many dogs and cats has been a huge challenge. While Ping An A Fu has tried its utmost to care for the animals, the shelter conditions and the high density of the dogs have attracted criticism. While she conducts sterilisation, Ms Ha does not believe in euthanasia. She could not do it even if she agreed that some terminally ill dogs and severely handicapped cats would benefit from it. "Euthanasia would be a weapon used to destroy Ping An A Fu by our opponents," Ms Ha added. She is right. The Chinese public, including animal lovers, are yet to accept euthanasia as a solution to end suffering.

Ping An A Fu is at a crossroads. With a huge financial and operational burden to feed so many dogs and cats, Ping An A Fu's relations with the government, and its own development, are being tested.[8]

Zhuzhou Animal Protection Association

For the Zhuzhou Animal Protection Association (ZAPA) in Hunan, seeking legal status has been a bittersweet experience. ZAPA's successful registration in 2013 was the result of a combination of factors. The founding members of ZAPA were a rare group of passionate activists who were also politically savvy, knowing very well the ability of local authorities to either help or undermine their cause. With this awareness, they took every opportunity to present themselves as the government's collaborators and assistants. In 2012, when the Zhuzhou city government launched a campaign to build a model city of civilisation, ZAPA members jumped on the bandwagon. They staged public events to call for responsible pet ownership and for dog owners to be sensitive to the feelings of others who did not have dogs or who

---

8   Interview with Ha Wenjin, 7 September 2009, Nanjing, China.

did not like dogs. These events were exactly what the local authorities needed in response to growing complaints about public sanitation and dog abandonment. "These events helped to project our organisation as a positive force that the local government can trust for promoting its agenda," said Wang Lisha, director of ZAPA.

ZAPA's founding members knew the power of the media and the importance of using media for their purposes. Besides the *Zhuzhou Evening News*, other local media such as Transportation Radio helped to publicise ZAPA's events and activities. "Whenever we have a public event, we extend our invitation to the media," Wang said. These public events to advocate for responsible pet keeping helped to promote ZAPA as a public interest organisation. Local media have on several occasions helped to promote ZAPA's needs to the public. The city's officials in charge of media even stepped in to persuade the director of the Animal Husbandry and Fisheries Bureau to be the supervisory office of ZAPA, a condition for ZAPA's successful registration as an NGO.

Name recognition has led to an increase in requests for help and a greater financial burden. By the end of 2016, ZAPA had rescued over 1,000 abandoned and stray dogs and other animals. It responded to distress calls all year round. "When a citizen spots a dog in need of help, she is most likely to contact us rather than any other rescue individuals or groups," said Ms Wang. To the city's animal loving residents, ZAPA is a trusted and reliable resource. The great number of dogs in its shelters has been a heavy financial burden. With limited financial help from the local government and restrictions on fund-raising, ZAPA founding members have long been the main donors.

ZAPA is not just a rescue and sheltering operation. In 2012, when the city authorities were planning a city-wide dog cull, ZAPA responded swiftly and urged the authorities to suspend the ineffective and hugely unpopular measure. To prevent future mass dog culls, in May 2013, ZAPA engaged the police department in talks to develop a longer-term solution for the city's dog abandonment problem. Instead of responding passively or reactively to dog bites and other incidents, ZAPA suggested that the authorities adopt proactive measures to anticipate common issues associated with pet ownership and human–dog conflict in a modern city, and to have in place a set of measures to prevent or reduce the number of incidents. These measures should include public education, incentives to encourage dog registration, free or subsidised micro-chipping, incentives such as discounted registration fees to encourage de-sexing, and strict regulation of pet breeding businesses.

For pet owners, ZAPA called on authorities to adopt policies to encourage pet owners to walk their dogs using a leash, to respect the sensitivities of people who do not like pets, and generally to be responsible pet owners. In July 2013, ZAPA signed an agreement with the police department. Responsibility for the city's animal control service was thereafter contracted to ZAPA. Having contracted the city's animal control and sheltering services, ZAPA succeeded in getting the city's legislature to budget RMB 300,000 yuan per year for these services. With the budget in place, the city's police department and the Animal Husbandry Bureau were able to reallocate RMB 250,000 yuan to ZAPA in 2016 for carrying out the contracted services. ZAPA was one of the few local NGOs that took over their cities' animal sheltering and care services.

ZAPA is still operating on difficult terrain. Hunan is one of the major markets for dog meat. Dog meat traders have aggressively promoted dog meat consumption. Zhuzhou, a major transportation hub, sits on the highway connecting the country's major dog meat markets in South and Central China. On 6 July 2017, with the help of the local law enforcement agencies (public security and animal disease control), ZAPA succeeded in ending a standoff between animal lovers from across the country and a truck driver who could not produce evidence of legal acquisition and health certificates for 240 cats and 121 dogs bound for Guangdong's slaughterhouses. Previously, animal activist groups across the country had agreed that no compensation should be paid to owners of the dogs on the lorries intercepted by animal activists, and that trans-provincial shipment of undocumented live dogs and cats must be punished by law-enforcement agencies. The July 2017 rescue put this into practice.

In 2018–19, ZAPA joined the Zhuzhou city government in efforts to draft a dog ownership management policy. As the city's officially registered animal charity, ZAPA submitted detailed proposals related to the duties of dog owners and the responsibilities of the city. ZAPA's proposals balanced the rights of society with the enforcement authority of the government. As Ms Wang stated, companion animals have entered the homes of many Zhuzhou people. "Owning or keeping a pet dog cannot be seen as a luxury," she said. "It is a right of citizens." However, she saw the necessity for the new policy to encourage responsible pet ownership and to penalise irresponsible pet owners. The collaboration between ZAPA and the local authorities has received the attention of the national government.

In summary, managing NGOs in a rapidly changing society is a new challenge for the Chinese government. Animal protection NGOs have grown out of an increasingly pluralistic society. The appearance of new groups suggests that the ruling authorities can no long assume that its social policies are supported by all. Voices questioning government actions and demanding changes to existing policies are getting louder. Authorities are adjusting to a society that is less likely to take things for granted (Tang Wenfang 2001, 890–909; Mertha 2009, 995–1012). The successful registration of the groups discussed above showcases the wisdom and tactics used by NGO founders to get legal standing. It also sheds light on local authorities' willingness to collaborate with civil society to offload some responsibilities that are new to them. The registered NGOs have in fact presented themselves as equal partners of urban social management, a situation that China's Communist state, like most 20th century Eurasian socialist regimes, has tried hard to avoid.

Animal protection NGOs in action

In his *Developing Democracy: Towards Consolidation* (1999), Larry Diamond identifies six kinds of activities that NGOs engage in. These activities, in the order of increasing involvement in a country's political process, are as follows:

1. To express their interests, passions, and ideas;
2. To exchange information;
3. To achieve collective goals;
4. To make demands on the state;
5. To improve the structure and functioning of the state; and
6. To hold state officials accountable (Diamond 1999, 121)

7 China's animal protection NGOs

As Diamond points out, the more an NGO is involved in activities further down the list, the more it impacts its country's political process and democratisation. While most registered animal protection NGOs in China have been involved in all six activities, the majority of unregistered groups have focused their efforts on activities 1, 2 and 3. Activities 4, 5 and 6 require an NGO to balance its demands, interests and position with those of the state. One view holds that the ability to participate in activities 4, 5 and 6 without inflicting harm to oneself also depends on the leadership's connections to the party-state and the resources it commands (Zhan and Tang 2013, 381-99). The following are two cases of animal protection NGO actions that highlight different success and risk factors.

China and foreign cruelty products

China's increasing participation in the global economy and its lack of animal protection legislation have attracted foreign businesses involved in cruel products and practices. In 2009, after the Catalonian legislature decided to outlaw bullfighting in the entire region, a Spanish company announced plans to build a large bullring in Beijing's Huairou County. The news elicited immediate opposition from Chinese animal activists who succeeded in stopping the plan (Mang Ping 2010). In 2011, Rodeo China, a newly founded American company, announced that it would stage a rodeo show at Beijing's Olympic Stadium. This event, with a prize purse of $8 million and a cast of 120 cowboys, 36 bulls and 90 steers, was reportedly part of a US–China cultural exchange program endorsed by both governments (Moore 2011). This exchange program was shut down by a nationwide coalition led by the Capital Animal Welfare Association (CAWA).

In 2012, Creek Project Investments, a foreign company, revealed that it intended to build the world's biggest foie gras plant by the side of Poyang Lake, China's biggest freshwater lake (Xu Cao 2012). The project died soon after it hit the news as a result of overwhelming opposition from Chinese activists. Earlier in 2004, both Shanghai and Beijing met with strong opposition when they attempted to introduce Spanish bullfighting into their cities (Wang Pei 2004). Not surprisingly, some businesses apparently still entertain the idea of staging and introducing Spanish bullfighting in China (Mang Ping 2010). More recent reports revealed that there were plans in Australia to export kangaroo meat and, more provocatively, dingo meat to China (Samuels 2016; Burton 2015).

The campaign against the Canadian seal trade

The success of Chinese animal activists in stopping the import of Canadian seal meat should serve as a warning or a deterrent to foreign companies engaged in animal cruelty and intending to market those products to China. In 2009, the European Union decided to ban the commercial seal trade in all 27 member countries. China was identified by the Canadian sealing industry as a potential "replacement market." In 2010, Canada jumpstarted its trade offensive, targeting the Chinese market in an effort to salvage its sealing industry. In January 2011, Canadian Fisheries Minister Gail Shea made a high-profile visit to Beijing and signed a Memorandum of Understanding with the Chinese government on marketing seal meat to China. The Minister's trade diplomacy in Beijing aroused much expectation from the Canadian sealing industry. Representatives of the industry were convinced that the Chinese habit of eating everything should be used to the industry's advantage (Watts 2011).

In response to the Canadian trade offensive, a nationwide alliance of Chinese animal groups was formed. The country's leading NGOs including CSAPA, the Capital Animal Welfare Association (CAWA), the Green Beagle Environmental Institute in Beijing, the Vshine Animal Protection Association, the Chinese Journalist Saloon for Animal Protection, and the Xiamen Animal Protection Association all joined the campaign in different capacities. A leading group was formed under Dan Zhang, one of the founding members of the Journalist Saloon for Animal Protection and a prolific writer on animal protection subjects. A campaign plan was put in place. The key components of the plan included dissemination of information, public outreach, government relationship-building, and seeking international support. The consensus of the leading group was that the Chinese public must be exposed to the facts about Canada's seal hunt; that the Chinese government must be approached and made aware of the health

7 China's animal protection NGOs

concerns related to seal products; and that the campaign needed help from international animal protection groups that had long worked on seal trade issues.

As to the tactics, the leading group agreed that a non-confrontational approach should be adopted and no protests should be staged against the Chinese government. Efforts were to be made to seek meetings with the national government agency involved in the China–Canadian MOU. The purpose of these meetings was to provide the Chinese government with information about the controversy surrounding the Canadian seal hunt and the World Trade Organisations (WTO)'s exception (Article XX: General Exceptions) on banning the import of immoral products, so that the government could make informed decisions about the Canadian seal meat proposal.

The coalition's public outreach effort consisted of three components. It first reached out to the media. On 30 November 2010, CAWA held a press conference in Beijing to launch the "China Campaign against Seal Trade." Invited to the press conference was Rebecca Aldworth, Executive Director of the Humane Society International, Canada who had documented Canadian seal hunt over the past 12 years. At the press conference, a seven-minute bilingual video about the seal hunt was shown. The Chinese media representatives were particularly shocked to see the killing of seal pups, "Canada's panda bears" in the eyes of many Chinese (Zhang 2010). Next, the campaign sought online publicity, in order to reach a greater number of Chinese consumers, particularly the younger generation. A special report, *Elegy for Seals: The Secrets behind Seal Products*, was published on the Tencent Internet portal (Tencent.com 2010). The bilingual video went viral immediately after it was posted on Tencent. Using Chinese search words such as "boycott Canadian seal trade," one is likely to pull up more than 240,000 results from Chinese language media reports on the controversy.

The next component of the outreach effort was mobilisation of the country's young people. In 2011, 2012 and 2013, some 6,000 students in Xiamen, in southeast Fujian Province, attended seminars, summer camps, and other events organised by Xiamen Animal Protection Association, a member of the campaign coalition. Seal protection was one focus of these events. Xiao Bing, director of the Xiamen Animal

Protection Association, supervised the outreach program and submitted petitions signed by the students to the Canadian Embassy in Beijing. In 2011, a "Seal Protection Poster Design Contest" was launched on 4 October, World Animal Protection Day. More than 240 entries had been received by the closing date in early November. The 15 award-winning posters captured the cruelty of seal hunting, the determination of the activists to boycott the trade, and the call for an end to seal hunting (Tencent.com 2011). Following a series of events in Xiamen schools in 2011–12, a banner signed by hundreds of Xiamen students calling for an end to seal hunting was sent to Mr David Mulroney, Canadian Ambassador to China (2009–12). These outreach efforts served to educate the public and to apply pressure on the Canadian government.

Government relations were a major component of the campaign. Alongside the outreach program, the coalition actively lobbied the Chinese government in ways that were away from public or media attention. In other words, the coalition approached the responsible trade office quietly, instead of publicly criticising the government. CAWA sent a package of information about seal slaughter, the potential health impact of seal meat consumption, and the questionable claims of the Canadian sealing industry to the office in charge of animal product imports. The Humane Society International (HSI) and its Canadian affiliate HSI-Canada provided most of the background information about Canadian seal slaughter, at the request of the Chinese coalition.

At the same time, the campaign team approached delegates to the NPC and the Chinese People's Political Consultative Conference (CPPCC), the two "chambers" of China's national legislature, about legislative proposals to ban seal trade. Their lobbying efforts paid off. In late February 2011, Zhang Kangkang, a famous writer and a CPPCC deputy, submitted the first proposal for ending seal product trade to the annual session of the 11th CPPCC (Zhang 2011). In 2013, a second proposal on marine mammal protection that included seal protection was submitted to the 12th NPC. This proposal called for an end to the import of polar bear skins, seal oil, seal pelts and other seal products. The proposals were forwarded from the Congress to the relevant trade offices.[9]

7 China's animal protection NGOs

In March 2011, in collaboration with China's official International Chamber of Commerce, the Chinese coalition held a one-day conference entitled "Stop Seal Trade, Promote Animal Protection and Pursue an Environmentally Friendly Trade." The conference was meant to gently push the Chinese authorities to reach a decision on Canada's seal meat trade offensive. Right before the conference, CAWA and activist representatives met with Chinese officials in charge of animal product imports. The officials confirmed the receipt of the information package regarding the Canadian seal industry. They admitted that the package provided a comprehensive and alternative view of seal slaughter unlike that given by the Canadian government. The officials also told the activists that the Chinese government had noticed media and public reaction to the Canadian seal meat trade proposal. It was looking into all options and would have a decision soon on Canada's seal meat export proposal.[10]

Meanwhile, protests directed at Canada and the Canadian sealing industry were vigorously staged. A protest letter co-signed by more than 40 Chinese animal protection groups was addressed and sent to Gail Shea, the Canadian Fisheries Minister, when she was in Beijing promoting Canadian seal products at the 37th Beijing International Fur and Leather Expo. Protesters in front of the Canadian pavilion at the expo held a sign declaring that "Chinese People Do Not Welcome Canadian Seal Products," causing a huge stir (Clifton 2011). The coalition also mobilised activists in 2012, 2013 and 2014 to protest at international fisheries exhibitions and fur exhibitions in Beijing, Dalian and Qingdao, where Canadian fisheries and seal traders were present (Wang 2011). The protesters presented an open letter to the Canadian Fisheries Delegation at the 17th Dalian International Fisheries Expo, asking the delegation to convey to the Canadian government the

---

9 An official letter of response written by the Agriculture Ministry to the head of the delegates who submitted the legislative proposal was received in July 2014.
10 I sat in the meeting when I was in China to attend the conference "Stop Seal Trade, Promote Animal Protection and Pursue an Environmentally Friendly Trade."

Chinese resolve to block seal meat from entering China (Sina.com 2013).

At the same time, a letter signed by more than 50 animal protection groups, led by CAWA, urged Canadian Ambassador David Mulroney to convey Chinese opposition to the Canadian sealing industry. The Ambassador's response to the letter repeated the claims of the sealing industry and of the Canadian government (Meng Si 2011). Chinese protests continued to be directed at the Canadian government. The Chinese campaign also wrote to Prime Minister Stephen Harper and the Canadian Parliament, calling for Canada to stop promoting the seal trade to China.

The campaign leaders confronted Canadian officials on several occasions. At the invitation of the Canadian embassy in Beijing, "an unprecedented move" as it was referred to by the embassy, the coalition leaders met Ambassador Guy Saint-Jacques at the Canadian embassy in 2013. To the shock of the Chinese activists, the ambassador, former chief of Canada's delegation to the global climate change conferences, used most of his talking time to defend the Canadian sealing industry (Zhang 2013). In April 2014, coordinated by Mr Zhu Chunquan, the IUCN representative in China, they met with Mr Mathew King, Canada's Deputy Minister of Fisheries and four other Canadian officials at the Canadian Embassy in Beijing. Like Ambassador Saint-Jacques, Mr King defended the seal hunt as humane, sustainable, compliant with international and Canadian animal welfare standards, and conducive to the livelihood of Inuit hunters and other fishermen. He accused the Chinese campaign of spreading incorrect information about seal hunting in order to influence others' consumption decisions.[11] The Chinese activists advanced a nine-point response, calling on the Canadian government and the sealing industry to stop promoting seal products to China; to stop using the Inuit people to defend a commercial trade that mostly benefited white Canadians; to be aware that the Chinese campaign would continue since China had its own seal species to protect; and to know that the seal trade tarnished Canada's reputation in China.[12]

---

11 Interview with Zhang Dan, chief coordinator of the China Campaign against Canadian Seal Trade, 6 May 2014.

The Chinese campaign swept across 14 Chinese cities. By the end of 2012, when CAWA attended the International Chamber of Commerce annual meeting, sources close to the trade office revealed that the Chinese government was considering tabling Canada's seal meat sales proposal. In an interview in early 2014, Canadian Fisheries Minister Gail Shea admitted that her attempt to market seal meat to China had failed. She blamed the Chinese animal activists and Canadian animal groups for the failure of her own misguided trade offensive (CBC 2013).

Success factors

This campaign could not have achieved its intended objective without a smart strategy. "We first of all had to tell the Chinese consumers what they could end up having on their dinner table," Qin Xiaona said, commenting on the importance of public education. The seven-minute video provided by the Humane Society International turned more than 2 million Chinese off in the first week of its release on the Chinese internet. "We can see that Chinese consumers do not want to be an accomplice of the ugly Canadian brutality packaged in the name of native Canadian livelihoods," she added.

Second, the alliance took the correct approach in dealing with the Chinese government. Instead of badmouthing the trade office involved in the MOU with Canada, they set out to provide information to the leading officials of the relevant office, to enable them to make informed decisions. The campaign presented the office with a complete package of information about the seal slaughter, international opposition to commercial sealing, Canadian domestic opposition to the industry, potential health impacts of seal products, and the WTO/GATT general exceptions that China could use to defend a trade ban on seal meat. "As an animal protection association, we were shared with important information and data on the seal trade by partner groups in Canada and the USA that had over the years accumulated tons of info and facts about the trade," Mm. Qin said.

Third, the campaign did not just work with the trade office of the national government. It also targeted China's national lawmaking

---

12   Telephone interview with Zhang Dan and Qin Xiaona, 6 May 2014.

bodies, the NPC and the CPPCC. Although China's national legislature is not an independent branch of the government, its influence over the country's political life has been increasing. Getting a legislative bill to the two legislative chambers could apply pressures on the trade departments of the executive arm of the Chinese government. As an indicator of the rising influence of the national legislature, legislative proposals have to be answered either by the NPC or the functional departments of the Chinese government. Both Zhang Kangkang's proposal and the proposal submitted by a different group of legislators in 2013–14 were handed over to the functional departments of the national government, whose leading officials were later emboldened to table Canada's seal meat trade proposal.

Finally, the campaign was pursued as an effort to assist the Chinese government in defence of the Chinese national interest, Chinese consumer rights, and the reputation of the Chinese nation. It was a bad idea for the Canadian industry to use a marginal culinary subculture of China, i.e., wildlife eating, as an argument for promoting seal meat. "The Canadians made a huge mistake," said Dan Zhang, the national campaign coordinator. "How can you humiliate and demonise your target customers? It was not only a racist bias, but also a reflection of some Canadians' lack of touch with the reality of a rapidly changing China." Dan added, "the outdated and controversial eating habit of a minority of people in China is no representation of the mainstream food culture of our country ... Seeing the Chinese people as a backward nation of wildlife eaters is less a poor trade strategy than a racist bias against China on the part of the Canadian sealing industry and some people in the Canadian government."

The campaign succeeded in blocking the entry of Canadian seal meat. However, Canadian seal oil and seal skins are still sold in mainland China. The campaign to end all seal product trade is continuing. In March 2016, the Chinese coalition sent a letter to Ambassador Guy Saint-Jacques calling for an end to all trade in seal products. In April the same year, 60 Chinese NGOs sent a letter to Zhao Shengrong, the China Director of the Always In Vogue chain of stores, urging him to stop selling seal fur products in China. On 23 April, a protest broke out in front of the Always In Vogue store in Shenyang, Liaoning. A 15-second advertisement against the seal trade was aired in public transportation in Dalian for two weeks. The seven-minute seal hunt video was reposted and generated more than 300,000 new views in the first week.[13] In March 2020, the campaign confirmed that the Always In Vogue branch store in Shenyang was closed.

Protection of China's bearded seals

While the Chinese campaign against the Canadian seal trade has scored a decisive victory, efforts to protect China's own bearded seals experienced a major setback. Unknown to most people in the general public, China also has a seal population. Of the eight main seal habitats, China's Bohai and Yellow Sea coastal regions are the southernmost habitat for the bearded seal subspecies (*Erignathus barbatus nauticus*). This is the only pinnipeds species that breeds inside Chinese territory. The exact breeding ground lies next to the Xiaodaozi Old Fishing Port, in Panshan County, Panjin City, in Liaoning. The Old Fishing Port sits at the mouth of the Liaohe River where wetland, swamp and a variety of fish provide a safe haven for the seals to breed and nurse their newborn pups. The area was originally inside the national Shuangtaihekou Nature Reserve, or Liaohe Nature Reserve, which was created in 1985. The reserve was elevated to become a national nature reserve in 1998 by the State Council. Both the Dalian Bearded Seal Nature Reserve and the Shuangtaihekou Nature Reserve are protected areas for seals in Liaoning Province.

The bearded seal population in China has long been declining. In the early 1930s, it was estimated that there were 7,100 seals in the Liaodong Gulf area, where the Liaohe River empties into the sea. By the end of the 1970s, the population had dropped to 2,269. By 1993, it had recovered somewhat to 4,500. However, by 2005, it had dropped to about 1,000. Over-fishing, water pollution, damages to the swamp and wetland, pollution on the Liaohe River, poaching, oil drilling, and increased tourism constituted the major contributing factors (Ding Weicheng and Luo Qi 2005).

---

13 Conversation with Yu Dezhi, Secretary General, Vshine Animal Protection Association, 20 December 2016.

Tian Jiguang, founder of the Panjin Bearded Seal Protection Volunteers Association (PBSPVA), has made seal protection his life mission. In 2007, Mr Tian registered PBSPVA as an NGO. By the end of 2011, Mr Tian and PBSPVA had established a good working relationship with the local government. PBSPVA responded to distress calls from fishermen who caught seals by accident or spotted stranded seal pups. Besides working for the rescue, rehabilitation and release of seals, Mr Tian and his team of volunteers also conducted public education programs in collaboration with government offices.

The partnership between PBSPVA and local authorities came to a halt when development projects began to encroach on seals' breeding grounds. In March 2011, a highway along the coast that would cut through the heart of the seals' core habitat was being built, reportedly before an environmental impact study had been completed. Citing relevant articles of the Law on Environmental Impact Evaluation, the *Wildlife Protection Law*, and the *Implementation Measures for the Protection of the Aquatic Wildlife*, Mr Tian filed an opinion of opposition to the Highway Department of Panjin City, the project evaluation authority, and the Northeast China General Design Institute of the Chinese Urban Construction Centre. On 8 April 2011, Mr Tian attended a "Protect Bearded Seals Forum" in Beijing co-sponsored by Beijing Capital Animal Welfare Association, the Nature University, and the Chinese Journalist Salon for Animal Protection. The forum was held at the Zoological Institute of the Chinese Academy of Sciences. As a keynote speaker, Mr Tian called on the media and the public to help stop the highway construction project (Feng Yongfeng 2011).

Having received no response from the construction authorities, Mr Tian began to petition the Party Secretary, the chairman of Panjin's People's Congress, the mayor, the chairman of the city's Political Consultative Conference, and the deputy mayors in charge of agriculture and transportation. Tian's revelation of the highway construction on social media paid off. A coalition of environmental groups across the country was formed, urging local authorities to move the highway away from the seal habitat. College students from campus environmental groups launched a "Send a Postcard" campaign, urging provincial authorities to intervene on behalf of the seals. A "Hundred Battalion" campaign, called by the media, started to pressure Panjin city government to revise the highway construction plan. Tian's Weibo post was shared more than 10,000 times. Chinese and international media such as the *China Daily, Science Times, ChinaDialogue, the People's Net, Hong Kong Cable TV*, and Spanish National Radio interviewed Mr Tian on the highway construction and the impact on the seals. Local officials had to respond to the rising pressure.

The pressure built by Mr Tian seemed to work. Panjin's department of transportation, instructed by the city's leadership, reportedly held four meetings to discuss Mr Tian's proposal on the need to revise the highway construction's original blueprint. In November 2011, led by the mayor of Panjin, the city's transportation, environmental protection and land departments undertook a two-day field investigation of the construction site. A decision was made to revise the construction plan to move the highway out of the seal habitat and to move a planned bridge seven kilometres from the original location. The revised plan suggested that the coastal highway would be longer by 37 kilometres, with an additional 170-million-yuan investment. The revision decision was a great piece of news to Tian and his supporters. However, this decision was later quietly abandoned because of the increased cost.

When Mr Tian learned in mid-2012 about the resumption of the original construction plan, the construction work had already been resumed for eight months. The highway cut through the core habitat area of the seals. Mr Tian, PBSPVA, and supporting groups across the country were shocked. On 16 August 2012, Mr Tian wrote on his Weibo blog, "Why have I opposed the construction of the Panjin coastal highway that cuts through the core habitat of seals?" He made public two points in support of his opposition. First, the seals that breed at Liaodong Gulf are the only group of pinnipeds that breed in China's territorial waters. Because of its relative isolation, this group of seals maintains unique genetic characteristics and has undeniably high scientific and ecological value. Second, Liaoning Liaohe River Mouth National Nature Reserve, where the seal habitat is situated, had already been reduced in size from 128,000 hectares to 80,000 hectares. Allowing a highway to cut through the swamp and wetland would create busy traffic. Increased human activity would lead to the fragmentation and decline of the wetland. He called for the authorities to return to the revised plan so that the highway would not cut through the nature reserve. He ended his blog by stressing that "The wetland is the most precious ecological resource of Panjin while the seals are one of Panjin's most valued ecological assets" (Tian Jiguang 2012).

PBSPVA's strong and uncompromising opposition to the highway construction was leading to a final showdown with the local authorities. The nationwide attention on Panjin was not what the local officials wanted. To the local government, the highway construction was part of the provincial and national project over which local authorities did not have much control.

PBSPVA began to encounter new problems in April 2013 when Mr Tian revealed in his blog that the Liaohe Oil Company had commenced oil drilling operations just 1,000 metres from the seal breeding and nursing sites. What was more, the *People's Daily*, the Communist Party's mouthpiece, reported the crisis faced by the seals. Under the headline "Adorable seals become homeless due to habitat loss from economic development," the *People's Daily* identified oil drilling and tourism – i.e., two key development projects – as the causes of the seals' homelessness. "Thanks to our advocacy efforts, even the fishermen have gained awareness of seal protection, in contrast to the obstacles to seal protection raised by some major companies and the local government," Tian was quoted in the report. This remark was hugely offensive both to the local authorities and to the oil drilling industry.

The *People's Daily* report alarmed the drilling company. It sent representatives to talk to Mr Tian, largely to explore how the company could quiet him. It was later revealed that a donation of RMB 100,000 yuan to PBSPVA was offered at this meeting. This was later used by the company as evidence of blackmail and extortion by Tian; although the donation was never made, the company alleged that Mr Tan exposed the drilling operation to the media in order to extort money out of the company. Following the meeting, drilling continued. In June, Mr Tian again made public the company's pollution problem. In response, the drilling company engaged Mr Tian in a new round of talks and offered to buy a high-resolution camera for PBSPVA. Who first proposed the camera donation in the meetings between Mr Tian and the drilling company representatives was a mystery. In October 2013, Mr Tian was arrested on charges of "using publicity of alleged environmental pollution to blackmail a business" (South China Weekend Review

2015). An additional charge against Mr Tian was "misappropriation of funds for personal use" allegedly involving RMB 480,000 yuan (Xu Gang 2015).

Mr Tian was indicted on 29 April 2014 and a verdict was issued on 11 September. Tian was found guilty of blackmail and misappropriation of PBSPVA funds. He was subsequently sentenced to 12 years in prison. Tian appealed to the Intermediate Court. In November 2015, the appellate court ruled in favour of the lower court's decision. However, in April 2016, the appellate court ordered that the case be re-tried by the lower court. A decision was reached on 11 August to revoke its earlier verdict on account of procedural violation. On 27 June 2017, a new sentence was issued by the court of Shuangtaizi in Panjin, reducing Tian's sentence to four years and six months in prison. Tian was still found guilty of blackmail and misappropriation of PBSPVA funds. He was also fined RMB 60,000 yuan (Liu Ji 2017).

Mr Tian's case was not only a personal setback but also a blow to the country's fledgling animal advocacy movement. Several lessons can be drawn from Tian's personal experience and his imprisonment. Although animal protection work does not directly challenge the party-state's power or its legitimacy, it can be viewed as a roadblock to the state's objective of development. Animal protection groups would be particularly disadvantaged when the targets of their criticism were big corporations of great national or local development significance, businesses that were involved in a traditional or culturally significant production, or enterprises that hired the rural and urban poor. Although economic liberalisation in the last four decades has allowed greater public participation in policymaking, China is still a top-down authoritarian state. The fact that protection of spotted seals, a protected species under the national Wildlife Protection Law, gave way to development projects in Liaoning demonstrates that environmental activists face an uphill battle when taking on such industries.

Reform politics and NGO professionalisation

In confronting businesses and local authorities over violations of the country's environmental protection laws, Tian Jiguang and others were in fact confronting a much more powerful force: China's developmental state. There was little doubt that Tian was a passionate seal protectionist. The highway construction and the drilling operation were both development projects supported by local government. Liaohe Oil Field is one of China's top ten petroleum producers. It is owned by China Petroleum (PetroChina), the second biggest corporation of the Top 500 Chinese companies. With 1.6 trillion yuan in revenue in 2016, PetroChina is a major contributor to the state coffers and a big employer, with half a million employees (PetroChina 2017). In 2013 PetroChina's Liaohe Oil Company employed more than 29,300 people and was a major taxpayer in Panjin. The objective of PetroChina and Liaohe Oil Company was the same as that of the Panjin government, whereas Mr Tian's mission contradicted or could potentially undermine the short-term interests of both industry and government.

Tian's case was not unique. Across the country, there have been similar cases in which environmental protection has to give way to development projects. According to one research report, 40 of the 303 national nature reserves have seen their sizes adjusted (i.e., shrunk) because of development projects. More of the provincial nature reserves have shrunk to make way for local projects. In order to bring Russian natural gas into China, a pipeline was built through Kanas Lake in Xinjiang, a nature reserve (Nanfang Zhoumo 2011). The construction through the nature reserve was reportedly approved by the SFB. In response to criticism, local forestry bureau officials said that the pipeline construction should be pursued because it was "a project of national strategic importance." In 2010, a railroad was built cutting through Anhui's national Yangtze Alligator Reserve. Similarly, a railroad through the Shaanxi Tianhua Mountain National Nature Reserve and Shaanxi Hanzhong Ibis National Nature Reserve was also planned in 2010. This project was part of a national endeavour to rebuild the earthquake-shattered Wenchuan in Sichuan. In Dongying, Shandong, chemical plants were built surrounding the Yellow River Delta National Wetland Reserve. Projects deemed to be of national or local "strategic importance" have taken precedence over nature reserves.

In fact, the construction of the pipeline through the nature reserve of the Kanas Lake did not violate the regulation on nature reserves.

7 China's animal protection NGOs

According to the Nature Reserve Regulation, a nature reserve consists of three components: core areas, buffer zones, and experimental areas (Article 18). Anyone or any work unit is prohibited from entering the core areas, while only scientific and research can be done in the buffer zones (Articles 26 and 27). Since the pipeline must go through the current core areas, the local authorities had only one choice for the project to proceed without violating the regulation. To achieve this, the Xinjiang forestry bureau had to resolve the issue creatively. It held an expert evaluation meeting to turn the core areas of the Kanas Lake Nature Reserve into an unprotected area. The evaluation meeting resulted in the removal of the core areas out of the way to allow the pipeline construction to proceed without breaking the law. A similar "adjustment" was done to the national wetland nature reserve in Henan. Since the highway construction would have to go through the core areas of the nature reserve, the "adjustment" succeeded in changing the core areas and buffer zones into experimental areas. This adjustment was approved by the SFB.

Instances of development taking precedence over the protection of nature reserves have happened more often at the provincial and local levels. In 1999, the State Environmental Protection Administration issued a *Notice on the Several Questions on Environmental Management Work of the Development Projects inside Nature Reserves* (State Environmental Bureau 1999). According to this policy notice, to allow key transportation, irrigation, and hydropower construction projects approved by the state to go through nature reserves, especially the core areas and buffer zones, relevant authorities could appropriately adjust the function, area, and boundaries of the reserves. With this notice, the state sanctioned the "adjustment" of reserves in order to facilitate development projects. There are many examples of such adjustments at the provincial and local levels. In 2008, to build a Yangtze Economic Corridor in Yichang, Hubei, the Chinese Sturgeon Nature Reserve, the only spawning site on the Yangtze River for the endangered sturgeons, was shortened from 80 kilometres to 50 kilometres.

Specific actions have been taken to resolve the conflict between development and environmental protection. In 2009 the Ministry of Environmental Protection issued a *Notice on the Adjustment of Five National Nature Reserves such as the Tianjin Ancient Coast and Wetland*.

This notice confirmed the adjustment of the core areas or buffer zones of five nature reserves in four provinces and Tianjin municipality. The adjustment of the Tianjin Ancient Coast and Wetland resulted in a drastic reduction of the protected area from the original 99,000 hectares to 35,913 hectares, a reduction by 64% (Ministry of Environmental Protection 2009; People.com 2011). Commenting on this "development-first" practice, Jiang Gaoming, a researcher at the Institute of Botany of the Chinese Academy of Sciences, said with great concern that no compromise to development projects should be made once nature reserves were established. If the current practice were not stopped, nature reserves across the country would be wiped out (Peng and Zhang 2011).

The building of "safe passages" for wildlife animals in nature reserves has been used to justify development projects inside these protected areas. In June 2006, Beijing's *Xinjing News* reported that 33 "safe passages" had been built together with the Qinghai-Tibet Railroad for the safe crossing of the endangered Tibetan antelopes inside Kekexili, the nature reserve of 45,000 square kilometres that Tibetan antelopes, Tibetan wild donkeys and other rare animals call home (Xu Chunlu 2006). In the eyes of some Chinese wildlife researchers, developers and local governments use the building of "safe passages" for wildlife, such as underground tunnels, bridges, and flyovers, to absolve themselves. To these experts, "safe passages" are not a panacea. Jiang Zhigang, a senior researcher at the Zoological Institute of the Chinese Academy of Science, pointed out that not all wildlife animals are like the Tibetan antelopes who can use the underground passages. Some animals may never use such passages since they are afraid of overhead structures. Jiang Gaoming of the Institute of Botany added that the so-called "safe passages" were being used as a shield against criticism of development projects' encroachment on the habitat of wildlife animals. The greater danger of allowing nature reserves to give way to development projects includes fragmentation of wildlife habitat, thus making it difficult for wildlife animals to migrate and causing inbreeding and damages to biodiversity (Peng and Zhang 2011).

Mr Tian was not merely standing up to one polluting company. He was confronting the "holy alliance" between business interests and local political power. The seal nature reserve in Dalian was "adjusted" to allow development projects to proceed. In Panjin, the Liaoning Liaohekou National Nature Reserve was reduced from 128,000 hectares to 80,000 hectares as a result of a similar "adjustment." What was most unacceptable to Tian was that the landing site of the seals was excluded from the reserve's core areas. The fact that drilling could happen so close to the seal's landing site was a direct result of the nature reserve's "adjustment" (People's Daily 2013).

The charge that Tian spread rumours and untruthful information about the drilling company was, in the eyes of his supporters, an act of retaliation. At the end of 2013, a similar case in Zhejiang province involving Cheng Meng, an environmental activist, led to his conviction of extortion. Cheng was subsequently sentenced to a 20-month imprisonment term (Li Xianfeng 2015a). Tian's sentencing to a 12-year imprisonment and its subsequent reduction to four and a half years made observers wonder whether the earlier conviction had been reached impartially. Despite the court ruling, Tian's extortion conviction has sparked speculation about retaliation by the businesses and local authorities concerned. The shortening of his sentence prompted even more questions. Had Tian entered into any agreement with the court in return for the reduction of the prison term?

Professionalisation

During Tian's trial, his defence lawyer pointed out that his client had never drawn a penny from the NGO and had received no fringe benefits. As a net donor to the association, Tian had no motivation for embezzling or misappropriating the organisation's funds for personal gain. Regarding the extortion charge, Tian said that the camera (valued at 50,000 yuan) was a donation to the association, not to himself. He denied that he ever asked for an 100,000 yuan donation from the oil company. The donation was talked about during a meeting between Tian and representatives of the oil company. Who first proposed the sponsorship donation will remain a mystery. Tian claimed that he had turned down 10,000 yuan in "hush money" offered to him by a representative of the oil company after he exposed the oil-pollution incident.

Tian himself admitted to the police that he did not take accounting seriously. Record keeping at the NGO was rudimentary. Expenses for rented boats, catering, fuel, printing, and other costs were usually not issued official receipts. Tian did use, illegally, unrelated receipts to cover expenses that had not been issued receipts. At the end of 2013, a receipt showed that Tian advanced 100,000 yuan from the association. He could not produce records or receipts to prove how he had spent this money. Besides the 30,000 to 40,000 yuan cash in his home, the rest of the 100,000 yuan, in his own words, was spent on "all kinds of activities of the association" unsupported by receipts (Li Xianfeng 2015b).

Zeng Xiangbing, an attorney and founder of the Environmental Public Interest Lawyers Group, made some insightful comments on the current state of affairs for Chinese NGOs. He said:

> Many grassroots NGOs were established because of the name recognition and motivation of their founders. These people grew their organisations by putting in time, using their own vehicles, and spending their own money without expecting financial payback. However, these NGO founders have not realised that they should separate personal property from that of their organisations. They are yet to take measures to professionalise their organisations so that they can solve funding problems like a self-sufficient social organisation. Professionalisation should start especially after their organisations have been operating, when their organisations are increasing their influence in the society, and at a time when environmental issues are drawing so much public attention. Since the founders are slow to professionalise the running of their organisation, problems are therefore unavoidable. (Li Xianfeng 2015b)

The lack of awareness of legal liability and knowledge of the law explained the fact that NGO activists could easily be brought to trial for "extortion," said Mr Zeng. There was barely a clear line separating "fundraising" from blackmailing (Li Xianfeng 2015b).

Chinese NGOs do encounter a funding challenge. Most NGOs are supported with financial input from the founding members and key supporters. A registered animal charity in North China spent a total of

2,600,000 yuan in 2016 on various programs and operations. A major donor contributed 66% of the organisation's operating costs.[14] Most other NGOs in China do not have major donors who can provide this level of financial support. As a result, most NGOs' staff members are not on the payrolls of their organisations. Record keeping, if done at all, is rudimentary. The poor financial record keeping of Tian's PBSPVA was common among China's expanding NGO community.

The lack of accountability and transparency is most serious among some of the private shelters maintained by individual owners. One private shelter in northern China was thrown into a major controversy. The owner of the shelter fundraised allegedly to support more than 4,000 dogs on a national TV program. However, a 2015 investigation by three senior activists found no more than 400 dogs in the facility. A follow-up report by the *New York Times*, published on its Sinosphere blog, confirmed that there were not 4,000 dogs in the shelter, that its facilities were filthy and littered with dog waste, and that the dogs were living in poor conditions (Chen Mincai, Chen Yunlian and Jiang Hong 2015; Huang Shaojie 2015). Donors to this shelter have generally not been able to get a report on how their donations have been used. A long-time local donor was even prevented from entering the shelter to see the dogs she had been helping.[15] A European donor of Chinese descent who had earlier dismissed the 2015 investigation as defamation and stood by the shelter owner was shocked to see the conditions of the dogs when she entered the shelter in November 2016.[16] Poor donation management, lack of transparency, suffering dogs, and lack of accountability have given rise to concerns and even suspicion that funds may have been misused.[17] This particular shelter has never made public full details of how donations from donors in China and abroad have been used.

---

14 Interview with a senior staff member of the organisation, 24 September 2017.
15 Interview with Ms Liu, a local police school director, 1 July 2017.
16 Hours of conversation with the Chinese-Spanish donor on her experience inside the shelter concerned, January, February and March 2017.
17 Interview with a Tianjin activist who volunteered at the shelter under investigation in 2015.

In 2017, a facility with a great number of suffering and diseased dogs in Xi'An that had similar problems was shut down by a coalition of local animal protection groups, activists, law enforcement, and the local village committee. The 100 or so dogs were handed over to the care of the Xi'An Small Animal Protection Association (XSAPA). In a public statement issued by XSAPA, the organisation listed a series of decisions aimed at building a set of rules for the responsible and transparent operation of shelters:

1. No person or organisation can fundraise or accept monetary donation in any form in the name of these dogs; violators will face criminal charges.
2. To ensure transparency and accountability, XSAPA will report to the public the conditions of the dogs accepted into XSAPA's facility.
3. XSAPA shall take a photo of and give a unique identification number to each dog before moving them into the dog houses. A record on each dog shall be established and their health conditions shall be released to the public to allow better societal supervision.
4. XSAPA will accept donations in kind such as medical supplies and dog food, to be recorded by a designated person and made public for societal supervision.
5. Should any dog die, XSAPA will report to the public the conditions and causes of the death of any dogs rescued from the hoarding facility.[18]

Financial accountability, operational transparency and good financial record keeping are yet to become the norm. Charity activities are a new development as a result of political liberalisation and the inability of the party-state to respond to new challenges. Individuals, volunteer groups and NGOs have moved in to fill the vacuum. And, like in most other countries, China has seen a delay in policy responses to address these new challenges. The NPC did not legislate wildlife protection until 1988, eight years after the authorities were confronted with runaway poaching and wildlife exploitation. Similarly, it was not until 1999 when the NPC made the *PRC Law on Charitable Donation*, which was

---

18 Social media post issued by Xi'An Small Animal Protection Association, 16 November 2017.

replaced in 2016 by the more stringent *Charity Law of the People's Republic of China*. NGOs in China are yet to standardise their operations in line with the stipulations of the Charity Law.

Finally, compliance with and enforcement of the Charity Law have been made complicated and difficult by the existence of a large number of unregistered NGOs. Many of these "illegal" operations are helping in various degrees the society's animal control services. The requirement that a non-profit organisation must have a supervisory unit from a government office has made NGO registration difficult. The result is the existence of a large number of "illegal" organisations. Those organisations that have registered have had a track record of activities serving the political objectives of local authorities; they have had a government office willing to act as their supervisor; and their founders have been relatively well connected or more effective in promoting the value of their operation to the authorities.

Conclusions

China in the reform era is an evolving, transitional society. Even though China remains a Communist one-party state, it is a completely different species from China under Mao Zedong. With the diversification of business ownership, for example, the society has been more vibrant economically. The increase in the disposable income of the average Chinese person has allowed many of them to adopt lifestyles that were ideologically and economically prohibited in the pre-reform era. With the increase of personal wealth and China's entering the rank of middle-income nations, a growing number of Chinese people are joining efforts to promote the public interest rather than personal gain. Environmental protection, nature conservation, and urban animal control and care have emerged as new policy issues for the authorities to deal with. While the authorities need help from NGOs to respond to these issues, the party-state's monopoly on political power has limited the space available for civil society.

There is a "love–hate" relationship between the Chinese authorities and the country's NGOs. After 40 years of economic reform, the Chinese government has learned that governance cannot be the sole prerogative of the party-state. To effectively manage a modern society, governments need to utilise the passion, time and expertise of social groups. Nongovernmental groups can serve an important purpose and can better deal with some social issues. To the Chinese government, however, NGOs can also be a nuisance. They can even become a threat or a roadblock to the fulfilment of the state's objectives. China's NGO registration policy was intended to minimise the negative impact of NGOs. Despite the political and institutional obstacles, however, Chinese civil society has continued to expand. In a range of issues, NGOs are playing an increasingly prominent role in Chinese society. Through informal and formal channels, they have scored some major victories. They are operating at the forefront of urban animal management and wildlife rescue. Some of them have encountered operational and legal problems, paying a heavy price for confronting business interests and for their own missteps. For NGOs, China is both a promising and a risky terrain. This challenge calls for a more friendly policy environment, greater societal support and participation, and NGO professionalisation.

Conclusion

In mid October 2015, I returned to Portland, Oregon to attend the 23rd annual Animal Law Conference at Lewis & Clark School of Law. Twenty years earlier, I had visited the city as a graduate student of international politics. At the Lewis & Clark School of Law, I spoke on the prospects of China's animal protection lawmaking. In my presentation, which covered the major challenges facing China's animal protection movement, I acknowledged the many stubborn obstacles in the way of legislative breakthroughs that are long overdue. I was however optimistic that China would eventually outlaw animal cruelty. The Chinese government, a one-party developmental state, has been adapting to the vast social changes brought about by the economic transformation of the last four decades. With the rise of new economic interests, China has seen the emergence of a much more diversified society where public interest groups are fighting for the attention of the country's authoritarian leaders.

The Chinese authorities are fully aware of social diversification and are revising and adopting policies tailored to this changed society (Hu and Zou 2018). China's urban dog management is a good example of the change in government attitudes. For the entire pre-reform era, the authorities viewed dogs in urban areas as undesirable bourgeois "playthings," a waste of resources, a public health menace, and a nuisance. This official attitude was challenged in the 1990s when dogs began to be kept as companions by millions of urban households. We have noticed authorities in a host of provincial and sub-provincial cities drop their formerly draconian policies, which were aimed at discouraging dog ownership, and shift to a new policy of active management, which seeks to balance the interests of dog owners with the wellbeing of the general public. A breakthrough was achieved in April 2020 when Shenzhen became the first mainland Chinese city to outlaw the trade and consumption of dog meat (BBC 2020). Following Shenzhen, Zhuhai became the second mainland Chinese city to ban dog meat consumption (Georgiou 2020). In April, commenting on the exclusion of dogs from the Livestock Catalogue, an Agriculture Ministry spokesman acknowledged dogs as companion animals, a recognition that was a milestone in China's attitude towards them. Although these were the remarks of just one spokesman, the acknowledgement of dogs as companion animals may open the way for legislative change in the future (Thomson 2020). China at present undeniably offers a much better environment for the rise, survival, and operation of public interest NGOs than in the past. Animal lovers, pet owners, and their supporters are an expanding force whose voice is heard more and more often. The Chinese authorities are rethinking and redefining the role of the country's public interest NGOs.

China is almost 200 years behind the most developed countries in terms of animal protection legislation, if we used the British Martin's Act of 1822 (the Cruel Treatment of Cattle Act) as the comparison point. As the world's second largest economy and a country with increasing global influence, China should be in sync with the rest of the industrialised world in animal protection legislation. In fact, China has the conditions for a legislative breakthrough in animal protection. Philosophically, China has a rich tradition of compassion for nature and for nonhuman animals. In the last three decades, it has also introduced progressive ideas about animal welfare and best practices for animal care from foreign countries. Materially, China is also ready. The Chinese people have never been able to spend so much on pet keeping and on animal rescue. This suggests that legislative action for animal protection is no longer out of touch with the material conditions of the country.

Conclusion

Moreover, policy making in China is no longer a prohibited area beyond the reach of the Chinese public. Public interest NGOs are active not only in cyberspace and traditional media, but also in the process of policy making. They understand that no effective actions can be sustained without policy or law change. Each year, delegates to China's national legislature, the NPC, and the Chinese People's Political Consultative Conference have submitted proposals related to animal welfare, such as those for ending the import of seal products, stopping the consumption of shark fin, suspending the domestic ivory trade, and cracking down on the dog meat trade. Since the early 1990s, animal activism has contributed to a change in dog registration policies in many cities. The end of the domestic ivory trade on 1 January 2018 was a response to domestic and global calls for a change in China's longstanding policy towards a so-called traditional artefacts. This was more than a symbolic act by the Chinese government. We are likely to see more policy changes and legislative actions in the years to come. However, considerable obstacles to animal protection lawmaking remain. China is still a Leninist party-state whose policy-making process is mostly closed to public view. The ability of society to shape the direction of politics and policies remains limited. The Chinese media, while increasingly rigorous in operation and more attentive to subjects of readers' interest, can influence the public agenda only in ways that do not make the authorities feel threatened.

It is true that China presents many challenges for animal protection. As the world's biggest livestock producer, it subjects the biggest number of farm animals to industrialised farming systems as part of the country's food security strategy. It has a wildlife farming operation that has drawn much domestic and international criticism. The outbreak of SARS and COVID-19 in China and its connection to the country's out-of-control wildlife exploitation have presented the Chinese government with a challenging question: which does it value more, the business interests of wildlife traders, or the safety of its 1.4 billion citizens. China has a dog meat industry that has been sustained by dog theft, illegal trans-provincial transport, and brutal slaughter, often in broad daylight. With a well-developed social media network via Wechat, TikTok, Weibo, QQ, and other applications, the transmission of videos of brutal killings of dogs and cats in chat groups of mostly young men is a new manifestation of this lawlessness. In shopping malls, restaurants, and resorts, penguins, polar bears, belugas, seals and other animals are displayed to attract customers, prompting condemnation from across the world. Other institutionalised animal cruelty, such as the practice of abandoning wounded laboratory animals after medical experiments, and using animals such as killer whales and elephants in performances, are all challenging the tolerance of the Chinese public.

However, attributing these practices to China's cultural traditions is neither fair nor convincing. The highly controversial bear farming industry, for example, is an invention of the 20th century. It never existed in China's dynastic past. Although bear bile and other animal parts were discussed in ancient traditional Chinese medicine books, ancient Chinese thinkers and medical practitioners did not believe in killing animals in order to save human lives. Business interests have been more motivated to promote the alleged curing power of tiger bones, bear bile, and rhino horn, to name some of the most controversial ingredients. The claim that there is "consumer demand" for wild animal parts as medicine is false. What I have seen and read are advertisements and other promotional literature produced by the industry, making claims about the allegedly irreplaceable properties of wildlife animal parts. Never have I encountered protests, demonstrations or petitions by consumers demanding a steady supply of wild animal parts as either medicine or food.

More importantly, cruelty to nonhuman animals was not sanctioned by Chinese culture. Both Buddhism and Daoism prohibited killing. Both called on their followers to exercise compassion through a meatless diet and the practice of mercy release. Confucianism, although a secular thought system, stood for benevolent governance. As Mencius suggested, a ruler who was kind to an ox would turn out to be a kind sovereign to his people. In ancient China, compassion for nonhuman animals was a state policy. Slaughter suspension was exercised by Chinese rulers when the nation was suffering or celebrating. This compassionate gesture was also introduced to Japan and Korea. Blaming China's traditional culture for animal cruelty in the contemporary era is not only unsubstantiated by the historical record, but can help to divert attention from the real culprit. As a recent study

Conclusion

in China's ethnic Korean region shows, kimchi (a fermented Korean vegetable side dish) is a traditional household Korean food, whereas dog meat is not. The designation of dog meat as traditional Korean food was the work of dog meat traders in Northeast China. Unlike kimchi, which is a daily household food for ethnic Koreans in northern China, dog meat is a commercial product promoted by commercial interests (Li, Sun and Yu 2017).

Animal cruelty in today's China is an outgrowth of the national drive for modernisation. The dog meat traders do not necessarily enjoy killing dogs, still less torturing them allegedly for making the meat taste better. They are in business to make a living. Since most dog meat traders are drawn from the least skilled and least educated of the former peasants, their business, heinous as it is to animal lovers, has been protected and tolerated by local authorities. To China's post-socialist developmental state, poverty reduction and employment of surplus labour, both of which are key to regime stability, are political imperatives. Similarly, bear farming and tiger farming were enthusiastically supported by Chinese government agencies in the 1980s. At that time, the authorities, together with the country's wildlife experts, did not see ethical, animal welfare, biosecurity or public health risks in the farming operations. They saw employment, revenue, and poverty reduction in using wildlife as a natural resource. The 1989 WPL, the first ever national legislation for protecting animals, turned out to be an endorsement of the country's wildlife farming industry. The 2016 revised WPL continues to define wildlife as a resource. Its main focus is still protecting and regulating the wildlife business. It remains to be seen whether China will extend its February 2020 ban on wildlife trade and consumption to other wildlife farming operations such as the fur industry, traditional Chinese medicine, display animals, and laboratory use. These wildlife farming operations are no less a potential breeding ground for pandemics.

The industry that "enslaves" the most animals – tens of billions of them – is livestock farming. This industry has received consistent policy support from China's developmental state since the early years of the country's economic modernisation campaign. Livestock farming is a major contributor to the state's political objectives of achieving food security, providing rural employment, ending rural poverty and growing local GDP. The introduction of the Western factory farming model was enthusiastically pursued to boost productivity. The Chinese authorities and the industry have failed to see the intrinsic cruelty of modern factory farms. This neglect is not uncommon in developmental states. To these governments, political openness, social justice, labour rights, environmental protection, and animal welfare are at best secondary to the primary objective of economic growth. To East Asian developmental states, only economic growth can secure the political objective of regime stability. To China's post-socialist developmental state, economic growth is essential for ending poverty and rebuilding the legitimacy of the CCP.

The state obsession with growth does have public support. Those who lived through the Maoist era's "tyranny of scarcity" have a collective memory of severe food deprivation. Food security is an overriding concern for this part of society, and the Chinese authorities respond to and rely on the support of this group. In the foreseeable future, the Chinese government is unlikely to drop the "development-first" policy, despite its awareness of the need to shift to a sustained development model. The adoption of a comprehensive animal protection law that could impact the livestock industry is unlikely to happen in the near future either. However, members of China's younger generation, who have no recollection of food deprivation, are forward-looking. Members of this generation are less tolerant of cruelty and injustice. Not only are they "rebellious" in their thinking, they are also action-oriented. Those who have confronted business interests connected with animal cruelty are the most active members of the younger generation (Bale 2017). As members of the thousands of registered and unregistered groups, they have stood firm against all sorts of cruelty practices. China is likely to remain divided over animal protection issues. It has already seen a "civil war" between the country's animal lovers and supporters of dog meat consumption. The "war" is likely to continue for the foreseeable future, despite the fact that two mainland Chinese cities have now outlawed the trade and consumption of dog meat.

Animal cruelty in today's China can be traced to the politics of development. China's economic reform was started to end hunger and poverty, which threatened the legitimacy of the ruling CCP. While the reform program has been hugely successful and lifted the entire nation out of poverty, the party has a new pressing task, i.e., to narrow the gap between urban and rural citizens. It is also the party-state's objective to propel China over the so-called "middle-income trap" so that the country will join the ranks of high-income countries by the middle of this century. To achieve this, sustained economic growth remains an overriding obsession of the party. Economic development continues to be the top priority of the Chinese government. Environmental protection, labour rights, women's rights, and animal welfare are all secondary.

China will eventually join the world's most developed countries in animal protection legislation. No modern society can tolerate widespread cruelty to nonhuman animals. In August 2016, I wrote to the *South China Morning Post* about a brutal cruelty case in Weihai, Shandong Province, where a dog was dragged to death behind a racing car. In this op-ed, I called on the Chinese authorities to introduce anti-cruelty legislation not only in the interest of deterring cruelty to animals but also to protect China's young people, who should not be exposed to such public brutality (Li, Peter 2016). In mainland China, businesses and individual traders who practise public animal slaughter should be informed that the practice can cause long-term psychological trauma to young children who happen to be at the wrong place at the wrong time. At the 3rd Global Animal Law Conference held in Hong Kong (4–6 May 2018), Professor Amanda Whitfort of the Law Faculty of University of Hong Kong argued that lawyers and prosecutors should use non-animal-related laws creatively to bring animal abusers to justice. Echoing Professor Whitfort's argument, An Xiang, a Beijing lawyer, used specific cases to illustrate how China's animal disease control laws, live transport regulations, and food safety regulations can all be used to prosecute animal abusers. However, these other laws, as Professor Whitfort pointed out, cannot fulfil the role of an anti-cruelty law. China cannot postpone for too long the legislation of a comprehensive animal welfare law.

China poses a comprehensive challenge for animal protectionists. But positive change is on the horizon. In the pre-reform era, "animal protection" was never heard of. Dogs as pets disappeared in urban China. Tigers were killed to the brink of extinction as part of the government's policy to wipe out the "injurious pests." Sparrows were condemned as pests to be mercilessly exterminated. These policies have all become history. Another noticeable development is the idea that China really does not need to look beyond its borders for ideas about animal welfare or animal rights (Chang 2010). It need only tap into the treasure box of Chinese traditional culture for inspiration (Mang Ping 2009).

Young Chinese people today have had entirely different experiences from their parents and grandparents. Those urbanites who were born in the 1980s and 1990s are much less tolerant of cruelty and more responsive to distress calls from fellow humans and nonhumans. They are much less desensitised than their elders (Zu, Li and Su 2005, 67–95). To build a more compassionate and humane society, China needs to rely on this generational shift. Mao Zedong had one thing right. In 1957, addressing young Chinese students studying in various institutions of higher learning in what was then the Soviet Union, he said "the world belongs to us and to you. But in the final analysis, the world belongs to you" (Shan Gang and Wang Yinghui 2007). He was absolutely right. China's future will be rewritten by the younger generations.

Acknowledgements

I am indebted to many people who have helped bring *Animal Welfare in China* into print. My thanks go to Denise O'Dea and Agata Mrva-Montoya of Sydney University Press for their tireless and invaluable suggestions for improving the manuscript. I am also grateful to Professor Amanda Whitfort of the Law Faculty of Hong Kong University and other reviewers for their comments and suggestions. While I own whatever remaining issues the book may have, I thank them for making it a more presentable work.

Animal Welfare in China is a product of several years of efforts. I thank the University of Houston-Downtown for providing me with resources for my research work. These include a sabbatical, a research grant, and many funded trips to academic conferences that have enabled me to pursue my research agenda. I thank the Social Sciences Department and my colleagues in particular for their accommodation of my requests and needs. I also want to thank the Humane Society International for the opportunity to serve as its China Policy Specialist and the many investigative trips to dog farms in South Korea, dog meat markets and wildlife captive breeding facilities in mainland China.

Finally, I want to take this opportunity to thank many animal welfarists, scholars, scientists and groups in China who have helped me, in different capacities over the years, to understand the unique challenges of human–animal relations in their country. Through their assistance, I was able to have a peek inside government shelters, wildlife breeding farms, wildlife markets, research labs, dog slaughterhouses, and intensive livestock farms. These field visits enriched my knowledge of China's animal welfare challenges and the need for policy change.

Appendix 1: offences and penalties in the revised Wildlife Protection Law

Offence and article number	Penalty
Dereliction of duties by wildlife protection departments. (42)	Concerned officials receive a demerit
Disturbing or threatening wildlife breeding; illegal construction; land reclamation in nature reserves. (43)	Penalty in accordance with relevant laws and regulations
Trading in wildlife or wildlife products under the guise of wildlife shelter and rescue. (44)	Confiscation of wildlife, products, and unlawful income; a fine between 2 and 10 times the value of the wildlife or products; publicising of the criminal records of the perpetrator; criminal prosecution if applicable.
Illegal hunting in areas closed to hunting, during hunting-free seasons such as migration periods, or along migration routes;	Confiscation of catch, hunting implements and unlawful income;

Offence and article number	Penalty
hunting and killing of wildlife under special state protection (1st and 2nd classes of species); hunting in violation of permission; indiscriminate hunting using poison, explosives, electric shocks, electronic trapping tools or other tools such as snares, traps, ground guns and volleys; hunting with night-time illumination; hunting by annihilation, by destroying nests or dens, or using fire attacks, fumigation or nets. (45)	suspension of special hunting licences; imposition of a fine between 2 and 10 times the value of their catch; where there is no catch, imposition of a fine between 10,000 yuan and 50,000 yuan; criminal prosecution if applicable.
Hunting in prohibited areas or seasons; hunting or catching of terrestrial wildlife under special state protection without a hunting licence or without observing assigned hunting quota; hunting or catching without observing prescriptions with respect to the species, quantity, area, implement, method, or time limit. (46)	Confiscation of hunting implements and unlawful income; suspension of special hunting licences; fine between one and five times the value of the catch; where there is no catch, fine between 2000 yuan and 10,000 yuan; criminal prosecution if applicable.
Breeding of wildlife under special state protection or without a breeding permit. (47)	Confiscation of wildlife and related products; fine between 1 and 5 times the value of the wildlife and products.
Selling, purchasing, using, transporting or mailing wildlife under special state protection (or their products) without permission, without a special marking, or without presenting a captive breeding permit or permission documents. (48)	Confiscation of wildlife, products and unlawful income; fine between 2 and 10 times the value of the wildlife and products; revoking of captive breeding permit; recalling of special markings;

Appendix 1: offences and penalties in the revised Wildlife Protection Law

Offence and article number	Penalty
	criminal prosecution if applicable.
Trading or transporting wildlife not under state protection without proof of their legal origin. (48)	Confiscation of wildlife and fine between 1 and 5 times the value of the wildlife.
Trading, transporting or mailing of wildlife or wildlife products without proof of quarantine. (48)	Punishment according to regulations in the Animal Epidemic Prevention Law.
Producing or trading wildlife for food without proof of legal origin. (49)	Issuance of an order to stop the illegal behavior; confiscation of wildlife, products and unlawful income; fine between 2 and 10 times the value of the wildlife and products; criminal prosecution if applicable.
Publishing or broadcasting advertisements relating to the illegal sale, purchase or use of wildlife, products and prohibited hunting tools. (50)	Punishment according to the Advertising Law.
Providing a trading platform for the illegal sale, purchase or use of wildlife, products or prohibited hunting equipment. (51)	Order for the illegal activity to cease; confiscation of unlawful income; fine of between 2 and 5 times the amount of unlawful income; criminal prosecution if applicable.

Offence and article number	Penalty
Import and export of wildlife and products whose trade is prohibited by international convention to which China is a party; import and export of wildlife or products under special state protection without import or export permits or certification of quarantine. (52)	Penalties in accordance with China's import and export laws and regulations; criminal prosecution if applicable.
Introduction of non-native wildlife species from outside Chinese borders. (53)	Confiscation of species; fine between 50,000 and 200,000 yuan; penalties in accordance with the regulations in the Law on Entry and Exit Animal and Plant Quarantine; criminal prosecution if applicable.
Release of non-native species into the wild. (54)	Order to recapture the released wildlife within a prescribed time limit; fine between 10,000 yuan and 50,000 yuan; liability for the costs involved government in recapture.
Forging, modifying, selling, transferring, borrowing or lending certificates, special marking documents or other permission documents. (55)	Confiscation of documents and unlawful income; fine between 50,000 and 200,000 yuan; civil penalty if in violation of public security administration regulations; criminal prosecution where applicable.

References

Ai Ta (2020). 捐赠熊胆粉抗击疫情？真的别把国人当傻子！(Donate bear bile powder to fight COVID-19? Give me a break. Don't underestimate the intelligence of the Chinese people), blog post, 29 February, http://bit.ly/369M0MX.

Anhui Forestry Bureau (2019). 安徽省林业局准予行政许可决定书 (Decision on the Administrative Permit issued by Anhui Provincial Forestry Bureau), Anhui Forestry Bureau Approval Document 547 of 2019, http://lyj.ah.gov.cn/public/9913203/39127794.html.

Antelope (1993). *Chairman Mao: The Last Emperor*, documentary, https://vimeo.com/53959962.

Agriculture Ministry of China (2002). 中华人民共和国农业部公告176号 (Agriculture Ministry Policy Document 176, on the use of antibiotics and other additives in livestock feed), https://bit.ly/3ochyrW.

Agriculture Ministry of China (2016). 疫情发布 (Information on Farm Epidemics: 2010–15), database, http://www.moa.gov.cn/zwllm/yjgl/yqfb/.

Anderson, E.N. (1988). *The Food of China*. New Haven, CT: Yale University Press.

Anhui Agriculture Commission (2006). 安徽省"十一五"畜牧业发展规划 (A Development Forecast for Anhui Livestock Industry for the 11th Five-Year Plan), 19 September, http://bit.ly/2Mlztzb.

Animals Asia Foundation (2015a). *Lies, Illegality and Stolen Lives: A True Crime Story (2011–2014)*, http://bit.ly/3afa7eH.

Animals Asia Foundation (2015b). Report reveals Chinese dog eating as minority activity with widespread support for ban, 12 June, http://bit.ly/36b8EVr.

An Xiang and Peter J. Li (2012). 活犬跨省运输与行政执法和食品安全: 4–15个案分析 (Trans-provincial dog transport and administrative law enforcement: The case of the 5 April 2011 dog truck interception), presentation delivered at the 3rd China Dog Ownership Management Symposium, Shanghai, China, 18 September.

Appleby, Michael C., Victoria Cussen, Leah Garces, Lesley A. Lambert and Jacky Turner (2008). *Long Distance Transport and Welfare of Farm Animals*. Cambridge, MA: CABI.

Ascione, F.R. (1998). Battered women's reports of their partners' and their children's cruelty to animals. *Journal of Emotional Abuse* 1(1): 119–33.

Ascione, Frank R. (2001). Animal Abuse and Youth Violence. *Juvenile Justice Bulletin*, September, http://bit.ly/3oeGFKv.

ASKCI (2014). 狗肉产业趋势和投资2014–2019年报告 (A Report on the Trend and Investment of China's Dog Meat Industry: 2014–2019), www.askci.com.

Associated Press (2007). China executes ex-head of food and drug agency. 7 October. https://nbcnews.to/2Ynvi8R.

Australian Financial News (2017). 澳大利亚活牛羊出口行业或将迎来发展的"春天" (A new expanding business opportunity is awaiting Australia's live cattle and sheep exporters). *Australian Financial News*, 14 November, http://www.afndaily.com/markets/10447.html

Bai Tongdong (2009). The price of serving meat: on Confucius's and Mencius's views of human and animal rights. *Asian Philosophy* 19(1): 85–99.

Baidu.com. 韩庄狗肉城 (总店) (An introduction to Hanzhuang Dog Meat City), http://baike.baidu.com/view/13510380.htm.

Baike.com. 归真堂 (Guizhentang), http://bit.ly/2M1sjA3.

Baker, Keiligh (2014). Chinese businessman is jailed for 13 years for hiring poachers to kill tigers so he could eat their penises. *Daily Mail*, 30 December, http://dailym.ai/3qOSSre.

Bale, Rachael (2017). Chinese youth embrace new attitudes towards pets and wildlife. *National Geographic*, 12 July, http://on.natgeo.com/3c831Lu.

Bartlett, Kim and Merritt Clifton (2003). How many dogs and cats are eaten? *Animal People*, September, http://bit.ly/2Y8yHIa.

BBC News (2006). China to promote wildlife hunt. BBC News, , 9 August, http://bbc.in/2LZlDCF.

BBC News (2008). Chinese scholar: increase of unemployment can lead to social instability. BBC News, 5 December, https://bbc.in/3p9HwgV.

BBC News (2016). Chinese woman sues over fatal tiger attack. BBC News, 23 November, http://bbc.in/3paJOfI.

BBC News (2017). Bear bites man in China "tiger death" wildlife park. BBC News, 22 August, http://bbc.in/39isDDH.

References

BBC News (2020). Shenzhen becomes first Chinese city to ban eating cats and dogs. *BBC News*, 2 April, http://bbc.in/3qN7iYH.

Becker, Jasper (1998). *Hungry Ghosts: Mao's Secret Famine*. New York: Henry Holt and Company, Inc.

Befly2000 (2014). 狗肉节之争 – 当代中国阶级斗争的一个缩影 (The conflict over the dog meat festival: a microcosm of the class struggle in contemporary China, 25 June.

Beijing News (2013). 归真堂主动终止创业板IPO (Guizhentang has all by itself withdrawn its IPO application from the Growth Enterprise Market), *Beijing News*, 3 June, A26.

Beijing Review (1994). Commercial raising saves Bears, *Beijing Review*, 7-13 March, 34.

Bell, Lorna (2001). Abusing children, abusing animals. *Journal of Social Work* 1(2): 223-34.

Berne, Piers (2004). From animal abuse to interhuman violence? A critical review of the progression thesis. *Society & Animals* 12(1): 39-65.

Boat, W.B. (1999). Abuse of children and abuse of animals: using the links to inform child assessment and protection, in F.R. Ascione and P. Arkow (eds), *Child Abuse, Domestic Violence and Animal Abuse: Linking the Circles of Compassion for Prevention and Intervention*. Indiana: Purdue University Press.

Bond, Anthony (2013). Customs officials seize 213 bear paws worth 293 pounds and arrest two Russian men for attempting to smuggle them into China. *Daily Mirror*, 18 June, http://dailym.ai/2Ya7mWe.

Bo Zhiyue (1996). Economic performance and political mobility: Chinese provincial leaders. *Journal of Contemporary China* 5(12): 135-55.

Broadway, Michael (1990). Meatpacking and its social and economic consequences for Garden City, Kansas in the 1980s. *Urban Anthropology and Studies of Cultural Systems and World Economic Development* 19(4): 321-44.

Browne, Rachel (2009). Sense of release. *Sydney Morning Herald*, 18 July, https://bit.ly/3sUNIeU.

Burton, Lydia (2015). Australia a step closer to sending kangaroo meat to China. *ABC News*, 7 July, http://ab.co/3pj0IsD.

CBC News (2014). Sale of seal meat to China thwarted by anti-hunt activists. *CBC News*, 14 April, http://bit.ly/39SWb9G.

CCP Central Committee (2018). The CCP Central Committee Document One for 2018. https://bit.ly/3sNg7Ul.

CCP Central Document Research Institute (2004). 邓小平年谱: 1975-1997 下 (*A Chronicle of Deng Xiaoping's Life: 1975-1997*, vol. 2). Beijing: CCP Central Documentary Publishing House.

Central Committee of the Chinese Communist Party (1972). 中共中央转发《国务院关于粮食问题的报告》的批语 (The Chinese Communist Party Central Committee releases comments and directives on the State Council *Report on the Question of Food Grains*), 10 December, https://ccradb.appspot.com/post/729.

CCTV (China Central Television) (2005). 西部大开发：西部特色经济篇 (Development of Western China: on the specialty economy of the region), CCTV News, 19 January, https://bit.ly/39dZ99W.

CCTV (2012). 江西野味餐馆大批宰杀猕猴 挂牌称公务消费定点 (Jiangxi exotic food restaurants as designated official catering venues were involved in massive slaughter of macaques), originally reported by *Xinjing News*, 28 November, http://bit.ly/3iJeQsF.

Central News of Korea (2017). 中国宠物市场位居全球第三位 (China has the third biggest pet product market in the world), 4 July, http://bit.ly/3sWc5cq.

Central People's Government of China (2015). 朝鲜族 (The ethnic Koreans in China), http://bit.ly/39alxkl.

Cha, Ariana Eunjung (2007). Pig disease in China worries the world. *Washington Post*, 16 September, http://wapo.st/3c6BfyQ.

Chang Jiwen and Gil Michaels (2010). 动物保护法与反虐待动物法：专家建议与各界争锋. (Animal Protection Law of the PRC and Prevention of Cruelty to Animals Law of the PRC: experts' proposal and the public response). Beijing: China Environmental Science Press.

Chang Jiwen, Guo Shunzhen, Wang Xin, Liu Kai, and Wei Zengchun (2015).《野生动物保护法》存在的问题与修改建议 (The remaining issues and revision suggestions to the Wildlife Protection Law), http://bit.ly/2Y9XoEj.

Chang Jiwen (2016). The current state of China's bear farming industry and recommendations on phasing out the industry: an investigative report in an internal government research journal published by the State Council Research Centre of Development, 5 July.

Chakraborty, Manab (2003). Wildlife trade and consumption threaten public health. *South China Morning Post*, 5 June.

Chebet, Caroline (2019). China's move to legalize use of rhino horn and tiger bones criticized. *Independent*, 2 January, http://bit.ly/2KILAWo.

Chen Bingan (2011). 大逃港. 香港: 中和出版社 (Great exodus to Hong Hong). Hong Kong: Zhonghe Press.

Chen Chunji (2003). The impact of SARS and the need to readjust laws and regulations: thoughts evoked by the outbreak of SARS. *Chinese Wildlife* 5.

References

Chen Fang, Liu Ming and Li Peng (2011). 瘦肉精: 何以十年难禁绝. (Why has it been so hard to crack down on Clenbuterol use in the past ten years?) *China Youth Daily*, 24 March, 3.

Chen, Laurie (2018). Chinese slaughterhouse staff force-feed cattle with water for 12 hours to artificially increase their weight. *South China Morning Post*, 21 November, http://bit.ly/3a4mbiN.

Chen Mincai, Chen Yunlian and Jiang Hong (2015). An investigative report on the conditions at Yang Xiaoyun's shelter, 27 September. A hardcopy of the report was provided to this author by the investigators.

Chen, Qin and Juliana Liu (2019). Chinese animal rights groups outraged about arrival of baby elephants. *Inkstone News*, 28 October, http://bit.ly/3qNv5HV.

Chen Ruo (2014). 毒金属危化品竟随意网购.广州日报 12月24日 (Hazardous chemicals are readily available online for purchase. *Guangzhou Daily*, 24 December, https://bit.ly/2MgumjE.

Chen Zhiye and Haihua Xie (2004). 道教的世俗化及其对中国民众的影响 (Popularisation of Daoism and its impact on the general public in China). *Hunan Daojiao*. Reprinted at https://bit.ly/3qNBvqK.

Chen, Zhiyuan (2013). 梁武帝与僧团素食改革-解读《断酒肉文》(Emperor Wu of Liang and vegetarian reform in the Buddhist temples: interpreting "On Abstaining from Wine and Meat." 中华文史论丛 (*Journal of Chinese Cultural and Historical Studies*) 3.

Cheng, Frances (2016). Cruelty to animals has no place in modern medical schools. *South China Morning Post*, 9 March, http://bit.ly/2MlNAo9.

Cheng Guangyan, Liu Shanshan, Yang Zhenni and Wang Dongyang (2015). 中国肉类消费特征及2020年预测分析 (The characteristics of China's meat consumption and a forecast for 2020). *Journal of Chinese Rural Economy* 2.

China Animal Husbandry Yearbook Compilation Committee (2004), 中国畜牧业年鉴 2004. 北京: 中国农业出版社 (*China Animal Husbandry Industry Yearbook 2004*). Beijing: China Agriculture Press).

China Animal Husbandry Yearbook Compilation Committee (2005). 中国畜牧业年鉴 2005. 北京: 中国农业出版社 (*China Animal Husbandry Industry Yearbook 2005*). Beijing: China Agriculture Press).

China Animal Husbandry Yearbook Compilation Committee (2014). 中国畜牧业年鉴 2014. 北京: 中国农业出版社 (*China Animal Husbandry Industry Yearbook 2014*). Beijing: China Agriculture Press.

China Animal Husbandry and Veterinary Science Yearbook Compilation Committee (2015), 中国畜牧兽医年鉴 2015. 北京: 中国农业出版社 (*China Animal Husbandry and Veterinary Science Yearbook 2015*). Beijing: China Agriculture Press.

China Animal Protection Network (中国动物关爱联网) (2013). 致玉林市人民政府 (A letter of petition to Yulin People's Government), 18 June, http://bit.ly/2Miy9Nm.

China.com (2006). 东北地区就业形势与对策分析 (The employment situation in Northeast China and an analysis of the solutions), 11 December, https://bit.ly/3oadckR.

China.com.cn (2012a). 归真堂"活熊取胆"引各界争议 能否上市仍存变数 (The controversy of Guizhentang's "bear farming" and the uncertainty of its IPO bid), 7 February, http://bit.ly/39emN5X.

China.com.cn (2012b). 速生鸡40天长5斤, 鸡肉流向伤害肯德基麦当劳 (Fast-growing chicken are fattened to 2.5 kilograms in 40 days and great quantity of such chicken sold to KFCs and McDonald's in Shanghai), 19 December, http://bit.ly/3qPeh3u.

China Daily (2013). Guizhentang drops IPO amid bile debate. *China Daily*, 4 June, http://on.china.cn/3i11g8O.

China Daily (2015). 风口浪尖上的玉林"狗肉节" (The "Yulin Dog Meat Festival" in the middle of a controversy). *China Daily*, 23 June, https://bit.ly/2YcDRTy.

China Daily (2017). China's TCM industry grows 20%. *China Daily*, 24 November, http://bit.ly/3sVDN8O.

China Development Research Foundation (2019). 国家'学生饮用奶计划'大事记 (A chronicle of the start of the state's "school milk" program), http://bit.ly/3qPfJms.

China Economic Information Net (www.ce.cn) (2012). 速生白翼鸡40天长5斤 喂食18种抗生素 (Broilers fed 18 antibiotics to grow 2.5 kilograms in 40 days), a collection of media reports about the fast-growth broiler scandal, https://bit.ly/3qOEuz3.

China Industrial Information Network (2018). 2018年我国宠物市场运行情况分析 (An analysis of the operation of China's pet market in 2018). 2 May, https://bit.ly/368NQ0S.

China Lab Animal Information Network (2018). 专访: 黄韧所长谈灵长类实验动物的重重瓶颈及行业发展之路 (An interview with director Huang Ren on the various bottlenecks and course of development of primate breeding for lab purposes). 16 December, https://www.labagd.com/Item/75197.aspx.

China News Network (2007). 国家林业局要求野生动物表演不得有悖人类情感 (State Forestry Bureau called for an end to wildlife animal performance that was offensive and provocative). *China News Network*, 6 October, https://bit.ly/2LSv4nz.

References

Chinameat.org (2015). 2014年生猪屠宰行业现状及趋势发展报告分析 (A report on the current state of the pig slaughter industry in 2014 and the trend of development), http://www.chinameat.org/detail_98.html.

China Statistical Bureau (2017). 2017年我国各地区野生动植物保护管理站数量统计 (Statistical summary of the wildlife protection management stations across the country in 2017), 26 August, https://bit.ly/3sUSI3a.

China Zoo Watch (2005). 中国野生动物园调查报告 (An investigative report of China's safari parks, Beijing).

Chyxx.com 2019. 2019年中国海洋主题公园继续保持良好发展,公园数量增至72家,游客规模突破8000万 (China's aquariums continued to display signs of great development in 2019, showing an increase to 72 display facilities and reaching a total number of more than 80 million visitors), 12 June, https://bit.ly/2Mgz7tw.

Clark, Campbell (2010). Facing backlash in Europe, Canada hunts for new seal market in China. *Globe and Mail*, 12 January, http://tgam.ca/2MlZlL0.

Clifton, Merritt (2011). Chinese activists object to Canadian deal to sell seal meat and oil to China. Animals24-7.org, 23 January, http://bit.ly/3r0St59.

CNN (2011). Live animals sold as keyrings in China. CNN, 15 April, https://cnn.it/3a2H1ib.

Cochrane, Gail M (2003). Problems associated with the free-dripping fistula technique as a method of bile extraction from Asiatic black bears. Presentation at the Animals Asia Foundation, Hong Kong.

Cohen, Paul A (1984). *Discovering History in China: American Historical Writing on the Recent Chinese Past*. New York: Columbia University Press.

Compassion in World Farming (CIWF) (2007). The role of the intensive poultry production industry in the spread of avian influenza, https://bit.ly/3oeKe3s.

Cummings, Bruce (1999). Webs with no spiders, spiders with no webs: the genealogy of the developmental state, in Meredith Woo-Cumings (ed.), *The Developmental State*. Ithaca, NY: Cornell University Press.

De Passille, A.M and J. Rushen (2005). Food safety and environmental issues in animal welfare. *Rev. sci. tech. Off. Int. Epiz.*(Scientific and Technical Review of the Office Internaitonal des Epizooties) 24(2): 757–66.

Deans, Phil (2004). The People's Republic of China: the post-socialist development state, in Linda Low (ed.), *Developmental States: Relevancy, Redundancy or Reconfiguration?* New York: Nova Science Publishers, Inc.

De Bary, Wm Theodore, Wing-Tsit Chan and Burton Watson (1960). *Sources of Chinese Tradition*. New York: Columbia University Press.

Deng Guosheng (2004). 中国非政府组织发展的新环境 (The new settings for the development of China's non-governmental organisations). *Xuehui Monthly* 10.

Diao Fanchao (2016). 亚洲黑熊种群数量急剧下降,动物保护组织呼吁终止活熊取胆业 (In response to a drastic drop in the wild population of Asiatic black bears, animal protection groups call for an end to the bear farming industry). *The Paper*, 30 March, http://bit.ly/365xc1W.

Diamond, Larry (1999). *Developing Democracy: Toward Consolidation*. Baltimore, MD: Johns Hopkins University Press.

Ding Qi (2007). Rules on meat reserves to stabilize prices. *China Daily*, 15 August, http://bit.ly/3sUsMF2.

DingShu (2014). 1970年一打三反运动纪实 (On the 1970 "One Crackdown and Three Opposition" campaign). *Huaxia Digest*, 12 April, https://bit.ly/39dFk2o.

DingWeicheng and Luo Qi (2005). 辽东湾斑海豹仅剩千只 专家吁保护措施刻不容缓 (With only about 1,000 seals remaining at the Liaodong Gulf, experts call for immediate protection measures), ChinaNews.com, 9 January, https://bit.ly/3sSZQx1.

Dongfang Morning News (2011). 河南双汇冷鲜肉查出瘦肉精 封存1877公斤冷鲜肉 (Clenbuterol was found in frozen meat produced by Henan's Shuanghui leading to the removal of 1,877 kg of meat from market). *Dongfang Morning News*, 21 March, https://bit.ly/39fojou.

D'Silva, Joyce (2006). Adverse impact of industrial animal agriculture on the health and welfare of farmed animals. *Integrative Zoology* 1, DOI 10.1111/j.1749-4877.2006.00013.x.

Du Li (2008). 从《齐民要术》看南北朝的素食 (The vegetarian food in the Northern and Southern Dynasties in Qimin Yaoshu). 扬州大学烹饪学报 25卷, 第3期 (*Culinary Science Journal of Yangzhou University* 25(3).

Du Mu. 杜牧诗全集 (A complete collection of Du Mu's poems), http://www.shujiu.com/wj/6/8.htm.

Economy, Elizabeth C (2004). *The River Runs Black: The Environmental Challenge to China's Future*. Ithaca, NY: Cornell University Press.

Elvin, Mark (2004). *The Retreat of the Elephants: An Environmental History of China*. New Haven, CT: Yale University Press.

Epstein, Gady A (2003). China dinner delicacies succumb to SARS scare. *Baltimore Sun*, 14 May, http://bit.ly/3ofpOYa.

Evans, Peter (1995). *Embedded Autonomy*. Princeton, NJ: Princeton University Press.

Fan Chunxu (2014). 中华鲟在葛洲坝建成32年后由1万余尾锐减至57尾 (A 32-year drastic drop from over 10,000 Chinese sturgeon at the time of Gezhouba's construction to 57 at the present time). *Xinjing News*, 25 September, https://bit.ly/3qS2Urh.

References

FAOSTAT (2013). Livestock Primary database. http://bit.ly/3t0YikT.
FAOSTAT (2014). Livestock Primary database. http://bit.ly/3t0YikT.
FAOSTAT (2019). Production: Livestock Primary. http://bit.ly/3t0YikT.
Farm Animal Welfare Council (1979). Five Freedoms. Published online 16 April 2009; archived by the National Archives (UK). http://bit.ly/369iF5i.
Feng Xiaoming (2004). 党建研究内部文稿 (2000–2004) (An internal manuscript of research on Chinese Communist Party construction: 2000–04). Shanghai: Shanghai Jiaotong University.
Feng Yongfeng (2011). Blog post describing the Forum for Protecting Bearded Seals, 8 April 2011, https://bit.ly/39Xpwjz.
Finance.ifeng.com (2012a). 张志鋆:熊活得很好 用社会资源救助失业工人比救熊好 (Zhang Zhiyun: bears are living a good life. Social resources should be used to help the jobless rather than rescue bears), 2 March, http://bit.ly/3pjO1he.
Finance.ifeng.com (2012b). 张志鋆:归真堂想上市才会被骂 有些人不希望它做大 (Zhang Zhiyun: Guizhentang was condemned for its IPO bid because some people do not want it to grow), 2 March, http://bit.ly/3a3Lt0n.
Finance.ifeng.com (2012c). 张志鋆:归真堂从来没有生产过保健品 (Zhang Zhiyun: Guizhentang has never marketed health supplements containing bear bile powder), 2 March, http://bit.ly/3sUWsle.
Fitzgerald, Amy J, Linda Kalof, and Thomas Dietz (2009). Slaughterhouses and increased crime rates: an empirical analysis of spillover from "The Jungle" in the Surrounding community. *Organization and Environment* 22: 158–84.
Food and Agriculture Organization of the United Nations (2016). *The State of World Fisheries and Aquaculture 2016: Contributing to Food Security and Nutrition for All*, http://bit.ly/3qP68w0.
Fur Industry Association (2013). The rise of the fur industry at a time of sluggish market, seeking efficiency by streamlining the industry, 2 February, https://bit.ly/2M4bc0u.
Gao Changli (2005). 代表建议发展经济不要忘了念"熊经"(Delegate does not forget to promote bear farming while speaking for economic development). *Dongbeiwang*, 28 January, https://bit.ly/39fVw3k.
Gao Lang (2017). 新余市野生动物驯养产业发展成效明显 (A great accomplishment and development of Xinyu City's wildlife farming industry). Jiangxi Forestry Bureau, https://bit.ly/365z3Us.
General Bureau of Quality Inspection and National Standards Commission (2018). 中华人民共和国国家标准公告2018年第2号 (A public notice on the issuance of national standards of the People's Republic of China, No. 2, https://bit.ly/3qLFdB4.

Georgiou, Aristos (2020). Eating cats and dogs banned in a second city in China in wake of COVID-19 pandemic. *Newsweek*, 15 April, http://bit.ly/2M1Ju4v.

Gerschenkron, Alexander (1962). *Economic Backwardness in Historical Perspective: A Book of Essays*. New York: Frederick A. Prager Publishers.

Ge Zhong-e and Xu Xianjiang (2009). 图说故宫六百年 (An illustrated account of the 600-year history of the Forbidden City). Hefei: Huangshan Books.

Gettleman, Jeffrey (2016). Closing China's ivory market: will it save elephants? *New York Times*, 31 December, http://nyti.ms/2MiEXuo.

GJ Financial Consulting (2005). *The Whale Meat Market: Study on Current Possible Markets and Cost of Operations in Minke Whaling*, https://www.mbl.is/media/65/265.pdf.

GongShaoqian 安定Bian Lizhen (2014). 母猪限位栏还要陪伴中国养猪业走多远? (How long shall sow crates accompany the Chinese pig farming industry?). *Northern Animal Husbandry* 14, 20 June.

Gold, Thomas B. (1986). *State and Society in the Taiwan Miracle* (New York: ME Sharpe).

Goulet, Denis (1995). *Development Ethics: A Guide to Theory and Practice*. New York: The Apex Press.

Gou Rou Hao Hao Chi Ba (Just enjoy eating dog meat) (n.d.). 吃猫吃狗杀猫杀狗这种行为是对伟大的中华民族的悠久的传统和历史的继承. (Eating dog and cat meat and killing cats and dogs are acts that continue China's great and time-tested traditional culture), a blog of Guo Rou Hao Hao Chi, https://tieba.baidu.com/p/5423554345.

Gu Xin (2020). 1800万只竹鼠被判死缓：10万养殖户的生计和20亿元生意 (The life of 18 million bamboo rats is on the line together with 100,000 wildlife farm workers and a 2 billion yuan business). *China News Weekly*, 6 April, http://bit.ly/3qStIrJ.

Guangxi Zhuang Autonomous Region People's Government (2015). 广西壮族自治区人民政府关于进一步做好新形势下就业创业工作的通知 (The People's Government of Guangxi Zhuang Autonomous Region notice on strengthening the work of promoting employment and business ventures under the new situation), https://bit.ly/2M3sye7.

Guizhentang (2017). 归真堂公司介绍 (An introduction to Guizhentang). http://www.gztxd.com/home/NewsDetail/45.

Gullone, Eleonora (2011). Conceptualizing animal abuse with an antisocial behavior framework. *Animals* 1(1): 144–60.

Guo Fang et al. (2012). 十八大代表企业家名单公布:当选关键是政治先进 (The list of entrepreneur delegates to the 18th Party Congress was released: their election was based on their political qualifications). *China Economic Weekly*, 6 November, https://bit.ly/2KII52b.

Guo Geng (2006). 鸟语唐诗三百首 (Birds and 300 poems of the Tang Dynasty). Beijing: Tong Xin Press.

Guo Peng (2012). 有关济南郊区盗狗与非法狗肉产业猖獗的调查报告 (Unpublished report on the theft of dogs in the suburbs of Jinan and the rampancy of the illegal dog-meat production chain, submitted to the Jinan city government, Shandong).

Guo Peng (2013). 玉林食用狗猫来源和社会背景的深度调查 (Unpublished report on the source of dogs and cats consumed as food in Yulin, with social background).

Guo Xiaojun (2006). "养熊取胆"场降至68家，林业局官员表示暂不取缔" (Bear farm number has dropped to 68 according to State Forestry Bureau officials who confirmed that the government had no plan to outlaw bear farming). *Xinjing News*, 1 March, https://bit.ly/2MgEvNg.

Haojinggui.com (2016). 2015年中国各省人均GDP排名 (2015 Chinese provincial per capita GDP ranking, 28 June, http://www.haojingui.com/gdp/1265.html.

He Hairen (2016). 野生动物保护法该如何"利用"野生动物? (How wildlife is to be "utilized" in the Wildlife Protection Law), https://bit.ly/3sTg2hS.

He Huaihong (2002). 生态伦理: 精神资源与哲学基础 (Ecological ethics: spiritual resources and philosophical foundations). Baoding: Hebei University Press, 2002.

He Zhengming et al. (2018). 写在《实验动物管理条例》发布实施三十周年 (On the 30th anniversary of the adoption of the Regulation on the Management of Lab Animals. National Lab Animal Expert Committee Briefing No. 45, https://www.labagd.com/Item/74298.aspx.

Heibao Pharmaceutical Company. 走进黑宝 (Company information), http://www.hbgroup.com.cn/nav/2.html.

Heilongjiang Provincial People's Congress (2002). 黑龙江省第十届人民代表大会代表名单(571人) (The delegate list of the 10th Heilongjiang Provincial People's Congress (571 delegates)), http://www.hljrd.gov.cn/info/1366/8105.htm.

Ho, Peter (2001). Greening without conflict? Environmentalism, NGOs and civil society in China. *Development and Change* 32(5): 893–921.

Ho, Peter (2007). Embedded activism and political change in a semiauthoritarian context. *China Information* 21(2): 187–209.

Hong Kong on.cc (2017). 中华鲟洄游产卵不足百条 长江江豚极度濒危(The Yangtze River dolphins were threatened with extinction while fewer than 100

Chinese sturgeon reached the upper reaches of the Yangtze for spawning). *Hong Kong on.cc*, 21 April, http://bit.ly/3oh3opn.

Hsieh-Yi, Yi-Chiao, Yu Fu, Mark Rissi and Barbara Maas (2005). *Fun Fur? A Report on the Chinese Fur Industry* (report jointly sponsored by the Swiss Animal Protection SAP, Care for the Wild International, and EAST International), https://bit.ly/369GABJ.

Hu Benzhen (2003). 白鱀豚: 中国的水中国宝 (Lipotes vexillfer: China's national treasure in the water). *Chinese Wildlife* 5.

Hu Mingqi (2015). 应光国: 十年"算账"抗生素 (interview with Ying Guangguo: a ten-year "chase" with antibiotics). *China Science News*, 10 July, https://bit.ly/3c9yRHM.

Hu Ping (1988). 怪黄河还是怪共产党? (Blame the Yellow River or the Chinese Communist Party?) *China Spring* 66 (November).

Hu Tianhua and Li Tao (2003). 宁夏贺兰山马麝资源的兴衰及保护管理对策 (The decline of the musk deer population and the protection measures at Ningxia's Helan Mountain). *Chinese Wildlife* 4.

Hu Zhanfen (1998). 触目惊心! 长白山仙人桥熊场血腥见闻 (A nightmarish experience: brutality we witnessed at Changbaishan's Xian Ren Qiao bear farm). Reprinted in *World Journal*, April 1998, and *China Week*, 2002, https://www.china-week.com/info/01031.htm.

Huang Hua (2008). 亲历与见闻 – 黄华回忆录 (Huang Hua remembers: a story of personal experience and an eye-witness account). Beijing: World Affairs Press.

Huang Shaojie (2015). Animal rights groups in China accuse Yulin dog rescuer of misleading public. *New York Times* Sinosphere blog, 22 September, http://nyti.ms/39gx8i1.

Huang Yongmin (2013). 中国抗生素年产21万吨成最大生产国 养殖业消费近一半 (China becomes the world's biggest antibiotic producer, producing 210,000 tons, half of which is used in animal farming). *Southern Weekly*, 8 March, http://bit.ly/3qJ0I5m.

Huang Zhen (2006). 王光美访谈录 (My interview with Wang Guangmei). Beijing: Central Documentary Press.

Hughes, Peter and John Heritage (2004). Antibiotic growth-promoters in food animals. In Samuel Jutzi (ed.), *Assessing Quality and Safety of Animal Feeds*. Rome: Food and Agriculture Organization of the United Nations. https://bit.ly/3sSvECf.

Humane Society International (2014a). China and cosmetics animal testing FAQ, https://bit.ly/2M4lC06.

References

Humane Society International (2014b). China implements rule change in first step towards ending animal testing of cosmetics, 30 June, https://bit.ly/3c8W2BK.

Humane Society International (2019). Breaking: campaigners outraged as Zimbabwe exports 30+ baby elephants to Chinese zoos, HSI/Africa releases last known video of the elephants taken days before shipment, 24 October, http://bit.ly/2KKBggJ.

Humane Society International (2020). Wildlife markets and COVID-19. Humane Society International White Paper, 6 April, https://bit.ly/3sSrp9E.

Huntington, Samuel P (1993). The clash of civilizations? *Foreign Affairs* 72(3): 22–49.

Huot, Claire (2015). The dog-eared dictionary: human–animal alliance in Chinese civilization. *Journal of Asian Studies* 73(3): 589–613.

International Fund for Animal Welfare (1998). Public opinion survey on animal welfare: an International Fund for Animal Welfare survey in collaboration with BMS & Associates, Inc.

International Fund for Animal Welfare (2006). *Ivory Market in China: China Ivory Trade Survey Report 2006*. https://g.ifaw.org/39fDDS2.

ITV (2015). Millions protest as China's controversial Yulin Dog Meat Festival begins. *ITV News*, 22 June, http://bit.ly/2NydKEJ.

Ji Xianlin (2009). 季羡林随想录四 国学漫谈 (Random thoughts of Ji Xianlin IV: on Chinese culture). Beijing: Metropolitan Publishing House.

Jia Qian, Du Yanyan, Chong Hailiang, Fu Junying and Yang Juping (2003). 中国药用濒危野生动植物保护战略研究 (A study of endangered animal and plant species for use in Chinese medicine), unpublished research funded by the China Science and Technology Information Research Institute and Beijing Tongrentang, a traditional Chinese medicine pharmaceutical company).

Jia Youlin (2001). 抓住机遇大力发展畜牧业 (Seize the opportunity and boost animal husbandry production). *The China Animal Husbandry Industry Yearbook 2001*. Beijing: China Agriculture Press.

Jiang Gewei (2014). 爱狗人士与食客发生冲突 行为艺术家遭围堵 (A conflict erupted between dog lovers and dog meat consumers while a performing artist was being stalked). *Rule of Law Weekly*, 24 June, http://on.china.cn/2LU9qzg.

Jiang, Jessie (2011). China: tainted pork renews food safety fears. *Time*, 23 March, http://bit.ly/3c6UBUw.

Jiang Jinsong (2011). 专家评审会如何才有公信力 (What does it take for an expert evaluation committee to stay credible). *Xinjing News*, 1 September, https://bit.ly/39ZoCDd.

Jiang Jinsong (2016). 野生动物保护与中医药发展 (The protection of wildlife animals and the development of traditional Chinese medicine), *China Weekly* vol. 11, republished at Science.net.cn, https://bit.ly/2MnVjlj.

Jiang Xuejiao (2017). 新疆自然保护区建立 五年内不得调整 (There will be no more nature reserve adjustments in Xinjiang in the next five years). CCTV News, 1 August, https://bit.ly/3a2VzOP.

Jiang Yuebo and Wu Zhiyuan (2006). 列车活猪输港完成使命 荆楚探索新渠道供应香港 (The end of Hubei's live pig transporation to Hong Kong and its exploration of new channels for pork supply). *Hubei Daily*, 18 March, https://bit.ly/3c6xObk.

Jiangnan University and China Food Safety Public Opinion Research Center (2015). 2005-2014 年间主流网络舆情报道的中国发生的食品安全事件分析报告 (An analysis of the mainstream online public opinion on the food safety incidents that happened between 2005 and 2014).

Jiangxi Provincial Government (2020). 帮助养殖户及时止损江西率先出台在养禁食野生动物处置意见 (Jiangxi takes the lead to compensate wildlife breeders by issuing a policy directive on banning the farming of banned wild animals for food). Press release, 16 May, http://bit.ly/2MkMIjs.

Jiao Jie (2000). 从唐墓志看唐代妇女与佛教的关系 (The epitaph and the relations between Tang Dynasty women and Buddhism). *Journal of Shaanxi Normal University* (Philosophy and Social Sciences Edition), 29(1).

Jin Junjie et al. (2012). The current state and measures for controlling and preventing the illnesses impacting the fast-growth broilers in Wenzhou City. *Livestock and Poultry Industry* 284.

Jing Jing (2012). 活熊取胆：两会上政协委员唱对台戏 (Bear farming: members of the Chinese People's Political Consultative Conference and the National People's Congress confront each other at the annual session). *Epoch Times*, 13 March. http://bit.ly/3c4ifB7.

Jinghua Times (2012a). Zhou Junsheng: let the stock market decide if Guizhentang should go public. *Jinghua Times*, 16 February, https://bit.ly/2MmaA6t.

Jinghua Times (2012b). 江西资溪野生猕猴遭疯狂猎杀 官方许可证成保护伞 (Poaching of wild macaques in Jiangxi Zhixi, protected by government hunting permits, is out of control). *Jinhua Times*, 28 November https://bit.ly/2Nud7Mh.

Johnson, Chalmers A. (1982). *MITI and the Japanese Miracle: The Growth of Industrial Policy, 1952-1975*. Stanford, CA: Stanford University Press.

Johnson, Tim (2006). China refuses calls to shut bile farms: critics say milking bears for medicines, makeup is inhumane. *Chicago Tribune*, 15 January, https://bit.ly/366EEdm.

References

Jones, Edwin F (1962). The impact of the food crisis on Peiping's policies. *Asian Survey* 2(10): 1–11.

Journal of the Chinese Dairy Industry (2006). 温家宝总理视察奶业基地并作重要指示 (Prime Minister Wen Jiabao inspects milk production base and makes important remarks). *Journal of the Chinese Dairy Industry* 5.

Joyce, Ed (2012). Californian shark finning bill creates cultural divide: traditional soup versus ocean conservation. *KPBS News*, 2 January, http://bit.ly/36crgEy.

Kai Chen (2017). 满族是从什么时候开始不吃狗肉的? (When did the Manchus stop eating dog meat?). *The Paper*, 10 November, http://bit.ly/3qUsb4t.

Kang Jianhai (2003). 百万广告效应是这样制造的 "非典" 时期非常策划记 (This is how a million-yuan advertisement was conducted: a special advertisement design at the time of SARS). Blog post, https://bit.ly/36bELnX.

Kaufman, Joan (2011). HIV, sex work, and civil society in China. *Journal of Infectious Diseases* 204: S1218–22.

Kirby, Alex (2000). Soup threatens sharks' survival. *BBC News*, 6 July, https://bbc.in/2KJp0No.

Kohn, Livia (ed.) (2000). *Daoism Handbook*. Leiden: Brill.

Krueger, Anne O (1980). Trade policy as an input to development. *American Economic Review* 70(2): 228–92.

Lam, Timothy, Xu Ling, Soyo Takahashi and Elizabeth A. Burgess (2012). *Market Forces: An Examination of Marine Turtle Trade in China and Japan: A TRAFFIC East Asia Report*, http://bit.ly/36bpEe5.

Lao Zi (2009). 道教 (Daoism). Changchun: Jilin Literature and History Press.

Le Aiguo (2013). 为天地立心: 张载自然观 (Creating peace for the world: a study of Zhang Zai's nature outlook). Xiamen: Haitian Press.

Li Bo and et al. (2011). 中国黑熊及其养熊业的发展现状 (China's Asiatic black bears and the current state of its bear farming industry). *Chinese Journal of Wildlife* 32(4).

Li Diqiang (2000). A brief account of the National Wildlife Management Work Conference. 生物多元性 (*Journal of Biodiversity*) 2.

Li Jin, Qin Fu and Ding Ping (2007). 我国居民畜产品消费特征及发展趋势 (On the characteristics of livestock product consumption and its development trend). *Research of Agricultural Modernization* 28(6).

Li Jing (2016). Animal rights activists petition Yulin city office in Beijing against annual dog meat festival. *South China Morning Post*, 10 June, http://bit.ly/3iMSkiz.

Li Jinxiu (2015). The current state of Fujian's open economic development and the opportunities and challenges it faces. *Foreign Trade* 255(9).

Li Maosheng, Lin Mingjiang, Ma Weihan and Zhang Qingkai (2011). 商业化/大型放生行为规范可行性评估研究计划 (Evaluation of the legislation of commercial/large-scale animal release, commissioned by the Forestry Bureau of the Agricultural Committee of the Executive Council of the Republic of China), 20 May.

Li, Peter J (2004a). China's bear farming and long-term solutions. *Journal of Applied Animal Welfare Science* 7(1): 71–81.

Li, Peter J (2004b). Rehabilitating rescued Chinese farm bears: results, limitations and implications. *Journal of Wildlife Rehabilitation* 27(1): 4–15.

Li, Peter J (2007). Enforcing wildlife protection in China: the legislative and political solutions. *China Information* 21(1): 71–107.

Li, Peter J (2009). Exponential growth, animal welfare, environmental and food safety impact: the case of China's livestock production. *Journal of Agricultural and Environmental Ethics* 22(3): 217–40.

Li, Peter J (2016). It's time to outlaw animal cruelty in China. *South China Morning Post*, 6 August, http://bit.ly/3sVXqh0.

Li, Peter J (2016a). Inside Yulin Dog Meat Festival: The silence of dogs awaiting slaughter is thundering. *International Financial Times*, 14 April, http://bit.ly/3sMOtGS.

Li, Raymond (2007). Scientists warn of new plague of mice at Dongting Lake. *South China Morning Post*, 17 July, http://bit.ly/3pgkfKl.

Li Rui (1996). 毛泽东的功过是非 (The accomplishments and failures of Mao Zedong). Hong Kong: Cosmos Books Ltd.

Li Shizhen (1994). 本草纲目 (Compendium of materia medica). Chongqing: Chongqing University Press.

Li Tiezhu (2020). 因野生动物祸害庄稼男子猎捕多只野生动物 获刑1年半 (A man was sentenced to one and a half years for illegal hunting of crop-damaging wild animals). *Beijing Youth News*, 1 June, ht.tps://bit.ly/39egyzl

Li Xianfeng (2015a). 环保人士发负面消息索要赞助费 被判敲诈罪获刑 (Environmental activists convicted of extortion for spreading negative information and demanding sponsorship donation). *Beijing Youth Daily*, 21 November, https://bit.ly/39fzGwJ.

Li Xianfeng (2015b). 斑海豹卫士背后罪与罚: 发负面消息向油田索赞助费 (The crime and punishment of the seal protector: spreading negative information about the oil company to extort for sponsorship donation). *Beijing Youth Daily*, 21 November, https://bit.ly/3c8FKZN.

Li Xiaoming (2018). 上海海昌海洋公园正式开园 震撼虎鲸表演首度亮相,还有唯美的美人鱼表演 (Shanghai Chimelong Ocean Park officially opens with breathtaking killer whale performance and stunning mermaid shows). SHXWCB, 16 November, http://bit.ly/3phsl5d.

Li Xiaoxi (2003). 修订相关法律是当前保护野生动物的当务之急 (The urgent task for protecting wildlife species is to revise relevant laws), unpublished report for *The People's Daily*, April.

Li Xinlian (2013). 麻雀劫难五十年祭 (On the 50th anniversary of the sparrow massacre). *China Report Weekly*, 3 February, http://bit.ly/3iKfKFb.

Li Yizhi (2018). 近代中国动物保护的先驱 (A pioneer of modern China's animal protection movement). *Legal Affairs News*, 12 July, http://bit.ly/369zL2Y.

Li Yuanbing (2016). 白马雪山已有2500多只滇金丝猴 (There are over 2,500 Yunnan Snub-nosed monkeys in Yunnan Diqing's Baima Snow Mountain). *Metropolitan Times*, 11 November, http://bit.ly/3qNAAq7.

Li Yumin (1994). 正确处理野生动物保护与群众生产活动之间的关系 (Correctly handle the contradictions between wildlife protection and the productive activities of the masses). *Chinese Wildlife* 77(1).

Li Zheng and Wang Yunjian (2009). 畜禽养殖中抗生素使用的现状, 问题及对策 (The current state, problem, and solution with regard to antibiotics use in livestock production). *China Animal Health* 11(7).

Li Zhuopeng (2013). 李作鹏回忆录 (The memoir of Li Zhuopeng). Hong Kong: Beixing Press.

Lian Chi (1535–1615). 戒杀放生文 (On prohibition of killing and mercy release). https://bit.ly/3iGVggG.

Liang Qizhi (2017). The two meanings of "Vegetarian China" in the Republic of China era, 21 August, http://bit.ly/2KIWvzm.

Liang Qizhi (2019). 素食曾在民初广受欢迎, 伍廷芳, 李石曾, 孙中山都大力推动过 (Vegetarianism was popular in the early years of the Republic of China: Wu Tingfang, Li Shizeng and Sun Yatsen made great efforts to promote it). *Information Express Network*, 9 May, https://dbsqp.com/article/110063.

Liang Zhiping (2016a). 梁治平: 野生动物保护法修订有多"民主"? 写在《野生动物保护法修订草案》二审之际 (How open is the process of revising the Wildlife Protection Law? A commentary in response to the deliberation of the second-draft revision). *China Law Review*, 31 December, http://bit.ly/3sTT3mY.

Liang Zhiping (2016b). 梁治平: 丧钟为谁而鸣? 写在新修《野生动物保护法》通过之际 (For whom is the death knell tolled? A commentary in the wake of the revised Wildlife Protection Law). *China Law Review*, 31 December, https://bit.ly/3iHoCLO.

Lieberthal, Kenneth (2004). *Governing China: From Revolution Through Reform*. New York: WW Norton & Company.

Lin Hui (2016). 农业部开展2016年生猪屠宰监管"扫雷行动" (The Agriculture Ministry launches 2016 "mine removal" campaign to strengthen the supervision of pig slaughter operations). *Xinhua News*, 18 May, https://bit.ly/36ccc9I.

Lin Yutang (1966). *My Country and My People*. Taipei: Mei Ya Publications, Inc.

Liu Bo and Yang Liu (2011). 太平天国灭亡的真相 (The truth about the collapse of the Taiping heavenly empire). People.com.cn, https://bit.ly/3oeL5RJ.

Liu Huoxiong (2010). 用生命做赌注偷渡香港：震动中央的"大逃港"风潮 (The wind and tide of the "mass exodus to Hong Kong" that shocked Beijing leaders: risking lives to cross illegally into Hong Kong). People.com.cn, http://bit.ly/2Yc0DLu.

Liu Ji (2017). "保护斑海豹第一人"田继光再审宣判：12年刑期改判四年半 ("First seal Protector" Tian Jiguang received a retrial verdict: 12-year changed to a four-and a-half-year imprisonment). *The Paper*, 27 June, http://bit.ly/3ceu9sl.

Liu Qin (2018). Why China's dogs need better protection. Chinadialogue, 16 February, http://bit.ly/369cTk5.

LiuShahe (2016). 发展野生动物养殖的巨大前景 (The great prospects of developing wildlife farming). *Information Reservoir for Rural Development* (July): 24–25.

Liu Yu-Yun et al. (2016). Emergence of plasmid-mediated colistin resistance mechanism MCR-1 in animals and human beings in China: a microbiological and molecular biological study. *Lancet Infectious Diseases* 16(2): 161–68.

Liu Xia (2012). 30余政协委员联名提案力挺养熊取胆：称不可取代 (Some 30 members of the Chinese People's Political Consultative Conference jointly proposed to support bear farming and called bear bile an irreplaceable ingredient of Traditional Chinese Medicine). *Xin Jing News*, 13 March. https://bit.ly/3sSOc5k.

Liu Xiaotong and Zhang Xinpei (2012). 黑熊梦魇：熊胆粉背后的商业江湖 (The nightmare of bears: the commercial interests behind the production of bear bile powder). *Times Weekly*, 1 March, https://bit.ly/3sVjEjg.

Liu Xing (2010). 王阳明社会思想探析 (A study of Wang Yangming's Social Ideas). *Journal of Chongqing University of Technology* (Social Sciences), 24(5).

Liu Yu and Ge Chen (2014). FAO hails China's success in achieving anti-hunger goal. *People's Daily*, 17 June http://bit.ly/3aivwUj.

Liu Yu-yun et al. (2016). Emergence of plasmid-mediated colistin resistance mechanism MCR-1 in animals and human beings in China: a microbiological and molecular biological study. *Lancet Infectious Diseases* 16: 161–68, first published online in November 2015.

References

Lo, Tiffany (2019). "Out of control" golden retriever is beaten to death by a policeman on a street in front of shocked pedestrians including children. *Daily Mail*, 2 January, http://dailym.ai/3a4tCGp.

Loeffler, Kati, Jill Robinson, and Gail Cochrane (2007). Animals Asia Foundation Report: compromised health and welfare of bears in China's bear bile farming industry, with special reference to the free-dripping bile extraction technique. March, https://bit.ly/36cBVPt.

Iotrade.com (2011). 瘦肉精事件大事记 (A chronicle of the incidents involving Clenbuterol), https://bit.ly/36bX0cF.

Lovgren, Stefan (2006). China's rare river dolphin now extinct, experts announce. *National Geographic News*, 14 December, https://bit.ly/3oml8Q1.

LuXiaobo and Jingping Lai (2011). 从反封建到发扬优秀传统文化——20世纪80年代以来中国共产党的历史认 (From opposition to feudalism to glorifying traditional culture – the change of the historical outlook of the Chinese Communist Party since the 1980s). *Journal of Academic Research 9*.

Ma Anyue (2011). 六部委联合发文要求全面禁止产销瘦肉精 (Six ministries issued a joint statement calling for a complete ban on the production and sale of Clenbuterol), 23 December, https://bit.ly/3cbvlMQ.

Ma Jianzhang, Chao Liancheng, and Luo Zexun (1985). 护、养、猎辩证关系的探讨 (A discussion of the dialectical relations among protection, domestication and hunting of wild animals), *Journal of Northeast-Eastern Forestry College* 13(1).

Ma Jianhua and Chen Chunji (2003). 反思"非典"影响,调整法律规范——由"非典"引发的思考 (The impact of SARS and the need to readjust laws and regulations: thoughts evoked by the outbreak of SARS). *Chinese Wildlife*, No.5.

Ma, Jianzhang et al. (2017). *A Research Report of the Sustainable Development Strategy of China's Wildlife Farming Industry*. Bejing: China National Academy of Engineering.

Magnier, Mark (2004). Bullfighting in Beijing? No way, say Chinese. *Los Angeles Times*, 11 May, http://lat.ms/3sXngRN.

Maisels, F., et al. (2013). Devastating decline of forest elephants in central Africa. *PLoS One* 8(3), DOI 10.1371/journal.pone.0059469.

Mang Ping (1999) 绿色生活手记 (On green life). Qingdao: Qingdao Publishing House.

Mang Ping (2009). 物我相融的世界:中国人的信仰、生活与动物观 (The world of the inter-related self and other: Chinese beliefs, lives and views of animals). Beijing: China University of Politics and Law.

Mang Ping (2010). 不宜引进西班牙斗牛 (Beijing should not introduce Spanish bullfighting). *Xinjing News*, 9 January, http://bit.ly/39fPQpH.

Mao Shoulong (2016). 爱狗有理，吃狗无罪 (It is all right to love dogs and it is not illegal to eat dogs). *New Beijing News*, 23 June, http://bit.ly/3iJLZ7J.

Mao Zedong (1991). 毛泽东选集第一卷 (Selected works of Mao Zedong, vols. 1 through 4). Beijing: People's Press.

Mei Shanyu (2007). 解剖帝王 (Remove the veils of the emperors). Beijing: Chinese Communist Party History Press.

Mei Zhiqiang (2003). 海南黑冠长臂猿 (Hainan black headed long-armed gorillas). *Chinese Wildlife* 4.

Meng Si (2011a). Snubbing the seal trade. *China Dialoge*, 20 April, http://bit.ly/3iLhVIM.

Meng Si (2011b). Licence to kill. *China Dialogue*, 23 August, article published on August 23, http://bit.ly/2NBe71j.

Menxius (372–289 BCE). 梁惠王-上 (Liang Hui Wang I), http://bit.ly/3ofE4Qr.

Mertha, Andrew (2005). China's "soft" centralization: shifting Tiao/Kuai authority relations. *China Quarterly* 184: 791–810.

Mertha, Andrew (2009). Fragmented authoritarianism 2.0: political pluralization in the Chinese policy process. *China Quarterly* 200: 995–1012.

Metropolitan Express (2017). An undercover investigation of China's tiger village of 1500 villagers who raise more than 300 tigers. Reprinted on Hangzhou.com.cn, 15 February, http://bit.ly/3t44kkL.

Meyer, David.S. and Suzanne Staggenborg (1996). Movements, counter-movements, and the structure of political opportunity. *American Journal of Sociology* 101(6): 1628–60.

Miao Song et al. (2014). Human rabies surveillance and control in China, 2005–2012. *BMC Infectious Diseases* 14: 212–21.

Miller, Dan and Edward Chow (2015). Chinese villagers beat dog thieves for nine hours, tie the dead animals' bodies around their necks before attacking police officers sent in to rescue the crooks. *Daily Mail*, 5 June, http://dailym.ai/36dOCJL.

Ministry of Commerce of the People's Republic of China (2007). 中央储备肉管理办法 (Central government management measures on the central meat reserves), http://bit.ly/3pjXR2L.

Ministry of Environmental Protection (2006). 中国环保民间中国环保民间组织现状调查报告组织现状调查报告 (A report on the survey of China's environmental NGOs), 29 April, https://bit.ly/3iNP9XO.

Ministry of Environmental Protection (2009). 关于调整天津古海岸与湿地等5处国家级自然保护区有关事项的通知 (Notice on the adjustment of five

national nature reserves such as the Tianjin Ancient Coast and Wetland), http://bit.ly/36dOmKN.
Ministry of Environmental Protection and Chinese Academy of Sciences (2015). 中国生物多样性红色名录—脊椎动物卷》 (China biodiversity red list: vertebrates), https://bit.ly/2YgJNLk.
Ministry of Foreign Affairs (2016). 2016年6月21日外交部发言人华春莹主持例行记者会 (Foreign Affairs Ministry spokesperson Hua Chunying's regular press conference), 21 June. http://bit.ly/3piWJwg.
Ministry of Housing and Urban-Rural Development (2010). 关于进一步加强动物园管理的意见:建城2010年172号 (Directive on further strengthening the management of zoological gardens: MHURD document 172, https://bit.ly/3qVc4mT.
Ministry of Public Health (1988). 《关于下达"引流熊胆"暂行管理办法的通知》 (Notice on the tentative measures for managing "extracted bear bile" Uuse"), 2 November, https://bit.ly/39hPa3b.
Ministry of Public Health (2007). 卫生部: 截至07年10月 全国报告狂犬病2717例 (By October 2007, 2,717 human rabies cases had been reported in China). China.com, 12 November, https://bit.ly/3sVpNfj.
Ministry of Public Health (2009). 我国狂犬病防控的现状 (The current state of rabies prevention and control in China). Joint report with the Ministry of Public Security, Ministry of Agriculture and the State Food and Drug Administration, September.
Money.163.com (2012). 张志鋆: 鼎桥创投投资归真堂的原因 (Zhang Zhiyun: the reason why top-bridge capital invested in Guizhentang). *Money 163*, 26 February, http://money.163.com/special/zhangzhiyun/.
Mong La (2016). Endangered breeds on menu in Myanmar border town. Anadolu Agency report, *Daily Sabah*, 29 February, http://bit.ly/3sZczhF.
Moore, Malcolm (2011). China's first rodeo triggers protests as 'trash' culture. *Telegraph*, 20 July, http://bit.ly/2NDcyzV.
Mu Jingjun (2014). 黑龙江三年攻坚 林业总产值翻一番 (Heilongjiang's three-year campaign resulted in doubling forestry industry revenues). China Industry Development Research Information Network, 18 March, https://bit.ly/39Y2CbK.
Murphy, Rex (2011). Seal hunt pieties die at the Chinese border. *National Post*, 22 January, http://bit.ly/3oh93fb.
Mu Yi (2013). 中国成全球遭受外来物种入侵最严重国家之一 (China has become one of the most impacted countries in terms of the invasion of non-native species). *Discovery*, 3 November, http://bit.ly/3pv8css.

Nanfang Zhoumo (2011). 中俄天然气管道或穿过喀纳斯湖区 (The China–Russia natural gas pipeline is to go through the Kanas Lake). *Nanfang Zhoumo (South China Weekend Journal)*, 22 March, http://www.infzm.com/content/56669.

National People's Congress (2004). 全国人民代表大会常务委员会关于修改《中华人民共和国野生动物保护法》的决定 (Standing Committee of the National People's Congress decision on revising the Wildlife Protection Law of the People's Republic of China), 28 August http://bit.ly/3sWh78E.

National People's Congress (2015). 中华人民共和国食品安全法 (The Food Safety Law of the People's Republic of China), http://bit.ly/2M3lpKO.

Nathan, Andrew J (1990). Why Does China eat its own? A culture of cruelty. *New Republic*, 30 July and 6 August, 30–35.

Nathan, Andrew (1993). Is China ready for democracy? In Larry Diamond and Marc F. Lattner (eds), *The Global Resurgence of Democracy*. Baltimore: John Hopkins University Press.

National People's Congress of the People's Republic of China (1988). 中华人民共和国野生动物保护法 (Law of the People's Republic of China on the Protection of Wildlife), http://on.china.cn/36cj1IF.

Ng Yew-Kwang (1995). Towards welfare biology: evolutionary economics of animal consciousness and suffering. *Biology and Philosophy* 10: 255.

Ngok King Lun (2002). Law-making and China's market transition. *Problems of Post-Communism* 49(2): 23–32.

Nguyen, Sen (2020). Coronavirus: China's bear bile "treatment" for COVID-19 alarms wildlife groups. *South China Morning Post*, 14 April at http://bit.ly/3c9vhxh.

Niu Tianjia (2013). Price hikes have led to a 50% reduction of Liaotong live cattle shipment to Hong Kong and Macau. *Inner Mongolia Daily*, 11 December.

O'Connell, Brian (2000). Civil society: definitions and descriptions. *Nonprofit and Voluntary Sector Quarterly* 29(3): 471–78.

Oi, Jean C (1989). *State and Peasant in Contemporary China: The Political Economy of Village Government*. Berkeley: University of California Press.

Paper, The (2020). 致天猫淘宝总裁蒋凡的公开信：请下架"鸟网"及非法猎捕工具，2020年让鸟儿自由飞翔 (An open letter to Jiang Fan, CEO of Taobao: please remove illegal bird catching tools and let birds enjoy the free sky in 2020). *The Paper*, 22 February, http://bit.ly/2KNk7Tv.

Peixian County Statistical Bureau (2016). 2016年沛县国民经济和社会发展统计公报 (Peixian 2016 statistical report on economy and social development), http://www.csmcity.com/zlzx/info-6380.html.

References

Peixian Fankuai Dog Meat Catering Management Corporation (n.d.). 公司简介 (Company introduction). http://www.fankuai.com/1/about.asp.

Peixian Fankuai Dog Meat Catering Management Corporation (n.d.). 闲话狗肉 (A talk on dog meat). http://www.fankuai.com/1/grwh.asp?NewsID=205.

Peixian County Government (2016). 2016年沛县人民政府工作报告 (Peixian 2016 government work report). 1 April, http://m.ahmhxc.com/gongzuobaogao/1761.html.

Peixian Information Centre (2010). 沛县以三种措施为困难人群提供工作机会 (Peixian creates job opportunities for people in poverty through three main measures). Peixian Information Centre, 15 November, http://bit.ly/3pdkk1j.

Peng Bo and Zhang Yang (2015). 野生动物保护法26年来首次大修：让它们更乐活 (Let them have a better life: on the first ever overhaul in 26 years of the Wildlife Protection Law). *People's Daily*, 26 December, http://bit.ly/3a7EfIR.

Peng Liguo and Zhang Jing (2011). 多少自然保護區被蠶食 (How many nature reserves have been eroded?). *South China Weekend Review*, 7 April, http://bit.ly/3a0WnUB.

People.com.cn (2011). 天津古海岸与湿地国家级自然保护区管理处——汪苏燕 (Wang Suyan of Tianjin Ancient Coast and Wetland National Nature Reserve, nominee of 2011 Marine Environmental Protection). *People.com.cn*, 26 March, https://bit.ly/3iKrR5a.

People's Daily (2012). 中科院专家称无管引流取黑熊胆不会对熊造成伤害 (A researcher at the Academy of Sciences Zoological Institute: free-dripping does no harm to bears). *People's Daily*, 23 February, http://bit.ly/2NsaLNU.

People's Daily (2013). 斑海豹"家"在何处：栖息地宁静不再 (Where is the home' of the seals? The quietness of the habitat is gone for ever). *The People's Daily*, 20 May, https://bit.ly/3piq0XV.

People's Political Consultative News (2017). How to deal with the 6,000 "home bred" tigers. Reprinted by *Beijing Digest*, 27 April, https://bit.ly/36eztrF.

Perkins, Carina (2012). FMD outbreak confirmed in China. *Global Meat News*, 26 January, https://bit.ly/3cekiT8.

PetroChina (2017). 中国石油天然气股份有限公司 (2016 Annual Report of PetroChina), 31 March, https://bit.ly/3pk5Z3h.

Piao Zhengji et al. (2012). 长白山自然保护区黑熊和棕熊种群数量动态分析 (Population size variation of black bear (*Ursus thibetanus*) and brown bear (*U.arctos*) between 1986 and 2010 in the Changbai Mountain Nature Reserve, China). *Chinese Journal of Zoology* 47(3).

Ponder, C, J Snyder and R Lockwood (2000). Cruelty to animals and family violence. *Urban Animal Management: Proceedings of the National Conference on Urban Animal Management in Australia*. Mt Pleasant, VIC: Chiron Media.

Qiu Huizuo (2011) 邱会作回忆录 (Memoir of Qiu Huizuo). Hong Kong: The New Century Press.

qq.com (2011). 今话题:纪念11只饿死的东北虎 (Today's topic: in memory of the 11 tigers starved to death), https://bit.ly/2M2O1Ut.

Ran Jingcheng (2020). 彻底取缔野生动物养殖产业? 你想过后果吗? (Have you thought about the consequences of a complete shutdown of the wildlife farming industry?), 28 February, http://bit.ly/3iQ6waz.

Ran Jingcheng (2020b). 养殖群众的利益轻于鸿毛? (Is the interest of the wildlife breeders really negligible?). Blog post, 28 February, http://bit.ly/2LUp5yz.

Ramzy, Austin and Ling Yang (2008). Tainted milk scandal in China. *Time*, 16 September, http://bit.ly/36c4kW2.

Red Guards of the School of Mao Zedong Thought (1966). 破旧立新一百例 (One hundred rules for smashing the old and building the new). http://ccradb.appspot.com/post/3870.

Reichsfuhrer-SS SS Office (1942). "Der Untermensch" (The subhuman). Republished by the Holocaust Research Project, https://bit.ly/3t4cHwH.

Ren Jiyu (任继愈) (2014): 中国佛教史 (The history of Buddhism in China). Beijing: China Social Sciences Academy Press. https://bit.ly/3iJhleG.

Rittenberg Sr, Sidney and Amanda Bennett (2001). *The Man Who Stayed Behind*. Durham, NC: Duke University Press.

Rowan, Andrew N et al. (2009). Animal welfare perspectives on pain and distress management in research and testing. *Proceedings for Pain Management and Humane Endpoints*. Baltimore, MD: Johns Hopkins Bloomberg School of Public Health, http://bit.ly/3sVx3YB.

RT.com (2016). Russian customs seize 500+ bear paws heading to Chinese black market. RT.com, 31 July, http://bit.ly/2M7qMZg.

Rush, Anthony (2009). *China's Labour Market*. Canberra: Reserve Bank of Australia. https://bit.ly/2KRwiPk.

Saich, Tony (2000). Negotiating the state: the development of social organisations in China. *China Quarterly* 161: 124–41.

Samuels, Gabriel (2016). Australian wild dogs should be killed and sent to China to be eaten, says wildlife expert. *Independent*, 17 August, http://bit.ly/36fref8.

Seimenis, Aristarhos and Darrem Tabbaa (2014). Stray animal populations and public health in the South Mediterranean and the Middle East regions. *Veterinaria Italiana* 50(2).

Seymour, James D (2005). China's environment: a bibliographic essay. In Kristen A. Day (ed.), *China's Environment and Challenge of Sustainable Development*. Armonk, NY: ME Sharpe.

Shan, Juan (2015). WHO warns of antibiotic overuse. *China Daily*, 16 November http://bit.ly/3pkDJ0a.

References

Shan Gang and Wang Yinghui (2008). 1957年, 毛泽东对留苏学生演讲 (Mao Zedong's speech in 1957 to Chinese students in the Soviet Union). Xinghua.com, 29 May 29, https://bit.ly/3pmGcr5.

Shang Xiaoyuan (2002). Looking for a better way to care for children: cooperation between the state and civil society in China. *Social Service Review* 76(2), https:/./bit.ly/3omzm3n

Shang Xiaoyuan and Xiaoming Wu (2003). The changing role of the state in child protection: the case of Nanchang. *Social Service Review* 77(4), https://bit.ly/369F1E0.

Shanshui Nature Protection Center (2020a). 分析了1552起野生动物犯罪案件后, 我们发现... (After scrutinising 1,552 wildlife crimes, we found ...). Shanshui Nature Protection Center, 29 February, https://bit.ly/3pjfD6a.

Shanshui Nature Protection Center (2020b). 野生动物非法贸易为何如此乱象百出? (What explains the lawless situation of China's wildlife trafficking?). Sohu.com, 21 February, http://bit.ly/3ccyRXA.

Shen Lin (1999). 动物王国里的维吾尔族夫妻 (The Uighur couple in the Kingdom of Animals). *Chinese Wildlife* 5.

Sheng Hai (2015). 伍廷芳 外交官中的素食主义者 (Wu Tingfang: a diplomat vegetarian). https://www.jiuchisu.com/ZhengTan/9685.htm.

Sheng Wei (2012). 力挺归真堂 中药协会抛"西方利益集团"论 (To support Guizhentang, Association of Chinese Traditional Medicine advanced the "Western interest group" thesis). *21st Century Economic Report*, 9 February, http://bit.ly/3c7DPop.

Shijiejingji.net (2016). 2015年江苏各市GDP和人均GDP排名 (2015 Jiangsu GDP and Per Capita GDP by cities). Shijiejingji, 19 February, http://bit.ly/3pvhVyY.

Shi Yi (2015). 新疆卡山自然保护区因开矿6次瘦身,曾被喻为"观兽天堂"(Xinjiang's Kashan Nature Reserve, a "heaven for wildlife watch," was reduced in size six times because of mining projects). *The Paper*, 9 June, http://bit.ly/3iMERrh.

Shu Xiqiang (2016). 国内狗肉来源调查: 多为盗抢 活狗死狗两条线 (An investigative report on the sources of dog meat: mainly from stolen live and dead dogs). *China Youth Network*, 23 November, http://bit.ly/2NBmudf.

Shuning Fur Industry Association (2015). 肃宁县裘革行业2014年经济运行情况及2015年工作思路 (The economic performance of Shuning's fur industry in 2014 and the forecast for 2015). Shuning Fur Industry Association, 2 June, https://bit.ly/3t4eQbJ.

Siebert, Charles (2010). The animal cruelty syndrome. *New York Times*, 11 June, http://nyti.ms/3c9AB3J.

Siegel, Matt (2011). Kangaroo meat producers weigh Chinese market. *New York Times*, 12 April, http://nyti.ms/3sTKLv7.

Silva, Lily de (2011). The Buddhist attitude towards nature. *Daily News* (Sri Lanka), 4 August http://bit.ly/3piuj5F.

Sina.com (2013). 大连国际渔博会: 动保人士抵制加拿大推销海豹制品 (Dalian International Fisheries Expo saw animal protectionists protest Canadian seal product trade). Sina.com, 17 January, https://bit.ly/3caVMCz.

Soho (2017). 广西考察吃穿山甲!? 广西官员请吃穿山甲被调查! (Eating pangolins on an inspection tour of Guangxi: Guangxi officials are investigated for offering pangolin at a catering event. Reprinted at Sohu.com, https://www.sohu.com/a/125666705_394156.

Song Xuelian (2014). 中国毛皮生产企业"换种"求生 (China's fur industry seeks survival by introducing "new breeding stock"). *China Economics Weekly* 27. https://bit.ly/2YfxZsM.

Song Yunxiao (2018). 城市流浪犬探因: 主人遗弃、行业混乱、监管缺失 (What's the root cause of urban stray dogs: abandonment by owners, unregulated pet market, and law enforcement problems). *Yangcheng Evening News*, 19 June, https://bit.ly/3qM7pUg.

South China Weekend Review (2015). 赶走公路，深陷油污: 一个动物保护明星的陨落 (From fighting a highway to getting smeared: the fall of an animal protection activist). *South China Weekend*, 11 June, http://bit.ly/36ft5k6.

Southern Metropolitan News (2006). 国家林业局等就动物福利答记者问:"活熊取胆保护了野熊" (State Forestry Bureau meets the press on animal welfare: "Bear farming has protected bears in the wild"). 南方都市报 (*Southern Metropolitan News*), 13 January, https://bit.ly/3a7A3Zk.

Southern Metropolitan News (2012). 中药协: 活熊取胆像开自来水一样无痛 (Association of Traditional Chinese Medicine: bile extraction is like the turning of tap water faucet, painless). 南方都市报 (*Southern Metropolitan News*), 17 February, http://bit.ly/3a3ijOT.

Standaert, Michael (2020). Coronavirus closures reveal vast scale of China's secretive wildlife farm industry. *Guardian*, 25 February, http://bit.ly/3iMuXFN.

State Council of the People's Republic of China (1962). 关于积极保护和合理利用野生动物资源的指示 (State Council order on actively protecting and reasonably utilising wildlife resources), https://bit.ly/3iIA1Ly.

State Council of the People's Republic of China (1989). 社会团体登记管理条例 (Regulation on the management of social organisation registration). State Council Order 43, https://bit.ly/3pkJaw7.

References

State Council of the People's Republic of China (1993), 国务院关于禁止犀牛角和虎骨贸易的通知: 国发 (1993) 39号 (Circular of the State Council on banning the trade of rhinoceros horns and tiger Bones). State Council Document 39 of 1993, https://bit.ly/3696aqj.

State Council of the People's Republic of China (2007). 国务院关于促进奶业持续健康发展的意见 国发 (2007) 31号 (State council recommendation for the promotion of the healthy and sustained development of the dairy industry). State Council Document 31 of 2007, http://bit.ly/3qNzLxF.

State Council of the People's Republic of China (2011). 危险化学品安全管理条例 (State regulation on the safety management of toxic chemicals), http://bit.ly/36c2nIO.

State Council of the People's Republic of China (2014). 关于印发中国食物与营养发展纲要 (2014–2020年) 的通知 (An outline on the development of food and nutrition: 2014–2020), http://bit.ly/3ooYUgE.

State Environmental Bureau of the People's Republic of China (1999). 关于涉及自然保护区的开发建设项目环境管理工作有关问题的通知 (Notice on the questions regarding the environmental management of development projects involving the nature reserves). 3 August, https://bit.ly/3t4gUjZ.

State Forestry Bureau of China (1994). Commercial raising saves bears. *Beijing Review*, 7–13 March.

State Forestry Bureau (2001). 全国野生动植物保护及自然保护区建设工程总体规划 (A general outline and plan for the protection of wild animal and plant species and for the construction of nature reserves), https://bit.ly/3piTapD.

State Forestry Bureau (2003). 国家林业局发布商业性经营利用驯养繁殖技术成熟的54种陆生野生动物名单 (The state forestry bureau announced the list of 54 land wildlife species whose commercial breeding technology is mature. *Chinese Wildlife* 24: 5.

State Forestry Bureau (2004). 全国林业产业发展规划纲要 (Outline of the National Forestry Development Plan: 2004–2010), https://ishare.iask.sina.com.cn/f/3WChTgkRGvn.html.

State Forestry Bureau (2006). 中国自然保护区的建设和发展 (The construction and development of China's nature reserves), https://bit.ly/2Nxf7Dv.

State Forestry Bureau (2009). 新中国60年林业部门预算改革的回顾与展望 (The past and future of the budget reform in the forestry bureaus in the last 60 years of the People's Republic of China), 30 September, https://bit.ly/2YeRXEg.

State Forestry and Grassland Bureau (2019). 国家林业和草原局 2019 年中央部门预算 (National government agency budget 2019: State Forestry and Grassland Bureau), http://bit.ly/3pkt8T1.

State Forestry and Grassland Bureau (2020). 国家林业和草原局 2020 年中央部门预算 ((National government agency budget 2020: State Forestry and Grassland Bureau), https://bit.ly/36d6iW2.

Sun, Celine (2018). Dog meat restaurant in Guangzhou closes amid "falling demand." *South China Morning Post*, 18 May, http://bit.ly/3a2FbOn.

Sun Jiang, He Li and Huang Zheng (2009). 动物保护法概论 (An introduction to the theory of animal protection legislation). Beijing: Law Press.

Sun Jingtan (1997). 《周礼》的作者、写作年代及历史意义新探 (A new effort at disclosing the author, year of publication and historical significance of the Rites of Zhou). *Nanjing Social Sciences Journal* 10, https://bit.ly/39iRE1n.

Sun Tingwen (2010). 新疆阿尔金山野生动物数量增长 (Wildlife animals at the Arerjin Mountain Nature Reserve have increased in number). *China News Network*, 13 August, https://bit.ly/2Mkf79o.

SWChina.org (2016). 调查结果显示中国公众强烈支持穿山甲保护 (A survey shows that the Chinese public strongly support pangolin protection. Swchina.org, 9 May, http://bit.ly/2LUuYM9.

Tan Youlin (1999). 中国就业压力的空间格局与区域经济发展 (The regional distribution of China's employment pressure and regional economic development). *Population Research* 23(6).

Tang Jingmei (2016). 玉林: 今年力争实现脱贫11万人 (Yulin authorities aim to lift 110,000 people out of poverty by the end of 2016). *Yulin Evening News*, 12 June, http://bit.ly/2YbXM51.

Tang Qing (2013). 中国狂犬病的传播和防控的进展 (The spread of rabies and the progress of its prevention). Presentation at the 5th China Dog Ownership Management Symposium, 16 November, Guangzhou, China.

Tang Qing et al. (2014). An expert opinion on mass dog meat consumption during summer solstice in Yulin. Open letter to Chen Wu, Governor of Guangxi, 10 June, http://bit.ly/3pleE5n.

Tang Wenfang (2001). Political and social trends in the post-Deng urban China: crisis or stability? *China Quarterly* 168: 890–909.

Tang Yifang (2014). 广东一养殖场涉非法交易保护动物 林业部门: 已立案 (A wildlife breeding farm is being investigated for involvement in trafficking of protected wildlife animals, confirmed by Guangdong's forestry bureau). *Nanfang Daily*, 31 October, https://bit.ly/3cclzKj.

Teets, Jessica.C (2009). Post-earthquake relief and reconstruction efforts: the emergence of civil society in China? *China Quarterly* 198: 330–47.

References

Teng Jingchao, Su Jun and Fang Xiuqi (2014). 中国西汉—清代饥荒序列的重建及特征分析 (An analysis and reconstruction of the chronicle of the famines and their characteristics between West Han and Qing Dynasty). *Journal of Chinese History and Geography* 4.

Terebess Asia Online. T'ai-Shang Kan-Ying P'ien: treaties of the Exalted One on response and retribution. http://www.terebess.hu/english/taishang.html#2.

Tencent.com (2010). 生灵的哀歌-海豹皮草背后 (Elegy for the seals: the secrets behind seal products). Tencent.com, 18 November, http://news.qq.com/photon/tpyk/haibao.htm.

Tencent.com (2011). 海豹! 海报! 拒绝海豹制品! 全球华人海报设计大赛 (Seal protection poster design contest). Promotional website, https://bit.ly/3a2wTGv.

Tencent.com (2014). 方舟子和赵南元谈动物权利利 (Fang Zhouzi and Zhao Nanyuan on animal rights). Tencent.com, 27 June, https://bit.ly/3ca2AAc.

Tencent Commentary (2016). 中国千年狗肉史, 梁实秋的说法最中肯 (China's history of dog eating in the last 1,000 years and the most relevant remarks made by Liang Shiqiu). Tencent.com, 22 June, http://view.news.qq.com/original/legacyintouch/d510.html .

ter Haar, Barend J (2000). Rethinking "violence" in Chinese culture. In Goran Aijmer and Jon Abbink (eds), *Meanings of Violence: A Cross Cultural Perspective*. Oxford and New York: Berg.

ter Haar, Barend J (2002). China's inner demons: the political impact of the demonological paradigm. In Woei Lien Chong (ed.), *China's Great Proletarian Cultural Revolution: Master Narratives and Post-Ma Counternarratives*. Lanham, MD: Rowman & Littlefield Publishers.

Thomson, Billie (2020). China recognizes dogs as "companions animals" in "game-changer" proposal that could prevent 10 million dogs from being slaughtered every year for food. *Daily Mail*, 9 April, http://dailym.ai/3sZEv5k.

Thornycroft, Peta (2013). Chinese man caught smuggling ivory from Zimbabwe. *Telegraph*, 25 October, http://bit.ly/3iMKt4P.

Tian Jiguang (2012). 我为什么反对盘锦滨海公路穿过斑海豹的核心栖息地 (Why have I opposed the construction of the Panjin coast highway that cuts through the core habitat of seals). 16 August. The link to the orginal article is no longer functioning, but Tian's main arguments are reflected in a related report at https://bit.ly/3qSpbWg.

Tian Song (2016). 再不罢手就晚了——写在新一版《野生动物保护法》颁布之前 (It is not too late to stop it now: a few thoughts on the eve of the release of the revised Wildlife Protection Law). Blog post, *China Environment*, March, http://bit.ly/3ocJdZG.

Tian Xiangbo (2008). 中国的立法体制现状 (The current state of law-making in China). *Modern China Studies* 3, http://bit.ly/2MmvFgX.

Tordesillas, Cesar (2015). Shanghai hopes to attract six million yearly visitors to new polar park. *Yibada*, 30 March, http://bit.ly/3qSfruS.

Tu Weiming (1998). Beyond the Enlightenment mentality. In Mary Evelyn Tucker and John Berthrong (eds), *Confucianism and Ecology: The Interrelation of Heaven, Earth, and Humans*. Boston: Center for the Study of World Religion/Harvard Divinity School.

Twenty-first Century Economic Report (2012). 中药协会力挺归真堂上市 抛"西方利益集团"论 (Supporting Guizhentang, Association of Traditional Chinese Medicine resorts to "Western interest group" charge). 9 February, https://bit.ly/2M6LNn5.

Twenty-first Century Economic Report (2016). 2015年各省份名义GDP排名 两省负增长 (GDP ranking of all Chinese provinces in 2015, two provinces experiencing negative growth). 17 February, http://bit.ly/3c9Gkqf.

UNDP (United Nations Development Program) (2015). China's success on Millennium Development Goals provides an example for others to follow for the post-2015 development agenda, says new UNDP report. 17 February, http://bit.ly/2Ybq4Na.

UNFAO (United Nations Food and Agriculture Organization) (2013). *FAO Global Capture Production Database updated to 2013: Summary Information*. http://www.fao.org/3/a-i4883e.pdf.

Venzmer, Gerhard (1968). *Five Thousand Years of Medicine*. Translated by Marion Koenig. New York: Taplinger Publishing Company.

Voice of China.com.cn (2012). 归真堂"堂主"一鸣惊人:反对我们就等于反对国家 (The shocking claim from the owner of Guizhentang: opposition to Guizhentang IPO bid is opposition to the government). Voice of China.com.cn, 19 February, https://bit.ly/36bNkiA.

Walder, Andrew G (1986). *Communist Neo-Traditionalism: Work and Authority in Chinese Industry*. Berkeley: University of California Press.

Wang Hebing (2011). 毛泽东的保健医生兼秘书的难忘回忆 (A Memoir of Mao Zedong's private physician and secretary). Beijing: The Long March Press.

Wang Hongyu (2004). 提高立法质量必须破除部门利益 (The making of effective and credible laws requires the prevention of the influence of departmental interest). *Xinjing News*, 16 September, https://bit.ly/3iMAFaH.

Wang Ming (1960). 太平经合校 (Compilation of the scriptures of the Great Peace [Taipingjing]). Beijing: Zhong Hua Press.

References

Wang Pei (2004). 必须考虑引进西班牙斗牛的负效应 (We must consider the negative impacts of the introduction of Spanish bullfighting). *China Youth Daily*, 20 October, http://bit.ly/3qSfZAW.

Wang Pu, Sun Xuan and Yu Ying (2010). 钟南山: 六成以上新传染病来自动物 (Zhong Nanshan: More than 60% of new infectious diseases come from animals). *Yangcheng Evening News*, 3 March, https://bit.ly/39jAhO6.

Wang Ru (2011). Unsealing the deal. *China Daily*, 6 December, http://bit.ly/3sV9xLq.

Wang Tianqi (2018). 八达岭野生动物园动物伤人: 老人骑骆驼被摔翻在地 (Badaling Wildlife Park injured visitors when they were thrown off the back of a camel). *Beijing Youth Daily*, 18 April, https://bit.ly/3qShmzA.

Wang Tong (2017). 湖北野生动物驯养繁殖业发展调查 (An investigation of the development of wildlife breeding industry in Hubei). *Hubei Daily*, 9 December, https://bit.ly/3a2hHZP.

Wang Xiaogang (2003). 中国濒危野生生物栖息地法律保护多元性之缺失和完善——与美国濒危物种栖 (The shortcomings of China's legal protection for the habitat of endangered species and proposals for its improvement: a comparison of Chinese legal protection with that of the US). *Chinese Wildlife* 5.

Wang Xiaoye (2016). 长春市首次实施"暖流计划" 六类群体直接或间接受益 (Changchun initiated for the first time the "warm currents" program to benefit directly or indirectly six groups of people). Chinajilin.com, 5 August, https://bit.ly/2NsyNZ8.

Wang Xile, Gong Wei, He Zhengming and Li Genping (2017a). 中国大陆地区实验动物机构, 人员和设施现状分析 (An analysis of the current state of lab animal institutions, personnel and facilities on the Chinese mainland). *Laboratory Animal Science* 34(3).

Wang Xile, Gong Wei, He Zhengming and Li Genping (2017b). 中国大陆地区实验动物生产现状分析 (An analysis of the current state of lab animal breeding on the Chinese mainland). *Laboratory Animal Science* 34(4).

Wang Xile, Gong Wei, He Zhengming and Li Genping (2017c). 中国大陆地区实验动物使用现状分析 (An analysis of the current state of lab animal use on the Chinese mainland). *Laboratory Animal Science* 34(6).

Wang Xuejiang (2004). 反思禽流感: 集约经营是养禽业的必由之路 (Reflections on the bird flu: intensive production is the solution that must be adopted). *Liberation Daily*, 22 February, http://bit.ly/3a501wx.

Wang Weijia (2016). 活熊取胆业: 苦撑七年 命悬一线 (The bear farming industry: a seven-year effort for the one final IPO bid. *First Finance and Economics News*, 14 April, http://www.yicai.com/news/5002833.html.

Wang Yangming (1998). *Instructions for Practical Living and Other Neo-Confucian Writings*. Translated by Wingtsit Chan. Quoted in Rodney L Taylor, "Companionship with the world: roots and branches of a Confucian Ecology, in Mary Evelyn Tucker and John Berthrong (eds), *Confucianism and Ecology: The Interrelation of Heaven, Earth and Humans*. Cambridge, MA: Center for the Study of World Religions.

Wang Yuexi and Wang Enbao (1990). 古文百篇英译 (*One Hundred Classical Chinese Prose Writings in English*). Beijing: Beijing Languages Institute Press.

Wang Zhengxuan and Cheng Haifeng (2020). 8000多个铁夹进熔炉 安徽歙县集中销毁非法狩猎工具 (In an Anhui She County crackdown, over 8,000 leg traps and other illegal hunting tools are destroyed). Social media post, 23 March, https://bit.ly/2YhjMeS.

Watts, Jonathan (2011). Canada "racist" for selling China seal meat, say Chinese activists. *Guardian*, 13 January, http://bit.ly/3sVPX1I.

Watts, Jonathan and Han Ying (2010). Chinese zoo closed amid tiger starvation investigation. *Guardian*, 17 March, http://bit.ly/3pkO2Bt.

Weary, Daniel M and Beverly Chua (2000). Effects of early separation on the dairy cow and calf 1. Separation at 6 h, 1 day and 4 days after birth. *Applied Animal Behaviour Science* 69(3): 177–88.

Weber, Bob (2015). Move over, America. Canada's polar bear fur has a new buyer: China. *Canadian Press*, 7 December, http://bit.ly/2Ye1mMb.

Wei Lingxue (2015). 吃肉与政治: 日本人为何禁止肉食近千年 (Meat consumption and politics: what made Japan ban meat consumption for almost 1,000 years). *The Paper*, 2 September, http://bit.ly/2KRVAge.

Welfare and Ethic Committee of the Chinese Association of Lab Animal Science (2013). On the drafting of Laboratory Animal Guidelines for Ethical Review of Animal Welfare. Internal and unpublished document shared by the committee.

Wen Wu (2010). 放生,要使之能够生存 (Mercy release should ensure the survival of the animals). *Environmental Protection* 12.

Wertheim, Heiman FL et al. (2009). Furious rabies after an atypical exposure. *PLOS Medicine*, 17 March, http://bit.ly/2MsOaQI.

White, G, J Howell and X Shang (1996). *In Search of Civil Society: Market Reform and Social Change in Contemporary China*. Oxford: Clarendon Press.

WildAid and African Wildlife Foundation (2015). *Rhino Horn Demand: 2012-2014*, https://bit.ly/2M3MoG6.

Wiley, Andrea S (2004). "Drink milk for fitness": the cultural politics of human biological variation and milk consumption in the United States. *American Anthropologist* 106(3): 506–17.

References

Wo, Tariq et al. (1991). Rabies in man handling infected calf. *Lancet* 337(8751): 1224.

World Animal Protection Association, China Veterinary Medical Association and Xinhua News (2016). *A Survey Report on the Pork Consumption of the Chinese Public.*

World Bank (2016). China. http://www.worldbank.org/en/country/china.

World Health Organization (2012). H5N1 avian influenza: timeline of major events. 25 January, https://bit.ly/3sVSjgS.

Wu Caili (2020). "禁野令"下, 贵州野生动物养殖产业如何转产? 听, 专家这样说! (How to move wildlife breeders out of wildlife farming at a time when wildlife farming was banned? Let's hear what the experts have to say). *Tianyan News*, 13 April, https://bit.ly/3a2dDJc.

Wu Hao (2016). 野生动物伤庄稼, 赔偿为何这么悬? (Why is it so difficult to get compensation for damages caused by wild animals?). *Sichuan Daily*, 24 February.

Wu, Harry (1995). *Bitter Winds: A Memoir of My Years in China's Gulag.* New York: Wiley.

Wu Hong (2015). "注胶牛"比"注水牛"还坑人 ("Gelatin-injected beef" does more harm to consumers than force-watered beef). *Shenyang News*, 31 March, http://bit.ly/3qNUl0T.

Wu Jun and Deng Yan (2004). 火锅店老板当街杀狗附近居民齐称太血腥 (Dog slaughter on the street by hotpot restaurant owners is condemned by residents as extreme cruelty). *Xiaoxiang Morning News*, 15 October, https://bit.ly/3a52wip.

Wu, Kun, Yue Longyao, Li Guijun and Shao Caimei (2011). 母猪蹄裂的原因及防治 (The cause of sow hoof cracks and their prevention and remedy) 饲料广角 (*Siliao Guang Jiao*; *Animal Feed Studies*) 10.

Wu Ningkun Wu and Yikai Li (1994). *A Single Tear: A Family's Persecution, Love, and Endurance in Communist China.* New York: Back Bay Books.

Wu Qianlan (2017). How has China formed its conception of the rule of law? A contextual analysis of legal instrumentalism in ROC and PRC law-making. *International Journal of Law in Context* 13(3), DOI 10.1017/S1744552317000039.

WWF and TRAFFIC (2016). A ban on commercial ivory trade in China: a feasibility study briefing. 2 September, http://wwf.to/3c83GMZ.

Xia Meide (2010). 论梁武帝的《断酒肉文》与佛教中国化 (On Emperor Wu of Liang's "On Abstention from wine and meat" and the Sinification of Buddhism). *Journal of Yantai University* (Philosophy and Social Sciences Edition) 23(3).

Xiang Jun and Wen Zhangzhe (2005). 汤锅店杀掉怀孕母羊取出胎羊当街叫卖 (Pregnant ewes slaughtered by a hotpot restaurant for unborn lambs pedalled on the street to attract eaters). *Chongqing Evening News*, 27 October, https://bit.ly/3cc81i0.

Xiang Sunan (2018). 宋徽宗为何下令在全国禁止杀狗? (Why did Emperor Huizong of the Song Dynasty prohibit dog slaughter across the country?). Sohu.com, 21 February, https://bit.ly/3iXZQYh.

Xie Xiaoting (2012). 归真堂二度上市再遇阻 亚洲动物基金会抵制IPO (Guizhentang's IPO bid was resisted for the second time and Animals Asia Foundation led the opposition). *Southern Metropolitan News*, 9 February, https://bit.ly/2LXKuH8.

Xin Wen (2016). 首届亚洲黑熊论坛召开 活熊取胆能否终结 (First Asia Black Bear Forum on the future direction of bear farming). China.com, 29 March, http://bit.ly/3cc2HeI.

Xinhuanet (2006). 海南野生保护动物驯养年产值达10亿元 (The annual revenue of Hainan's wildlife farming reached 1 billion yuan). Xinhuanet, 10 October, https://bit.ly/3sWKQ1f.

Xinhuanet (2015). 我国每天销售一亿多公斤牛奶 (China sells over 100 million kilograms of milk a day), Xinhuanet, 18 August, https://bit.ly/39jqU0G.

Xinhuanet (2016). 广西高速路货车起火 300头活羊变"烤全羊" (Fire on a transport truck burned 300 sheep alive and turned them into "roast whole sheep"). Xinhuanet, 16 February, https://bit.ly/3qRi7cb.

Xinjiang Academy of Social Sciences (2013). 1962年新疆"伊塔事件"历史渊源 (The historical roots of Xinjiang's "Yili-Tacheng Incident" in 1962). Xinjiang Academy of Social Sciences, 12 January, https://bit.ly/3qQ3S7B.

Xu Cao (2012). 环保组织呼吁抵制全球最大鹅肝酱厂落户鄱阳湖 (An environmental organisation opposes building the world's biggest foie gras plant at Poyang Lake). Caixin.com story, 1 March, http://bit.ly/3a7tyG7.

Xu Changwen and Jing Xu (2007). 解析佛教的动物权利思想 (An analytical examination of the animal rights ideas of Buddhism). *Lanzhou Academic Journal* 9.

Xu Chunlu (2006). 青藏铁路为藏羚羊安全迁徙设置33处通道 (The Qinghai-Tibetan Railroad is built with 33 safe passages for the safe migration of the Tibetan antelopes). *Xinjing News*, 22 June, https://bit.ly/39YBvxe.

Xu Gang (2015). 中国环保名人田继光在盘锦受审 涉嫌敲诈勒索罪 (Tian Jiguang, a well-known Chinese environmental activist, in court for alleged extortion and blackmailing). *Liaosheng Evening News*, 28 May, https://bit.ly/39i7CZx.

References

Yan, Alice (2012). CCTV report says KFC chickens are being fattened with illegal drugs. *South China Morning Post*, 19 December, http://bit.ly/36cBsN3.

Yan Chunxiang (2015). 依法惩治刑事犯罪 守护国家法治生态–2014年全国法院审理刑事案件情况分析 (Deal with criminal violations in accordance with laws, safeguard the state's rule of law: an analysis of criminal cases handled in 2014 by courts across the country). *People's Courts News*, 7 May, http://bit.ly/39ixwMJ.

Yan Dong (2007). 改革时期中共和民间组织的关系 (The relationship between CCP and NGOs during China's Reform Era). *Modern China Studies* 14(3).

Yan Ge (2007). 浙江人大常委建议工农与企业家人大代表分开选举 (Zhejiang Provincial Congress Standing Committee member proposed to elect delegates representing peasants, workers and entrepreneurs separately). China News Network, 9 March, https://bit.ly/3on7rAl.

Yan Jiaxin (2014). 吃狗肉会感染狂犬病吗? (Does eating of dog meat cause rabies?). Sciencenet.cn blog post, 7 December, https://bit.ly/3r4FcZl.

Yan Mingshen (2006). 行政立法权扩张的现实之批判 (A critique of the reality of the expansion of law-making by administrative agencies). *Journal of Law and Commerce* 2.

Yang Jisheng (2013). Tombstone: *The Great Chinese famine, 1958–62*. New York: Farrar, Straus and Giroux.

Yang Kuisong (2010). 中国成立初期清除美国文化影响的经过 (How did the new government eliminate American influence in China). *Journal of Studies on the History of the Chinese Communist Party* 10, https://bit.ly/2MtEeqw.

Yang Kuisong (2013). Uncovering the bloody history of the Suppression of Counter-Revolutionaries campaign. *Wenxue City News*, 3 October, http://bit.ly/2LUW7yz.

Yang Siqi (2016). The Chinese elite's new love of hunting has conservationists worried. *Time*, 14 April, http://bit.ly/3piFvzb.

Yang Wenming (2017). Wildlife animals: protect us if you care about us. *People's Daily*, 17 April, http://bit.ly/36cRnLDh.

Yang Xuyu and Li Hongying (1995). A discussion of the current state and management measures regrading bear farming in Sichuan. *Sichuan Journal of Zoology* 14(3).

Yang Ying, Yu Gang and Li Zongchang (1991). 黑熊圈养繁殖初报 (A first report on the captive breeding of bears). *Sichuan Journal of Zoology* 10(4).

Yang Zhaoquan and He Tongmei (2001). 中国-朝鲜-韩国关系史 (A history of the relations between China and Korea, vol. 2). Tianjin: Tianjin People's Press.

Yeh, Emily (2014). Do China's nature reserves only exist on paper? *China Dialogue*, 2 March, http://bit.ly/3sVZzJQ.

Yi Weekly (2020). 野味帝国 (The kingdom of wildlife eating). *Yi Weekly*, 5 March, http://news.ifeng.com/c/7uafDESh3po.

Yicai (2012). 亚洲动物基金会回应中药协指责"八国联军"之说很荒谬 (The Animals Asia Foundation calls the "Eight Allied Nations" allegation made by China Association of Traditional Chinese Medicine ridiculous). Yicai.com, 15 May, https://www.yicai.com/news/1726833.html.

Yin, Xuean (2005). 深圳市解密档案:1962年的大规模逃港风波 (The turmoil of 1962, mass exodus to Hong Kong: declassified Shenzhen documents). Sina.com, 24 December, https://bit.ly/3c8ENkc.

Ying Jian (2007). 试论佛教在中国的传播远胜道教的原因 (A preliminary discussion of the causes underlying the greater success in the spread of Buddhism in comparison with Daoism). *Examination Weekly* 23.

Yong Xinzhong and Zhang Wei (2014). 玉林"狗肉节": 错位的对峙 (Yulin Dog Meat Festival: a misplaced conflict). *South China Weekend*, 26 June, http://www.infzm.com/content/101786.

Yu Shoujun (2012). 狗肉火锅险取七命 (Dog meat hotpot almost killed seven people). *Jiangnan Metropolitan News*, 31 December, https://bit.ly/3ogL53K.

Yu Suyun and Xue Mayi (2014). 昆山父子菜场买来熟狗肉 吃后上吐下泻竟是中毒 (Father and son in Kunshan vomited and had diarrhea after eating dog meat). *Yangtze Evening News*, 15 December, http://bit.ly/39g7XvK.

Yu Xiguang (1993). 位卑未敢忘忧国: 文化大革命上书集 (The commoners' concern for state affairs: a collection of letters to government leaders during the Cultural Revolution). Changsha: Hunan People's Press.

Yulin City Government (2011). 玉林市人民政府关于加快玉林市住宿餐饮业发展的意见: 玉政发(2011)25号 (Yulin government recommendation on accelerating the development of the hospitality and catering industry). Yulin government document 25, http://www.foodmate.net/law/guangxi/182024.html.

Yulin City Statistical Bureau (2015). 2014年玉林市国民经济和社会发展统计公报 (Yulin 2014 statistical report on the economy and social development of Yulin). 11 May, http://bit.ly/3qR5z4D.

Yulin City Statistical Bureau (2016). 玉林市2015年国民经济和社会发展统计公报 (2015 statistical report on the economy and social development of Yulin). 12 April, http://www.tjcn.org/tjgb/20gx/32768.html.

References

Zeng Fanchao (2018). 要做事 先做人: 立己修身最为先 (Be an honest person before being successful: personal moral cultivation is most important). Beijing: Zhonghua Books.

Zhan Xueyong and Tang Shuiyan (2013). Political opportunities, resource constraints and policy advocacy of environmental NGOs in China. *Public Administration* 91(2): 381-99.

Zhang Ailin (2007). In response to rapacious rabies, Yulin started the storm of "dog culls". Xinhua.net, 2 January, https://bit.ly/3ojzgtA.

Zhang Dan (2013). 当枫叶红了的时候 (When the maple leaves turn red). Blog post, 7 August, http://bit.ly/3t4M6j5.

Zhang Endi (2002). 不要给野生动物扭曲和错误的爱 (The wrong and distorted love that wild animals should not be subjected to). *China Youth Daily*, 12 June.

Zhang Guangyou (1995). 万里在1975-1986 (Wang Li in 1975-1986). Hong Kong: Qiwen Books.

Zhang Jianfeng (2011). 马建章:让外国人来打猎是为了保护动物 (Ma Jianzhang: Giving hunting permits to foreign hunters is for protecting wild animals in China). *Nanfeng Chuang* (*South Wind Window*), 13 September, https://bit.ly/2LWim7i.

Zhang Kangkang (2011). 关于禁止进口加拿大海豹制品的提案 (A legislative proposal on banning the import of seal products). 27 February, https://bit.ly/2MjQdGV.

Zhang Ke (2012). 林业局首谈归真堂: 只要合法就应上市 (State Forestry Bureau talked about Guizhentang's IPO bid for the first time: it can go public if it is legal). *First Finance and Economics News*, 6 June, https://bit.ly/3a3maLU.

Zhang Ke (2014). 姚明等众多名人联合呼吁终止活熊取胆 (Yao Ming and other celebrities jointly appealed to outlaw bear farming). *First Financial Times*, 22 February, http://www.yicai.com/news/1450436.html.

Zhang Ke (2020). 养殖蛇类能保护野外资源? 知情人爆料称"这是弥天大谎" (Can captive breeding of snakes help protect snakes in the wild? An insider discloses the "biggest lie"). *Yicai* , 19 March, http://bit.ly/36fZDui.

Zhang Liutao (2014). 团伙用氰化钠毒杀1600条狗 (Using cyanide, dog theft gang killed 1,600 dogs). *Oriental Morning News*, 16 July, https://bit.ly/369lPpK.

Zhang Muhan (2007). 在中国狗的登记比抚养费用还要高 (It costs more in China to register than to keep a dog: on the hefty registration fee). *Market News*, 20 April. https://bit.ly/39k4AEm.

Zhang Ping (2002). 唐代的"断屠钓" ("Suspension of slaughter" in the Tang dynasty). *Journal of Classics and Culture* 4.

Zhang Qian-qian et al. (2015). Comprehensive evaluation of antibiotics emission and fate in the river basins of China: source analysis, multimedia modeling, and linkage to bacterial resistance. *Environmental Science & Technology* 49(11): 6772–82.

Zhang, Sarah (2017). Resistance to the antibiotic of last resort is silently spreading. *Atlantic*, 12 January, http://bit.ly/2KO3HKB.

Zhang Songhui (2006). 道家万物平等观与儒家人类中心观 (On the Daoist idea of all lives being equal and the Confucian anthropocentric ideology). *Hunan Daojiao*, https://bit.ly/2NxKBtb.

Zhang Tianfu (2017). 可可西里藏羚羊"保护神"今昔: 生命禁区再无枪声 (The present-day "guardian" of Kekexili Tibetan antelopes: no more gunshots on the Tibetan Plateau). *China News*, https://bit.ly/2NBgQb4.

Zhang Wei (2013). 内蒙古活羊"特供"中东 与约旦协议出口活羊20万只 (Inner Mongolia will supply 200,000 live sheep specially for Jordan and other Middle East countries according to a signed agreement). *China News Network*, 16 January, https://bit.ly/3pklp7E.

Zhang Xingjun (2017). 河南推行畜牧业供给侧改革 鼓励农民发展"牛家乐" (Henan implements supply side reform in livestock production encouraging peasants to develop integrated beef cattle production). *Xinhua News*, 17 March, http://bit.ly/36ci2rS.

Zhang Xuebing and Pan Lina (2013). 剧毒化学品网上仍有售卖 卖家称能带走就卖 (Highly toxic chemicals are still sold on the internet: dealers willing to sell if buyers can arrange for their shipment). *Nanfang Daily*, 14 May, https://bit.ly/3qY0eJ3.

Zhang Yan (2012). TCM expert accuses animal welfare group of anti-China activities. *China Daily*, 15 May, https://bit.ly/3qScmLv.

Zhang Yi (2008). China has become the world's third largest milk producing nation. People.com.cn, 22 April, https://bit.ly/2Yi0plO.

Zhang Yu (2002). 微波炉活烤小狗 某名牌大学学生恶行令人震惊 (A college student from a well-known college shocked the country for microwaving a live puppy). *Chengdu Commercial News*, 21 March, https://bit.ly/2YcX9Iq.

Zhang Zai. "The Western Inscription." http://bit.ly/3qSV7d6.

Zhang Zuoliang (1998). 周恩来保健医生回忆录: 1966–76 (Zhou Enlai: the memoir of a private doctor, 1966–76). Hong Kong: Joint Publishing.

Zhao Chali (2014). 吃狗爱狗的民间博弈, 应体现在公共政策中 (The conflict between the dog lovers and dog eaters should be regulated through public policies). Blog post, 23 June, http://bit.ly/3iMb0z2.

Zhao Min (2006). 广西宾阳一村村民吃狗肉中毒 四五十人腹泻不断 (A villager in Village One of Bingyang, Guangxi, was poisoned from eating dog

References

meat, some 50 others having diarrhea). *Southern Morning Post*, 12 May, https://bit.ly/3qMIIqM.

Zhao Nanyuan (2010). 答复郭鹏副教授—点评《中国人与中国动物—与赵南元先生对话》 (Zhao Nanyuan's response to associate professor Guo Peng: a commentary on "The Chinese and Animals in China"). https://bit.ly/2YgeoJa.

Zhao Nanyuan (2012a). 动物权利论的要害是反人类 (The essence of animal rights theories is anti-humanity). First published in November 2002; reprinted 18 January, 2012, *Nanfang News*, http://view.news.qq.com/a/20120118/000013.htm .

Zhao Nanyuan (2012b). 养殖、利用是动物保护的重要途径 (Domestication and utilisation are important approaches to animal protection). http://opinion.m4.cn/2012-04/1160732.shtml.

Zhao Rongguang (2006). 中国饮食文化史 (A history of China's culinary culture). Shanghai: People's Publishing House.

Zhao Xiaoli (2013). 论全国人大代表的构成 (On the make-up of the delegates to the National People's Congress). Research paper, http://www.calaw.cn/article/default.asp?id=8437.

Zhao Xiaona (2013). 严惩食品安全犯罪 让它成为"过街老鼠" (Severely punishing food safety violators and making them a target of active government crackdown efforts). *Southern Daily*, 4 May, https://bit.ly/2KOAX4x.

Zheng Shaozhong (2003). 陕西畜牧业农民人均增收350元 (Shaanxi livestock farmers saw 350 yuan per person added to their income). *People's Daily, Overseas Edition*, 21 January, http://www.china.com.cn/chinese/huanjing/265104.htm.

Zheng Yi (2001). 中国之毁灭 (China's Ecological Winter). Hong Kong: Mirror Books.

Zhong Lianhai (2009). 魏晋南北朝佛教传播的三大策略 (On the three tactics used in the spread of Buddhism in the Wei, Jin, and North and South Dynasties). *Forum of Social Sciences* 5.

Zhou Chao (2016). 去年北京生猪养殖量减5% 不影响肉价 (Beijing's pig farming went down by 5% last year having no major impact on meat price changes). *Rule of Law Evening News*, 15 April, https://bit.ly/3pkT5SD.

Zhou Chonglin (2004). 浅谈素食与道教的关系 (A brief discussion on Daoism and its impact on vegetarianism). *Chinese Taoism* 2.

Zhou Hang et al. (2016). Human rabies in China, 1960–2014: a descriptive epidemiological study. *PloS Neglected Tropical Disease* 10(8), http://bit.ly/3pjx9ad.

Zhou Hongmin (2010). 浅谈佛教的因果报应论 (A preliminary discussion of the Buddhist concept of karma). *Science and Technology Information* 11.

Zhou Jie (2017). 中国毛皮业:"动物福利"践行者产业 (China's fur industry: a practitioner of "animal welfare"). *China Commercial News Network*, 14 May, https://bit.ly/3sVdT5l.

Zhou Ke (2010). 动物保护组织呼吁中国对海豹产品说不 (Animal protection organisations call on China to say no to seal products). *Yicai*, 30 November, https://bit.ly/3iKQnTX.

Zhou Ke (2016). 野生动物保护法修改稿专家评论集 (A collection of expert views and feedback to the draft revision to the Wildlife Protection Law). Unpublished electronic document.

Zhou Tianyong (2009). "Employment creation through business ventures" should become a national strategy. *Beijing Daily*, 4 May, http://bit.ly/2NsSi3M.

Zhu, Shu (2003). Let's have a national mobilisation to illuminate "Clenbuterol". *New Security* 10, http://bit.ly/2NwCZah.

Zhu Weiyi (2010). 是该吃狗的时候了？(Isn't it time to eat dogs?). *Xinmin Weekly*, https://bit.ly/3sS29k9, 13 January.

Zhuang Zhou (1990). 庄子全译 (A complete translation of Zhuangzi). Guiyang: Guizhou People's Publishing House.

Zhu Xing and Hou Jiafa (2007). 笼养蛋鸡骨质疏松症的研究进展 (A progress report on the study of cage layer osteoporosis). *Heilongjiang Animal Husbandry and Veterinary Science* 2.

Zhu Xuesong (2013). 规模化肉鸡养殖与疾病防控—2013 (临沂)第七届中国健康养殖论坛 (Intensive farming of broilers and disease control: 2013 Linyi 7th China Healthy Farming Forum). *Veterinarian Orientation* 9.

Zhu Yong-guan et al. (2013). Diverse and abundant antibiotic resistance genes in Chinese swine farms. *Proceedings of the National Academy of Sciences* (PNAS), 11 (9).

Zou Jiang (2014). 玉林养猪户如何应对肉价下跌？(How is Yulin pig farming responding to the decline of the pork market?). *Yulin Daily*, 25 April, https://bit.ly/3qRc07N.

Zu Shuxian, Peter J Li and Peifeng Su (2004). Animal welfare consciousness of Chinese college students: findings and analysis. *China Information* 19(1): 67–95.

Index

All China Association of Traditional Chinese Medicine (ACATCM) 167
amphibians 151
animal agriculture
   and animal welfare 195–200, 201–212
   and rural employment 123, 194, 212, 213, 215
   expansion of 180–189, 212–214
   adoption of Western intensive farming methods 190–200, 204, 215
   traditional practices 190
Animal Husbandry and Fisheries Bureau 286
animal protection associations 93, 270, 275, 284; *see also* non-government organisations (NGOs)
animal protection legislation 43, 51, 91, 124, 168, 217–266, 311; *see also* Wildlife Protection Law (1989)
animal sacrifice 70, 72, 84
animals as entertainment 17, 106, 241, 314; *see also* aquariums, zoos

Animals Asia Foundation (AAF) 3, 19, 25, 115, 149, 154, 156, 160, 166, 270
antelopes 50, 280, 304
anthropocentrism 70, 71, 103, 105
antibiotics 163, 199, 200, 202, 203
aquaculture 180
aquariums 2, 17, 19, 241
Asia for Animals Coalition 19
Australia 13, 37, 211, 290
authoritarianism 54, 58
avian influenza 194, 201; *see also* viruses

Bai Juyi 90
baiji *see* dolphin, Yangtze River
battery farming 193, 195, 204; *see also* chickens
bear farming
   and animal cruelty 4, 153, 163–166
   and conservation 152–155, 166–171, 234
   bile extraction and use 3, 153, 157, 162, 167, 226, 314
   campaigns against 3, 6, 149, 166, 220

government support of 154–160, 155, 173–176
bears 2, 219
beef 117, 124, 141; *see also* meat production
biodiversity 220, 222
Boxer Rebellion 47
British Farm Animal Welfare Council 4
Buddhism 64, 75–89, 91, 103–107, 314
bullfighting 37, 289
butchers 86, 87, 114, 207

Canada 36, 219, 290–295, 296
Cao, Deborah 51
Capital Animal Welfare Association 10, 111, 126, 131, 138, 139, 148, 289
captive breeding 15, 151, 152, 218, 225, 231, 244, 253–255, 257
cats 7, 285
Centre of Disease Control, China 133
Chen Mincai 111
Chiang Kaishek 48, 93, 114
chickens 114, 117, 179
  beak trimming 195, 198
  drugs and hormones 201, 202
  injury and illness 196, 201
China Small Animal Protection Association 6, 52, 270, 277, 282
China Zoo Watch 19
Chinese culture
  and environmental protection 50, 80, 104
  and the party-state 60, 94, 145
  as an explanation for animal cruelty 53, 60, 91, 106
Chinese literature 63, 83, 88, 89, 105
Chinese Social Sciences Academy 145
Chongqing Animal Protection Association 111
civet cats 154, 226, 261, 263

civil society 56, 92, 267–270, 274, 288, 309
civil war 47, 48, 93, 94
Cixi, Dowager 47
class 69–75, 95–98, 102, 143
collective farms 59, 96, 123, 190
Communist Party National Congress 160
companion animals 7–9
  during the Mao era 49, 98, 99, 102, 317
  in pre-revolutionary China 93, 114
  since the reform era 110, 125, 131, 136, 144, 287, 288, 312
Compassion in World Farming 204
Confucianism 38, 41, 44, 55, 64, 65, 69–75, 91, 104, 106, 314
conservation 15, 50, 233–234
  and wildlife industries 26, 152, 154–160, 166–171
  in Chinese history 80, 152
COVID-19 17, 52, 150, 215, 217–218, 226, 263, 266
cows 81, 185, 198, 209, 211
Cultural Revolution 47, 98, 99, 100, 101

dairy consumption 185, 185, 213
dairy production 85, 125, 185–187, 198
Dalian Vshine Animal Protection Association (Vshine) 111
Daoism 64–68, 76, 80, 83, 91, 103, 105–106
de Silva, Lily 76
deforestation 50, 101
Dehuai, Marshall Peng 39
democracy 56, 58, 59, 95, 269
Deng Xiaoping 57, 115, 123, 174, 194, 217, 269, 273, 282
desensitisation *see* violence
developmental states 53–61, 302, 316

Index

disease control 133–136, 193, 196, 204
dog meat
  and contemporary Chinese food culture 115–117, 147
  and employment 117–122, 124, 128, 132, 145–147
  and nationalism 141–144
  and the fur trade 114, 117
  campaigns against 8, 111, 129, 139
  dog meat restaurants 8, 36, 112, 117, 119–122
  government support for 110, 112, 125, 127, 147
  in Chinese history 91, 113–115
  promotion of 117, 126, 315
  regulation and banning of 138, 312
dogs
  as companion animals 7, 110, 122
  culling of 46, 135, 283, 286
  disease control in 133
  farming of 110, 121, 130, 144
  illness and injury 110
  public slaughter of 139
  registration of 52, 131
  rescue and shelters 129, 283, 307
  theft of 130–133
  transportation of 129, 137
dolphin, Yangtze River 224
Dong Zhongshu 69, 70, 71
Du Mu 90
Du Yufeng 111
ducks 179, 187, 190

economic growth 4, 23, 28, 50, 52, 53–58, 92, 147, 160, 176, 236, 316; *see also* developmental states
economic reform 28, 47–52, 59, 123, 217, 269, 271, 309, 316
Economy, Elizabeth C. 50
eggs 67, 75, 81, 187, 204

elephants 15, 106, 219, 313
employment 113, 118, 127, 133, 145–147, 194, 195, 213, 215, 217
endangered species 2, 217, 219, 222, 224, 227, 231, 233, 258
entrepreneurialism 55, 160
epidemics 15, 150, 201, 202, 206; *see also* pandemics, viruses
Evans, Peter 55

factory farming *see* animal agriculture
Falun Gong 274
famine 1, 14, 38, 58, 101, 210, 212
Fan Kuai 116, 126
Fan Xian-tao 126, 128
farming *see* animal agriculture
fast food 201
fishing 66, 74, 104, 180
foie gras 36; *see also* geese
food safety 11, 12, 22, 35, 136–139, 140, 196, 239, 263, 317
food security 12, 14, 26, 122–125, 179, 187, 210, 212, 214, 316
foot and mouth disease 206
forced watering 12, 210
Friends of Nature (FON) 245, 270, 278
fur animal farming 16, 151, 241

Gaozu, Emperor 86
geese 36, 105, 151, 190
Genghis Khan 82
gestation and furrowing crates 197, 205
goats 31, 179, 211
gorillas 224
Goulet, Denis 57
grain production 59, 101, 124, 191, 207
Great Leap Forward 1, 39
Greenpeace 278
growth-promoting additives 11, 201
Guizhentang 149, 158, 170, 172, 176

Guo Geng 89
Guo Peng 131

habitat protection 250, 304
Hanzhuang Dog Meat City 125, 128
Harrell, Steven 38
Hastings, Alcee 109
Heibao bear farm 158
Hinduism 76
Hong Kong 36, 43, 49, 51, 58, 203, 209
horses 45, 67
Hu Ping 46
Hua Chunying 112
Huan Yu 131
Huizong, Emperor 113, 143
Humane Society International 112, 115, 246, 291, 292, 295
Huntington, Samuel 142
hunting 74, 80, 82, 88, 102, 104, 237, 242, 244, 245, 250, 255, 261

imperialism 43, 44, 51, 59
importation of animals 124, 211, 219
India 51, 77, 105
industrialisation 53, 56
ivory *see* elephants

Japan 54, 56, 87, 91, 94, 142
Ji Xianlin 64, 65, 76
Jiajing, Emperor 114
Jilin market 121, 125, 128, 146
Johnson, Chalmers A. 54

kangaroo 37, 290
karma 78
KFC 12, 198, 201
Korea 54, 58, 87, 115, 142, 153, 314
Korean communities in China 116, 121, 125, 315

Kuitun Small Animal Protection Association 283

laboratory animals 20, 151, 241, 314
Lao Zi 65, 68
Le Aiguo 71
Lee Seong-gye 87
legal protection for nonhuman animals *see* animal protection legislation
Li Keqiang 147
Li Lianda 168, 242
Li Rui 42
Li Shizeng 92
Li Zhizao 88
Li Zhuopeng 39
Lian Chi 86, 88
Liang Congjie 278
Lin Binyan 40
Lin Yutang 70, 79, 106
Liu Shaoqi 39, 268
live export 211
live feeding 31
live transport 206–212; *see also* dogs: transportation of
livestock industry *see* animal agriculture
Lord, Bette Bao 39
Love First, Guangdong 111
Lu Bicheng 93
Lu Di 46, 52, 282
Lu Xun 41

Ma Jianzhang 151, 242
Mao Shoulong 148
Mao Zedong 1, 39, 42, 45, 47, 48, 57, 60, 94–103, 115, 122; *see also* Cultural Revolution, Great Leap Forward
Martin's Act (*Cruel Treatment of Cattle Act*) 51, 312

Index

May 4th Movement 41
meat consumption 13, 85, 92, 105, 179, 180, 211, 213
meat production 124, 179, 180–184, 191
medicine *see* traditional Chinese medicine
Mei Sangyu 42
Mencius 69, 72, 73, 87, 314
mercy release 78, 88, 105
milk *see* dairy production
Millennium Development Goals 187
minke whales 36
monkeys 35, 227
musk deer 224

Nanjing Ping An A Fu Animal Protection Group 132
Nanjing Society for the Prevention of Cruelty to Animals 93, 276
Nathan, Andrew 38, 39, 41, 44
National People's Congress (NPC) 51, 173, 245, 260, 262, 296
Nationalist Party of China (Kuomintang) 92, 94, 115, 268
nature reserves 230, 280, 297
  encroachment by development 237, 298, 302
New Life Movement 93
non-government organisations (NGOs) 267, 269, 274, 288, 306, 309
  animal protection groups 270, 275–280
  registration of 281
  supervision and surveillance of 273, 281, 309

pandas, giant 1, 217
pandas, red 3

pandemics 52, 215, 226, 231, 247, 254, 262, 263, 266; *see also* viruses
pangolins 219, 220, 227
Panjin Bearded Seal Protection Volunteers Association (PBSPVA) 298
Peixian market 120, 126, 128, 138
pets *see* companion animals
pheasants 236
Pian Shan Kong 111
pigs 10, 179, 191, 191, 209
  early weaning 198
  pig farming 195, 197, 199, 205
  illness and injury 205, 206, 208
  tail docking 198
Ping An A Fu Animal Protection Association 284
Ping Jingya 93
poaching 33, 217, 219, 234, 280; *see also* hunting, poaching
pork 12, 114, 122, 179, 184, 206
  strategic pork reserve 179
poverty reduction 58, 187, 212, 217, 262
primates 21, 152
privatisation 56
Pu Yi 47
public executions 100
public slaughter 139; *see also* violence

Qian Muzhai 88
Qiao Wei 132
Qin Xiaona 131, 138, 139, 148
Qiu Huizuo 39
Qiu Shuhua 150, 158, 170

rabbits 179, 190
rabies 52, 133–137
Red Guards 99, 102

369

religion *see* Buddhism, Daoism, Hinduism
reptiles 151
rhinoceros 16, 33, 219, 220, 259, 266
rodeos 36, 289
Rongguang Zhao 34
Royal Society for the Prevention of Cruelty to Animals (RSPCA) 93

safe passages for wildlife 304
seals 36, 236, 292, 297–301
Severe Acute Respiratory Syndrome (SARS) 15, 33, 52, 221, 226, 245, 262
Seymour, James D. 46
shark fin 36, 51, 313
sheep 179, 207, 211
Singer, Peter 13
slaughter suspension 86, 105, 314
social media 8, 9, 29, 143, 150, 298, 308, 313
Soviet Union 33
sow crates *see* gestation and furrowing crates
Spain 289
sparrows 101
Spence, Jonathan 38
Su Shi 89
Sun Jiang 141
Sun Simiao 69
Sun Yat-sen 91, 92
supermarkets 140
Survey of Intangible Cultural Heritage 127
State Forestry Bureau 26, 151, 157, 166, 170, 171, 176, 233, 238, 243, 265

Taiwan 43, 48, 51, 54, 56, 58
Tang Qing 133
Taoism *see* Daoism
technocracy 59

ter Haar, Barend J. 39–41
Tian Jiguang 298
tigers 2, 16, 34, 259, 266
tourism 2, 110, 127, 147, 156, 266, 297
traditional Chinese medicine 33, 34, 41, 46, 89, 151, 155, 167, 170, 240
trafficking 32, 219, 239, 255
transport *see* live transport
Tu Long 88
Tu Weiming 71
turtles 32, 219

United Nations 187
urban animal management 8, 52, 283, 284, 309
urbanisation 27, 148, 195, 207, 209, 210

vegetarianism 77, 78, 82–85, 91, 92, 105, 106
violence 38–42, 41, 44
    desensitisation to 100, 101, 103, 139–140
viruses
    COVID-19 *see* COVID-19
    foot and mouth disease 206
    H5N1 203–205
    H7N9 202

Wang Anshi 89
Wang Hongju 245
Wang Yangming 72
Wei Jingsheng 272
wet markets 35, 140, 207, 219, 263
wildlife eating
    as a response to famine 1, 85, 102, 225
    as status symbol 227, 232
    in Chinese culture 219, 225, 226, 233, 296
wildlife farming *see also* bear farming and conservation 218

Index

and poverty reduction 217
government support for 217, 243, 257, 261
Wildlife Protection Law (1989) 151, 152, 155, 221–225, 228, 249–253, 264
wildlife trade 219
World Health Organisation 200, 203
World Wildlife Fund 1, 277
Wu of Liang, Emperor 75, 80, 83, 86
Wu Tingfang 92
Wu Zetian, Emperess 80, 86

Xi Jinping 109, 115, 247
Xi'An Small Animal Protection Association (XSAPA) 308
Xu Mengxin 113
Xuan, Emperor 72
Xuan, Emperor Wen 86
Xun Zi 70, 71
Xunzi 69

Yang Yuhua 111
Yao, Emperor 113

Yin Guang 88
Yongzheng, Emperor 114
You, Lu 89
Yuan, Emperor 88
Yulin Dog Meat Festival 9, 109, 112, 127, 147
Yutang Lin 64

Zhang Songhui 71
Zhang Zai 71, 73
Zhao Chali 142
Zhao Jianzi 88
Zhao Nanyuan 136, 141, 142
Zhao Yixia 283
Zhao Ziyang 42
Zhen Banqiao 90
Zheng Yi 42, 50
Zhong Nanshan 231, 262
Zhou Tianyong 147
Zhu Wei-yi 144
Zhuang Zhou 65–68
Zhuzhou Animal Protection Association (ZAPA) 285
zoos 2, 17–20, 241